CAMBRIDGE LIBRARY COLLECTION

Books of enduring scholarly value

Travel and Exploration

The history of travel writing dates back to the Bible, Caesar, the Vikings and the Crusaders, and its many themes include war, trade, science and recreation. Explorers from Columbus to Cook charted lands not previously visited by Western travellers, and were followed by merchants, missionaries, and colonists, who wrote accounts of their experiences. The development of steam power in the nineteenth century provided opportunities for increasing numbers of 'ordinary' people to travel further, more economically, and more safely, and resulted in great enthusiasm for travel writing among the reading public. Works included in this series range from first-hand descriptions of previously unrecorded places, to literary accounts of the strange habits of foreigners, to examples of the burgeoning numbers of guidebooks produced to satisfy the needs of a new kind of traveller - the tourist.

Travels in the East

This work, first published in 1847, is an account by Constantin von Tischendorf (1815–74) of his journeying in the Middle East at the beginning of the 1840s. It is part travel log and part account of the Christian history of the area. After encounters with such men as Mehmet Ali and Ibrahim Pasha, he visits the library of the Patriarch of Alexandria. The German biblical scholar then travels to the monastery of Saint Catherine on Mount Sinai, where he makes the extraordinary discovery of a previously unknown fourth-century manuscript, one of the main witnesses to the Septuagint, before reaching the main goal of his long journey – Jerusalem. This lively narrative by a controversial scholar–explorer also entertains the reader with some of the more unexpected elements of his travels, such as an attack by robbers who are routed when he draws his sword.

Cambridge University Press has long been a pioneer in the reissuing of out-of-print titles from its own backlist, producing digital reprints of books that are still sought after by scholars and students but could not be reprinted economically using traditional technology. The Cambridge Library Collection extends this activity to a wider range of books which are still of importance to researchers and professionals, either for the source material they contain, or as landmarks in the history of their academic discipline.

Drawing from the world-renowned collections in the Cambridge University Library, and guided by the advice of experts in each subject area, Cambridge University Press is using state-of-the-art scanning machines in its own Printing House to capture the content of each book selected for inclusion. The files are processed to give a consistently clear, crisp image, and the books finished to the high quality standard for which the Press is recognised around the world. The latest print-on-demand technology ensures that the books will remain available indefinitely, and that orders for single or multiple copies can quickly be supplied.

The Cambridge Library Collection will bring back to life books of enduring scholarly value (including out-of-copyright works originally issued by other publishers) across a wide range of disciplines in the humanities and social sciences and in science and technology.

Travels in the East

Constantin von Tischendorf

CAMBRIDGE
UNIVERSITY PRESS

CAMBRIDGE UNIVERSITY PRESS

Cambridge, New York, Melbourne, Madrid, Cape Town, Singapore,
São Paolo, Delhi, Dubai, Tokyo

Published in the United States of America by Cambridge University Press, New York

www.cambridge.org
Information on this title: www.cambridge.org/9781108014793

© in this compilation Cambridge University Press 2010

This edition first published 1847
This digitally printed version 2010

ISBN 978-1-108-01479-3 Paperback

TRAVELS IN THE EAST.

TRAVELS

IN THE EAST.

BY

CONSTANTINE TISCHENDORFF,

EDITOR OF THE

"CODEX EPHRÄMI RESCRIPTUS," "CODEX FRIDERICO-AUGUSTANUS,"
ETC.

TRANSLATED FROM THE GERMAN,

BY

W. E. SHUCKARD.

LONDON:

PRINTED FOR

LONGMAN, BROWN, GREEN, AND LONGMANS,

PATERNOSTER-ROW.

1847.

PREFACE.

I HERE offer my Travels in the East to friendly readers. The great sympathy I myself received during my pilgrimage, inclines me to hope that these reminiscences will also attract favourable regard. The very aspect of my book proves that the tone of its communications is not addressed to the learned: my heart rather than my head has dictated them. He who has travelled in the East, possesses at least all that a Swiss has in his native mountains ;- if he have them not before his eyes, he bears them in his heart. I say that the East attracts the traveller at least to this extent; for in reality it enchains him far more, provided he brings a right mind and spirit to behold the memorials which it preserves of the origin of Christianity and of the sacred past history of mankind.

The eye which I myself brought to the contemplation of the East, will be readily detected in what I have written. The impressions which personal inspection made upon me, it has been my chief object here to compress into a permanent form, as an enduring memorial. It is to be regretted that a work like mine necessarily puts the first person to a certain extent in the foreground ; but I conceived that an unreserved outpouring of the heart, an open ingenuousness of narrative which should place writer and reader as it were in immediate contact, would be appreciated by many.

Questions indicative of hearty sympathy have often been put to me by unlearned persons, as to the scope and tendency of the

Biblico-critical labours which I prosecuted during my five years' travels. For the purpose of meeting this request I have introduced a Chapter addressed to an Illustrious Patroness.

I consider it a great good fortune to have travelled in the East, but to describe my travels there I consider to be a still greater. At least I have experienced this in writing this book, as will be readily detected in its style. I indulged the hope that such a representation, a contribution as it were from the Pilgrim's own heart, would be peculiarly adapted, not only to promote a familiarity, but also a sympathy, with the Holy Land. I shall rejoice greatly if I have succeeded.

I have endeavoured to appear as little learned as possible in these pages. When, however, it was indispensable to discuss learned questions, as for instance, in that relating to the Holy Sepulchre at Jerusalem, I have sought to adopt a course which should give umbrage to no reader. Perhaps the omission of a map will be chiefly felt, where I treat of the site of the Holy Sepulchre. I could indeed have supplied one suited to my purposes from among those extant. But I thought that, even for this purpose, as also for the object of the entire compass of the Travels, I might without any prejudice to the sense refer to the many maps of this particular locality which are in almost every body's hand, and whence it would be easy to gather the details of my pilgrimage, and of my views.

     *   *   *   *   *   *

As it is possible that many readers might pass by the Epistle which relates especially to my Biblico-critical labours, I take the opportunity here of soliciting for it a kindly regard.

A new opinion has recently been started which disputes the claim of Sinai to the celebrity of being " God's mountain." I gave a short notice of this at the commencement of this year in the Allgemeine Zeitung. A particular refutation of this view, the strong foundation of which is not upon many points to be disputed, I did not think suitable for incorporation in my Travels. But I shall shortly endeavour to do so elsewhere.

I have still only to express the wish that, amid the mighty struggle of ecclesiastical interests, a salutation will be welcome to many from that land of palms, whence the imperishable Word of Peace has resounded to every one that has a heart fitted to be its receptacle.

CONSTANTINE TISCHENDORFF.

Leipzig, 1846.

CONTENTS.

MONASTIC EXCURSIONS IN CAIRO.

THE PATRIARCH OF ALEXANDRIA AND HIS WALLED-
UP LIBRARY.

THE PYRAMIDS.

VISIT TO ORIENTAL LADIES.

THE COPTIC MONASTERIES IN THE LIBYAN SANDS.

MEMPHIS AND HELIOPOLIS.

EXCURSION TO OLD CAIRO.

ARRIVAL AT JERUSALEM.

JERUSALEM.

THE HOLY SEPULCHRE.

THE INHABITANTS OF JERUSALEM.

THE ANGLICAN BISHOPRIC AT JERUSALEM.

MONASTERIES IN AND ABOUT JERUSALEM.

CONTENTS. XV

TRAVELS IN THE EAST.

TO MY BROTHER JULIUS.

Leghorn, 12th March, 1844.

HERE am I on the eve of an earnest day : to-morrow I depart for the East. I address you once more to bid you a long farewell; a joyful one doubtless ; yet the tear drops upon my page. It is indeed a road over rocks, — a giddy path over an abyss, where it is easier to be precipitated than to proceed. Hence have you not ceased to dissuade me. At home, you write, a happy hearth awaits you. No ! no ! my heart exclaims. And, behold ! my wings are expanded. — What a happy fate is mine ! Do you remember the October of the year forty ? There was then no one to believe in my creed ; nor any to cherish my hopes. But I at last succeeded in catching hold of a twig although possibly resembling the thorn of the fox in the fable. I started upon the anniversary of the Reformation, intending to return in a few months. Then came the labours at Paris, and their results : I visited Holland, England, Switzerland, Italy, and found a harvest rich beyond all expectation.

My heart throbbed with fervent desire. The man who has said to himself, " I will see Jerusalem," is not to be diverted from his object by the attractions of happiness, or pleasure, or affection. Its accomplishment was protracted ; but a few words, vibrating from the very depths of hoar antiquity, resounded both day and night within my ears. They are those of Priam to Hecuba repelling every entreaty to desist from his intention of visiting the camp of the Greeks to redeem the body of Hector. But, indeed, you must read them in the original to feel the full force of their expression.

> " Seek not to stay me, nor my soul affright
> With words of omen like a bird of night ;
> 'Tis heaven commands me, and you urge in vain ; —
> Had any mortal voice th' injunction laid,
> Nor augur, priest, or seer had been obey'd ;
> A present goddess brought the high command,
> I saw, I heard her, and the word shall stand.

B

I go, ye Gods! obedient to your call,
If in yon camp your powers have doomed my fall,
Content ———" POPE.

Then at last came the longed-for letters. In imagination I have already returned, and that prompt faculty has conveyed me through all the countries of my pilgrimage. Mentally I have already listened to your greeting, and with heart pressed to heart have seen my rejoicing eye vividly reflected in yours.

Thus I go forth with cheerful confidence: it cannot be a delusion which dazzles me. Do you still ask me what I seek? Does it not suffice to behold the Pyramids? — to gaze upon Mount Sinai? — to view Jerusalem? Goethe said of Naples, that he who has visited it may at least compute some days of happiness even in the most miserable life. Naples I have enjoyed, yet how happy shall I be when I shall have seen the Pyramids, Mount Sinai, and Jerusalem. But I have a still more definite purpose to accomplish. How much more prolific will be my study of the Bible when I shall have beheld the Holy Land with its memorials and its inhabitants. The history of the Church has no theatre grander than the East. And is not the East at this very moment in the act of a political as well as religious development? This must be beheld, examined, comprehended.

Nor does hope fail me as to the success of my researches with respect to manuscripts. It is thence that Europe has derived its riches, and many a monastery still contains unexamined recesses. No one has explored recently with so definite a purpose as myself. I have learned to distrust the labours of my predecessors. Should however nothing present itself, we can then proceed with so much greater energy to reconstruct with the materials we possess.

Should I never return, I know that I shall have fallen in a worthy cause. The warrior falls upon the battle-field; you know my field of battle: and if this be its termination, I shall find the heavenly, in seeking the earthly Jerusalem. The blooming earth is beautiful; how far more beautiful must the holy heavens be. Whether my permanent abode be here or there, the route will I cheerfully pursue. Farewell, my beloved one! and, oh! fare ye well, ye dear ones in my paternal home. Think of me whilst traversing the dark waves, when wandering in strange lands; for,

" Where'er I roam, whatever realms to see,
My heart, untravell'd, fondly turns to thee:
Still to my brother turns, with ceaseless pain,
And drags at each remove a lengthening chain."

Malta, 26th March, 1844.

The French mail-boat, the Lycurgus, was in vain expected upon the

13th at Leghorn; the violence of contrary winds had blown her to Elba. The rough sea looked cheerless, indeed; before me lay the wrecks of two vessels. On the afternoon of the 14th the anxiously expected steamer made her appearance, covered to the very summit of her funnel with foam. She lay so far from the shore, that none but courageous sailors would venture to go aboard in the customary frail little boat.

During the two following days we had a charming passage. I thoroughly enjoyed the delights of a sea voyage, pacing the deck with an undimmed eye and a firm step: the blue sky above, the still deeper blue of the water beneath, and the vanishing shore upon our left, I greeted with a painful smile. In the imprisonment of a ship there is a sensation of freedom seldom experienced elsewhere. We lay to several hours at Civita Vecchia and Naples; but scarcely had we turned our back upon the smoky column of Vesuvius, when the sky gave indication of its previous stormy disposition, and therefore, when La Valetta received us in its splendid harbour on the 19th, I resolved upon remaining for a week at Malta. This island is remarkable from its soil, the peculiarities of its inhabitants, and its history. Surveyed from one of its elevated points, we observe many districts in their aboriginal state of naked rock, for the whole of the very superficial soil that lies upon it has been brought from Sicily. Nevertheless, Malta possesses a luxuriant vegetation. The palm grows nobly by the side of the olive; and its oranges are of singularly delicate flavour. Unfortunately the splendour of its roses I knew only by repute, and yet gardens and meadows glowed with variegated beauty. The heat would be insufferable were it not relieved daily by refreshing breezes. Its aspect is wholly African, in spite of the act of parliament which has incorporated Malta with Europe.

The climate of the island is considered as very salubrious, and its extreme fertility may possibly be a concurrent result; and so rapid is the increase of population, that her sons have to seek a domicile away from home, and with them she has enriched the proximate coasts of Asia and Africa. A suggestion was recently made to colonise the Peloponnesus with Maltese, but only under an especial guarantee from the Greek government. It was, however, followed by no result, as that government would not be responsible for every contingency. These Maltese would, in my opinion, be just the people for Greece, which, absorbed in musing over its sad political visions, allows the soil to sigh for the plough.

The population comprises a variety of different elements. The women, with their olive complexions, their dark and sparkling eyes, their perfidious mantillas of black silk reaching from head to foot,

belong, as the very first glance convinces, aboriginally to the island.
The Italians harmonise readily herewith; the charming Neapolitan at
my *Hôtel del Mediterraneo* is exactly in her place. But we find here
stiff Englishmen in multitudes, and, indeed, as lords of the island.
The Scottish garrison, clothed above in the vesture of the North,
and beneath in that of the South, are not here exposed to the chance
of having their naked legs frost-bitten. But every feature of its
northern protectors does not as congruously blend with the characteristics of the island. Hence a certain trait of Maltese nationality
stands prominently forth in harsh contrast, notwithstanding the
inscription glittering in gold opposite the palace of the governor:
*Magnæ et invictæ Britanniæ Melitensium amor et Europæ vox has
insulas confirmant*, 1814. It is well known that Englishmen carry
with them the stamp of their origin on the brow, and in the eye
and in the heart, even to the very farthest recesses of the earth ;
and at Malta they conspicuously avoid all assimilation with the
peculiarities of the place. How absurd does it seem that the present
governor does not even understand Italian ! Italian is the written
language, as well as that of superior society ; whereas the Maltese,
which is a dialect of the Arabic, is confined to familiar intercourse.
To the expressed wish of the Maltese, that the former governor should
remain with them longer than the usual time, the English minister
for foreign affairs could only object, that places were few, but ex-
pectants many.

There are but few French in the island. British influence is
unlimited; although an attempt was made to restrain it a few years
ago, when the Russian fleet repaired to Malta to recruit, after the
battle of Navarino. I was told that the Russians then made such an
enormous expenditure, and gave such profuse presents to the natives,
that the local government hastened by all possible means the oft-
delayed departure of their fleet. Russia's friendly advances, before
the island reverted to the protection of the English, were also
remembered. It is very natural that Russia should not forget that
the Emperor Paul was Grand Master of the order of St. John, who
was only prevented by his assassination from opposing his claims to
the appropriation of the island by the English.

The truly splendid period of Malta's history still dwells in the
memory of all, though the present generation, within its own experience, beholds but the faint reflection. I refer to the time of the
Knights of St. John of Jerusalem. Originally a colony of Car-
thaginians ; then belonging first to Rome and next to Byzantium ; and subsequently wrested from the hands of the Goths
by Belisarius ; in the ninth century under the dominion of the
Saracens, who were driven thence by the valiant Norman, Roger,

in the eleventh, whereby it became annexed to Sicily ; Malta was presented by Charles V., in the sixteenth, to the Knights of St. John, when Rhodes was taken from them by Solyman II. I say presented, for they held it by the small tenure of delivering a falcon annually at Palermo. Shortly afterwards these noble knights maintained, under La Valette, their glorious war of defence against Mustapha. Twenty years later they built the magnificent church of St. John, which, by its marble splendours, its tombs of the grand masters, and its conquered standards and flags, still exhibits to the eye the glory of the past. This order of knighthood harmonised admirably with the religious disposition immemorially characteristic of the Maltese. The island contains now but one of these chivalrous knights : his sword is fixed in its scabbard, but he still wears the cross upon his breast. He spoke to me very particularly about the incomparable hospital, to whose service he had been attached. Fifteen hundred sick were attended there ; religious distinctions were unknown ; all were served upon silver. He also told me much about Bonaparte, who passed the six days succeeding the disgraceful surrender of the citadel at his house, without once at night taking off his uniform.

But I hasten to another reminiscence of the Maltese, less clouded than those of their chivalric period, and which has grown as it were into their very hearts. I allude to the visit of the Apostle Paul. Every reader of the Acts of the Apostles knows that St. Paul, upon his stormy voyage from Cæsarea to Rome, suffered shipwreck upon the Island of Melita. This Melita is Malta, although, following the example of Constantine Porphyrogenitus, the question of their identity has been seriously and learnedly debated, both in the present and preceding centuries. Meleda, on the coast of Illyria, has been cited in preference. But this assault made by the Benedictine Giorgio was valorously refuted. The chief point of the assailants is the express mention made of the Adriatic Sea by St. Luke, in Acts, xxvii. 27. : " But when the fourteenth night was come, as we were driven up and down in Adria, about midnight." But what was easier than to confound the idea of the sea around Malta with the Adriatic, particularly since we are quite certain that it was formerly customary to apply this name to the whole sea between Greece and Italy. On the contrary, no artifice of interpretation can do away with the account of the arrival at Syracuse and at Rhegium (Acts, xxviii. 12, 13.): the expression steering downwards has no disturbing effect upon it. Another cause of doubt was adduced in the circumstance that no poisonous snake is now to be found in Malta. This has certainly surprised me : there is indeed, in great abundance, a small species of snake, above an ell

long, but it is not poisonous. The pious faith of the Maltese finds
little difficulty in the matter : according to them the entire species
was divested of its venom through the one thrown into the fire
by St. Paul. For a certain mode of interpretation nothing would
be more simple than, under such circumstances, to strip the miraculous from the miracle. But it was the natives themselves, thoroughly conversant with their indigenous animals, who expressed
their fear, according to St. Luke (Acts, xxviii, 6), and founded their
faith upon the miraculous proceeding. The matter, in my opinion,
presents but the semblance of a difficulty. But neither in the
grotto of St. Paul, nor elsewhere, did I find any indication of
the serpents' eyes and serpents' tongues, the healing powers of
which have been so much lauded by pious travellers ; but indeed
this may have ceased.

I made a Sunday's excursion in very agreeable society to
St. Paul's grotto. We went in a carriage from La Valetta to the
Citta-vecchia, which consists chiefly of stately villas. I thus
became acquainted with a peculiar class of people, the Maltese
drivers, who, as their two-wheeled vehicles have no seat for them,
gallop along beside it, in spite of heat, storm, or rain. I venture to
call in question the justice of the fame which this grotto has acquired
in connection with the history of St. Paul. It is said to have been
the Apostle's domicile during the three months of his sojourn. But
how is it possible that the shipwrecked Paul, who was instantly recognised and revered as a worker of miracles, and who likewise saved the
sick father of the governor (Acts xxviii. 8.), should have been offered
such a grotto for an abode ? It is reputed never to diminish in size,
notwithstanding the fragments that are incessantly being carried
away. This peculiarity I left unproved.

To me St. Paul's bay was far more interesting. We may recognise
there, I believe, the actual spot of the shipwreck, which St. Luke
has distinctly indicated as " a place where two seas met." (Acts
xxvii. 41.) The north-east wind, which the Evangelist had also
previously named, drove the vessel to this tongue of rocks, whose
extreme apex forms two reefs, which appear, indeed, more or less
separated according to the violence of the waves, but which are certainly connected under water with the tongue itself.   Close by
stands St. Paul's tower, and about two short leagues distant lies
the Casale Nazzara, a village which is said to have derived its name
from the community of Nazarenes founded by St. Paul.

Thus have I quickly reached the proper field of my researches.
Twelve months ago I stood in Puzzuolo, where St. Paul first stepped
upon Italian ground.

I now behold him in the midst of the conflict of the waves ; he stands like an immovable rock amidst the waters. " For there stood by me this night the angel of God, " said he to the terrified sailors. (Acts xxvii. 23.) The angelic promise resounded joyfully within his heart. Hence did the shining Pharos blaze for him each night, and in every storm was there a haven open for his reception. It is delightful to think of St. Paul within view of this sea. Two thousand years have elapsed; much splendour, infinite grandeur, have passed away : but his word, like the enduring sea, still incessantly resounds throughout the world, conveying the heart to this Island of Islands.

Alexandria, 6th April, 1844.

It was on the 28th of March that I quitted, on board the Scamander, the remarkable island, which had become very dear to me from the kind and courteous reception I had experienced. The sombre powers of the waters were insensible to my need. Shortly after our departure I shut myself up in my cabin: the Scamander danced and pitched unmercifully. My young ship's surgeon, familiar as he was with the sea, was out of all humour with his patients. He prescribed for me a solid piece of ham and a glass of claret ; but as I should doubtlessly have failed in this bravoura, I preferred being reported at the table as a *nature faible*. On the 31st of March, shortly before midnight, we cast anchor. The ship was still, the sea was tranquil. I then sprang up from my couch as if moved by the spirit, and got upon the deck. I was in Greece ! How enchantingly delightful was the view ! Syra lay before us ; the full moon shone down upon us. The white houses leaned pyramidically against the perpendicular bright-red rocks of the island. There were many vessels in the harbour, having at the mast-head a solitary lantern, which traced a long and flickering reflection in the crisped dark blue wavelets. " Hail, fair Greece! " I exclaimed ; " thou blessed land, whose charms are enhanced by universal praise. Like a bride in her wedding garment, mute, yet eloquent, I behold thee before me." A host of dreams fluttered over her. What might they be whispering to Young Greece?

Palm Sunday was drawing to a close. For four days concealed behind the scenes, and now suddenly at midnight dreamily pacing up and down the stage, I felt the oppressive half-consciousness of a sleep-walker.

The following morning I hastened to the island : every thing there was new to me. I beheld, for the first time, the variegated mixture of Greek costumes, the display and pride of Palikars promenading with their weapons stuck in their silken garments. Amongst them the Frankish coat wanders like an alien. Even without their red and blue ribbons, suspending the crosses upon their breasts, each individual seemed to say, " I, too, am a hero." Truly not of Marathon or Salamis. The events of September still glittered in their eyes. As a German I could not sympathise with this: who can sympathise with ingratitude ? *

I here became intimate with a young travelling companion of mine, a lieutenant of artillery from Switzerland, who was going to Odessa as tutor in a family of distinction. I was astounded when he told me that he was a passenger of the third class. What self-denial is requisite for such an act! I also became acquainted here with a young French physician, who had been domiciled for several years at Cairo, but who had made a trip to Paris to recruit his health, and was now on his return.

In the afternoon I embarked on board the Dante, which was to convey me to Egypt. Thenceforward I found myself tolerably solitary in the cabin ; there was only a young Russian prince with me. The deck, on the other hand, presented a very singular party. A Turkish slave-dealer with his people, and five slaves, crouched around the funnel. Two of the slaves, — a handsome white lad and a dark brown girl, especially excited interest. I was astonished that a French ship would convey such passengers. We had scarcely taken these people on board, who embarked direct from a Turkish vessel, when ours hoisted the pale-coloured plague ensign, whereby our further intercourse with Syra was strictly prohibited.

In the evening we had a gorgeously beautiful sky ; a storm was brewing, and every preparation was made on deck for its reception. The slaves and the rest of the passengers of the fourth class remained where they were ; there was nothing but a very thin covering to protect them. At last our expectations were realised :—the storm burst. Such a scene cannot be described. The vessel rolled upon the boisterous sea ; I clung closely to my cot ; whatever was not fixed in the cabin was upset ; glasses, cups, plates, all tossed and tumbled about. The lightning glittered through the broad arch of heaven ; the thunder rattled amongst the creaking beams ; the rain fell in torrents upon the ship, and oozed even into the cabin. I was apprehensive of danger to our steam-boat. This very morning neither of the two French mail steam-boats lying at Syra were disposed to proceed : the Dante, as the commander himself assured me, had already suffered considerably. But in such a situation we are taught resignation. My soul clung fast to my guardian angel. Has it, so said I to myself, brought me thus near to my anxiously desired goal to plunge me and all my hopes into the solitude of a watery grave ?

* This refers to the revolution of the 14th of September, 1842.

All went off favourably. In the morning I inquired of my companion, who had just come down from the deck, about the poor slaves. I had thought with pity on them during the dreadful deluge of rain : they were exposed to the whole of this cold night-bath, but they were again in good spirits ; the negress alone had suffered severely from fever, produced by the nocturnal frost.

Late in the evening of the 3d of April we arrived at Alexandria. We had there also to endure a wretched night. The approach to the harbour of Alexandria being too dangerous to be navigated during the obscurity of night, our vessel tacked to and fro in front of the entrance for several hours ; and, as often as it turned, it produced the most unpleasant motion. How rejoiced was I when we cast anchor the following morning. The harbour presented a most animated scene ; I was particularly struck with the number of black labourers on the vessels. Slender minarets shot upward high above the houses : the palace of the viceroy glittered on the left, close to where the celebrated Pharos once stood : upon the right, along the quay, is a string of bustling marine warehouses : palm-trees presented themselves here and there ; and in the distant background, Pompey's Pillar rose in solitary state. But what noise and confusion enveloped us the instant we landed on the quay ! Camels and asses lay or stood around us in multitudes ; stout Turks, clad in gay silks, strutted amongst the brown Bedouins, clothed in their simple dirty frock : the splendid turban, the red tarbusch, and the French hat were intermingled.

On board the vessel we had already engaged with the landlord of the *Hôtel de l'Orient,* who speedily arranged all the difficulties of the custom-house ; and we then galloped, upon spirited asses, through the Turkish city, up to the European square. This noble square, surrounded by entirely new and stately houses, the creation of Ibrahim Pasha, has a festal appearance when, as happened the day after my arrival, the national flags, which are hoisted upon towers rising from the flat roofs of the consular residences, flutter in their various hues afar in the breeze.

I immediately visited several of the consuls, — the Sardinian, the French, and the Danish. I was also delighted to see again the chief physician of Alexandria, Dr. Grassi. We had met the preceding October in Upper Italy. His return visit, truly, was not very welcome to the guests in the hotel, for during the last few days about thirty persons had died of the plague ; and the plague is Grassi's favourite occupation. He indeed seriously indulges the hope of realising Butard's scheme of eventually extirpating this scourge of the East. He had already made me a convert, in Italy, to his views, that only direct contact renders it contagious. I therefore, without hesitation, accepted his invitation to accompany him to visit a patient that instant announced; but I greatly regret that I allowed the anxiety of the landlord to prevent my accomplishing it.

Special animation had been given to the Mahometan population by the government having just discharged the pay which had been long due. In addition to this, one procession of the Circumcision followed the other across our square. A camel decorated with silken cloths, and carpets, bore the hero of the fête, almost always a boy of at least six years of age. The women whimpered their musical concords ; a great drum was lustily beaten ; nor were there wanting a tamburin and a couple of squeaking fifes. One or two skilful tumblers played a prominent part in the affair. A large multitude of jubilant people accompanied the procession. The dominoes of the women were least to my taste ; yet did their dark eyes glitter pretty roguishly through their white linen masks. But, singularly enough, there was no difference between the festive music of to-day and that which accompanied the lugubrious spectacle of a burial on the morrow.

The same evening I took a walk in a splendid garden of palms. What a magnificent sight is this. How proudly and majestically does the palm-tree rear its head aloft; yet its branches sweetly vibrate in the evening breeze, as if it would whisper in playful confidence.

On Friday I visited Cleopatra's Needles. They conjointly form a truly mournful couple ; the one an upright bright-red granite obelisk, inscribed with the names of Thothmoses III. and Rameses, the two creators of the most wonderful structures of Egypt, and the other, its companion, lying beside it on the ground. What vicissitudes have they not beheld ! Once may they not have stood like two faithful brothers, side by side, before the palace of the charming queen ! Still more tragically did the dark-red granite column, called the pillar of Pompey, or perhaps more correctly that of Diocletian*, present itself to me. It stands upon an insulated eminence, behind it pale sandy dunes, and the lake Mareotis, and in front widely spread ruins, and a Turkish cemetery. But the eye with delight takes a wider survey, and settles upon modern Alexandria ; there death

---

* It has often been a question how this pillar first received the name of Pompey. Von Prokesch says it has received his name as has the grave of Themistocles the renown of his on the shores of the Piræus. It is agreeable indeed to the imagination to conceive that at the foot of this pillar Pompey's haughty soul expired. The inscription noticed by Villoison and Wilkinson, which assigns its erection to Publius the Eparch of Egypt, in honour of Diocletian, would not necessarily exclude its earlier attribution to Pompey, were there any ancient testimony to this effect.

celebrates the resurrection ; and it at last rests upon the widely glittering mirror of the sea, where life is in incessant action, and has not slumbered for an instant during all the ages that are past. These pillars and that obelisk are the only remains of the famed splendour of the city of Alexander. The gigantic catacombs, a real city of the dead, with the adjoining bath of Cleopatra, which bears her name without the least foundation, recall less its passed splendour than its passed greatness. The impression which hangs as it were a veil of crape before the eye sparkling with the reflected tints of variegated life, was to mine not new, and therefore less mysterious ; and yet was I pleased to entomb it again within my soul. How did I rejoice in the rays of the bright sun, although now near high noon, upon quitting this obscure scene of desolation. But the visit was well suited to Good Friday. May the dead, whose bones moulder here—and doubtlessly many a martyr has here borne his own bloody cross—now rejoice in the beams of an Eternal Easter Sun.

The street of marble pillars from the door of the sun to that of the moon—who can adequately conceive its splendour ?—can be only recognised by the remains of its foundations, and the course of its cisterns. The spot can scarcely be traced where stood the Temple of Serapis, once one of the architectural wonders of the universe, but there are mounds of ruins upon ruins. Thence, possibly, may be obtained by exhumation many a fragment of the great and beautiful past, and many a treasure of art, although it is hopeless to expect that we should recover a single manuscript of the library of the Ptolemies. To compensate us for that loss, the names of an Eratosthenes, of a Clemens, and of an Origen, float over this waste of the dead in imperishable freshness.

This is the triumph of mind over matter : — cities disappear with their power, which defied all competition, — with their splendour, which dazzled the eye, — with their magnitude, which bordered upon the miraculous, — cities built in centuries by the hands of myriads. You stand upon their formless ruins, and you ask, where are they ? A thinker scarcely called a wretched hut his own ; but he bore genius in his bosom, and the thoughts which he conceived and uttered stand prominently throughout all time, imperishable as a mountain, streaming forth their lustre like a star throughout the realm of intellect.

Cairo, 12th April, 1844.

I found myself obliged to leave Alexandria earlier than I had at first wished. It was upon the morning of Easter Sunday that I embarked on board a vessel to proceed up the Nile to the ancient capital of the Caliphs.   On the preceding evening, for the first time this year, the terrific Chamsin had begun to blow ; what I had mistaken for the twilight rosy hue, was nothing but the bright-red sandy dust swept up from the desert and filling the whole atmosphere.   Even after 6 p.m. the heat had remained excessive ; during the night the howling storm had interrupted my slumbers, but this morning it seemed as if even the sun of Egypt was celebrating the Easter Holidays.   The cheerfulness of the morning surprised us all, and a wind was blowing which rendered the navigation of the Nile practicable.   This was quite a new adventure for me ; but as I travelled with the physician who was on his return from Paris to Cairo, it was rendered easy enough.   We were provisioned for several days, and we had both cooking utensils and a cook.   In our vessel we had, besides, seven Arabs as sailors.   Upon our embarking they were at their meal : seated in a circle, they scrambled for their pilau with their scrubby fingers out of a large family dish common to all ; and this during the whole of our excursion was their main sustenance. Frequently, indeed, they gathered a species of green weed from the fields bordering the Nile, which they devoured with great satisfaction, while I should have thought it fitted only for the digestion of quadrupeds.   On separating from them they were pleased with being presented with a solid piece of mutton, nor did they by any means despise a glass of our wine.

My first direct intercourse with our Arabs consisted of the significant question *Waue deyib ?* (Is the wind fair ?)   The word *deyib* (good) did me many a good turn, and I believe it makes a favourable impression even when the stranger has nothing better to say than the word *good.*   There are besides two other words with which the stranger in Egypt becomes early familiarised ; they are the first and the last which resound in his ears ; they are the compendium of a characteristic of the East.   The one is *bukra* (to-morrow), the other *backschisch* (drink-money).   Every thing that the Oriental can defer until to-morrow he certainly will not do to-day, for he has a very different idea of time from what we have.   The word *backschisch* children seem to learn immediately after " father " and " mother :" it might be called their a b c.

I had not reflected upon the possible dangers of our Nile voyage, until, close to the junction of the canal with the river, we met a vessel that had been blown on her beam-ends by the wind.   This vessel was but a trifle smaller than ours.   Six men, all good swimmers, were carrying on shore a female passenger who was drowned.   The result of this melancholy spectacle was, that without hesitation we permitted our sailors to take refuge in a cove whenever the current appeared oo violent, or the place at all dangerous.

The banks of the Nile are not to be compared with those of the Seine or the Rhine, but they have their own peculiar beauty ; and my eye revelled in many a new delight. The whole course of the canal is cheered by broad, flat, green plains and numerous villages. Upon the approach of evening we reached Hatfeh. Clumps of acacias formed its outposts, and its palms, poplars, and sycamores, interspersed amidst its white manufactories and high minarets, make a most agreeable impression ; besides this, the fragrance of orange blossoms was wafted towards us. We disembarked to solicit the lock-keeper to open the passage. This was easily effected through the familiar address of my travelling companion, and a significant squeeze of his hand. We passed through the narrow bazaar, and purchased oranges and dates.

But now we again floated upon the proud waves of the sacred stream. Sunk in the contemplation of those distant and obscure ages which are interwoven closely with our own infantile reminiscences, I looked down into the majestic river ; evening was at hand and I noticed to-day, for the first time, that in Egypt there is no twilight. We found the splendid view of Fuah was already obscured.

The following morning we perceived that we had made but very little progress. The wind, as our reis assured us, had been quite still. The colour of the water of the Nile was the light muddy yellow of the *flavus Tiber* at Rome. I was anxious to taste it. Who knows not how celebrated is its excellence ! My physician told me it was most wholesome without filtering, as was usually practised in earthen or stone vessels, or by the infusion of bitter almonds. And in fact, notwithstanding its suspicious appearance, it had not the least unpleasant taste.

We passed now almost constantly between delightful banks ; the green of the meadows and clover fields was much darker and more luxuriant than along the canal : here and there we beheld a row of palm-trees, or a group of dark sycamores shading doubtlessly the white gravestone of an Arabian saint. We occasionally beheld solitary, stately villas beside the earth-coloured villages, the latter scarcely observable but for their white or reddish-white minaret. Thus, at Terraneh, there is a splendid house, built by the Italian Cibara, and which looks haughtily down from its wooded heights into the broad stream, with all the dignity of a European. The Nile was not at present high. We saw several vessels aground, and particularly two laden with wool ; and we also observed the wreck of others, which had been totally lost, floating upon the surface. We ourselves frequently grated upon shoals ; but our sailors immediately jumped into the water to set us again afloat.

The navigation of the Nile derives considerable animation from the custom of the Arabs of always singing whilst at work. This bears, to be sure, no manner of resemblance to what we call singing, but even their uniform tones are agreeable to hear. The text was no doubt always religious. Allah, or Ya Allah, the great exclamation of the East, was the predominant sound. I invariably found a religious bearing amongst these people, the result doubtlessly of their frequent prayers. It often made an elevating impression to behold at the instant that the sinking sun cast the last ray of its red and golden glimmer upon the sky, our own Arabs, as well as all who were walking on the shore, suddenly, as by one impulse, cross their arms and then raise them upwards, and kneel and prostrate themselves upon the earth. The Arabs have, possibly, derived this custom from the Jews of preferring to pray on the banks of rivers. They think that thereby their souls become purified and more holy.

On the fourth morning we disembarked upon the left bank of the Nile where the river makes a large bend. After passing through fields, exhaling refreshing odours, and animated by innumerable birds, we arrived at a sandy district which was elevated considerably above the river. It was alarming to look down upon it, for the fine sand lay heaped to a depth of from thirty to forty feet, and it seemed that one false step would precipitate us without the chance of a staying point. My companion told me that this dune might give me some idea of the desert : it was, in fact, a portion of the Lybian desert, which in its rapacity had stretched forth an arm towards the fertile and beneficent waters of the Nile ; but thick and luxuriant shrubs peered forth singularly enough from the lofty ridges of the sand.

During the whole voyage we frequently landed. Every morning, when rejoicing to quit my hard berth and the nightly tormentors natural to the vessels of the Nile, we found ourselves at some village. Then the wind invariably failed every evening for our Arabs ; and we were thus in the morning enabled to purchase fresh milk and eggs, even if nothing else offered. Our Arabs met with friendly acquaintances in all the villages: we were incessantly obliged to urge our departure. The Fellahs whom we beheld upon the banks, both men and women, all looked poor and dirty ; but their eye, methinks, sees not like ours : they do not miss what we want. Among the men I saw many a countenance with an agreeable expression of energy ; the sun had always burnt them dark brown, which harmonised admirably with their features. The women looked pretty only at a distance, walking along with a graceful bearing, their water-pitchers upon their heads.

At noon of the fourth day we saw the point of the pyramids. I took them at first to be the tops of the masts and sails of craft not far from us,—but it was really the pyramids! The idea is deeply affecting. Yonder are the pyramids! Who has not beheld them in his mind's eye, these imperishable pyramids, these mysterious monuments of a bygone age, grand in its reminiscences? how delighted was I to see them with my own eyes! The fancy, however, still retained full freedom to attribute a most imposing bulk to these points that were alone visible.

As evening approached, and as we yet saw nothing of Shubra, we gave up the hope of reaching Cairo before nightfall. Suddenly, however, a favourable breeze sprung up, but so strong that it wanted but a couple of inches to plunge one side of our vessel in the water; we flew rapidly on past Shubra, glittering in its brilliant light. Between eight and nine, after being carried about forty paces through shallow water upon the shoulders of our Arabs, we landed in good condition at Bulak. It is true, we arrived at an unpropitious moment at Cairo, for we found the gate already closed, and we were ignorant of the parole; but my companion knew how to untie the knot. He called through the gate to the guard that he came as Hakim Baschi (a first physician) direct from Mehemet Ali, at Shubra, whither he had been suddenly called. So soon as the credulous guard had opened the gate, even in absence of all identification (for every physician bears a diploma), we entered without further hinderance.

In the *Grand Hotel de l'Orient* I met with my previous travelling companion from Syra to Alexandria. He immediately told me that there was here quite a peculiar fruit. " Go to Shubra," said he to me, " and there you will see it hanging." This I found to be the sheikh of a neighbouring village, who, because he had not immediately delivered up or sent back to his village a countryman who had fled from it, on account of the tyranny of the imprisonment consequent on the nonpayment of the poll-tax*—whether ignorant or not of his being there—was strangled without any trial, and hung for three days

* The nature of this poll-tax. Every village pays its peculiar tribute. If an individual cannot contribute his portion, it is unhesitatingly levied upon his nearest neighbour, or if he be as needy as the other, upon the next, and so on. It often happens that deceased persons are mulcted. The survivors, or even the relatives of the household, must pay for him. The revenue will lose nothing: this is the state maxim. This maxim was recently followed out in a very peculiar manner upon the transport of some horned cattle to Lower Egypt: the majority had died either before, or immediately upon, their arrival. The physicians declared the meat unwholesome. But how now was the revenue to be indemnified? The physicians were constrained to pay for their opinion. This sounds absolutely incredible, but it was related to me by several trustworthy persons at Alexandria.

upon a tree in the splendid promenade of Shubra, as a spectacle and a warning. This proceeding surprised me exceedingly, for only a few days before the French consul at Alexandria had told me that as soon as Mehemet Ali had condemned the man, he had gone to him and represented that such terrific measures would be very prejudicial to his good repute in Europe. Thereupon Mehemet Ali promised him to consider the condemnation as merely *in terrorem,* and that it should not be carried out. Lavalette had been congratulating himself upon this successful achievement of diplomatic authority ; the conclusion of which was, that upon a tree in one of the most lively and splendid streets of Cairo a sheikh was suspended, who, I was assured by many persons, was a very estimable individual.

The following day I rode with the Austrian consul-general to Shubra. We had scarcely gone a few steps in the company of the dragoman of his highness, when we met Mehemet Ali, who was taking a walk with his suite. When he perceived us he remained standing, and I was immediately introduced to him. He gave me one of his usual glances with his sharp eye, and said he would summon us to him instantly. Mehemet Ali has noble and sharply marked features, to which his long white beard is an admirable adjunct. Between his eyes he has a more than serious wrinkle, which made me desire never to have him for an enemy. From the haleness of his appearance, he looks younger than he is. The most striking portion of his dress is his fine fur robe. He wore no trinkets, nor did he bear any sign of his rank. He did not wear a turban, but a red fez.

We might have sauntered for about five minutes in this paradise of a garden, which has probably no equal, when Mehemet Ali called us to him. We took our seats with him upon his divan. He gave me, through his dragoman, the heartiest welcome, but said to the consul-general that he did not think it requisite to welcome him, he being at home. Upon expressing my astonishment to him that he was about to quit Shubra precisely at the time when it became the most charming residence in the world, he replied that we in Europe were very differently circumstanced to him. With us, whatsoever the government ordained was done, whereas, unless he were present, his orders, whatever they might be, would surely be neglected. He purposed, he said, to visit his agriculturists near Alexandria, and overlook their labours. After a cup of coffee, the conversation diverged to all kinds of topics. With respect to the gold-washing in Upper Egypt, Mehemet Ali had learnt foresight, and had become suspicious. The wealth that may be acquired by an improvement of the rude system now practised is said to be enormous ; but all the experiments yet made by Europeans, for the Viceroy, have had no other result than to cost his generosity large sums of money. He circumstantially related to us that he was now much busied in increasing the size of his breed of horses, and that for this purpose he had ordered some large Mecklenburg steeds. Upon this subject he was pleased to be witty. We were discussing whether the size of the stallion or of the mare contributed most to that of the race. My companion was of opinion that it was the size of the mare ; but Mehemet Ali thought differently. Take, for instance, said he, my step-son* Ibrahim and his mother. He is big enough truly, and yet his mother is small. This observation was the more surprising, as the Orientals, as is well known, rarely ever in conversation with Europeans refer to the ladies.

On the whole, Mehemet Ali spoke freely and well. We passed about two hours in the company of the old man.

MEHEMET ALI.

No Eastern name has, since the commencement of this century, been more frequently mentioned in European circles than that of Mehemet Ali. Our sympathies with the East, the deeply rooted sentiments of our early childhood, must necessarily be kindled into active energy when reflecting upon a man who has evoked the light of a new day over the ancient land of the Pharaohs. What a chorus of voices, in English, in French, in German, have resounded upon this phenomenon ! But when we listen to their strange discords, how the one raises the great reformer to the skies, and how the other tramples upon the tyrannical monster, that land of unfathomable mysteries seems to have produced in this man the newest mystery of all ! These differences of opinion continue to this very hour. At the moment that the author of the " Briefe eines Verstorbenen " decks Mehemet Ali in the most festive garment by the splendour of his narration, the " Correspondenzen vom

* Ibrahim Pasha is the step-son of Mehemet Ali, who married the widow of his commanding-officer. He was born at Cavata in Roumelia, in 1789. He is a little taller than the Viceroy, but with an appearance much less prepossessing. The preponderating influence of the amiable character of his mother has produced permanent and beneficial results upon his natural disposition. He is evidently a *bon vivant*, also a courageous soldier, and tolerant in his opinions, he is fond of agriculture as a recreation from the exacting claims which his position makes upon his time and inclinations. He has several children ; the eldest, Achmet Bey, was born in 1825.

Nil" resound their implacable arraignments against the accursed barbarian.

I am far from presuming that I can harmonise these differences. Edward Rüppel was the man best adapted to effect this, from his long residence in the Egyptian states, from his profound knowledge of the historical development and present condition of Egypt, and from the acuteness as well as the correctness of his judgment. But in the course of three months I had many opportunities for observation, and many an opinion was disclosed to me by men who have been intimate with the country for years. Since my return from the East, I have been too frequently called upon to express my sentiments upon Mehemet Ali, not to avail myself eagerly of the present opportunity to record here my matured judgment.

Forty years ago Mehemet Ali was at the head of four hundred Albanian soldiers; that was the entire amount of his importance. Involuntarily the present attendant upon strangers in the monastery of St. Catherine upon Mount Sinai is present to my memory, — a venerable old man, with delicate Greek features and a handsome white beard, who commanded at that same time a thousand Mamelukes. What a career lies between the position of the Colonel of Albanians of 1803, and the Egyptian Viceroy of 1845! The Turkish governors of Egypt, such as Kosruf and Kurschid Pasha, were, notwithstanding their official representation of the Porte, but sorry opponents compared with the Mamelukes, who, like indestructible ramparts, pertinaciously opposed the ambitious plans of the young Albanian. But in a few years he compassed their total destruction, aided no doubt mainly by the weapons of sanguinary intrigue. To what contests and bloody conflicts has not the Porte constrained him, to wrench from the Wechabites the holy land of the Mahometans, and to elevate himself to the rank of an Arabian prince! This he has successfully accomplished, in spite of rebellion in the very heart of his own dominions. Upon what enormous districts in Upper Egypt has he not ventured to cast his eyes! and he has victoriously acquired them from the madly excited native hordes. He wished to possess Syria, and he took it. And all this in the very face of the Divan, which has earnestly watched the rebellious vassal from the commencement of his ambitious career, has encompassed him with treachery, and has often warred against him with the sword. The infidelity of his European alliances and the superiority of European arms have, it is true, deprived him of the possession of Syria; but Constantinople itself has not gained one victory over him.

And what is Mehemet Ali doing in the interior of his country, during this warlike agitation upon its confines? He creates a costly

navy,— if only for the imperiously pressing instant,— a navy such as
the East never before had ; he disciplines his troops upon European
principles ; he opens amicable relations with the wild tribes of the
Desert; he cultivates the soil with plantations of cotton, indigo, the
sugar-cane, and by the propagation of the silkworm in Syria. Further,
he embellishes his land with charming pleasure-grounds and with
splendid buildings : he increases the fertility of the country by canals ;
the noblest, of incalculable importance, incessantly absorbs his attention and care. He lines the banks of the Nile with factories ; he
founds a multitude of schools for the arts of war and peace, and
establishes hospitals ; he introduces vaccination, and calls the landed
proprietors together for deliberative consultation. Is that not performing something extraordinary ? — Is that not labouring towards a
noble regeneration of the East ?

It is very true that, to a head full of such plans,— a mind which
combines such rare talents, is not conjoined the heart of a Christian philanthropist ; but this, I most assuredly believe would never
have produced the results he has effected. His eye can view
blood without blenching, whether righteously or unrighteously shed.
He has an iron hand, and every blow leaves its victim dead upon the
ground. Assassination weighs lightly upon his soul : and the wants
of his oppressed people harass him but little, if all but conduce
to his great ultimate aim. The suppression of the slave-trade is
more indifferent to him than to Guizot or Aberdeen. And he im-
presses upon all his subjects, imperatively, what Napoleon urged upon
his princes and kings, the maxim, " Your paramount duty is my
service ;" and that royal dictum, " L'état c'est moi," he has more
efficiently proclaimed than did its author, Louis XIV.

We may therefore be fully justified in withholding from Mehemet
Ali the attribute of humanity, which is indispensable to a Christian
sovereign if he will not be styled an accursed tyrant ; and we are
also justified in contemplating with sorrow the grandeur which has
made so many wretched corpses the foundation of its triumphal
arch. But let us view the East as it is. The present age of that
country the author of the " Briefe eines Verstorbenen" compares,
not injudiciously, with the middle ages of Europe. Viewed from
this point, we shall form a right judgment of his cruelties ; and
although religious zeal may be urged in extenuation of the atrocities
of our own middle ages as a cloak to shelter them from the nakedness of those perpetrated by the Egyptian Viceroy, yet is that cloak
died deep in carnage. And has not poison stood ready prepared for
Mehemet Ali in his own palace during the last forty years ? Did not
the bowstring constantly await him ? Has not the sword of rebellion
been repeatedly wielded in bold hands against him ? We seek in vain

c 2

for parallels to all this in modern Europe ; — and equally in vain
may we seek them to the immeasurable and shameless deceptions of
Egyptian officials, notwithstanding Mehemet Ali's sanguinary
severity.

If we wish to appreciate correctly, the complaints made, by many
European travellers, of the treatment of the poor Fellahs, we must
first acquire a thorough knowledge of the native population of Egypt,
and of their obstinate indolence, which has not an ear for the voice
of exhortation ; and we must also lay aside our acquired notions of
well being in a people with whom freedom from want is alone imperative, and who care not for any luxury. And even if it be repeated
again and again that Mehemet Ali's selfishness is the sole motive
to all his acts — that he calls the whole country his own — that he
possesses all the manufactories — that he is the universal specu-
lator as well as the sole and all-monopolising merchant; still it is
not to be forgotten, that all that Mehemet Ali gains he spends
again upon the whole country, and thereby, even if it be not within
the compass of his wish, or at least the direct and immediate object
that he seeks, yet is it unavoidable that it must prepare a future
which shall place Egypt in the enjoyment of a new and beautiful era.

An unpropitious star may, doubtless, rise upon Egypt upon the
death of its Viceroy. Ibrahim Pasha may possibly trample down with
heavy footsteps the tender seedlings which require a careful hand
to nourish. Yet it is very questionable how far Egypt's fate will be
at his disposal. The part of an Abd-el-Kader may be his, and thus
would the fruits of Mehemet Ali's exertions advance rapidly to their
full maturity.

Mehemet Ali has been considered as the protecting stay of Mahometan orthodoxy, or rather it has been declared that he is considered
as such in the East ; but on the other side this has been as absolutely
denied, and this assertion has been supported by his self-willed and
irreverent proceedings against the property of the mosques. The
appropriation of this property, viewed abstractedly, was certainly
the act of fraudulent might against right, but it received a tinge
of justification in the dissipated and deceitful guardianship of the
clergy themselves : besides, Mehemet Ali has very recently declared
the amount of the whole of his possessions in *Wagf,* whereby he
places it under the all-potent protection of the mosques; and in case
of the total extinction of his family, he makes the mosques his lega-
tees. This was doubtlessly one of the most skilful strokes of policy
on the part of Mehemet Ali. And whether the Mahometan Prince
upon the banks of the Nile is as free-thinking and enlightened in religious matters as the present Rex Christianissimus upon the banks
of the Seine, he has nevertheless acquired from the latter his pru-
dent toleration of orthodox principles.

But the point upon which humanity may be most cordially greeted is that of religious toleration, so widely disseminated by Mehemet Ali. Nowhere, throughout all the countries where Mahometanism prevails, is the Christian, as such, so highly regarded as in Egypt. One principal cause of this is, doubtless, the many European Christians, chiefly French and Italians, who are in the service of Mehemet Ali, many of them in high stations. Egypt has been led undeniably by Mehemet Ali a great step towards its ultimate conversion to Christianity, however little probability there may be of its immediately taking place, through his open and decided opposition to the determinations of the Porte in the affair of the renegades.

This recals to mind an interesting communication made to me by a member of the diplomatic circle at Cairo. The object was to annul, with Mehemet Ali, the renegation of a subject of his government. Mehemet Ali said, " Let him go home." That might be called cutting the knot, not untying it. For, in this case, Mehemet Ali's protection was not needed. It is to be understood that the renegade wished to stop in Egypt. Mehemet Ali then advised that he should not reside either in Cairo or in Alexandria, as he could not be responsible for the tranquillity of the population in those capitals. In the course of the interview he denied that he was already apprised from Constantinople of its most recent decision of the renegade question. Upon quitting him the consul-general met the minister, who still had with him the note of the Porte to Mehemet Ali. Presuming that Mehemet Ali had already acquainted the consul-general with it, he imparted its literal contents. The following is the peculiar mode of expression of the note : — " Many instances have hitherto occurred of depraved persons having become converts to the doctrines of the Holy Prophet, and having then again withdrawn from them to betray the holy mysteries, and to desecrate them. When detected, the Sultan has condemned them to be beheaded and hanged. But he has now resolved no longer to inflict upon them such punishment, but to leave these perjured outcasts of mankind, who are not worthy to soil the executioner's hands, to their own shame and wretchedness. They may therefore now with impunity return to the heart of their own community, bearing with them the poison of their perjury."

We may not, I believe, consider this language as the candid opinion of the Divan in this matter, although its enthusiasm is possibly great enough for it ; but its policy towards Mehemet Ali is reflected therein, which causes it to give its forced condescension towards the European powers the colouring of an act of unbiassed determination and religious forbearance. The old cunning Viceroy can as readily as any other interpret the style of the Porte.

In his political relations with the European powers, Mehemet Ali has always been crafty enough to derive advantage from their dissensions. He is fully aware that, were it not for these dissensions, the East would long since have assumed a very different form ; and the absolute certainty that, nevertheless, the Turkish empire is incessantly hastening towards its great and final catastrophe, is an important element in the calculations of his policy. He well knows that his own kingdom does not occupy the lowest place in the great roll of proscription. If he has become vacillating and disingenuous towards his European friends, he in that course follows his head as much as his heart.

The plan was very subtly conceived, which, in opposition to Russia's conquests, already accomplished upon paper, boldly erected a stable bulwark, by stretching his arm forth over Syria to the very confines of Persia, and thus as it were conjunctively creating a large asylum for Mahometanism. He was justified in reckoning upon the alliance of England ; for if England would, conjointly with its own interests, have a regard for the interests of Mehemet Ali, it must necessarily acknowledge itself as his natural ally. But England looked with other eyes. The death struggle of the Turkish empire could not be averted by the restoration of Syria ; therefore the Holy Land was, without hesitation, given back to its original oppressors. But Mehemet Ali, by the successful working out of his plans; might win an importance which would have effectually disarranged foreign speculations. It was only when he found himself disappointed in his expectations of England, that he thought of an alliance with the French. His experience of the conduct of this ally has, had it even been necessary, fully opened his eyes. For the same idea which withheld the policy of England from a defensive alliance with the Viceroy, doubtlessly influenced France when it so unsparingly compromised the interests of its confederate.

Verging now so closely on his departure from the all-cheering sun, his cares must lie the heavier upon his heart, the more clouded the future presents itself to his apprehension. In all his transactions with England, even when only petty interests are concerned, he is more than cautious. He dreads too much the long fingers of this guest. If acquainted with Roman history, he will certainly think of the Romans, who only desired to be invited and admitted into a country where they purposed speedily to plant their eagles. Mehemet Ali, moreover, is not without diplomatic friends to tickle his ears with flattering tales ; although policy therein frequently subserves commercial speculations, which have evoked a phantasmagoria of the discovery of an Eldorado, the projectors having meanwhile filled their own pockets at his expense.

With respect to the event which took place at the Egyptian Court in July 1844, it is indeed difficult to form an accurate judgment. People profess to see in it a manifestation of the old fox, — a new artifice of the practised conjurer. If we look back to the history of his life, and especially to the first decisive steps in his career, we shall not long seek in vain for an analogy ; for at the very time when he first cast his eagle eye upon the throne of Egypt, he concealed himself beneath the mask of tranquil resignation, and thereby weathered successfully the tempest of events. But it is also a positive fact that, for some time past, he has exhibited striking indications of decrepitude of mind. To this we may add that he has recently dismissed his harem by the express advice of his physicians. And an attack of melancholy which is sufficiently explained by the communications made to him of the sad state of his country, may have effectively contributed to so remarkable a display of his policy.

Cairo, May 8th.

To become speedily better acquainted with the ancient Saracenic city, it was indispensable that I should immediately quit my hotel with its superior European tinge, more costly to the purse than agreeable to the palate. It is true that from my windows there I had a very delightful view of the beautiful Esbekieh square, encompassed with its acacias and sycamores, and celebrated by the memory of the Mameluke festival held there, as also by that of Bonaparte who resided in it in the palace of Elfy Bey, and of Kleber whose breast was there transpierced by Turkish fanaticism through the dagger of Soleyman ; beholding at the same time displayed before me the very praiseworthy creation of the existing government, which has secured this square from its annual inundation, and transformed it to its present cheerful appearance.

A few days after my arrival in Cairo I changed to the Casa Pini, a near neighbour of the English Consulate, in a genuine Cairo street, where even the meeting of a rider upon an ass may have its disagreeable results, and a loaded camel wends with difficulty through.* I have no view here except from the flat roof, whither I do not neglect frequently to repair towards sunset to walk. I am there

---

* A short time since it was proposed to widen many narrow streets by removing the stone seats before the doors, as well as all the projections of the lower portions of the houses. But one after the other of the aggrieved parties came to lay their complaints before the minister of police. The minister called the director of police, and censured him for having adopted his measures so heedlessly that every body came with loud complaints to him. He appears to have thought that his commands could have been executed like a thief in the night, and in obscurity.

surrounded by innumerable minarets, and scattered palm-trees
which elevate themselves above the houses huddled together. I also
behold small gardens, planted with stately trees, laid out upon some
of the neighbouring roofs.   Close to me I regularly find one or two
Catholic friars in their capuchin robes.

As many of the houses are, in a certain sense, open above, the
muezzins, or prayer criers, might look down from the madneehs of the
mosques upon many an agreeable family party, were they not almost all
blind. But their very blindness may be the recommendation to their
post; for the Egyptian is extremely jealous of any participation in
his domestic recreations, and especially of even the most harmless
glimpse of his wives.   Yet did these muezzins, although their voice
to a German ear has any thing but a musical tone, produce a serious
impression with their exclamation " There is no God but God," and
what ever else constitutes the theme of their exquisite psalmody.
The loud prayer from the many hundred minarets, especially when
resounding at the hour when the foaming waves of this land of the
Thousand and one Nights are lulled to rest, envelopes Oriental life as
with a holy temple wall.   To the Mahometans the muezzins are
what our bells are to us.   In Christian Europe we commercially
measure hour after hour by quarters, that the transactions of civil
society may proceed in orderly course.   But how rarely do our
bells resound through the heavy atmosphere of our daily toil, to utter
their beautiful peals, like the voice of heavenly conciliation per-
meating with our earthly handiwork !

I now pass rapidly for an instant to the bazaar which is close in
my neighbourhood.   It is there that the life of Cairo flows in its
fullest currents. However intensely the sun may burn, we may ride
coolly through the narrow unpaved streets, the high houses of which,
with their projecting stories, shade them from the hot rays.   The
bazaar itself, which is about ten paces wide, is enclosed above by light
drapery which hangs suspended from one roof to the other.   On
each side the stalls are laid out with their costly and beautiful temp-
tations.   There the salesman sits with his legs crossed, his pipe
in his mouth, and a cup of mocha in his hand, which he handles
with the most contemplative seriousness.   Coffee houses are met
with at every step, and they are as rarely empty as the mosques.

The assemblage of so many nations of the East recals to mind
the Whitsun festival at Jerusalem.   There are seen Arabs in their
dreamy repose ; Turks in thoughtless self-sufficiency ; Persians with
pride in their eyes, and splendour in their attire ; Armenians with
their manly handome features and dark beards ; Copts with their
brownish-yellow visages full of dark mistrust ; Greek monks in their
black gowns, and with cunning falsehood in their treacherous glance;

Bedouins most picturesque with their keffijeh, and hemp lace round the brow, the freedom of the desert in all their movements; handsome negro boys who are happy enough, in the red tarbusch and the gay clothes with which their masters decorate them; Fellah women with a dirty shift over their broad trowsers, large rings in their ears, and frequently also one in the nose, and many gold coins around their necks. Suddenly an Englishman, with his lady on a donkey, presses through the crowd. A French physician, with his sabre at his side, comes riding upon a splendid nag, his footman making way for him. On one side a harem is proceeding to the bath, enveloped from head to foot in black silk mantillas; the face, excepting the eyes, concealed by a white curtain. These women, riding upon handsomely caparisoned asses, are guided through the miscellaneous mob by their silent and collected seis. The baths themselves next to the mosques are the most conspicuous places of resort. The scene enacting within a barber's stall attracted my attention. It is perfectly ridiculous to see the process; a head thickly covered with a lather of soap, and then the razor dexterously applied in smoothing it to the appearance of a full moon with but the single tuft of Mahomet fluttering in its centre.

On my return I passed the English hotel. A caravan was that instant arriving from Suez with passengers from India. A hundred camels are standing still unpacked in a long and immoveable train. Such a troop of silly faces formed in line makes a remarkable impression.

The dust at this season of the year would be a most oppressive nuisance were not more than a thousand asses incessantly going up and down the city with open water vessels for irrigation; a regulation which does infinite credit to the board of health, for it is of the utmost importance to the poor ophthalmic sufferers who abound here in melancholy multitudes. The number of the totally blind in Cairo itself is greater than is to be found in the entire population of many other countries. One of the privileges of these blind people struck me, it is that they alone may be in the streets after night fall without a lantern. The corners and angles of the streets and the public gardens are but too frequently their only homes. How often upon returning late have I not stumbled over the bodies of the poor blind natives who were lying about! At Cairo great attention is paid to the education of the blind, and the office of muezzin is not the only one open to them.

On the 12th April I went to the citadel. My Cairo dragoman rode by my side in his long white shirt, which he had thrown over his ordinary dress, in his red tarbusch with its blue tassel, beneath which glanced his small dark eyes, full of roguish cunning. Our asses

carried us over many of those disagreeable dogs which, notwithstanding the throng of passengers, lie crouching everywhere about. The
" Riklek dschemalek," and the many other expressions, often seasoned
with flattering forms of speech, to induce people to make way, which
the seis or ass-conductor is incessantly crying to the crowd, echoes
long afterwards in one's ears.   I have often been as much astonished
at the imperturbability of these donkey-drivers as at the cautious
agility with which the crowd at their call made room for the un-
believing Frank.

We found soldiers upon guard knitting, whilst their arms stood
quietly in a corner: a pleasing picture. Indeed, those wretched
Fellahs, with their chopped off forefinger, broken front teeth,
and blinded eye, are better fitted to knit stockings than to wield
arms.   Mehemet Ali has acted very judiciously in not allowing
people who have made these absurd self-mutilations to be exempt
from military duty.

The first place we visited upon the height was the ménagerie with
four lions, one tiger, and several hyenas, which here, in the land
of their nativity, make a very different impression from our
European exhibitions. We then descended into the remarkable
and deep Joseph's well, but we were obliged to wait until the female
visiter, who was in it at the time of our arrival, had cleared the
place, although there would have been space enough for a very large
party.

The citadel upon the declivity of the Mokattam is an extensive
and very strong building.   Many cannons are directed full upon the
city : in Cairo there is no chamber of deputies.   But two objects
especially attracted my attention : the one was the solitary granite
column which once formed a portion of the palace of Saladin, who
founded this citadel ; and the other the incomparable and splendid
alabaster mosque of Mehemet Ali, which conspicuously rears its
glittering crest as a new wonder of Egypt in the very face of those
ancient ones, the pyramids.   At the feet of the citadel reposes this
" sea of the world," in the grandeur of its fulness and beauty, this
" victorious " queen of cities, which, a new Memphis, has built for
herself a glittering throne out of the ruins of the ancient one.   I was
absorbed in the contemplation of its majesty and the splendour of
its view.   But as the magnet turns to the north, so does the eye
here fix itself upon the pyramids.   And viewed from the citadel,
they exercise their full power upon the admiring stranger.

Close to the two sides of the view of the city solemn objects repose.   In the south and north-east, separated only by the Mokattam,
are the two large cemeteries, spread forth with their many beautiful
monuments and mosques. The Desert itself lies beyond and contiguous

to them, thus interposing, as a holy land-mark, between the noisy
bustle of time, and the seriousness of illimitable eternity.   My
attention was drawn particularly to the north-east by the tomb of
the caliphs, with its strong towers, remarkable remains of the ancient
Saracenic style of architecture.   Upon visiting, subsequently, this
silent and yet eloquent region of the dead, I inspected, amongst other
things, the family tomb of Mehemet Ali, consisting of a double
chapel, receiving from above an obscure light through two cupolas.
The marble sarcophagi placed in the centre are simple and noble.   I
plucked a few leaves from the palm-tree branches which waved over
it.   An Oriental tint is given to it by the splendid carpets which lie
spread on each side of the monument.

I stood also by the simple grave of Burckhardt: he died a noble
death.   From the midst of his inquiries into the mysteries of a
venerable antiquity and a sacred region, he was summoned into the
halls of eternity.   But his bones he has left in the land of the imperishable dead, close to the ever-during monuments of the Pharaohs,
in the very land wherein he has erected to his own name a widely
glittering pyramid of fame.

IBRAHIM PASHA.

I have been with Ibrahim Pasha.   Clot Bey, whose obliging disposition makes the wanderers on the banks of the Nile so willingly
his debtors, accompanied me to him.   At first our conversation did not
flow smoothly ; the dragoman to the Pasha was absent, and Clot
Bey is not a good Arabic scholar.   But I had already observed to
my astonishment that even consuls who had been more than twenty
years in Egypt could not communicate without the intervention of a
dragoman.   A misunderstanding occurred when Ibrahim Pasha asked
to what period the most ancient original codex of the Bible extended.
(I had already been given to understand that he was interested in
theological researches.)   I told him as far back as the fourth century.
He was surprised that we had nothing older, as they themselves
possess originals of the time of the prophet.   I naturally hastened to correct the mistake.   It is possible he misunderstood the
calculation of our centuries.   But I rejoiced that at this moment the
dragoman entered.   The Pasha told me, through him, that in the
course of a few years no dragoman would be required at the court
of Egypt, for all the young princes learned Italian and French.   I
replied, that the language which he had already so distinctly spoken,

both by land and sea was in Europe also universally comprehensible.
In the golden age of Egypt, he continued, three pests were unknown,
writers, interpreters, and the plague.   The dragoman was compelled
to give me this explanation, but he did not seem to take it much to
heart.

Amongst other things, he spoke of Prince Albert, the consort of
Queen Victoria.   He had read that the prince, upon visiting his
home, had renounced his patrimony.   I replied that England had
given the prince the best patrimony.   To this he added, in his own
peculiar style, a very good remark upon the celebrated talents of the
princes of the Saxon line.

Ibrahim Pasha has far less noble and delicate features than his
stepfather, the Viceroy.   The soldier is not to be mistaken in his
expression : he has a constantly cheerful smile about his mouth, yet,
even this trait wants delicacy.

The island Roda, in the Nile, is a delightful possession of Ibrahim
Pasha's.   It forms a large and luxuriant garden, with the laying out
of which, however, very critical eyes are not thoroughly satisfied.
I found it in the fullest luxuriance of its bloom.   In one of the
princely buildings constructed entirely in the European style, I
visited the Swedish Consul, and the Greek Anastasy, with his two
charming foster-daughters.   Directly opposite his windows we beheld the pyramids of Gizeh, which hardly appeared two miles
distant.   I saw also in the garden the beautiful giraffe which
the Consul intended as a present to the King of Sweden.   This
transition will scarcely be agreeable to the delicate animal.

But the most venerable object in the island is the ancient tower,
as it is supposed to be at a distance, but which is an octagonal marble
pillar contained within an enclosed wall, and is called Mekkias, or
the Nilometer.   It is upon the same level with the bed of the
stream, and indicates, by the scale marked upon it, the exact rising
and falling of the Nile.   It was formerly mysteriously withheld
from the eyes of Europeans.   If it be not of the very highest
antiquity, as has been sometimes asserted, yet it can be proved to
have stood for more than a thousand years upon its present position,
as prophetic of weal or woe to the valley of the Nile.

My dragoman explained to me that the island Roda was the
pleasure-garden of the daughter of Pharaoh, who had found the
"goodly child" Moses in the flags of the Nile. (Exod. ii. 5.)
Tradition could not have chosen a better locality ; indeed, were
this the case, Memphis which is most probable, and not Zoan, would
have been the royal residence.

MONASTIC EXCURSIONS IN CAIRO.

I was very anxious to visit the monasteries at Cairo. I had an excellent guide in the dragoman of the Austrian Consulate, a native Copt. In the Catholic monastery we found but a single monk: he was most hospitably inclined ; we were obliged to partake of a multiplicity of refreshments before we got access to the library, which appeared to have but little of his regard. When we at last entered it, we found it buried within a densely enveloping cloud. "We have no manuscripts," he said. Yet I found some Arabic ones of little value.

I became acquainted with a highly interesting person in the Armenian bishop. He cherished fondly the idea of a peaceful union of all the Christian sects. This trait appears so very natural when living in the midst of the Mahometan opponents of the cross, yet is it so rare ; the harsh distinctions of the several Christian sects are, particularly in the East, most unpleasantly apparent. I wished to obtain from the bishop a couple of lines in writing for a friend of mine, an autograph collector at home ; but he had a singular apprehension of any publication of his opinions ; and even a biblical maxim, which he could have written, he was fearful might compromise him. Amongst his manuscripts he considered some leaves attached to a modern manuscript as very old, but he was not able to decipher a single word of them as the character was one totally disused.*

Upon reaching the Greek monastery of the Sinaïtes at Cairo, the whole of the brotherhood was in the chapel. We therefore joined them in their religious services. There were multitudes of tapers ; the hymn, of which we remembered the " Ho tu paradoxu thanatos," it being repeated by many, one after the other, was sung so ridiculously out of tune, that the choir boys could scarcely repress their laughter. How melancholy does one quit such worship ! The Kyrie eleison, constantly repeated, was the frame to the whole ceremony.

At its conclusion, some of the bread just consecrated was brought to us : we were also presented with honey and water before we took our coffee. In Paris a whole day may be spent in visits, without the offer of as much refreshment as is presented at every fresh step in a

* Among the Armenian fragments which I have brought with me from the Holy Land, there are several leaves of parchment inscribed with the same extremely ancient characters.

house at Cairo. The standing custom is coffee and a pipe ; but frequently, especially among the Greeks, I was first handed honey or a very sweet preserve. And it is the custom with the natives of the East, and those acquainted with their manners, that before the coffee and the pipe no subject of importance, or that for which the visit is especially made, becomes the topic of conversation. Business is thus rendered to a certain extent agreeable ; one is no longer an entire stranger when sitting with pipe in mouth and cup inhand.

Upon asking at length to see the manuscripts, they told me that they possessed none at all, but that I should find many good ones upon Mount Sinai. Their own library contained printed books only, which were entirely at my service. I then requested the cupboard full of books standing opposite to me to be opened. A full half-hour may have elapsed before the key could be found, and the operation of open-ing accomplished. The libraries in these monasteries are mere orna-ments. They occupy the place that ladies' what-nots do with us. I took several volumes out, and found nothing but manuscripts. Perfectly astonished at my discovery, I mentioned it to them ; but with still greater astonishment they heard me and inspected them. Manuscripts ! manuscripts ! they re-iterated, and seemed to entertain some doubt of it. An ancient manuscript was to them a perfect novelty, for they seemed to be acquainted with such things only by repute ; and no sooner had they heard of their riches in manu-scripts, than they began to dream of their inestimable value. After examining this bookcase, I inspected another in the chapel of the monastery, which proved to be still more productive.

I returned again to this monastery, and a study was in the most friendly way provided for me. The results of these studies I shall elsewhere show. But my discoveries in this library were my first joyful proofs of the incorrectness of the dissuasions made at home against my journey, founded upon the supposition that nothing new was to be discovered, after the exploration of so many who had pre-ceded me. A man of widely celebrated name, and whose pursuits were the same as my own, had visited this monastery twenty years ago, and reports thus baldly upon it : " It contains no manuscripts of any literary interest ! "

THE PATRIARCH OF ALEXANDRIA AND HIS WALLED-UP LIBRARY.

I was informed by many persons of a treasury of manuscripts that had reached Cairo from Antioch, about twenty years ago. It

consisted of an entire library conveyed to Cairo as security, and was
in the immediate possession of the patriarch. No person conversant
with such matters had seen these manuscripts, and therefore the
stories about them were exaggerated into romance. The incredible
addition was soon made, that this library was walled-up. The
Austrian consul-general endeavoured, in the kindest manner, to obtain for me an elucidation of the mystery. To effect this he
thought the best plan would be to make a direct application to the
patriarch, with whom he was personally acquainted. We therefore
rode, one Sunday, in company with a native Greek to Old Cairo,
where the patriarch resides when absent from Alexandria.

After the preliminaries of reception by an aged female domestic,
who hospitably entertained us with coffee and pipes, the patriarch
himself appeared in his home costume, which was sufficiently distinguished to indicate his high rank. Pope Gregory XVI. was more
simply clad when he admitted me to a private audience. The
patriarch, who is now in his ninety-first year, has great dignity in
his appearance, his long white beard, which falls down upon his
breast, becomes him very well; his stature is above the ordinary
height. We exchanged a few friendly words, in the course of which
I told him, that the chief ecclesiastic of my own country was, like
him, a wonder also in his reverend appearance; for he equally resisted the attacks of extreme old age by the indestructible bearing
of a cheerful temperament.

We rapidly approached the object of our visit. The consul-
general told him, that I was a profound Hellenist, although I had
never been in Greece. The patriarch then called for a printed Greek
book in folio, I think it was a volume of Chrysostomus, and he requested me to read in it. I presumed he wished to hear how we
un-Grecians pronounce Greek, and I read him a couple of lines
according to our Leipsic pronunciation. To my great mortification,
I did not succeed in this examination; I may fairly record it as a
failure. The patriarch upon this experiment was of opinion, that
I had scarcely yet learnt the alphabet. We intermingled a little
mirth in our hasty explanations, but the mishap was not to be re-
repaired. I conversed also in Greek with him; but the least mistake
in the Romaic pronunciation, or even a false accent — I had latterly
become accustomed to pronounce the Greek according to its quantity
— he urged harshly in confirmation of his opinion. It would seem
that the patriarch had the delicate ear of a Parisian lady. It was
now, indeed, difficult to make him comprehend, that my studies of
manuscripts could be of any consequence. My *Codex Ephræmi
Syri rescriptus* sounded like a pleasant fable. Upon hearing of it,
he retorted with how could I read manuscript, when I could not
even read a printed text?

The consul began to lose his temper, and told him, he might wholly rely upon him, and that our great object was only to obtain the privilege of the sight of his concealed library. Upon wishing to know why we so eagerly sought to see it, we informed him, that my object was to inspect the ancient codices of the original text of the New Testament, in order to derive a text from their combination, which might approach as closely as possible to what was written by the Apostles. But he added, we have all that we require — we have the Evangelists, we have the Apostles, what can we desire more ? * The idea of criticism seems to have struck his ears for the first time in his ninety-first year. He became thoughtful and distrustful upon our explanations. At last he availed himself of the circumstance that the library was walled-up, and could be entered only at a great outlay ; whereupon we mentioned that we were willing to bear all the charges. Nevertheless he seemed only apparantly to concur, and we very speedily withdrew.

That I did not kiss his hand as my two companions did, may possibly have given him an unfavourable impression of me. Upon this occasion, as upon many others, when I have observed this mark of respect paid by ecclesiastics to their superiors, I remembered the dignified words of the patriarch of Constantinople, who said to a young clergyman, who wished to kiss his hand, " We require preachers, not actors." The want, however, seems to have become reversed ; and even on the banks of the Tiber I heard no echo of this noble sentiment.

From the patriarch we went to Solyman Pasha. Solyman Pasha is a Frenchman by birth, and has obtained great distinction in Egypt by the organisation of Mehemet Ali's army. How much this is appreciated by the Viceroy is proved by the princely rank to which he has elevated him. It is true, indeed, that he is all the Gospel the poorer ; he has sold himself to the Koran, and doubtlessly he has purchased therewith for his conscience many an hour of bitter remorse. When with him I had nothing to do with old Palimpsests, nor even with Greek. The instant he was apprised that I was from Saxony, an opportune inquiry suggested itself to him. Do you know, said he to me, the two daughters of an apothecary living at M——? I was not indeed so lucky as to have such agreeable acquaintances at M——. But Solyman Pasha now related to me in pleasant detail, that he had been in Saxony under Napoleon, and being billeted in the house of an apothecary at M——, had had some trifling and innocent adventures there. This may not, indeed, be called an old love affair, but it certainly belongs to the unfading forget-me-not of ancient affection. Here

* Τὸ εὐαγγέλιον καὶ τὸν ἀπόστολον.

is a man of French blood, and a soldier, who, after living thirty years in the full practice of Oriental customs, thinks still with hearty affection of two apothecary's daughters on the Elbe, to whom he dedicated, before the battle of Leipsic, his transitory gallantries. I met with another Frenchman in Cairo, who had been in Saxony with Napoleon as regimental surgeon. His weak side was, as all his friends knew, to speak about Saxony whenever an opportunity presented, and he was delighted when we met one evening in the garden of Clot Bey, beneath the shade of the pomegranates, where with impunity he could give animated expression to all his sympathies for Saxony.

During our trip back to Cairo, my companion told me of the excavation, some few years back, of the rubbish of the ramparts at Cairo, and of the discovery therein of an ancient Greek church, the walls of which contained a kind of Palimpsest. There were paintings, namely, upon it, which had been executed one over the other, accompanied with Greek inscriptions. The Austrian consul-general had gathered thus much from it, that the original pictures were representations of passages in the lives of Saints, coloured over and obliterated, and replaced by others of a similar character. He was deprived of the opportunity of further examination ; for upon his return from a short excursion to Cairo, he found that all the remains had been destroyed. In explanation of this Palimpsest we must recur to the period and the course of the Iconoclastic fury, which, judging hence, must also have raged at Alexandria.

But to revert to the walled-up library of the patriarch — we induced several Greeks of distinction to attach themselves to our interests ; nevertheless we were still unsuccessful, for as an opponent, we had to combat with a narrow-minded dogmatism, which saw in my critical labours upon the sacred text, some undefined danger threaten the *status quo* of the faith of the Greek church.

At last I found a powerful auxiliary in a German physician, a man whose name had been already very long dear to me. He made his professional intercourse, as family physician to the procurator of the patriarch, available for my object, and upon him some influence was gained by the representation that, upon my return to Europe, I should make an unfavourable report respecting this unapproachable walled-up patriarchal library. The procurator promised that he would have this library opened for me ; but I was not present personally when this took place, and the number of manuscripts that I had the opportunity of examining from it was very small, whereas the remaining contents of the library consisted ostensibly of many thousand printed books. I strongly suspected that I was not ingenuously dealt with, yet those few manuscripts have yielded most

D

welcome results.*   I occupied a whole day in this investigation in
the house of the learned secretary of the procurator.

This secretary had very recently married ; he had a very youthful
wife.   Her share in my visit consisted in nothing more than handing
me pipe after pipe, which she lighted herself, and cup after cup of
coffee ; and at our meal she waited upon both of us, without partaking
with us of the repast.   German wives will scarcely envy the condition of the wife of this secretary.

THE PYRAMIDS.

On the 16th of April, I visited the pyramids.   I have become
rich in never to be forgotten hours.   At the distance of a day's
journey the enraptured eye beholds the queen of all the pyramids :
an hour spent upon its summit glitters with its reminiscences
throughout the entire length of our earthly years.

It was before sunrise that I traversed with my Ali the rubbish
and ruins of the Babylon of the Nile.   Upon both banks we already
found the market in full activity : at Gizeh there were heaped at
our feet large piles of beans, millet, and lentils.   We rode through
a delightful country, planted with palm trees and acacias.   Many
cornfields were ripe for the sickle, others stood widely extended,
high and luxuriant.   We easily forded the canal ; it was almost
empty.   And now, instead of smiling verdure, we had speedily
beneath our feet nothing but the barren sand of the Desert.   We
thus rode cheerfully onward to the objects of our attraction.   And
now hastened from all sides towards us, what seemed from their
familiarity friends and acquaintances ; and yet we had never seen
them before.   They were the Bedouins of the neighbourhood, a
people of robust stature, burnt deep brown by the sun, and with a
vivid fire glittering in their dark eyes.   Although I had strongly impressed upon my dragoman not to burden me with more than a couple
of these intrusive guides to the pyramids, yet we were totally unable
to discard any that came, and they all wandered on with us.

During a journey of four hours' duration the pyramids gained
nothing in imposing effect : they almost appeared to familiarise
themselves into objects of common occurrence.   But, upon ascending
the rocky base, the most considerable portion of which lies buried
in the sand, and we stood at the foot of the greatest among them, this

---

* I have published elsewhere the particulars.   Consult the *Wiener Jahrbücher*, 1845. vol. ii.

mountain, created by the hands of man, had an incomparable effect. Horace must not have stood here when he wrote his *Nil admirari.*

I know not how it happened, but I was impressed at this instant with the remembrance of the Strasburg Cathedral standing upon the banks of the Rhine. It must have been an affinity to the inspired mood which I once felt there in the contemplation of Erwin's wonderful structure, at once Germany's obelisk and Germany's pyramid, that I now experienced.

It was as the sun was sinking in the west that I gazed insatiably upwards at its cloud-capped summit. It appeared to me like the prayer of the German nation, cast in a splendid eternal and tangible form, clear and open as the German eye, bold and decided as the German heart. The inspiration which had so shortly before drawn so many valiant swords from their scabbards, and so much dear blood across the waves towards Jerusalem, to battle for the lost tomb, was suddenly infused as by the voice of an angel : in lieu of the earthly they sought the heavenly Jerusalem, and for a mere temporary earthly grave, an ever-enduring life above. There, in the presence of that monument of inspired Christian faith, there it was, that a religious sentiment thrilled to the profoundest depths of my soul, and loosened within my eyes the fountain of their tears.

Here stood I paralysed by the lightning of Genius ; here stood I gazing upon this venerable mystery. For centuries, the curious have examined it in the dazzling light of the noonday sun ; but the profound son of Egypt has wisely enveloped it in a nocturnal veil. It stands forth like a gigantic thought, conceived in a great age by the mind of an omnipotent ruler : the triumphal festival of the human will and of human art over the kingdom of death and mutability. My eye did not become here moist with emotion ; I was fixed in silent admiration ; methought, I saw before me the human mind, hovering with the heaven-embracing pinions of a cherub.

My Bedouins no doubt were engrossed with other thoughts ; they consider the pyramids as their dear grand-papas, who never cease tossing a trifle to gratify their light-hearted grand-children. This may be easily forgiven them ; for they alone share their great and desert country with the pyramids ; they are both equally faithful to the sands of the Desert. But what makes their society disagreeable is their incessant appeal for backschisch, which even in its most tranquil moments slumbers with only a half-closed eye. They thus hang, notwithstanding their volatile nature, as heavy weights to the pinions of intellectual contemplation.

We had now lying before us the two hundred and six decreasing quadrangular terraces of pale grey fine limestone *, many of which were

* Schubert calls it nummulitenkalk.

D 2

more than three feet high. We instantly ascended: four Bedouins, two before me and two behind, insisted on assisting me. This, considering the confinement of my European clothing, was not unnecessary. We rested twice in the ascent, although I felt no particular fatigue. We reached the platform in about twenty minutes, and this is at about five hundred feet above the rocky base of the pyramid. Upon this platform which is a square surface, twenty persons could conveniently find room. Probably, this pyramid had originally no platform but ran up to a point ; yet the supposition that originally a colossus stood upon its summit, as upon other similar monuments of Egypt, contradicts this opinion.* Besides the whole gradual structure was formerly covered with a polished species of marble. Thus was it that Herodotus beheld the pyramid of Cheops ; and the second, named after Cephren, has still at its apex the remains of such a shining encasement.

Here stood I upon the very summit of the largest pyramid, and my eye surveyed a wide extent of this wonderful and most remarkable land. What a circuit did I not behold ! In the north-east lay the city of the caliphs with its ancient mameluke fortresses, its slender minarets, and its lofty palms, and its citadel which is as superb as it is strong. It leans against the Mokattam, which like a sage looks over it with his white beard. On the east, and on the west, the illimitable Desert in its nakedness glared upon me with its dazzling sand ; here and there only were sparingly scattered tufts and spots of a stunted shrub, which dotted the Desert like the shadows of clouds. In the north the eye was refreshed with the view of the fertile valley of the Nile, with its dark green herbage, the luxuriant vegetation of its trees, and its golden cornfields. In the centre flowed the sacred Nile itself, this all-sustaining element, the very quickener of life. Like a favourite child of the Almighty, it looks with grateful eye to heaven : enclosed by the blank borders of the Desert, it lies there like the joyful token of a dear and distant friend. Lastly, in the south are the ruins of Memphis, reposing in death-like sleep ; the Desert has entombed them ; by their side lies the repository of the mummies, truly the battle-field of Death, and above it tower, like strong and faithful brothers armed for every chance, the pyramids of Abusir, Sakkara, and Daschur.

As the daughters of grief these pyramids were themselves brought into being by the hands of an oppressed people, whose tears and sighs cleave to every stone. But a bold thought was conceived in a human heart, and willed the erection of an ever-during monument, that should baffle the vicissitudes of fate. Thence

* Wansleb, in the year 1673, asserts that the cavities wherein the colossus was fastened, were still to be seen upon the platform.

was the rude and unshapely stone of the wilderness moulded into form, and a second mountain was heaped upon the mountain that had sprung from God's mandate.   It is the work of man's hand, yet to man's eye it is a wonder.

What have not these pyramids beheld in the course of ages! Around them fluctuate the spirit of the mighty Pharaohs ; even if their bodies do not still repose within them.   They beheld Joseph and his brethren.   They are witnesses of the journey into the promised Land, and of the punishment of the hardened Pharaoh.   They have beheld the profound wisdom of Egypt, its arts, its fortunes, and its power ; they have beheld, also, the setting of its sun.

Herodotus, the father of history sat at their feet ; and Alexander, the conqueror of the world.

The torch of Christianity was but lighted over these cities and over these wastes, and instantly they beheld the self-sacrificing enthusiasm of the primitive hermits, and the triumphant wisdom of the Alexandrian sages.

But notwithstanding this, the cross of the Saviour speedily succumbed before the crescent of the Prophet.   A modern Memphis arose : the city of the caliphs towered upon the Mokattam, the sacred centre of Islamism.

Speedily afterwards barbarism wrestled with civilisation, and at last the long-enduring beautiful festival was succeeded by the horrors of a dismal night.

But another ray broke through, towards the close of the last century. *Du haut de ces pyramides quarante siècles vous contemplent,* said Bonaparte to his army ; this nerved them to victory.   Had not the mischances of Aboukir intervened, Egypt would, perhaps, have owed its regeneration to the great son of the French revolution.

Thus wholly absorbed in the contemplation of the present and the past, I stood upon the summit of the pyramid.   Even at the present hour, I still rejoice that my whole soul revelled in the auspicious and glorious moment.   What imports it that' the harmony of the bell call to the revel, if the heart does not feel the resonance?

In descending I again availed myself of the assistance of my four Bedouins.   I found the descent not only more irksome than the ascent, but in some spots even almost dangerous.   Having descended without casualty to the base, I visited the interior of the pyramid. It is well known that this is accomplished by a very unpleasant and difficult path.   I can willingly believe the esteemed Von Schubert *, who says, that he would rather thrice ascend the pyramid, and as

* Reise, t. ii. p. 200.

frequently descend the deepest shaft in his native land, than explore
this path a second time.

The two crooked, narrow, low passages, of which the one leads
upwards and the other downwards, were, although admitting of only
a very curved position of the body, more endurable than that part of
the way where the ascent was made by alternately projecting and
receding portions of the wall on each side, just wide enough to hold
one half of the foot.*

It appears, from very ancient testimony, indeed that of Makrizi,
Masudi, and Abd Allatif, that this opening into the pyramid was
effected in the reign of Al Mamoon, the son of the celebrated
Haroun al Raschid, after he had been dissuaded from destroying
one of the pyramids for the gratification of his curiosity. But
Sylvestre de Sacy supposes, upon very good foundation, that Mamoon
found the opening, and possibly only carried it further.

The result was, however, but slightly productive. We reached, it
is true, a wide chamber, called the Queen's Chamber, which our four
torches but sparingly lighted; we also saw there an empty sarcophagus;
but we were unimpressed with any ennobling sentiment, and were
only conscious of being in the heart of the admired wonder of the
world. The Bedouins wished to conduct me still higher to another
chamber, or further to two others ; but I preferred leaving the field
clear to its inhabitants, the large bats, which we had disturbed.

* Père Sicard, who wrote at the commencement of the eighteenth century,
has given a somewhat particular account of the passages in the interior of
the pyramid. I obtain the following extract from his account from Paulus
Sammlung der merkwürdigsten Reisen in den Orient. 4 Th. pp. 341, 342.

" An attached canal is passed through, which is 85 feet long, and 3 feet 6
inches wide: another diverges from this, which goes upwards and is 96 feet
long, and 3 feet 4 inches wide. At the extremity of this second canal there is
on the right a dried-up well. It runs downwards, and its termination is ob-
structed with sand. A level passage, 113 feet long, and 3 feet wide,
runs from this well, and terminates in a chamber 18 feet long, 16 wide,
and is 21 feet high as far as the commencement of an irregular vaulting.
At present, in this chamber there is neither grave nor mummy. Both have
been removed many centuries ago.

The return is made by the same road as far as the juncture of the second
canal, thence it is necessary to climb over a glacis 136 feet long ; upon each
side is a bench, each with 28 apertures ; the glacis is 6 feet wide, and as far
as the base of the irregular archway 24 feet high. At the upper end of the
glacis there is an even space, and level with its floor runs a canal lined with
granite, 21 feet long, and 3 feet 4 inches high. This canal leads into the
large chamber destined for the reception of the dead. This is 32 feet long, 16
broad, and as many high. The pavement, the roof, and walls are lined with
granite. The sarcophagus is placed upon the ground, 4 feet 4 inches away
from the wall. It is of granite, hewn out of one block, and without a cover.
It is 7 feet long, 3 feet wide, half a foot thick, and 3 feet high. When struck,
it resounds like a bell.

We may, however, be quite certain, that the inside of this, as well as of the other pyramids, contains many interesting secrets. Were it even to be confirmed, that these structures were intended merely to be royal tombs, there would, no doubt, be conjunctively discovered many peculiarities of structure as well as other secondary purposes. And relative to the large canals within the depths, mentioned both by Herodotus and Pliny, we shall some day certainly acquire further intelligence.

The two most considerable contiguous pyramids, those of Cephren or of Sensuphis, and of Mykerinos or Moscheris, I was satisfied with modestly enjoying from the exterior and below, although one of the Bedouins was very willing to clamber, in our presence, to the summit of the second, that of Cephren, which is about 400 feet high.

In the materials of construction the two last do not essentially differ from the first; for it was a mistake to consider, as was formerly the case, that the third pyramid was built of the splendid reddish-black granite, of which only its coating consisted. The costliness of this coating was very tempting, and yet its wilful abstraction first occurred during the centuries immediately preceding ours: remains of it still lie at the foot of the pyramid, whilst upon the second the remains of the former coloured-marble coating, still well preserved, glitter at its summit. Several of the other pyramids of Egypt, as is well known, are built of bricks and tiles; and amongst the smaller ones at Daschur there is one constructed of the same kind of bricks as were made by the Israelites, according to the express account of the Mosaic books. These bricks consist of clay, or rather of the slime of the Nile, mixed up with small pieces of straw to give them greater consistency, and then hardened in the sun.

The two first pyramids, at a small distance apart and with similar angles of elevation, appear to be of similar size. Thence might the Arabic poets, " in the intoxication of their enthusiasm," as Abd Allatif very judiciously remarks, call them " a twin pair of arched breasts rising upon the bosom of Egypt."

It is known that the inside of the second pyramid has been explored, and that the first modern attempt was made by Belzoni in 1816, not without result. The large sarcophagus found in a chamber contained the bones of an Apis. He met also with an inscription, which indicated a previous visit of one of the caliphs.

The third bears traces upon each of its four sides of a rude and destructive hand. Abd Allatif was present when, in the year 1196, the caliph, Osman Ben Jussuf, " by foolish advice," undertook with great energy the destruction of the pyramids. He relates that the very hills shook and the earth trembled at the thundering of the precipitated masses of rock. And yet, after eight months of incalculable labour and heavy cost, the result exhibited merely the weakness of the foiled attempt.

Of the smaller pyramids of inferior elevation, I was chiefly interested in the ruins of that which was built by the royal daughter of Cheops with the gold of her lovers. This reflection occurred to me: " What might in this age be built by such sacrifices?" Such antediluvian gallantry presupposes antediluvian attractions as well as equally gigantic darts of love. What imagination can construct sufficiently colossal images of it? The text of Herodotus is an interesting contribution to the lost giants' chronicle of antiquity.

Whether Herodotus is right in attributing the queen of the pyramids to Cheops, or Manetho, who ascribes it to Pharaoh Suphis, archaeologists have not yet determined, although, in a recently discovered chamber, the name of the latter has been deciphered from inscribed hieroglyphics. Still it is gratifying to consider, like Herodotus, the three great pyramids as having a family connection, for Cephren was the brother of Cheops, and Mykerinos Cheops' son. To these may further be added the partially destroyed lovers' pyramid of the daughter of Cheops.

Herodotus has furnished us with a highly interesting memorandum of the cost of the building of the pyramid of Cheops, which, in his time, was still found inscribed upon the flat marble covering of that pyramid. According to this, a hundred thousand men, during a period of thirty years, were occupied in its construction, and consumed in that time 600 talents' worth (somewhat more than 225,000*l.*) of onions, cabbages, and radishes.

What the positive age of its construction may be, whether the 30th century before Christ or the 40th, or still earlier.* Bunsen and Lepsius will, doubtlessly, soon determine from the most satisfactory data yet extant.

The hieroglyphics of the pyramids, even those only of the two largest, which Abd Allatif says, probably with Oriental exaggeration, would have filled in their transcription ten thousand leaves, although, subsequently, they have been so frequently overlooked, will also, it is expected, be opened to the learned world by these, the most recent inquirers.

It was simple, yet natural, for pious pilgrims to have very early considered the pyramids as the granaries of Joseph. Gregory of Tours, in the 6th century, even explained their mode of structure from this designation of their uses. Thus, he says, they are built narrow above, that the grain should be thrown in through a narrow aperture, whereas, below, they had capacity to contain vast quantities. Even science itself seemed to substantiate the conjectures of piety; for the Greek word, pyros, which signifies wheat or corn, recurs in the word pyramid.

I must mention here a surprise I met with at the very entrance of the pyramid of Cheops. There, in gay colours, flaunts the hieroglyphic inscription with which Lepsius and his coadjutors recently celebrated the birthday of King Frederic IV. of Prussia. It is a most appropriate embodiment of a festal idea. Germany may be as proud, as it will naturally rejoice, if the expectations of the results of the Prussian expedition be realised; if a light, at once clear and remarkable, shall be thrown upon the mysteries of a former world, here upon the banks of the Nile, through the liberality of a German prince, and the skill of patient German investigation. Then will this inscription be viewed by the latest ages with gratitude and respect.

After walking round the pyramid (which took me a quarter of an hour to accomplish), I inspected the colossal Sphinx, which the sand of the Desert has swallowed with its voracious jaws, excepting only the head. This genial creation forms a worthy termination to the groups of architectural wonders : it should not, however, be viewed too closely ; for then the mutilations, especially the missing nose, disturb the harmony of the whole. We cannot now repeat, with Abd Allatif, " It seems to smile and to look kindly down upon us." Yet, in spite of all these disfigurements, we can yet comprehend the admiration which even Denon, the most competent of critics, has bestowed upon the Sphinx, and especially upon the graceful and gentle expression of the entire head, as well as the life-like delicacy and loveliness of the mouth. To the question, What was the most wonderful of all that he had seen? Abd Allatif might well reply, " Abu'Chaul's face."* And even Denon says, that, at the period of such a work, art must have attained a high degree of perfection, and that it is unjust to regard the colossal size of this statue with astonishment merely, for the perfection of its details is even still far more admirable.

The head of this gigantic statue, hewn out of a single block, is about 20 feet long. According to Pliny, King Amasis is entombed within it; but, according to the inscription in hieroglyphics, its originator was Pharaoh Thotmes IV., in the 15th century before Christ, whom it was intended also to represent. That in fact between it and the pyramids there was a subterranean connection which was made available for oracular purposes by the priests, who thereby could get into its head, future inquiries will make more apparent.

The endeavour made by the French expedition to free this colossus from its sandy grave would have been long since renewed, were it not to be apprehended that the Desert would again, speedily, inexorably reclaim its prey.

* It is thus that the Arabs call this Sphinx. Abu'Chaul means *worthy of astonishment*, or properly, *father of astonishment.*

Intending to make my visit to the southern group of pyramids, as well as to the ruins of Memphis, a special excursion, I now returned direct to Cairo. My dragoman, who had been so frequently to the pyramids, led me through a high wheat-field, in ignorance of the proper way, and this he excused with the observation that the paths changed yearly in consequence of the inundations of the Nile.

But I have forgotten my leave-taking of my guides the Bedouins. I paid five of them. They had scarcely quitted us when they sat themselves down to gamble. My dragoman informed me that it was their custom to gamble on until all the perquisites fell to the share of one individual.

Early in the afternoon I was again at my Casa Pini. The following day I felt extremely fatigued in my lower extremities, occasioned, I believe, by nothing more than the importunate and officious services of my Bedouins, which led me to make very unnecessary haste. My dragoman, who followed after more slowly and without help, felt no similar inconvenience.

The day before my excursion on the Nile to Terraneh I met with a little adventure. I called to visit Mr. von L., who was not at home; but his little mis-shapen crafty sister-in-law played the joke of conducting me to the apartment of his wife, who sat in the midst of eight Oriental and indeed purely Levantine females. M. von L. had previously told me that he himself durst not visit the apartment of his wife when she received the harem of a Pasha or any other grandee. I was therefore not a little surprised to be introduced suddenly into this circle, and was still more so when, upon my entrance, these ladies rose simultaneously from the divan where they were sitting with crossed legs, and stepped down to receive me standing. I subsequently learnt that this courtesy is a general rule. I call it courtesy, but it is in intimate connection with the profound respect which both by law and custom, woman pays to man in the East.

Amongst these ladies there were several very pretty faces. The full contour of their forms reminded me of the much-praised Rebecca, whose significant name (fat) in the taste of the East even yet indicates charms of a peculiar character. The one sitting nearest to me understood a little Italian. I expressed to her my astonishment that the ladies received me unveiled. She replied that they had nothing to fear from us Franks, they regarded us as well behaved persons. I did not know exactly if this was intended to be a flattering compliment. " Look," continued she, " there is one who has already veiled herself; but she is the ugliest of all :" and this was really the case.

With what splendour were these ladies dressed ! All of them wore diamonds, and I was especially attracted by a crescent which

glittered upon a beautiful brow. She who wore it hastened to take
it off that I might more closely admire it.

Thus the Mahometan women wear their crescent as the Christians
do their cross, and as Jewesses wore their golden crown in the form
of the city of Jerusalem ; hence we see that the vain ornaments of
women have been every where made to resemble their most significant religious symbol.

The long tresses of these ladies, which are braided in broad plaits,
were no trifle. On each of them more than a thousand gold pieces
were suspended. When the seis, gallant as he ought to be, throws
his arm around the lady as she sits upon the ass, it is not at all surprising that he casts a sly side glance upon the head of the gentle
rider ; indeed, one of these very ladies whom I met at M. von L.'s
lost several of these coins upon her ride homewards. These tresses
are not always false or artificial. It is well known that Oriental
ladies devote the most careful attention to their long and beautiful
hair. I might refer in confirmation to the testimony of a most authentic witness, Lady Mary Wortley Montagu, who assures us that
she has nowhere seen handsomer heads of hair than in the East. She
says, with emphasis, " I counted upon one lady a hundred and ten
long tresses, and all of them natural." She also adds, that all kinds
of beauty are more general in the East than with us. Opinions, however, upon this point will differ.

We may, nevertheless, observe in the rich ornaments with which
both the beautiful and the ugly adorn themselves in the East, that
the misery wherein they pine is at least a splendid one ; for the
ladies of abolitionist Germany would doubtless consider the social
position of the ladies of this country a misery.—I speak especially
of the ladies of the harem, in their prison-like exclusion from
public life, from intellectual cultivation, and even from the light of
the sun. But nothing can well be a greater source of wretchedness
than their being constrained to share the possession of their husband
with others. Woman will sacrifice her all not to have a rival ;
and if she spring from a more distinguished family than her husband, she binds him by the fear of her relatives' revenge. It must
not, however, be thought that here even two or more wives dwell
together in a harem ; so far the arrangement does not extend. People
of the lower classes, when, as is not often the case, they have more than
one wife, are always anxious to obtain for them separate apartments.

Notwithstanding all this, the women in the East have perhaps
greater power over their husbands than with us. We know how
the Oriental clings to enjoyment, how he dreams away his most
agreeable hours in the sanctuary of his domestic dwelling—this unapproachable asylum, and how he seeks to enhance the splendour

of his establishment in nothing more than in the splendour of his harem and the ornaments of his women. Wives have here also certain legal rights, with regard to their husbands, which cannot be made so legally valid elsewhere ; and at the present moment married plaintiffs possess here their main stay in the daughter of Mehemet Ali, the widow of that notorious defterdar whom his own father-in in-law caused recently to be poisoned whilst governor of Señaar.*

Whilst the Mahometan has considerable doubts if he may ascribe as rational a soul to woman as to himself, he thinks himself the more bound to mark with consideration her corporeal *eidolon :* whence it happens that even upon dismissing their harem, as Mehemet Ali recently proposed doing, they by no means require that the ladies should remain unmarried. It presents a strong contrast to our manners, that it should be considered a high honour to obtain a wife from the harem of Mehemet Ali. It was a matter of honourable competition amongst the grandees of his court.

Every Oriental would give Madame de Staël the same answer as Napoleon, who, when she asked him who was the first woman in the world, the reply was, "She who is most frequently a mother." As it was in the East four thousand years ago, at the time of the tender-eyed Leah and the beautiful Rachel (Gen. xxix. 17), so is it now. The beautiful but unfruitful Rachel is unhappy, and envious of Leah's maternity, in spite of her "tender eyes" (Gen. xxx. 1). Besides, Oriental wives, and especially those of the Bedouins and the Fellahs, enjoy an enviable privilege in escaping the fulfilment of the threat delivered to Eve, "in sorrow thou shalt bring forth children" (Gen. iii. 6). They therefore know nothing of European childbed. It is nothing extraordinary for a female, with a new-born infant in her

---

* I heard many stories told of this remarkable man, Mohammed Bey, usually spoken of as the defterdar. He generally had as companions at Cairo upon his divan, a lion and a tigress, both unchained. His features are said also to have closely resembled those of a tiger. His visiters he likewise received in this uncomfortable society, which necessarily led to more than one adventure.

His heartless ferocity towards one of his black wives, whom he shot with the pistol at his girdle on account of some trivial neglect, produced a very dangerous mutiny of his black body-guard. They would have laid instant hands upon him, had he not escaped by a side-room, whence he called into the garden for help. Ibrahim Pasha helped him out of the difficulty with a battalion of soldiers; but not one of the guard yielded before he was shot down.

I must give an instance of his justice. A milk-woman complained of a soldier who denied having drunk a glass of her milk. The defterdar asked when the soldier had drunk the milk; and hearing that it was but a few minutes since, he ordered the soldier's body to be ripped open. The milk was found, and the woman was paid. This is, indeed, making an example.

arms to rejoin the caravan, from which she had withdrawn but a few hours before with empty arms. Morier tells a story of a female vine-dresser who carried home with her her new-born infant for circumcision. And nothing could be more desirable to depopulated Egypt than the renewal of such productiveness as Aristotle ascribes to the Egyptian woman who four times bore five children.

THE COPTIC MONASTERIES IN THE LIBYAN SANDS.

On the 18th of April, at four in the afternoon, I rode with my Ali to Bulak. The Austrian flag was waving over a large Nile boat, which was conveying the consul-general, his family, and establishment, to Alexandria. I also embarked in the vessel, to accompany them a portion of the way ; my intention being to go to Terraneh, and from Terraneh to the Coptic monasteries of the Libyan desert.

Our voyage was pleasant ; twice we landed on the banks. There were turtle-doves, plovers, and other birds in multitudes, of which we speedily shot an ample supply for the kitchen. Early on the 20th I took my leave of this amiable family, after the consul-general had most impressively recommended me and my concerns to the governor of Terraneh. The chief building of Terraneh belongs to the Italian Cibara, who enjoys from the viceroy the monopoly of nitre. It glitters upon the borders of this inconsiderable village like a magic creation. After having sufficiently recreated myself in the fragrant garden which surrounds it, I bathed in the Nile ; but I found that one might easily stick in its slimy bed.

At five in the afternoon I commenced my ride to Castello Cibara, the settlement on the lakes of nitre, in company with a large caravan. This was my first expedition into the Desert. The *tout ensemble* was singular enough : thirty camels, some twenty buffaloes, a strong escort of armed Arabs, chiefly mounted on asses, and also several women and children : such was our procession. I myself had my eyes protected by double spectacles, each of which, with its four blue glasses, shaded my eyes from the dangerous reflection of the sun upon the sand ; and my head was decorated with a large straw hat, from which hung suspended an ample green veil : hence I must have cut a remarkable figure in this remarkable company. A powerful Arab carried me on his shoulder over the canal ; and, upon the extensive stubble field adjacent, the caravan collected together.

The sun sank as we broke up. Shortly afterwards we rode forward into the apparently interminable desert, gleaming with a pale ruddy light from the hues of the setting sun.

The night was magnificent: the stars appeared to me to shine here with a brighter light than in the European North. The temperature was pleasantly cool. My spirited ass, which was conspicuous beyond all its companions by its more stately bearing, as well as its more superb accoutrements, frequently conveyed me to the head of the caravan; but my cautious guides overtook me with earnest expostulations, and I remained in the heart of the company, being only cautious not to come into contact with the herd of buffaloes, which repeatedly fell into a rapid motion, while the camels, on the contrary, conducted themselves like decent respectable "snobs."

Shortly after midnight the caravan indulged in a short repose, which was most welcome to me, for the unusual exertion had made me excessively drowsy. We encamped close to a spot covered with green shrubs, which our cattle browsed whilst their guides collected round a fire to enjoy a cup of coffee. I had slept perhaps about two hours, enveloped in my woollen rug, when I was aroused to depart, and after the refreshment of a cup of coffee, I remounted my vivacious animal.

Shortly after daybreak we saw in the distance upon the left, in the middle of the Desert, a lofty stone wall, and still further on, a second. These were two of the Coptic monasteries. Presently afterwards one of the salt lakes glittered in the distance, with its obscure reddish blue waters, and a flock of flamingoes sprung out of its reeds. Upon the right was the Castello Cibara; in the background the low Libyan hills formed a dark-red border to the whole scene. About nine in the morning we reached our destination, and I found in the midst of the Desert a hospitable hearth. An Italian, who is chemical overseer of the nitre works, occupies the mansion, or rather castle, of which, notwithstanding its name, we must not form too grand an idea. We, the only two Europeans amongst these sons of the Desert, conceived a fraternal feeling towards each other. This castle deduces its origin from an ancient building called Kassr, and is partly built of nitre. Cibara has considerably enlarged the castle, and the tenements about it are almost exclusively of his building.

In the afternoon we made an excursion to the fields and lakes of nitre. What a singular scene! In the midst of this sandy waste, where uniformity is rarely interrupted by grass or shrubs, there are extensive districts where nitre springs from the earth like crystallised fruits. One thinks he sees a wild overgrown with moss, weeds, and shrubs, thickly covered with hoar frost. And to imagine this wintry scene, beneath the fervid heat of an Egyptian sun, will give some idea of the strangeness of its aspect. The existence of this nitre upon the sandy surface is caused by the evaporation of the lakes. According to the quantity of nitre left behind by the lake do these fantastic shapes assume either a dazzling white colour, or are more or less tinted with the sober hue of the sand. The nitre lakes themselves, six in number, situated in a spacious valley between two rows of low sand hills, presented—at least the three which we visited—a pleasing contrast, in their dark blue and red colours, to the dull hues of the sand. The nitre which forms a thick crystallised crust upon these shallow lakes, is broken off in large square plates, which are either of a dirty white, or of a flesh colour, or of a deep dark-red. The Fellahs employed upon this labour stand quite naked in the water, furnished with iron rods. The part which is removed being speedily renewed, the riches of its produce are inexhaustible. It is hence that nearly the whole of Europe is exclusively supplied with nitre ; and this has probably been the case for ages ; for Sicard mentions, at the commencement of the last century, that then six and thirty thousand hundred weight of nitre was broken annually for the Grand Signior, to whom it yielded thirty-six purses.

By the side of one of the lakes, piled in large layers, was heaped the produce of the last week's labours. My companion had occasion to find fault with the result of the work of one of the villages. The sheikh of the village stood before us. He sharply rebuked him, and to give greater effect to his words he crossed his naked shoulders two or three times with his whip of elephant's skin. The sheikh sprang as nimbly as a gazelle into the lake, and received his further instructions beyond arm's length. Such was the impressive discipline which even this Italian, who was a man of gentle manners, considered it necessary to adopt towards these Fellahs.

The plates of nitre, after undergoing a preliminary cleansing upon the banks of the lake, are carried to the castle, where, by various processes, they become a dazzling white powder ; and in this state it is conveyed in large quantities to Terraneh.

What Varsi, my companion, told me of the excellence of the water in this vicinity is remarkable. Several places he caused to be dug, and almost everywhere spring water was found not far from the surface, but with, here and there, a chalybeate taste in different degrees of intensity. He was now even about sending six different kinds of water to Mehemet Ali: one of these I tasted, which was excellent. This phenomenon may possibly be ascribed to the fact that the Nile once had a branch flowing through the Libyan desert. For, even were it not an undoubted circumstance that this branch of the Nile flowed through the Desert (to which the so-called Bahr belama, *river without water*, of the Arabian geographer evidently refers), it might receive collateral confirmation from these corroborative particulars.

In the small collection of natural curiosities made by Signor Varsi, I was especially struck by a beautiful queber, or weber the first specimens of which that had been seen at Paris were conveyed thither by Leon de Laborde ; but some few years earlier, specimens had been transmitted to Berlin and Frankfurt by Ehrenberg and Rüppel. That which I saw here agreed tolerably with the coloured print of it in Leon de Laborde's travels. Most probably none of the specimens, either at Paris, Berlin, or Frankfurt, were obtained from the Macarius desert, or from any portion of the Libyan desert. Laborde says it is of frequent occurrence in the peninsula of Sinai. Arabian writers describe it as being between a weasel and a cat ; the little tail given to it by Bochartus, in his figure of it in the Hierozoicon, after Arabic writers, is found only upon paper.*

It was early in the morning of the 22d of April that I commenced my trip from Castello to the neighbouring Coptic monasteries. I was accompanied by my dragoman, the secretary of the castle, a native Copt, called Malem Saad, and eight armed nitre guards. It was considered requisite to have so strong a military escort on account of the wandering Bedouins; yet it was not our fortune to meet with any, and the only quadrupeds we saw were several graceful gazelles, and a wild sow with her young. Sicard, on the contrary, relates that he saw every morning in the sand, traces of bears, hyenas, and wolves. At the commencement of our journey we occasionally saw flamingoes, ducks, and other water-fowl ascending from the lakes; but they were difficult to shoot.

There are four Coptic monasteries at the distance of a few leagues apart. Ruins and monasteries, and heaps of rubbish, I observed scattered in great numbers throughout the district. I was told that there were formerly about three hundred Coptic monasteries in this desert, which derives probability from the historical fact that the Emperor Valens, towards the end of the fourth century, turned five thousand monks into soldiers in these wastes. The conductor of the Abbé Sicard, the superior of the monastery of St. Macarius, told

---

* It is thus described by Laborde :— " These animals, active in their motions, endeavoured to bite when caught ; their fur is of a yellowish brown, becoming paler and longer with the age of the animal. Their form, by the vivacity of their eyes, the head close to the shoulders, the compact crupper, and the absence of tail, approaches to that of a Guinea pig. Their legs are of equal length, but the feet are peculiar: instead of nails or claws they have three toes in front and four behind, and they walk like rabbits upon the whole length of the hind legs.— *Voyage de l'Arabie Pétrée.* Paris, 1830, p. 47.

him that formerly there were in this desert of Scete, and upon the
mountains of Nitrien, as many monasteries as there were days in the
year.   And Sicard himself discerned the remains of fifty monasteries
in a single district.

Both externally and internally these monasteries closely resemble
one another.   Sometimes square, at others in the form of a parallelo-
gram ; they are enclosed by walls tolerably high, and usually
about a hundred feet long.   From their centre a few palms frequently peer forth, for every monastery has a small garden within
its circuit, and is also furnished with a tower slightly elevated
above the walls, and containing a small bell.   The entrance, an
iron-bound gate, is so low that the asses upon which we rode could
not creep in without their saddles being removed.   Close to each of
these doors is deposited a large block of sandstone, fashioned like a
millstone, to protect this entrance still more effectually in case of a
hostile attack.

Within the walls are seen nothing but old and dilapidated ruins,
amongst which the monks find a habitation.

The tower I have just described is insulated from the body of the
monastery, and approachable only by means of a drawbridge supported
on chains, offering thus an asylum against enemies, who may have
mastered the monastery.   This tower commands the entrance.   The
interior consists of a chapel, a well, a mill, an oven, and a storeroom
(all required in the event of a long siege), and the apartment assigned
to the library.

The churches or chapels, of which there are three, or even more,
in every monastery, are indeed more considerable than the cells ; yet
they too retain the character of a mean simplicity.   Here and there,
in the mural structure of the entrances to the cells and chapelries, we
obtain a glimpse of the fragment of a marble pillar, or of a frieze, or
some similar decoration.   Thus has the sordid present been built out
of the ruins of the splendour and grandeur of the past.

The distance to the first monastery that we visited was about
eight leagues.   We were received very hospitably, for my Coptic
guide was well known to the brethren.   We mutually performed our
salam, or salamalek, by placing our hand on the breast and the forehead.   This monastery bears especially the name of St. Macarius.
I say especially, because the whole of this portion of the desert is
called the desert of Macarius, and the four monasteries are called those
of Abu Macar.   We found fifteen brethren in it; while Sicard saw
here only two monks and two secular deacons.   Their countenances
were all sallow, and several of them of a sickly yellow ; they almost
all suffered in their eyes, and the superior was totally blind.   The

cells are dark chambers upon the ground-floor, looking as if hewn in
the rock, and without any windows; and the light is admitted only
through the doorway.

One of these cells was my chamber.   After dark I had a little
lamp burning in a corner.   I sat upon the ground : on my right sat
my Coptic secretary, with his white turban, his silken girdle, in
which were placed a brace of pistols and his writing materials, conjunctively fit emblems of peace and war : on my left sat my small-
eyed dragoman, enveloped in his long white shirt, and with his red
tarbusch on his head; and to complete the circle, there were six
Coptic brethren, with their dark garments and dark turbans, long
beards, and woful countenances.   Our pipes passed from hand to hand.

The cloister fare is more than meagre.   Meat is indulged in but
on few days in the course of the year.   The chief food consists of
nothing but bread steeped in a concoction of a disagreeable flavour,
consisting of lentils, onions, and linseed oil.   Besides this they have
coffee and pipes.   I had very prudently provided myself with some
fowls, rice, and a few other articles, upon this excursion.

Before sunrise the little bell rang to mass, which lasted more than
three hours.   The biblical readings were partly Coptic and partly
Arabic.   What was sung struck me as singularly discordant.   The
Kyrie Eleison and the Hallelujah were frequently repeated.   The
service I found extremely defective.   The reader was whispered to,
during his occupation, and replied also to the questioner.   One
commenced a wrong portion, another corrected him, and the correction was made with perfect good humour.

The Copt, however, who accompanied me, was serious and reverential.   After reading or recognising who it was, he prostrated
himself before every holy image so absolutely that his forehead
touched the earth.   Upon entering the church he performed the
same ceremony.   During the service he remained in the most appropriate position, and also read aloud to the community.

The reception of the Eucharist was very peculiar.   Instead of
wine, they used a thick juice of the grape, which I at first mistook
for oil.   The officiating priest took it out of a glass vessel with a
spoon, and shared it between himself and the deacon standing
opposite him; he then scraped out the remainder with his bare finger,
and licked it, and poured into the vessel and its glass plate some
water which he and the deacon also drank.   And lastly, with his
hands still wet with the remaining drops, he touched all the other
brethren upon the forehead and cheek.   I also took part in the final
ceremony.

During the whole rite I stood, together with the monks, outside the sanctum (called heikal, *within*), at the lattice of the main

aisle, supported, like all beside me, upon a wooden staff with a straight handle. This is called the staff of Macarius, and is an attribute which always accompanies his representation.

It is difficult to say what could possibly be edifying in the entire celebration of the mass, the most prominent acts of which consist in the incense-burning before the individual images, the hand-kissing of the officiating priest, the laying-on of hands, and the passing round with the image of the Virgin. Many of its parts had an ancient-Egyptian character, and the whole was coloured with a mysterious tint, to which the locality itself greatly contributed. Only one incident in the scene was affecting to me. The blind senior of the monastery, with his wrinkled but venerable countenance, his long white beard, his head covered with a dark-blue turban, enveloped in a robe of the same colour, and barefooted, like his brethren,—this aged man walked thrice round the altar, ringing his metal bell, which had a harsh, melancholy tone, and singing a triumphant Hallelujah. He looked like one who had risen from the grave, and was still dreaming of the gloomy pictures he had beheld within that sacred bourne.

Two peculiarities struck me in the arrangements of the church. The one is the oven behind the sacristy, employed in baking the sour sacramental bread used fresh at every mass. These loaves are round, like a small cake, of the size of the palm of the hand, not over-white, and stamped at the top with many crosses. One is eaten at the altar, and the remainder are distributed amongst the community after mass. I also received mine. The other peculiarity is a four-cornered stone basin, in front of the church, which is used for a certain sacred bathing ceremonial.

The chief pictorial representations, in all the four monasteries, were those of St. Macarius and St. George. In the third, which bears the name of the Syrian, or the Virgin of the Syrians, St. Ephraim is held in high honour. A tamarind tree was there shown me, which had miraculously sprouted forth from the staff of St. Ephraim, who, upon entering the chapel, had stuck it in the ground outside.[*] In the second, St. Ambeschun was represented as the patron. In the fourth, besides St. George, St. Theodore was represented on horseback, with the vanquished dragon beneath his feet. The name of the monastery is El Baramus.[†]

---

[*] Compare p. 55.

[†] Russegger, in his tour to the salt lakes, mentions only two of these monasteries, and calls the one Labiat, and the other U-Serian, whereas Andreossy, in his " Mém. sur l'Egypte," calls the one El Baramus, and the other Amba-Bischay. Ritter, in his geography, follows Andreossy. This Amba-Bischay is evidently identical with Ambeschun, as well as Amba-

But I must also advert to what was my main object in exploring these monasteries, namely, their libraries. The special locality set apart for the library in the several monasteries, as I have already mentioned, is the tower chamber, which is accessible only by means of the drawbridge. No spot in the monastery could well be safer from the visits of the fraternity than this. Here are seen (I speak of the first monastery) the manuscripts heaped indiscriminately together. Lying on the ground, or thrown into large baskets, beneath masses of dust, are found innumerable fragments of old, torn, and destroyed manuscripts. I saw nothing Greek; all was either Coptic or Arabic; and in the third monastery I found some Syriac, together with a couple of leaves of Ethiopic. The majority of the MSS. are liturgical, though many are biblical. From the fourth monastery the English have recently acquired an important collection of several hundred MSS. for the British Museum, and that at a very small cost. The other monasteries contain certainly nothing of such consequence, yet, much might be found to reward the labour of the search. The monks themselves understand extremely little about the matter. Not one amongst them, probably, is acquainted with Coptic; and they merely read mechanically the lessons of their ritual. The Arabic of the older MSS. but few can read. Indeed it is not easy to say what these monks know beyond the routine of their ordinary church service. Still their excessive suspicion renders it extremely difficult to induce them to produce their manuscripts, in spite of the extreme penury which surrounds them. Possibly they are controlled by the mandate of their patriarch. For my own part, I made a most lucky discovery of a multitude of Coptic parchment-sheets of the sixth and seventh centuries, already half destroyed, and completely buried beneath a mass of dust. These were given to me without hesitation; but I paid for the discovery by severe pains in the throat, produced by the dust I had raised in the excessive heat.

In the second monastery there remain now only four monks. The superior was an old man of a hundred and twenty years of age. He has been blind a long time. He sits all day long upon a cross bench, and sings aloud both day and night: he sleeps but for one hour at a time. This evening of life has something pleasing in

Beschoi, cited below, at p. 55. Sicard, however, gives a particular description of the four monasteries I visited. The second he calls Amba-Bischoi (but writing in French he calls it Bichoi; as does Andreossv. Bichay), or that of St. Abisay. Of the fourth, Elbaramus, he says that it received its name from the two disciples of the Abbot Moses, the Ethiopian, Maximus and Timotheus. Elbaramus or Piromaus is but a corruption of El Romaus, signifying Greek. See " Paulus, Collection," v. 15., &c.

it. To this old man heaven hangs down its holy lamps so low into the narrow valley of the earth, that his eye, already closed to the world, sees God only, and his lips do nothing but pray. I visited him in his cell the instant I heard his unceasing prayer. Upon taking my departure from the monastery he came forth, supported by his staff, and appeared to me to speak with perfect intelligence. A benediction from these aged lips deeply affected me.

In the third monastery, that of the Syrians, or of the Virgin of the Syrians, there are more than forty brethren. It is the handsomest and richest of all. Hence it was that they least of all thanked me for what I supposed the considerable present, which, according to custom, I left with them at my departure. My strong escort, further increased here by three other cavaliers on their asses, who had welcomed my arrival with a salute of musketry from the walls of the monastery, had excited great expectations. They are, besides, too much accustomed to the visits and to the gold of the English.

A Madonna in the grotto chapel of this monastery passes for the production of the evangelist St. Luke. She is of the same dark brown colour as the many others which I saw in Egypt. By the same analogy would she be transformed into a Moor in the country of the Moors. If, as there is every appearance of probability, this monastery has received its appellation from this picture of the Virgin, there can be no doubt of its being the work of an ancient artist. Not one of my Arabs was permitted to step into this grotto.

In this monastery I was consulted regarding every possible disease, many of which were already of several years' duration. I was sorry I had not my small medicine-chest with me. I therefore only gave homœopathic advice, and referred my patients for further instructions to my friend in the castle.

In the fourth monastery, called El Baramus, I met with twenty monks. Here the cells were the blackest and narrowest of all. The superior had a peculiar custom ; he sat beside me in the cell, and as often as a pause was made in the conversation he interposed the formula of welcome, Salam, Salam, and repeated the pantomime of his hands.

What I inquired for everywhere and in vain, was manuscript accounts of the history of the monastery. Not a line of such a record was known. Thus they live on carelessly from day to day. To such an existence, what is the past and what the future? Yet there is not one of these monasteries to which, if you ask the date of its foundation, they will not give fifteen centuries of age. This is possibly the age of the original monasteries on whose ruins the present structures are built. The latter are, in my estimation, much more recent. In all these monasteries my advice and aid were in request by people

with sore eyes: many of whom were hastening towards total blindness.
If there be a mode of life which leads directly to blindness, it is certainly that of these monks.   Their monasteries lie in the midst of
the dazzling sand, and under the sun of Egypt, both most hostile to
the sight.   Their cells are dark chambers, lighted of an evening alone
by a small lamp or candle.   Their daily fare, consisting of linseed
oil, is said of itself to produce disease of the eyes.   They almost all
smoke tobacco, and this in considerable quantities.   And, lastly, they
pass the greatest part of the day and night in their gloomy chapels,
with ever-burning lamps and lights, and the incessant smoke of their
incense.

Thus the entire existence of these Coptic communities is an unna-
tural and unscriptural penitence.   There the spirit of Christianity
slinks stealthily about like a gloomy demon, infusing poison in life s
joyous draught.   The path it indicates as the road to heaven is a
sunless shaft, where the nearer we approach the hour of death, we
become hourly more paralysed both in body and soul.   Yet the sky
is spread over our heads with its cerulean tints.   How many a pious
eye, directed upwards, sheds tears of joy when absorbed in holy contemplation !   Dost thou inquire the way that thither leads ?   If no
other voice be near to give reply, ask the lark that soars aloft, jubilant
in its Maker's praise.

During the night of the 25th I rode back, with an excellent escort,
from Castello to Terraneh.   I retain a most grateful remembrance of
my hospitable reception in the desert.   In the afternoon of the 26th
a vessel, with a freight of about thirty women and children, passed
Terraneh en route to Cairo.   I engaged for myself and my dragoman
the still unoccupied cabin.   The party was cheerful enough.   On the
27th we again entered the gates of Cairo.   Since my excursion I
look doubly intently into the face of every Copt I meet; but few
of those who dwell here appear so sickly and poverty-stricken as
the brotherhood of the Libyan desert ; but they have all the same
reserved and suspicious aspect.   There may be about ten thousand
of them in the metropolis, and about a hundred and fifty thousand
dispersed throughout the whole country.   One is inclined to regard
them as the genuine descendants of the ancient Egyptians.   The peculiarity of their Christian doctrine is, that they hold the tenets of
Eutyches and Dioscurus, to whom the names of Jacobites, or Mono-
physites, are usually applied.   The following is the confession of faith
they make before communion, as forwarded from Egypt by the
Jesuit du Bernat to the Jesuit Fleuriau : —

" I believe, I believe, I believe, and confess to my dying moment,
that this is the living body which thy only Son, thou, our Lord and
our God, our Saviour Jesus Christ received from our dear Lady, the

pure and unspotted Mother of God. He has united it with his
divinity without mixture and without change. He nobly confessed before Pontius Pilate, and submitted willingly for us to the
holy tree of the Cross. I believe that his divinity has not been an
instant separated from his humanity. He gives himself up for the
salvation of the world, for the forgiveness of sins, and for the
eternal life of those who receive him. I truly believe this.
Amen." *

They are placed under the spiritual dominion of their own
patriarch, who resides in Cairo. The most remarkable peculiarity
that I heard related of them, was the excessive facility with which
they dissolve the matrimonial tie. Their practice of circumcision
is possibly more their peculiar view of the historical advent of the
Saviour in the world, than a forced accommodation to the prejudices
of the Mahometan lords of their home. Yet this custom may have
probably descended to them from their forefathers.†

By way of appendix, I may state that John Michael Wandsleb,
of Erfurt, undertook, during his travels in Egypt, in 1663, an excursion to the Coptic monasteries of the Libyan desert, although,
from the dangers which attended it, he did not succeed in his object.
Paulus, in his " Sammlung der merkwürdigsten Reisen in den
Orient," reprints Wandsleb's Travels ‡, wherein the traveller gives
the following account of these monasteries : —

" From an ancient Arabic manuscript, I found that there were
formerly seven celebrated monasteries in the desert. 1. That of St.
Macarius. 2. That of St. John the Less. 3. Amba-Bischoi. 4. St.
Maximus and Timotheus. 5. Amba-Moyse, called the Black. 6.
Amba-Kema ; and, 7. that of the Holy Virgin of the Syrians. Besides these seven monasteries, it is said there are 300 houses for
hermits. But of all these monasteries, only two may be considered
of any importance, namely, that of the Syrians and that of Amba-
Bischoi.

" In the monastery of the Syrians a tree is shown which grew
miraculously out of the walkingstaff of St. Ephraim. This saint,
whilst visiting one of its holy inmates, left it standing at the door.
That instant it struck root, and leaves and blossoms sprouted from
it. It is said, that throughout Egypt this species of tree is no
where else to be seen.

" Between the monasteries of St. Macarius and Amba-Bischoi,
and thence onward into the desert, there is a long series of small
earth hills, standing a single step apart, and indicating a path.

---

* See Paulus, Sammlung, t. iv. pp. 276, 277.
† See p. 64., below.   ‡ See vol. iii. p. 255, 256.

These, the monks say, were made by angels, that the hermits might find the road to church on a Sunday, when they wished to hear mass, as they had probably often lost their way. Hence this path is called The Angels' Path to the present day."*

MEMPHIS AND HELIOPOLIS.

MEMPHIS and HELIOPOLIS; two names which, like the shadows of gigantic mountains, look down upon us from the past. But little more than the names remain to us of these two seats of Egyptian splendour and art — of Egyptian religion and philosophy. But few that can be compared with them has the world ever seen; they have now become a dirge on the decay of all that is earthly.

Was not this Memphis, which called the pyramids her children, the queen of the cities of the earth, both of the past and of the future? For tens of centuries have the children survived their mother; children who, like invincible heroes, have passed victoriously through the conflicts of all ages. They faithfully protect the graves of those who bore and cherished them; they tell, although in obscure language, our transitory generations of their labours and of their fate. Were Abraham to return from the tomb, he could bear testimony with the pyramids to the wonders his eyes once here beheld.

Upon the great sandy plain of shapeless ruins, where formerly Memphis stood, occupying 3¾ geographical miles† in circumference, there now stand, close to a grove of acacias, a couple of wretched huts, which bear the name of Mitrahenny. They form a bitter contrast, the impression of which one in vain endeavours to shake off, to the remembrance of the past grandeur and splendour of this selfsame spot. To enhance the force of the contrast, there lies close to the hamlet, like a stranded whale, one of those colossal ruins which metamorphose dwarfish man into a fabulous giant. It is forty feet long. It is with great probability considered to be one of the six colossal statues which Pharaoh Rameses II. caused to be made to represent himself, his consort, and his four sons, and which stood before the temple of Phtha. Possibly, therefore, I now stand upon the ruins of the celebrated temple which Egypt's mystical faith erected to Phtha, the world-creating spirit dwelling eternally in primeval fire. Here also it was where the black steer, with the white star upon its forehead, roamed about amongst the magnificent

---

* Sicard at the place cited also mentions this " Angels' Path."
† According to Diodorus Siculus.

columned halls — the Propylæa, — before the eyes of the silent and anxious multitude.

The very destruction of Memphis reaches far into antiquity ; and even Strabo relates that, amidst the other splendid works of architecture, he found the temple of Serapis, together with its sphinxes, destroyed and buried beneath the sand : but even so late as the 13th century, Abd Allatif was overwhelmed with lofty feelings, when wandering to the extent of half a day's journey amongst its ruins ; and he writes — " It would be in vain for the most eloquent tongue to attempt to describe these wonderful ruins." The longer they are contemplated the greater does our admiration increase. Each glance inspires us with fresh delight.

At Abd Allatif's visit the reputed green-house was still standing, nine ells high, eight ells long, seven ells wide, formed of a single mass of granite, and covered with mysterious characters, and with as mysterious hieroglyphics of sun and stars, and men and animals. And this " wonderful" house was in its solitariness, as it were, the embalmed heart of a majestic temple, probably of that very temple which was dedicated to Phtha.

Abd Allatif also found idols in great numbers. He describes one formed of a single stone, covered over with red varnish, and more than thirty ells high. Two colossal lions rampant also attracted his attention.

What he, a physician, most admired in all these gigantic works, was the great correctness of their proportions, judging them after the small models offered by living nature.

Although since the time of Abd Allatif the ruins of Memphis have been continually plundered to furnish materials for new buildings at Cairo, (to which the beautiful granite of Syene, so extensively used in the structures of Memphis, was a paramount attraction,) I still think it very probable that the deep sand of the desert has engulfed much of the former city, which, were it once more excavated and exposed to the light of day, would fill European investigators with astonishment and admiration.

As I proceeded further through the grove of acacias towards Sakkara, I could not resist the inclination to ascend several of the heaps of rubbish, and to take a survey of the entire circuit of the adjacent pyramids. Nineteen large ones, including the three of Gizeh, were grouped before my eyes. Even this very day the thought struck me, that here upon this spot, centuries ago, a race possibly held sway, towards whom the present race may look up as a child to its father, as Astyanax the playful boy to the helmed Hector. It is very remarkable that we in no instance find, upon the theatre of their reminiscences, that the Egyptians have ever peopled their antiquity with giants.

The great depository of mummies at Sakkara admits of no comparison.   There lie dispersed, for miles around, skulls, hands, feet,
and other fragments of mummies, which had reposed for centuries
undisturbed in their subterranean caverns.   If we ask ourselves
what may possibly have occasioned this destruction of the once so
carefully preserved bodies, we are disposed to ascribe it rather to
jackals in search of their prey than to Bedouins in search of treasure,
or even to European antiquaries.

It is also suggestive of much reflection when we consider the
conscientious, the significant care with which the ancient Egyptians
treated those who had departed from amidst the living to await their
eventual resurrection.   How beautifully painted are these chambers
of the dead, in the niches of which the mummies reposed , how regularly are they constructed, and how perfectly were their occupants
arranged !   And these mummies themselves, their empty bosoms
filled with the symbols of their divinities, enriched with papyrus
rolls of deep significance, adorned with costly ornaments, and prepared for an interminable duration by their imperishable bandages;
all this necessarily gave death the character of a gentle, but significant
slumber.   The light of day was not extinguished, it was only
obscured, the fibres of the heart were not sundered, they were but
loosened.   The dwellings upon the earth, and the dwellings beneath
it, were not separated by the frightful partition-wall which our
imagination, notwithstanding our Christian belief, has interposed
between them.   Hence these Egyptians made mummies take a share
in their festivals.   This happy familiarity with the dead necessarily
cast a serious aspect over the mirth of their rejoicings, but, in compensation, it brightened the dark side of life with the purple streaks
of the morning.

From the receptacle for human mummies we passed to another of
greater extent, where were preserved the mummies of sacred animals,
and especially of various kinds of the Ibis, and of other birds.
These were also deposited in deep and artificially arranged chambers,
or rather in broad long corridors, hewn in the rock.   We descend
into them, as into the shaft of a mine, or a well.   The number of
animal mummies preserved here in earthen vessels with earthen lids,
and arranged in extensive rows in these subterranean chambers, is
still very considerable, notwithstanding the plunder that has long been
perpetrated amongst them.

I have classed Heliopolis with Memphis.   Its Egyptian name, On,
renews our remembrance of Joseph, the favourite of the Lord.
Pharaoh gave Joseph, as Moses (Gen. xli. 45) relates, a wife, named
Asenath, the daughter of the priest Potipherah, at On.   In the
time of Joseph the City of the Sun may have been in its most flourish-

ing condition. It was the chief city of the Egyptian priests, and of their wisdom. In conjunction with their sacerdotal office, these priests cultivated philosophy and astronomy.

As late as the time of Jeremiah, Heliopolis appears to be the very centre of Egyptian religious worship ; for he exclaims, in his prophecy (xliii. 13), " He (Nebuchadnezzar) shall break also the images of Beth-Shemech, (which is, House of the Sun, or City of the Sun,) and the houses of the gods of the Egyptians shall he burn with fire." The fearful prophecy was speedily fulfilled ; what Nebuchadnezzar spared, Cambyses trampled, in his destroying wrath, beneath his feet. In his measureless zeal against religious monuments he seemed to war more against the gods of Egypt than its mortal inhabitants.

Plato also visited Heliopolis to behold its remaining ruins, to enquire and to wonder. Some centuries later, Strabo was shown the house where the " Divine Plato" had dwelt.

The statues referred to by Jeremiah must be understood to be the obelisks, which were doubtlessly numerous at Heliopolis. Strabo, when he visited it, still found very many, and tells us that two of them which belonged to the Temple of the Sun, which was erected by Sesostris, were conveyed to Rome in the reign of the Emperor Augustus. And even Abd Allatif in the thirteenth century speaks of the sublimity of the ruins which he beheld here. He says, amongst other things, that there was scarcely a stone to be seen which was not inscribed with a variety of those significant characters and figures. Hence there can be no doubt that here also many interesting remains of ruins are concealed beneath the rubbish.

But even at the present day there still stands one witness of the past grandeur of the City of the Sun ; as if supported by a magic hand, it has stood erect amid all the tempests of three thousand years. A tall obelisk of red granite still rears its unbent head to heaven. All the four sides are covered with hieroglyphics.

It is agreeable to consider this obelisk with Wilkinson as contemporaneous with Joseph, and as a monument of that same Pharaoh who appointed the inspired "dreamer" steward of the land. All its fraternal companions have fallen, together with the gods to whose vain service they were dedicated : this one alone was distinguished amongst them as Joseph once was amongst his brethren in his father s house. The Ruler of fate has stamped it with the impress of durability. The God of Abraham, Isaac, and Jacob has supported it with his strong arm. As the announcer of the salvation that shall come from Israel, it stands there in its venerable antiquity ; but its prophetic words are not understood by the children of its native home.

The village of Mataryeh lies close to the obelisks, just as Mitrahenny is situated beside the fallen colossus upon the ruins of Memphis.

Two other curiosities presented themselves to me there; a very ancient sycamore and the so-called Fountain of the Sun. To the ears of innocent faith both respond to the prophecy of the obelisk; for they announce to it the Salvation that shall come out of Israel. Beneath the sycamore, says tradition, the Infant Jesus with his parents reposed in their flight to Egypt; or, as the tradition more circumstantially relates, the tree concealed them from their pursuing enemies,—I know not whether in its sunken and umbrageous boughs, or by cleaving its stem. This sycamore now stands in a pleasant orange grove: it is greatly revered, and is hung with many fragments of clothes, the gifts both of Mahometan and Christian pilgrims. If these fragments could be converted by the imagination into lighted tapers, it would closely resemble a Christmas tree.

This sycamore bears the very aspect of high age. Its bole is of extraordinary circumference. Hence I doubt if the great Danish traveller of the preceding century was right in estimating its existence at no more than two hundred years.

Contiguous to the sycamore is Ayin Shemech, or the Fountain of the Sun. Pious pilgrims call it in preference the Fountain of the Virgin; for, according to tradition, it is said to have miraculously burst forth when the Child Jesus was suffering from severe thirst.* The Trappist Geramb finds it very natural — in opposition to the philosopher, who might possibly ridicule it — that God should have done for his Son, for Joseph, and for Mary, that which He had previously done through Moses for a murmuring and ungrateful people.

This fountain formerly gave its name to the whole district; Abd-Allatif calls the whole of Heliopolis Ayin Schemech. It is very probable that its water, which was peculiarly good, and was even esteemed medicinal, might have stood in some relation to the Temple of the Sun.

Heliopolis has again become celebrated in recent times by the battle fought there at the commencement of the present century, and won by Kleber, with the French army, against a very superior force of the grand vizier. It was immediately after this battle that the valiant Alsatian fell by the dagger of the fanatical assassin Soleyman, who expiated his crime with incredible coolness, being impaled after having had his hand burnt off.

---

* The apocryphal literature of the New Testament speaks both of this miraculous fountain, and of the venerable sycamore tree.

EXCURSION TO OLD CAIRO.

The chief object of this excursion was an inscription, involved
in mysterious obscurity, said to be extant in a Coptic monastery.
Wilkinson, as I was told, was even unable to ascertain with certainty
the language in which it was written. Fragments of a copy in an
English lady's handwriting were shown to me: they had something
of a Greek character.

Myself upon an ass, Lieder on horseback, and Bonomi upon a
camel, in company with several Arabs, in the afternoon of the 9th
of May set out on our excursion to Old Cairo. On our arrival
we left our cattle at the walls, and proceeded on foot through several
narrow streets to the Coptic monastery. The inscription was in a
remote corner of the monastery, in a small and almost square apartment. We raised an artificial but dangerous scaffolding, to enable us
to reach the inscription. It was without much difficulty that I deciphered it. It was in Greek raised characters carved upon hard
wood, and consisted of several lines containing a pious eulogium.
Most probably it referred to some solemn act, such as the dedication
of a monastery, for appended to it were the names of the abbot, the
deacon, and the œconomos, with a date according to the Diocletian
chronology. Wilkinson, it appeared, as I subsequently found in
his published account, had by no means mistaken the character of
the inscription.

After making the best copy we could of the inscription, as well as
of the pictorial illustrations surrounding it, we visited another Coptic
monastery, which is in possession of a grotto that is said to have
sheltered Joseph and Mary, with the Infant, on their flight into
Egypt. This ancient monastery, named after St. Sergius, is of a
very solid style of architecture: within, it is thoroughly Coptic both
in its simplicity and penury: its only riches and its only ornaments
are its reminiscences. From the chapel we descended on the right
of the altar several steps, and thus reached the grotto, where, in consequence of its damp walls, we made but a hasty survey. It is supported by several low columns, and contains a font and an altar.
From the larger grotto we passed into a small apartment cut out of
the rock, which is separated from the larger one by a picture upon
wood, representing the flight into Egypt, together with the pyramids.
Pious faith believes that it is upon this very spot that the Holy
Family sat. We re-ascended into the little chapel by some steps
which led up to the left of the altar. These two flights of steps are
not without their peculiar object. By one the Copts descend into

the grotto, and by the other the Greeks; for the latter also perform religious ceremonies within this holy place.

It is readily to be imagined that in Egypt, the very home of hermits, Christian reminiscences should willingly attach to grottoes. And if we compute collectively the grottoes which ecclesiastical history has raised into holy importance, we might thence deduce an actual Christian grotto worship.

We visited near these monasteries the great mosque of Amru. It is of the form of an amphitheatre, open above, and surrounded by several arched colonnades. I was told, that the number of the pillars which form them are three hundred and sixty-five, corresponding with the number of the days of the year. Yet, even were they a hundred less, as I found elsewhere stated, we may still easily imagine the noble impression made by these galleries.

In the centre of the court, near the marble bath, there is a little house, enclosed within a stately building, which has been compared, not inaptly, with the celebrated mill at Potsdam. A poor Jewess would not consent, by any means, to give it up to that Amru whose arm was as familiar with conquest as a child with its toy. This Jewish hut merits as much as the Potsdam mill its place in history.

The native of the East does not readily belie a certain poetical or superstitious cast of character. This same Amru, who it is known conquered Egypt, founded old Cairo by the name of Fostat; the occasion of which was the nestling of a dove upon the pole of his tent. He would not allow this pole to be removed, but erected his Fostat (tent) on the very spot.

The great Amru mosque has become, in the course of centuries, much dilapidated. But as a belief prevails that the fall of this mosque will be portentous to the dominion of the prophet,—a belief which, in the present day, methinks, is willingly entertained,— Mehemet Ali has caused it to be repaired. But even in its present condition it is still used upon great festivals.

Two other curiosities attracted our attention within this mosque. Upon one of the pillars Amru tried the strength of his powerful arm; he endeavoured to cut it in two by a blow of his sword. This he did not accomplish, but we still see how deeply his Damascus blade has pierced. And close to the entrance there are a couple of columns, between which none but a man of honour is said to be able to pass. We made one of our Arabs, who could not complain of spareness, put his integrity to the test. We soon saw that he would not succeed, and, so, speedily recalled him from the attempt, amidst the mirth and laughter of the spectators.

After having admired the beautiful arabesques adorning the portal, with which I was already acquainted, through the admirable collection of sketches made by Mr. Beaumont, we rode home. On the road, in one of the streets of Cairo, I beheld an aged man, with a long beard and very long hair, going about completely naked. He was described to me as a celebrated saint.

On the morning of the same day I visited, in the friendly company of Mr. Lieder, the celebrated collection of Egyptian antiquities belonging to Mr. Abbot. This gentleman is an Englishman, as learned as he is amiable. To him the science of Egyptian archæology is greatly indebted for its advancement, and more especially by his exertions in the Egyptian Literary Association, of which he is the secretary. This society, as well as its rival of similar name and with similar objects, likewise in Cairo, proves that the Franks, located in Egypt, consider it their duty worthily to represent, in the very presence of the pyramids, so sadly neglected by their compatriots, that quarter of the world, wherein, as in no other, learning is a kind of common property.

The other Egyptian society to which I have alluded, offers to the traveller a costly treasure in its admirably selected library. Its secretary, Mr. Walmass, is now establishing also a European printing press, to which we must heartily wish the most complete success.

Were I to describe all that I found interesting in the antiquarian collection of Mr. Abbot, I should have a difficult task. His greatest treasure he considers to be a gold ring, discovered not a great while ago, and supposed to be the signet ring of the great Sesostris. He told us that he had been offered two thousand pounds for it. A bronze helmet also he estimates highly ; its antiquity is reputed to be very great, and it is surmised to have belonged to a man of note.

As in the Pompeian cabinet at Naples, so here many very ancient articles of pottery, and other curiosities of a domestic character are preserved ; the entire wheel of a chariot, several portions of an ancient plough, and other implements. Also bundles of papyrus,— for thus I consider they are more fitly called, than rolls of papyrus,— and fragments with Coptic inscriptions are not scarce.

A remarkable curiosity Mr. Abbot showed us, in a delicate gold leaf, of a pyramidal shape, such as have been found upon female mummies, and which, from their peculiar significance, could only be found there. Abd Allatif mentions such gold leaves, as also other similar ones, which covered the forehead, nose, and eyes of mummies. That which was now exhibited derives its celebrity from its having suggested to a learned Englishman, who supports his opinion in perfect seriousness, and has elucidated it in detail, that the pyramids themselves are analogous to the gold leaf upon a large scale, and have the most intimate affinity with that signification. I should

like to become more intimately acquainted with this theory of the
pyramids ; only, unfortunately, it is a subject that does not well admit
of discussion in good society.

Among the amulets, Scarabees and other curiosities, there were also
many specimens of the Phallus, which Egyptian women, as in other
countries, used formerly to wear round the neck, either as a talisman
or as an ornament. Thence we derived a confirmation of the still disputed opinion,
that circumcision was very customary amongst the ancient Egyptians,
although possibly not universally prevalent.

I must also tell you my adventure in the book bazaar at Cairo.
A young Russian, in Turkish garb, and attached to the Russian consulate, told me that he had there made some desirable purchases of
Arabic manuscripts. I accompanied him upon his next visit; but
I was totally unsuccessful. I have elsewhere found that my Frankish hat and coat were an authority to which the Orientals paid all
respect; but here my costume was an offence, or more properly a
traitor. Scarcely had we passed through a narrow entrance into this
bazaar, and inspected the MSS. spread out before us, when we heard
some hostile remarks in the dense crowd which surrounded us, and
especially the cry, " Close your stall ! Close your stall ! " My companion became alarmed, and urged me to a speedy retreat. The
Mahometan proceeds with his Koran quite differently from what
the Christian does with his Bible. It is well known that our Missionaries distribute the latter in profusion, whereas the Mahometan,
on the contrary, considers it a sin to sell the Koran to a Christian.
Undoubtedly it is easy enough to obtain it by cautious stratagem; but
public dealing for it is liable to produce a public disturbance.

JOURNEY TO SINAI. — FROM CAIRO TO SUEZ.

I HAD spent above a month very agreeably at Cairo and in its
vicinity, industriously occupied with my peculiar pursuits, when I
became impatient to visit Mount Sinai. The temperature was certainly not the most propitious ; we had a succession of days of
oppressive heat, far more enervating than the Neapolitan Sirocco in
July, according to my experience of the preceding year. This was
called in Cairo the temperature of the Chamsin. On the 10th of
May I went out about three o'clock. Upon passing from my own
narrow cool street to the large garden abutting upon it, the atmosphere was so suffocating that I turned back, fully assured that it

could be but noon. But no delay was propitiatory : the days glowed with increasing fervour towards summer. I now became an absolute convert to the doctrine of predestination, and, indeed, possibly more to the Turkish than the Christian.

On the eleventh some Bedouins arrived in Cairo, who offered to conduct me to Mount Sinai. I fell in with them encamped with their camels opposite the Austrian consulate. I had good advisers, and therefore took care not to offer them too much. We had already come to terms. It was agreed that I should pay a hundred and forty piastres for each of three camels — the fourth, rode by the Sheikh the leader of the caravan, was to be included without cost. The Bedouins now fell out amongst themselves; they were dissatisfied with the price. I thought the matter would be soonest settled by subjecting them to the alternative of taking the proposed offer, or of going about their business. But I was mistaken. They directly broke up, and departed homewards. The consular authority brought them back again. I now consented to give four hundred and eighty piastres for four camels. The requisite Cairine notary drew up the agreement upon a long strip of paper which lay upon his hand as he stood in front of us. I subscribed it, and the Sheikh made in lieu of his signature an impression under it with his seal dipped in ink.

I wished to start on the forenoon of the twelfth, but it was noon before the camels appeared in front of the Casa Pini. My active Ali had sufficient to do to prepare all my travelling and cooking apparatus as well as the necessary supply of provisions. At three in the afternoon the camels proceeded with their burdens, friends surrounded me at my departure, besides two Arabs and a Copt who had rendered me several essential services, all of whom with the consular kawass accompanied me on asses. But I did not quit Cairo with much regret, for in a few weeks I expected to return within its gate enriched by that time with imperishable reminiscences.

The weather was agreeable. We had got about half a league beyond the gates when we drew up in the neighbourhood of some considerable tombs ; for my Bedouins still had preparations to make. I was astonished to find myself so comfortable upon the " Ship of the Desert." I had read in travels that the motion of the camel resembles that of a ship at sea, and consequently produces a kind of sea-sickness ; but I sat securely, and as comfortably as I could wish.

We pursued a path which lay somewhat to the south of the usual caravan road to Suez. The latter has within the last few years become tolerably permanent from its being the English post and conveyance road, and furnished for this purpose with seven stations, as

well as with a succession of telegraphic towers. The road to the
south was said to be nearer ; but it led us (and this was doubtlessly
the chief cause for its selection) direct to the native village of my
Bedouins ; and this we reached shortly after nightfall.

This village, at this particular hour, had a sort of gipsy effect. In
the midst of the barren desert, and beneath the tranquil canopy of
heaven, there was spread before our eyes a multitude of black tents,
arranged without art. In front of most of them a fire was flickering,
around which the Bedouins were lying or standing, covered with
their simple dirty white frocks. Upon approaching nearer their
figures became quite grotesque in the glimmer of the fires. We soon,
too, heard the four-footed occupants of the village. Camels bellowed,
kine lowed, sheep bleated, dogs barked, and we were welcomed in the
most friendly manner by the inhabitants, who hastened towards us.

I now for the first time caused my tent to be pitched. I rejoiced
like a child at the raising of this small Bedouin habitation : it was
the first house that I had called my own. The tribe of Bedouins
with whom I was now associated, and to which my three guides
belonged, had for two years past encamped here in the vicinity of
the Mokattam. They had previously dwelt between Gaza and Jerusalem : but having vanquished a neighbouring tribe, and acquired a
booty of several hundred camels, it was thought advisable to make
this change of residence. The impression I received from these
children of the desert was so favourable, that I lay down to repose
in my tent with the most perfect feeling of security.

At sunrise on the 13th all were cheerfully on the alert. My
Bedouins brought me good milk. After I had drunk a cup of tea,
and my guides had finished their coffee, we broke up.

Our road across this desert was thickly sprinkled with dark flints,
amongst which my eye frequently detected red jasper and other
similar minerals of a beautiful colour; and often the road was strewed
with various-sized pieces of fossil palms. I immediately recognised
that they had precisely the appearance of the fossil forest a few
leagues distant from Cairo, from which I brought home many speci
mens. On our right lay, from the Mokattam onwards, a gradually
decreasing mountain ridge : on the left the view was bounded by
sand-hill upon sand-hill.

Between ten and eleven we encamped to take our meal. My guides
selected for this purpose a spot overgrown with green shrubs. I
found there some very tall and beautifully coloured thistles. To my
astonishment, our camels browsed upon these thistles with much
satisfaction ; whilst to me the very sight of their thorns was painful.
How happily must the camel's mouth be constituted !

Having consumed my fowl, and slumbered a little, I stepped out of the tent to survey the widely extended sandy plain. All was still around me. The dragoman and the Bedouins slept; in the far distance camels were browsing. A pair of cicadas alone chirruped; and a desert-bird whistled its melancholy tones, resembling those of the willow-finch in Voigtland. I now fully felt that I was in the desert. Nothing absorbs the mind so entirely as the desert.

One thought, however, was dominant in my soul. I had shortly before, in my tent, read in the books of Moses. I was now on the very spot where Moses had wandered with his brethren. Whilst reading it as a child, beneath my mother's eyes, how could I have thought that I should once read it upon this spot! Thus did the Bible recal home with its associations. And the plaintive voice of the little bird sounded also like a call from home. Oh ye beloved ones at home! Not that I would exactly and willingly exchange your green hills and your solid houses for my little white tent in the desert sandy plains; but I said to myself, " Oh that there was here an eye to reflect my delight, a heart that I could ardently clasp, and two lips to join me in a hymn of joy ! "

About four I aroused my Bedouins. The camels were speedily collected; having found themselves quite at home, they had mean-while wandered as far as any vegetation could be seen. I placed myself in front of one of these animals, which was stooping upon its knees to receive its burden. No sooner did it see my straw hat, and my streaming green veil, than up it sprang and galloped away; so shy had this large animal, and of such a phlegmatic tempera-ment, become at the sight of my straw hat. The sheikh told me it had never before seen one. But I much wondered that our camels were never panic-struck when they saw upon the road the scattered bones and skeletons of their dead brethren. They may possibly be accustomed to this sight; for from Cairo to Suez, after we had rejoined the main route of the caravans, we found sure guides for our direction in the numerous skeletons of these animals that we met with, and which shone brightly white in the distance.

Shortly before sunset we passed close to a mass of colossal dark-coloured stones, which had more than a solemn, even an awful effect. They were, doubtlessly, aboriginal mountain fragments. We rode on till late at night; it was tolerably dark, our pathway was a flat plain, but upon our right lay a long low chain of hills, above which towered a considerably higher brown-coloured mountain, called Dschebel Gharbun. Suddenly, close upon our right, and amongst some low shrubs, I beheld a wanderer, still blacker than the night; it was a great *zingale*. This apparition was the less agree-able, as my dragoman had told me that the zingales in this desert sometimes attack the traveller.

Upon stopping to bivouac for the night I did not at first allow my tent to be pitched. I caused my blanket and lamb and sheep skins to be spread between the long provision basket, made of palm leaves, and my travelling chest, and wrapped myself up in them. By my side lay my loaded double-barrelled gun, and around me slept my Ali and the Bedouins. The camels could only hop about to graze, having their fore-feet tethered to prevent their wandering.

I may have slept for about an hour when I awoke. I shall never forget the moment ; I had a second time a full consciousness of the desert. I lay there in the fearful waste, whose savage inhabitants might be now seeking their prey. All was deadly-still about me ; the pigeons only fluttered in their cage, and the camels bellowed in the distance. Above me was the nocturnal sky, splendidly studded with stars. Canopus shone down with his eye of fire. In such a situation, were we not fully impressed with the watchful guardianship of heaven, it would be difficult to recompose oneself to sleep. But in the desert one acquires confidence, even when not constitutional. I felt as if from the stars the paternal arms were reaching downwards to me, which had so faithfully sustained me throughout my wanderings, and I then reclosed my eyes with comfort.

During the whole of the 14th, the rugged Ataka lay to the south-east on the right, before our eyes ; it has a reddish appearance, slightly tinged with brown. About mid-day we observed, upon bending towards the high road of the caravan, at some distance from us, one of the seven English halting-places, and a telegraphic tower, which singularly surprised me as it shot upwards with its summit from behind the sand-hills. As we were passing the white station in the evening, our camels were seized with an extraordinary panic. This house, standing here in the midst of their peaceful home, where a feeling of boundless freedom prevails, may possibly have appeared to them as an usurping stranger. Such adventures are any thing but pleasant. Fortunately I was going before the camels on foot, and the ,camel laden with the cooking apparatus was led by the bridle; but the three others sprang wildly right and left. The few utensils of my Bedouins were dashed to atoms by this catastrophe, but they soon succeeded in pacifying the animals. We passed this night close to Abscherud, the fortress, with a deeply sunken well of bitter water, which welcomes the pilgrims to Mecca with hospitable solicitude. But we saw less of the fort than we heard of it, for the dogs barked loudly.

We reached Bir Suez early on the 15th, after a two hours' journey ; there we found two wells enclosed within a square building, and surrounded by four towers ; and a very numerous party of Arabs had assembled. This retarded the approach of our camels to the drinking-place. This water is fitted only for camels, although at Suez it is also applied to domestic purposes; it is strongly impregnated with salt. It was the first water we had met with since we left Cairo. We had taken for our use upon the road two large bottles of filtered Nile water, which at first constituted a tolerably complete lading for one camel.

We had now distinctly in view Suez, and the mirror of the Red Sea. In the south the reddish-brown Ataka stretched down to the coast, and on the opposite coast we also observed another long mountain-chain trending to the south likewise, of a darkish-red colour. It was called Toraha. Between eight and nine we reached the gates of Suez. Instead of resorting to one of the two European hotels, I preferred adhering to the custom of the desert; and a little to the northward of the gate, close to the sea, and under the protection of a sand-hill, I pitched my tent.

SUEZ.

Suez itself has a modest appearance. Comparing it by a European standard, it appears like a large village; but it has many stately houses, especially upon the quay, which reflect themselves in the blue waters of the sea. The vessels lying here were very numerous, but generally small. The steam-boats plying between India and Suez lie at some distance to the south, at anchor, on account of the shallowness of the water. The interior of the city, owing to the entire absence of all vegetation, has a melancholy aspect. Even in water it is poor; that which is brought from the eastern side of the sea is, doubtlessly, better than the water of Bir Suez, and yet even that is not entirely free from a brackish taste.

After a refreshing dip in the sea, during which the ground alone, with its numerous corals and shells, was uncomfortable, I paid a visit to the consul of France and Austria. Although a native Greek, he did not understand a word of Romaic.

Whilst sitting with him, a man of middle age, and in the ordinary costume, entered the apartment, seated himself in the Oriental fashion upon the floor, quite unceremoniously, and commenced a narrative. Thereupon the son of the consul handed him a coin. The stranger continued his narrative, and received a second coin. He then arose, and took his leave.

I now learnt that he was a Turkish beggar who related that in the course of his travels he had reached Suez, and could not resist paying a visit to the distinguished and wealthy consul. Upon this he had received the first coin ; this he thought too little : he therefore added, that with such a trifle he could buy nothing worth having, which certainly would be inconsistent with the dignity of the consul ; and upon this plea he had received the addition. All this had taken place in such a becoming and friendly manner, that not the least idea of a beggar had entered my head.

Mr. Costa and his son told me they had gone frequently for weeks together for recreation to the monastery upon Sinai. They spoke of the richness of its library, but had no positive knowledge of its contents.

I now purposed visiting Mr. Manoli, the agent to the East India Company, and purveyor to the monastery ; but I was told he was at present in his harem, where no intrusion was allowed, nor was it even possible to announce us. Here, then, the same custom prevails as with the Italian princess when she is *inamorata*, at least according to the description of Madame de Stael. I returned a few hours later, and found in Mr. Manoli a gentlemanly well-educated Arab, who even spoke English. In one of his rooms he had a portrait of Rüppel, and spoke of this profound inquirer with the greatest esteem : Rüppel is possibly the only German who may have had his portrait taken upon the Red Sea. Both Manoli and Costa offered me, in the most pressing manner, letters of recommendation to the monastery upon Sinai. I had reasons for accepting them from both parties.

Upon returning to my tent I found a multitude of dark brown Arabs collected in front of it. They urged upon me that they were the true guides to Sinai, that their own domicile was upon Sinai, and that they had the most complete knowledge of every nook and corner of the Desert ; that I might therefore dismiss my companions and engage them in their stead ; but that in making this change I should not pay a fraction more than what I had already agreed for. I was fully aware that other travellers had met with the greatest danger under such circumstances, for one tribe is ready to contest with another their supposed rights. I consequently asked my Bedouins if they in fact had perfect right to guide me, when they assured me they had. I now explained to the others that I had given my word to my Bedouins, and that my word was an infrangible obligation. They then quitted me. But upon visiting the consulate a second time in the afternoon, I found them assembled before it : they had laid their claim before the consul. The consul explained the matter to me. I asked him upon whom the decision depended, and he replied that it depended upon me. I then repeated to the consul the explanation I had already given to the Bedouins, and he himself dismissed them with a rebuke.

The result of this affair made so deep an impression upon my Bedouins, that they swore they would sacrifice their lives in my defence; and that they were in earnest, and although but three, were certainly a match for a dozen enemies, I had subsequently a positive proof.

At a short distance from my tent, towards the north, I found ruins and traces of the cities that had previously stood here. I did not go far enough in that direction to convince myself actually of the correctness of the conclusion which Linant de Bellefonds formed of the former extent of this arm of the Red Sea; but the soil clearly shows that the drift sand of the Desert has made an attack upon it.

The traces of an ancient canal are also visible. Yet Karl von Raumer, in his researches upon the limits of the Red Sea at the time of the passage of the Israelites, has inappropriately referred to this to prove that its extent at that period was not essentially different from what it is now; for the construction of this canal dates no further back than the time of the caliphs.

At night we had a beautifully starry sky; I ascended to the summit of the hill, adjoining which my tent was pitched, and thence enjoyed a splendid view of the sea. There was it, then, that the powerful arm of the Omnipotent was revealed! The waters roared; they still repeat the ancient holy tale. With respect to the diameter of the strait, Linant de Bellefonds, who is profoundly conversant with the subject, repeated several times at my request the information he possesses. It is well known that Mehemet Ali has commissioned him specially with this matter, and that he has for years studied the locality. The difference of level of the two seas was certainly not the most serious consideration. Ptolemy stopped the progress of the canal to the Nile already extending to the salt lakes, from the fear of injuring the quality of the water of that river. Linant de Bellefonds has clearly enough proved that its completion would not make a very extraordinary demand upon the energy and means of an age like ours accustomed to gigantic undertakings; and that the results of the cutting would be of incalculable importance to European trade, and of such a nature that the cost in comparison would appear but a bagatelle, is certainly clear to all the world.

Why the undertaking is not commenced, but, on the contrary, delayed by the most recent post arrangements between Cairo and Suez, may be best answered by that state whose interest it chiefly affects. England could not, without serious prejudice to its own interests, share with any other country the advantages of the conjunction. If this were now to take place, how would England claim the exclusive advantages of it? Who can be ignorant of the policy of England with regard to Egypt? The necessary complication of relations will not fail at the proper moment, to enable the hand to seize what the eye has long been fixed upon. In one word : until Egypt is English, England, more than any other power, will retard the undertaking. As soon as Egypt is English, it will instantly take place, and the age will be immediately conscious of the great fact. But to anticipate impatiently the course of great events in the East would be to mistake hugely the present policy of the great powers. And Mehemet Ali will so much the less accelerate this great undertaking from not caring to make both friend and foe more eager for his country. Besides, the proposed damming of the Nile occupies all his energies, and is far more important to his country than the cutting through of the isthmus.

The following morning, very early, I caused my camels and Bedouins, together with my dragoman, to ford the sea at about ten minutes' distance from Suez; for it was a complete ebb tide. The water nowhere reached the thighs of the camels; a spot in the middle was completely dry. In rather more than a quarter of an hour they had reached the eastern side of the sea.* The circuit that must be made at flood tide round the extreme arm of the sea would occupy several hours, as I was told. I myself had accepted the invitation of young Mr. Costa, to accompany him in his boat to Ayin Musa, where he possessed a villa. But we were obliged to await the return of the tide to enable us to start, and, in conjunction with the flood, to depend upon a favourable wind.

Meanwhile I paid a visit, in company with Mr. Costa, to the governor of Suez. We found, under the entrance archway of his palace, this athletic and muscular man, who had seen much military service. We immediately seated ourselves beside him. I presented him with the credentials which had been made out for me for my journey to Sinai by the governor of Cairo. The governor received them with the customary mark of respect, but he could not read them. His secretary was called, who read them to him, and then subscribed them, to show that they had been viséd by the governor of

---

* Niebuhr accurately measured the present breadth of the sea at Suez, upon which we may observe that the portion immediately north of Suez is considerably wider than that opposite the place. Yet the breadth of the sea to the north of Suez, at the spot where the Arabs usually ford it at ebb tide, approaches to its breadth at Suez itself. These are Niebuhr's calculations.— "I placed the astrolabe on the shore on the east side of the sea, and found the angle between my meridian line of 83 double paces and the south-east angle of the city in the first position, 76° 5', and in the second 97° 52'. The breadth of this arm of the Red Sea is therefore 757 double paces, or about 3450 feet."

Suez. I had no occasion to make use of his offer of protection and other incidental civilities.

About nine we commenced our excursion to Ayin Musa. I observed in the middle of this arm of the sea an extensive shoal, as well as a second, which reached over from the east like a slightly covered tongue of land. Our boat was obliged to avoid most carefully any approach to it, and could not pass straight across. On the trip, Chalil, the consul's dragoman, mentioned the services he had rendered to Alphonse de la Martine. We were about two hours upon the water, although the wind was not unfavourable. When we were directly opposite Ayin Musa, we observed there what appeared a small glittering pyramid; this was, however, nothing more than my tent, which my Ali had already pitched. The small white tenement looked down proudly and imposingly from its elevation into the beautiful dark blue sea; but the optical delusion was temporary; and I might compare it with Niebuhr's, for he also, in the vicinity of Suez, saw an Arab upon his camel who appeared to be riding in the air, "higher than a church."*

The entire circuit of Ayin Musa, or the Wells of Moses, contains many mounds of rubbish; and the ruins of many ancient structures, undoubtedly, lie buried here. During the French expedition it is well known that General Bonaparte himself discovered the large canal through which the water of these springs, eight in number, was conveyed to the seashore. This canal probably supplied the Venetians with water, for the fleets which they equipped against the Portuguese, after the latter had discovered the passage to India round the Cape of Good Hope. It is, indeed, better than any of the rest found in the neighbourhood, although not entirely free from a milky or nitric taste, nor yet without a slightly aperient effect. Solitary palm-trees are dispersed around in their completely natural state, densely covered with branches from the root to the summit. Several very ancient stems of trees presented a remarkable appearance. One of the largest of the Moses' fountains is enclosed within the pleasure grounds of Signor Costa: this agreeable villa, with its delightful green foliage, and with its luxuriant growth of vegetables and fruits, created in the very midst of the Desert, looks like the cheerful eye of the waste; and we distinctly here perceive, that the soil bounteously rewards the labour of its cultivation. Several Englishmen have imitated Signor Costa in laying out pleasure grounds with villas, and I may safely prophesy a still more luxuriant future to these establishments.

It is very doubtful if the naming of these fountains after Moses

* See Niebuhr's Reisebeschreibung, vol. i. p. 253.

may be ascribed to a very high antiquity. But as there can be no doubt that the great leader of the Israelites rested here after the passage of the Red Sea, later generations, whether Mahometans or Christians, and most probably the earliest pilgrims to Sinai, were fully justified in attaching the name of Moses to these refreshing fountains. Peter Belon, who was here three hundred years ago, says positively, that these fountains, twelve of which he enumerates, are the bitter waters of Moses. (Exod. xv. 23.) But in opposition to this opinion, in the first place, the waters are not bitter enough ; and, secondly, the situation does not agree — a circumstance long since noticed.

Whilst sitting alone beneath an ancient palm-tree, by the side of one of these fountains, I was wholly absorbed in a reverie on the mighty past. I read the hymn which Moses, together with the children of Israel, chaunted to the Lord by the same fountain, after their miraculous escape from the waters and their enemies' hand. " I will sing unto the Lord, for he hath triumphed gloriously ; the horse and his rider hath he thrown into the sea." The song could never be forgotten when once read here. I saw Miriam the prophetess with the timbrel in her hand, and the women that went out after her with timbrels and with dances — " Sing ye to the Lord," thus did it peal in my ears, " for he hath triumphed gloriously ; the horse and his rider hath he thrown into the sea." (Exod. xv. 21.)

I cannot deny myself halting here in my travels, to introduce the result of my researches upon the passage of the Israelites through the Red Sea. But I shall try to avoid giving my relation the character of a strictly learned treatise, purposing, as I do, to publish one upon this subject shortly.

PASSAGE OF THE ISRAELITES ACROSS THE RED SEA.

Moses' narrative of the miraculous assistance given by the Lord to the people of Israel, in their flight from the Egyptian bondage to the promised land, has been recently attacked, on the ground, that from an inspection of the scene itself, the simplest natural circumstances will account for their preservation, without requiring the interposition of the divine power. All else has been attributed to the exaggerating poetical colouring of tradition. It is very natural to suppose that these attacks raised opponents, who have erected a new bulwark about the faith of our fathers. Possibly, however, both sides may be in error ; the one party having divested the miracle of the miraculous altogether, and the other having made it too miraculous. Whereas, to me it appears that a thorough investigation of the facts leaves both faith and science all their dues.

Above all, it is important to follow closely the biblical narrative in all respects, from the exodus to the passage. The children of Israel journeyed from Rameses to Succoth, as is expressly stated in Exodus, xii. 37. Where lay Rameses? In my opinion, on the site of Heliopolis. Instead of this, Heroopolis has been recently named.* I say recently; yet it is only the same thread again taken up which was spun by Du Bois Aimé, in 1810.† This requires confutation, and a few words will suffice.

In the first place, the passage cited in proof that Heroopolis and Rameses are identical, proves, on the contrary, most decidedly that they cannot be identical. Thus in Genesis, xlvi. 28., it says, " And he sent Judah before him unto Joseph, to direct his face unto Goshen." The Septuagint has here, instead of Goshen, " Heroopolis in Rameses."

Rameses is identical with Goshen. This is evident from Genesis, xlvii. 11., where the Hebrew text itself has Rameses instead of Goshen. But if in Genesis, xlvi. 28., it distinctly says, " Heroopolis in Rameses," this certainly cannot be " Rameses in Rameses." The name of the CITY Rameses, says Hengstenberg, had fallen into disuse. This assertion is absolutely contradicted by Exodus, i. 11., for here the name of the city Rameses is left quietly even by the Greek translators.

Secondly, Heroopolis cannot be Rameses, and, as such, the place whence the Israelites took their departure, for the road from Heroopolis, the site of which is well known, is perfectly incomprehensible as leading to any transit across the Red Sea. So far is this from being the case, that from Heroopolis the northern extremity of the gulf which was called the Gulf of Heroopolis, from its so closely adjoining it, would have been doubled.

It may not be objected, that we can know nothing of the road which Moses MUST have taken. Moses had his definite plan, or rather, the express direction of Heaven, to go across Sinai to Canaan. To effect this, it was improbable that he should be required to strike into an unreasonable path; and it would have been unreasonable to have gone from Heroopolis by any other way than to the east of the gulf.

Moses had indeed promulgated, for the purpose of deceiving Pharaoh, that the Israelites were only going to hold a festival in the Desert. But the Desert was both on the east and on the west of the gulf. And

---

* See Hengstenberg, " Die Bücher Moses und Egypten," 1841.
† See Description de l' Egypte, tom. viii. p. 111, &c.

76

if we are reminded of the anxiety Moses may have suffered in apprehending an attack from the frontier garrisons of Egypt, we may reply, that Heroopolis itself was a frontier fortress, and would consequently be garrisoned. Besides, the miracles performed must certainly have made a deeper impression upon all the Egyptians than upon the obstinate Pharaoh; and therefore possibly nobody but Pharaoh was desirous to force the wanderers back again. But Moses could not more securely escape all pursuit than by hastening at once to the east side of the gulf, which might, thence, have been accomplished in a few hours. Moreover, had any apprehension actually been entertained of the Egyptian frontier garrisons, there would certainly have been mention made of it in the text, as is the fear of war with the Philistines; for the former was of more immediate consideration.

There is but one point that has some degree of plausibility in its favour, viz. the reference made by Du Bois Aimée to Exodus, xiii. 18.: " But God led the people about through the way of the wilderness of the Red Sea." Du Bois Aimée says, " It could only be by making the exodus from the valley of Sebabyar, where Heroopolis itself lay, that it is at all conceivable how the Israelites should have wandered for three days by the Red Sea." But this the passage itself by no means intimates. The way through the Desert by the Red Sea, is in contradistinction to the land of the Philistines, which lay close to the Mediterranean. It does not even refer to the first three days. The passage in question stands at the outset of the journey, and refers to its whole course. Besides, it does not say, the way by the Red Sea, but, "the way through the Desert by the Red Sea." The direct road from Heliopolis to Canaan, through the land of the Philistines, would have been by Belbeis, and towards the lake Menzaleh upwards towards Pelusium and Gaza, the very road I myself took. Upon this road the Israelites would have met with cultivated land; whereas, in accordance with the divine direction, they took the way through the Desert by the Red Sea, through which the road led to Sinai.

Another objection to the adoption of the exodus issuing from Heroopolis is, that Moses must be considered to have been in the immediate vicinity of the royal residence; for, during the night of the last plague, he was called to Pharaoh. But Memphis lies too far distant from Heroopolis; and Zoan, which is indeed much nearer than Memphis, can hardly be considered as the royal residence.

Lastly, the direction of the journey commanded in Exodus, xiv. 2., supposing it to have proceeded from Heroopolis, is scarcely possible.

Therefore, according to my view, the Israelites started from Heliopolis. Josephus agrees with this, in as far as he allows the Israelites to have been stationed at Heliopolis, and thence directs their way by Bessatin. And the requisite proximity of Moses to Pharaoh at Memphis concurs with this supposition. And lastly, Heliopolis agrees admirably with Rameses. This is proved by the old Arabic translator Saadias, who gives Heliopolis as the equivalent of Rameses; in favour of which Jablonsky's etymology, from the Coptic, may at least be cited. And in conclusion, the Greek translation of Exodus, i. 11., speaks directly in favour of it; whereas it has been customary to deduce thence the objection. For " Rameses" this has, in the ordinary text, "Rameses and On, which is Heliopolis." The addition, " and On, which is Heliopolis," I consider as a more definite designation of Rameses. We find, consequently, more correctly, in the splendid MS. of the sixth century at Milan, not "and On," but, "or otherwise, On;" whilst two Arabic translations place "and On," and " which is Heliopolis," in apposition, as two different additions. It would also have been surprising had the Greek translator, fifteen hundred years after the original was written, added to the ancient text a new and positive fact; whereas it is perfectly in his manner to explain the strange Coptic name Rameses, in the first place, by the better known Egyptian name On, and also, at the same time, with the corresponding Greek name Heliopolis.

From Heliopolis it has been preferred to trace the course of the exodus through Bessatin; the main cause of which is that Josephus mentions this course. But did Josephus possess in his time any other anthority than perhaps a vague tradition? Where the Israelites dwelt could and must have remained more permanently impressed upon the memory of the people than the way Moses took across the Desert.

The further course of the exodus Sicard especially has endeavoured to trace south of the mountain chain Mokattam. In Gendeli he discovered Succoth, Etham in the plain of Ramlie, Pihahiroth in Thuarek, and made the passage of the Red Sea take place nearly opposite Ayin Musa, from south-west to north-east, just where existing traditions, possibly in favour of Moses' fountains, have chosen to place it. The gulf is there from five to six leagues wide.

It is not to be denied that much may be said in favour of this being the road; but certainly much more may be said against it. I will only mention in the first place, that Sicard, to shorten the road of three days' journey, causes the exodus to commence from Bessatin, recognising in Bessatin, Rameses. This appears to me to be quite untenable; for, without referring to aught else, Bessatin lies beyond the frontiers of the land of Goshen: besides, the road still remains very long. Sicard himself, indeed, accomplished these twenty-seven French miles in three days; but for that host of two millions the task was considerably more difficult, and would be certainly im-

possible, if we add thereto the road of several leagues lying between
Heliopolis and Bessatin.   Raumer has therefore recently suggested
that in the Mosaic account we are by no means to understand days'
journeys.   But this is certainly erroneous : days' journeys must just
as surely be understood here as subsequently (when Raumer himself
derives his proofs from them).   But in these days' journeys we are
not to understand the intervening repose to consist of a night, or
indeed as limited to any precise time.

Besides, the breadth of the sea being from five to six leagues,
which would be a journey of at least from nine to ten hours for the
host of Israel, it is scarcely reconcilable with Moses's account of the
eventful night.

It is also improper to give great weight to the tradition that points
out that particular spot, as another tradition fixes upon a place a
couple of days' journey to the south of it, at the so-called Hamam
Pharaun, whereby the miracle would become still more miraculous,
and its historical investigation would amount to an absurdity.

If, now, the Israelites issued from Heliopolis, and not by way of
Bessatin, the distance in a direct line to the sea would amount to
twenty leagues.   But I conclude that Moses, with clear eye and
decisive plan, directed the course to the northern extremity of the
gulf.   Early in the second day's journey they arrived at the border of
the wilderness, in Etham ; for the commencement of the journey
still bordered upon the fruitful land of Goshen.   But both Succoth
and Etham are without definite location, unless we may take note
that, immediately about Suez, both east and west of the sea, the
Desert bears the name of Etham.   (Exod. xiii. 20.)

From the second station of Etham, the Lord points out the road
that the children of Israel shall take ; and at the same time mention
is made of Pharaoh's pursuit of them.   Induced by the latter circumstance, Moses may — indeed, to some degree, by compulsion —
have thought of the possibility of a passage through the sea at both
of the fords well known to him, to the north and south of Suez,
whereas Pharaoh was advancing as nearly as possible from the north,
to cut off the only passage from the emigrants.

Moses encamped before Pihahiroth, between Migdol and the sea,
over against Baal-zephon. (Exod. xiv. 2.)   Baal-zephon may have
stood, as is usually considered, upon the present site of Suez.   Pihahiroth, or Hahiroth, is the present Adscheruth. The further description
of the encampment " between Migdol and the sea " is perfectly consistent, if under the name of Migdol the mountain Ataka is understood ; and in no respect can any thing of moment be urged against
the admission of this.   Mountain and sea are very congruously
placed in conjunction, whilst the city Baal-zephon is named in
apposition.

But it appears perfectly incomprehensible to me how Hengstenberg can suppose that Migdol indicates the frontier fort of this name in the vicinity of Pelusium. A single glance at the map shows, that two points at a distance of three days' journey from each other cannot be cited as the opposite extremities of a place of encampment. The Migdol, situated closely to the Mediterranean, lies beyond all connexion with the exodus. Besides, to the Israelites issuing from Heroopolis — as Hengstenberg assumes — that Migdol would have been nearer to them during the two first days than on the third, to which especially this encampment refers. But now the Israelites were, in fact, in the most dangerous position in the world. On the right they had Mount Ataka, which seen from Suez appears to have but the very narrowest strip of land free between it and the sea, below them the sea, and behind and on their flanks the army of Pharaoh.

In opposition to those who prefer contemplating the miracle through their own magnifying glasses — sometimes indeed from religious zeal, but certainly foolishly so — it is dangerous to take into consideration the alternating phenomena of ebb and flood. But the text itself guides us decidedly to this : "And the Lord caused the sea to go back by a strong east wind all that night." (Exod. xiv. 21.) The north-east wind is still that which to this day increases the ebb. Besides, even to the present day, as I myself have twice seen and taken advantage of, the ebb occurs during the early morning. The Red Sea, as I have before said, has near Suez, two fords, one to the north and the other to the south : at ebb tide both are still made use of by the Arabs. But at that period the sea extended considerably further northward than at present : it reached — only compare the maps of Du Bois Aimée and Laborde — nearly to the valley of Sebabyar ; and therefore an easy circuit round the sea, as Raumer says, was not to be thought of. If the fords were, as is very credible, then in existence, the passage must have occupied a longer time than now, and therefore the whole matter would have seemed much more extraordinary than at present.

The Israelites made the passage successfully during the night ; at the first watch they were already across, and the Egyptians in the midst of the waves. All this is possible only at Suez. Whereas the passage of six leagues at Ayin Musa, and which, besides, must have been considerably longer for the Israelites, and cannot be rendered dry by even the most powerful east wind — had Moses intended to speak of an absolute miracle, he would not have referred at all to the east wind — this passage, I say, deprives the event of all connection with the ordinary divine ordination.

The most prominent aspect of the miracle is indeed not so much the safe passage of the Israelites as the destruction of the army of Pharaoh, although it has been in vain that the requisite quantity of water has been anxiously sought for to effect it ; for no thought was taken of the different extension of the sea at that period.   If, however, the question be absolutely decided in favour of the southern ford, at which it is scarcely possible to hesitate, a similar phenomenon may be still observed.

Notwithstanding all this, I still clearly behold in that event, viewed from either side, the protecting arm of the Lord miraculously extended over his people.   But that he made natural means serviceable, though in the most peculiar manner, we have the authority of the sacred text.   To go beyond the text is, in my opinion, less pious than inconsiderate and capricious.

" The Lord hath triumphed gloriously.   The Lord shall reign for ever and ever." (Exod. xv. 18.)   This triumphal song of the chosen servant of God will, as long as there is history and faith upon the globe, float truly and for ever over the passage of the Israelites through the Red Sea.

FROM AYIN MUSA TO SINAI.

On the afternoon of the 16th of May I quitted Ayin Musa.   We took the reddish Toraha on the east, whose southern summit, the Dschebel Sadr, casts far away its whitish glitter, as our faithful companion upon our immediate journey, whilst in the west we had at first the brows of Ataka towering imperiously over the mirror of the sea, but subsequently this was supplanted by the Dschebel Kuaib. As evening sank, the Kuaib enveloped itself in dark-blue vapours, which clung magically about its reddish rock.   We now again wandered through a sandy plain, strewed with fire-stones : the sea had disappeared from the eye.   But I was forcibly attracted to it, and my guides were obliged to lead me again this evening close to it. We had scarcely fixed our nocturnal bivouac, when I hastened with my lantern to the foaming flood ; my eager desire was too great even to let me collect the beautiful shells upon the shore.   But on my return I had all my pockets filled with them.

The next morning we proceeded for hours along the shore, which was still moist with the retiring tide.   I now beheld it in the completeness of its grandeur.   The shells of the Red Sea merit their celebrity; upon no other coast is there exhibited such a spectacle.   My Bedouins sought, instead of shells, the fish that the ebb had left behind. Towards mid-day we found ourselves in the Wadi Sadr, which has the appearance of a forest, from the multitude of its tamarisks, and its lofty shrubs, and bushes.   I saw there also many leverets.

Having passed through the Wadi, I directed my course westerly again, by the sea-shore.   Here I reaped my chief harvest of shells ; I collected, especially, a small white- and grey- sprinkled species, which Egyptian women hang round the necks of their children, as a talisman, to protect them from the evil eye.   And at my next bivouac by the sea, I dreamt of a bright eye far away.   " Look," said I, to its possessor, " here have I found a talisman against the evil eye, but where shall I seek for one to protect me from thy heavenly eye ?"

The Egyptian women fully believe in the evil eye.   I have myself repeatedly experienced, to my annoyance, that mothers have covered up their children when I was looking kindly at them.   They have a similar apprehension of shrieks.   If, indeed, we are as completely surrounded by evil spirits as the Egyptians surmise, then certainly can we not be too cautious.   Here, in the desert, where the visible demons of social cultivation are not found, a belief in invisible ones may be better justified.

During the forenoon of the 16th, our course lay for a long time between white chalk ridges.   After proceeding for some leagues, we came to a guard-house, which looked like a deserted orphan in the midst of a heartless world.   Immediately behind it lay, according to the information of my companions, the Howara fountain, with bitter water; but still drinkable, in case of need.   It is well known, that this fountain is assumed to be the Marah of Scripture, where "the Lord showed Moses a tree, which when he had cast into the waters, the waters were made sweet." (Exod. xv. 25.)   The distance of three days' journey agrees very well with the position of this spot ; naturally the three uninterrupted days' journey must only be so understood, that during them no encampment of any duration took place.   The means of sweetening the waters have also been investigated ; and Burckhardt found that the berries of the Gurkud, which grows profusely about the fountain, may have contributed to this effect.   But at the present time the Bedouins are not aware of any such application of them.   At Cairo, however, I was informed, that the Marah of Scripture is a fountain lying to the east of Howara, the water of which is more decidedly bitter : possibly we shall shortly have this point thoroughly determined.

The heat towards mid-day became almost insupportable.   I never experienced it so intense.   It rose certainly to from 30 to 35 degrees in the shade ; and what increases the sensation of this heat, is the precaution adopted to protect from a *coup de soleil*.   During a hot summer in Germany, I have not willingly kept my head so warm as I did in the Arabian desert ; I, besides, wore silk cloths over my face. This a friend at Cairo imposed upon me as a duty ; for he, on his

return from a journey to Sinai, during the same summer time,
brought back with him a complete metamorphosis of his countenance.

We had already proceeded for a league through the Garandel-
valley, before we reached the fountain which is supplied by a little
brook that rills to the sea. It is a magnificent oasis ; where we rested
it lay, enclosed like a jewel, between precipices of limestone. We
waded for a long time through reedy grass as tall as ourselves.
Tamarisks and low palms formed a wreath through it from east to
west. The face of the precipice in front of us was enlivened by
numerous swallows and small birds of prey ; and the trees swarmed
with turtle-doves. Notwithstanding the intensity of the sun's rays concentrated in this beautiful valley, so that even the least refreshment
was difficult to obtain, and the water of the fountain itself tasted warm,
yet was the idea paramount, that we were in the Elim of the Bible,
that Elim where were twelve wells of water, and threescore and ten
palm-trees. (Exod. xv. 27.)   Elim had ever attracted me ; I had delighted to contemplate the children of Israel refreshing themselves
beneath these palms, and by these cheerful wells, after their exhaust-
ing journey through the desert and the steppe.   Hence I rested
long and happy to-day in this blessed valley.   Towards evening
however, contrary to their usual custom, the Bedouins urged our
proceeding, dreading the attack of the insects upon their camels.

Shortly after our departure we descended from a considerable elevation.   We were then enclosed on both sides by whitish-grey limestone
rocks, which, towards the west, assumed the most fantastic shapes.
A strong wind arose. After a two hours' journey I missed my straw
hat, which I had fastened to my gun. The loss was irreparable.
Slen and Attayo and Ali immediately ran back.   Meanwhile, I lay
down in the sand in the dark, with the sheikh and the four camels.
We here interchanged, as well as we could, reciprocal friendly cour-
tesies and I smoked out of his tchybuck. The seekers at length re-
returned, but without the hat. At their desire we at once halted,
as they made sure of recovering it on the following morning. They
had even themselves previously lost the blue linen mantle used in
common among them, and had found it again, after retracing their
steps for many leagues. And, in fact, my hat was also found the next
morning.

On the 19th we felt the effects of the Garandel water, whose smooth
milky taste had made me immediately suspect its quality. Our experience at the Moses fountains had been lost upon us. We reposed at
midday beneath a gigantic mass of rock, insulated in the middle of
the plain, like a lost son of Dschebel Pharaun, which far in the
north-west looked frowningly upon us.

At night our camels became suddenly shy. Attayo ran fearlessly in the direction which seemed to create their apprehension, he discovered nothing but a deserted wandering camel. Later we had a symphony howled by the wolves.

About eight in the morning of the 20th we met with a small encampment of tents. The ground was perforated with several cavities for water, but the contents were very trifling. A maiden was watering her lambs at them ; she had reason to refuse us a participation in her scanty store. The Wadi was called El Bada (rain water). My Bedouins now fetched water from a distance, from a spring called El Malha (bitter) ; but they thus exposed me to the intensity of the mid-day sun, so that, to the indulgence of their social propensities I was compelled to remain at the village until evening. When we broke up I was obliged to take several drops of naphtha as a restorative, from the excessive exhaustion I had suffered during the intense heat.

Our course now lay over a stony and mountainous road, which was often even dangerous ; but the camel has a sure foot. Upon bivouacing for the night we were enclosed by mountain rocks ; yet our camels found green shrubs to browse.

On the 21st we reached the wildly romantic Nasseb-valley. How sublimely here are the masses of sand-stone and granite piled about ! As frowning bulwarks they lay lowering upon our right and upon our left ; often they took a pyramidal shape, and assumed the strangest forms, mimicking, as it were, the ruins of a city of Egyptian colossuses. The colour of these rocks was charming. Now they appeared enveloped with a grey cloud ; they were now of a light or dark red, with veins of slate ; and now they wore a bright green robe over a greyish white mantle. Our road was always serpentine ; and we could never see at once more than a few hundred steps before us. At mid-day the wind again blew hot ; but I had fortunately recovered from the preceding day's exhaustion. Two of my Bedouins fetched water from a fountain, which they called Om Nagla. My dragoman translated it *mare degli arbori,* and told me that two date-trees stood by the spring.

Still riding on in constant view of the masses of rock which encircled us, I could not forbear surmising that we were passing through the dried-up bed of a river. The rocks presented frequent indications of the action of water, and our path was constantly strewed with heaps of pebbles. At all events, even in the present age, the winter floods may rush through this valley.

About half-past four we quitted our halting-place, that we might still reach by sunlight the Wadi Mokatteb. Upon the valley of Nasseb widening into the valley of Mokatteb, we advanced into a splendid amphitheatre. Opposite us stood the majestic mountain range of Feiran. I hastened to the remarkable rock, the inscriptions of

G 2

which give the valley its name. A singular impression is made by these incomprehensible monuments. I long wandered silently around: a forgotten dream as it were floated before my eyes. Here, then, have men roamed, whose language at this day no being comprehends. Here, in the midst of the silent desert, have they experienced their joys and their sorrows, and dedicated these stone tablets of nature to the perpetuation of the record. Were they children of the wilderness who dwelt here, as in the security of a happy asylum? Were they prisoners who torn from their distant homes here deplored their wretched lives; or were they pious wanderers from distant zones, whose hearts impelled them to Sinai, the holy mountain? I could have exclaimed, "Stand forth, ye sleepers! Stand forth! and reveal to us the mysteries of your dark and distant days! Why do ye involve us in delusive dreams? Ever since the sixth century, when these inscriptions, as well as the other similar ones of the peninsula of Sinai, were discovered, no certain clue towards their interpretation has been found. Cosmos Indicopleustes is the first who speaks of them. This makes us necessarily inclined to refer their origin to a very early antiquity. But, in contradiction to this, we may urge the Christian cross, which is found interspersed amongst the inscriptions, as also, .that the Greek inscriptions which occur amongst the strange characters, have certain letters, and especially the Ω, of exactly the form which first occurs upon stones in the early Christian period. As far as I am aware, this has not been before noticed. To my astonishment, I found that Leon de Laborde has most remarkably deviated, in his transcript of them, in several Greek words, which contain a particular sense.* This induces us to place but little confidence in his copy of the other characters ; but, fortunately, they have been more accurately copied by Grey.

Had my countryman Beer been in my place at this moment,—but fate has, unfortunately, too early torn him from his serious pursuits, — he would, without doubt, have remained for days chained to these, his favourite study ; and he would also, more probably than any one else, have penetrated their mysteries. According to his opinion, these characters, as well as the inscriptions upon Serbal and upon Sinai, have an affinity to those of Palmyra, and take a place between the Syrian Estranjelo and the Kufic inscriptions ; and in the dialect in which they are composed, he has discovered Aramaic and Arabic elements. With Quatremere de Quincy, he considers their authors to be the Nabathees, who in the fourth century after Christ occupied Arabia Petræa; but he also surmises that pilgrimages may have led to the sculpture of these inscriptions.

---

* Κακον γενος τουτο and στρατιωτης εγραψα I found upon the rock. Leon de Laborde has published in lieu κακον λεγος λουγος and στρλτιω της εγραυα.

Were not more skilful philologers at hand, I might hazard the observation, that I detected in these inscriptions an affinity with the Samaritan.

The idea of pilgrims concurs with the little which Beer considered he had deciphered. Thence the initial exclamations frequently occur, " Peace ! Salvation ! " or, as it stands undoubtedly in the Greek remains, " In remembrance of," &c. The terms " Pilgrim " and " Priest" also occur frequently. But, in opposition to their having originated at least exclusively with pious pilgrims, we may mention the occurrence of the repeated representation of petty combats as between two bowmen, and referring to armed warriors, as well as the Greek inscription cited above in the original text, wherein a soldier speaks, and that in a completely soldierlike tone.

Besides, it is incredible to me, that those with whom the inscriptions originated, should have been inhabitants of those parts, like the Nabathees. They were, more probably, strangers from Egypt or from Asia, who, starting from Suez, came across these deserts. A learned German at Cairo gave me as his opinion that these characters most closely resemble the Bactrian, and were inscribed by prisoners, amongst whom were· probably Christians, who had all worked here in the quarries. He also asserted that in Upper Egypt, in the quarries of Arwan, similar inscriptions were still extant.

Upon quitting this remarkable valley, my dragoman told me of the neighbouring Sarbut el Kadem, which is of a grander character than the valley Mokatteb. A wonderful oasis of profound and speaking monuments, it lies amidst naked rocks in the heart of the noiseless desert. The impression it most forcibly makes is that of a cemetery, by its multitude of monuments, profusely covered with hieroglyphics, erected, as it were, over graves. But in the midst of these stones are the remains of temples, as well as numerous columns in ruins. These less consistently indicate a cemetery ; and how happened it, might we ask, that precisely here in the solitary desert so splendid a cemetery should have been founded ? Besides, up to the present time no mummies have been discovered, which would, however, necessarily under such circumstances, have been extant. I therefore concur entirely in Lord Prudhoe's supposition, that this Sarbut was an ancient place of Egyptian pilgrimage, the origin of which, notwithstanding the so beautifully preserved hieroglyphics, must reach back to more than a thousand years before the Christian era.

About midnight we stopped at a small building, wherein the government stores up corn for the use of the pilgrimages to Mecca. In the morning my dragoman and the Bedouins showed me the footprint of a tiger impressed in the sand close to our bivouac. They assured me that even now tigers and other feline animals are found amongst these mountains.

We had a splendid day upon the twenty-second ; we then entered the enchanting valley of Feiran.   At its entrance I saw upon my left a precipice of rock profusely covered with inscriptions similar to those of the valley of Mokatteb.   Shortly afterwards, the high rocks, namely, those to the left, presented traces of ancient buildings.   They resembled the rocky habitations at Siloam.   Probably they were ancient excavations.   The nearer we approached the village the more beautiful did the valley become ; shrubs of tamarisks as tall as trees, exhaling the odour of honey, or rather the scent of manna : figs, almonds, pomegranates, oranges, olives, and many of the usual fruit trees of central and northern Europe were around us.   Flocks of doves and small birds fluttered about.   I beheld splendid butter- flies ; and lofty torch weed blossomed, and reminded me of the friendly hills at home ; rills of water, bright and clear, trickled through the green plain.   But, above all else, the valley derived its character of beauty from the luxuriant and gigantic date palms, which here acquired the richest exuberance.   Close to the village they form a dense wood, and by the side of the living fresh ones towering upwards with their summits, lie the worn-out ones stretched along the plain.   The sight of them reminded me of the Egyptian Titans.   Thus lay these palm trees there like gigantic warriors fallen upon the battle field.

Besides those rocky excavations, there are many other ruins in the valley of Feiran, although none of any particular beauty.   I have not the least doubt that even at the period of the exodus there were settlements here.   Possibly, the names given to the stations of the host before Rephidim, Dophka, and Alush may refer to this spot. (Numb. xxxiii. 12—14.)   Here must the children of Israel have found pleasant refreshment.   We know that at the commencement of the seventh century of the Christian era, the Monothelite Theo- dorus was bishop of Feiran, and that at the council of Constanti- nople, in the sixth century, " a priest and legate of the holy church of Pharan," of the name of Theonas, occurs.

Our camels, also, were happy enough in the valley of Feiran.   The young tamarisks must be the greatest delicacy to their palates, for they extended their long necks insatiably both to the right and to the left.

I fixed my tent in the Wood of Palms.   The Bedouins resident here were handsome and friendly.   As I lay in my tent I was visited by many children ; yet they kept themselves at a respectful distance.   All that they saw about me was interesting to them : they thrust their little fingers under the tent, to touch my shoes and my hat.   I gave them a handful of the small dry fruit which grows in the valley, and which resembles cherries, and is of a yellowish red ; and yet they remained, to my astonishment, very well conducted : hot one of them uttered the horrid " Backshish."

Shortly after quitting the valley we were enclosed on each side with high grey rocks, intersected by many copper-coloured and beautifully angulated veins. In front of them lay ruins which looked like solitary precipices of plaster. Our road was skirted by many green shrubs, especially tamarisks : the ground was strewed with small glittering stones, sprinkled with red, grey, and white. At this instant the sun was setting, which increased the magical effect of the landscape. Upon an ancient wall, which we rode by, we observed two large lizards, the one of a slate colour, and the other of the colour of plaster. At midnight the wolves howled around us : it was almost too terrific to think of resting there ; yet my Bedouins had courage, I had confidence, and so we all reposed in peace.

Early on the 23d we broke up, shortly after the first ray had greeted us, and reached, in about an hour and a half, the Sheikh-* valley, with the celebrated manna-tamarisk or, as it was there called, the Darfa tree. The Feiran valley, indeed, possesses the same tamarisk, and in much greater profusion than the Sheikh valley ; and the tamarisk plantations there were, as I have before said, completely enveloped in the peculiar odour of the manna ; yet was I universally assured that the manna itself is exclusively collected from the tamarisks of the Sheikh-valley. I rejoiced exceedingly that I had arrived at the spot at the commencement of the time at which the formation of the manna takes place : the months of June and July are considered as this period ; and I strayed eagerly from branch to branch, to discover by my eye what was so apparent to the smell. How rejoiced I was upon shortly finding upon the branches of one of the largest and tallest shrubs excrescences hanging like glittering pearls or thick dewdrops. I broke off some of the finest ; for I felt convinced that I held in my hand manna in the process of its formation. These thickish lumps were clammy, and had the same powerful scent emitted by the shrub. I tasted it, and its flavour, as far as I could find a suitable comparison, greatly resembles honey. On many shrubs I found small excrescences upon the twig, which resembled at a distance those described, but close to them I observed that they consisted of a round thick web, similar to what are found upon other shrubs, and which are but the cocoons of insects.

The twigs with the drops of manna I placed in a tin box : they are very well preserved. Indeed, after several weeks of great heat, the drops appeared melted, and the whitish glitter had assumed a dark brown hue. But at the very instant that I am writing the twigs brought home by me still retain these brownish masses of

G 4

manna, still feel clammy, and have also the complete smell they had in the Sheikh-valley.

My Bedouins told me that no manna had been collected for three years, but that this year a rich harvest was expected. In the month of July, the Bedouins, and also the monks of St. Catharine's monastery, collect it in small leathern bags, chiefly from the ground, whither it drops from the branches upon hot days. As it is not produced in very large quantities, it is sold tolerably dear, and chiefly to the pilgrims to Mecca and Mount Sinai. Yet do the Bedouins themselves sometimes indulge in it; they eat it spread upon bread, like honey.

Ehrenberg, who was during the summer in the Sheikh-valley, has given the most satisfactory account of the formation of manna. According to him, a small insect, which he calls *Coccus manniparus*, punctures the twigs of the tamarisk, and the manna consists of its exuding juices. I, for my part, could discover nothing of this coccus, and only those small webs already alluded to indicated its existence. On the contrary, these tamarisks were surrounded by a large and beautiful kind of bee, which made it almost difficult to approach them. If Ehrenberg's theory be correct, I believe that the tamarisks of the valley of Feiran possess the same capability of producing manna, and that only the coccus is wanting to enable them to yield it, and which might be, it would seem, easily enough conveyed there. What further confirms Ehrenberg's investigation is, that the medicinal manna of Calabria and Sicily exudes from ash trees during the summer months from the puncture of a cicada.

But what gives this manna of the Sheikh-valley its great interest, is the recollection of the heavenly bread which fed the Israelites in the desert. And, whatever may be objected to the comparison of the one with the other, I am nevertheless convinced that the present manna of the Sheikh-valley has intimate relation to the Biblical manna; for this spot closely agrees with the spot where the Israelites first received manna. The book of Exodus, namely, places it near Rephidim, and Rephidim is nowhere else than between the Sheikh-valley and Sinai. And the Biblical description of manna is also surprising (Exod. xvi. 31), " and its taste was like wafers made with honey;" as well as (xvi. 21), " and when the sun waxed hot it melted," perfectly agrees with the present manna; although that produced in Persia from an Oriental kind of oak, and the manna which drops in Mesopotamia from the shrub Gavan, more closely agrees with " white coriander seed." (Exod. xvi. 31.) Indeed there are varieties enough of it. The Biblical manna fell during the night from heaven, and lay in the morning like dew upon the fields: on the sabbath it did not fall; but on the previous day it fell in double quantity: after a short keeping, maggots were produced in it.   Besides, it had the property of sustaining a host of two millions for forty years. The statement of its falling has recalled what Aristotle says, that sometimes on the rising of large stars honey falls out of the air ; a statement which Pliny further elucidates in saying that this honey falls upon the rising of the Pleiades so thickly that the leaves of shrubs and the clothes of travellers become quite clammy with it. With this has been compared the account given by the monks at Tor, who, in the morning, frequently find traces of honey upon the roof of their monastery.   Lastly, Wellsted has recently informed us that a Jewish Rabbi told him, that in the desert of Damascus, at the present day even, a kind of manna falls from the open sky.

Hereby, indeed, the tamarisk-manna of Sinai is somewhat lessened in its importance, especially as, in the manna of the Israelites, we must not overlook the miracle.   But does not the miracle retain its true character when we conceive the present manna, by the operations of Divine grace, deducible on every side from the preceding food of the Israelites ?   Were it not apparently too far fetched, I should say that the exhalations rising from the groves of tamarisks might very readily fall back again to the earth like dew : at least, this idea may be as admissible as that which surmises the present manna to be the enfeebled continuous result of the Biblical heavenly bread.

It may have been about two hours after quitting the manna tamarisks when I obtained a sight, probably, the most magnificent that I ever beheld in my life.   We were riding up a gentle acclivity : on both sides the rocks approached closer and closer.   Suddenly, we stood before two colossal smooth granite precipices, which rose perpendicularly in the air — a majestic structure.   They are like petrified palm trees, melted into one mass, brown, grey, and red ; irregular stripes of a dark blue steel colour undulate downwards, as if the lightning had thereby traced its course.   It is a portal as if to the throne of the Lord of Lords.   I was silent and astounded.   " Here is holy ground " was my feeling : here has the angel of God held sway, to arrest the mortal eye for some grand purpose.   We rode through the portal; we rode upwards as over invisible steps : the walls of rock widened.   We stood in a cheerfully overgrown wide space, enclosed like an amphitheatre, interrupted only by solitary masses of rock resembling seated judges.

In the midst of these impressions, methought I heard bells chiming in the distance : this perfected the festal feeling.   For months I had not heard a bell : now they broke loose suddenly, like suppressed, but sweet, though painful, reminiscences.   When I spoke to my dragoman about it, he replied, almost sneeringly, " here are no bells."   Nevertheless, we were here, in fact, near the remark-

able Dschebel Nakus, or Bell Mountain, which, by the bell-like tones
it produces when a footstep traverses its loose sand, has led to the
belief that a buried monastery lies beneath it. As we stepped forth
from this amphitheatre the road resumed its previous sublime character: it was a real triumphal way directly before me ; and in
communion with the clouds stood, majestic and solemn, the summit
peaks of Sinai.

During the mid-day siesta I dreamt of the little garden of my paternal dwelling ; the playfellows of my childhood sat beside me : I
was telling them tales as I used to do. · On opening my eyes a flock
of little birds, which once in autumn were my whole delight, flew
away over my tent. Greetings from home they seemed of my earlier
happy days. Thus did my childhood re-awake within view of Sinai.
It was delightful to renew here those feelings. Thus was it also
once, when in my childish fancy I first saw Sinai, the mountain of
God. This instant, methought, that childlikesoul was restored
to me which life, alas ! so deeply buries with its storms. When I
first read that the Lord descended upon the mountain, in the midst
of fire, to deliver his law into the hand of his servant, that the very
mountain heaved, then in that religious thrill I may have felt the
first consciousness of God's proximity, the greatness of a holy sublimity. Happy the soul in which a festal echo can renew this
sentiment !

But I was speedily torn from this round of sentiment and thought.
Several bands of Bedouins of the Sinai-deserts, men, women, and
children, upon stately and decorated dromedaries, accompanied by
flocks of lambs and animated by a widely echoing shout of joy, came
winding past us. Several sheikhs joined my guide ; and the celebrated guide of strangers, the sheikh Tualeb, stepped to me in my tent,
and invited me to the great festival of the day, the festival of the
prophet Salech. This festival was to be celebrated near the tomb of
the prophet, which was distant from my encampment about a league,
and about two leagues from the monastery of St. Catharine. I told
the sheikh I could not be present at the festival, as I wished to proceed at once to the monastery, although I promised to stop a moment
on passing. But upon riding to the encampment the sheikhs, conjunctively headed by their leader, advanced thirty steps to meet me,
to renew their formal invitation to the festival. I was surprised at
this extremely pressing invitation : the Bedouins seemed to attach a
real value to my presence at the festival. As I still hesitated giving
the desired answer, I was suddenly addressed from among these
foreign faces in the language spoken on the banks of the Seine. I
considered it almost as an illusion of the ear ; but a little being
stepped forth before me, dressed in a Turkish habit, with little red-

dish eyes, and of a delicate white tint, no production of this hot
sandy steppe. He was, in fact, a Frenchman, who had pursued a
peculiar career. From being an apothecary at Lyons he has proceeded camel doctor to the Bedouins in this desert. He was
now returning from the Hedschas, or rather from their camels. The
wealth produced by his successful practice ran beside him upon four
legs, consisting in a considerable flock of goats and lambs.

I now resolved upon stopping during the festival of Salech: my guides
were rejoiced at this, although they had not dared to express one wish
for it. In company with the troop that had advanced to meet me, I
entered the large common tent. I carried my woollen blanket and my
tiger-skin to be spread out, and seated myself there amongst the chieftains. This tent, in which from forty to fifty sat in a circle, was completely closed only on two sides. On the north it offered a view of the
herds, dromedaries, and camels, and the baggage; towards the south,
a fire was burning, at which coffee was made with all despatch; and
forty steps beyond it stood the grave of the prophet, freshly coloured.*
The prince, or superior of the chieftains, sat by the fire with his
coffee, as the general host. His appearance was dignified and pleasing.
He was one of the largest of the number, with manly, energetic
features, brown eyes, and a dark beard. On his head was a white
turban, from the centre of which was perceived the red fez. He had
no covering upon his feet; but his chief garment was an unusually
long white gown, of light woollen stuff. This costume reminded me
of the Camaldulense garment worn by Gregory XVI. when I had
an audience of him. Thus do extremes meet: the prince of the
warlike hordes of Bedouins at Sinai, and the holy father in the Vatican
at Rome, dress apparently after the same fashion. Several smaller
tents were connected in a line with our large one; and these were
closed on all sides: even the entrance was hung with carpets. In
these their women and children were contained. Immediately behind
me the first tent adjoined ours: by this means I made an acquaint-

---

* This tomb and some others which I met with in the desert made the
application of our Saviour's words very clear to me, where he says to the
Pharisees, "Woe unto you, Scribes and Pharisees, hypocrites! for ye are
like unto whited sepulchres, which indeed appear beautiful outward, but are
within full of dead men's bones and of all uncleanness." (Matt. xiv. 27.)
Even to this day the custom prevails in the East of occasionally whitening
the tombstones that they may glitter at a distance in the desert; although
frequently their whole grandeur consists of nothing but a stone placed upright, the rest being strewed upon their graves. Possibly the Mahometans
may have had a similar object in view to that which once prevailed amongst
the Jews, who made it a matter of so much importance to colour their graves
that they might thereby warn the priests, the Nazarenes, and the pilgrims
wandering to the paschal feast, of the unclean proximity.

anceship of the most innocent description, *dos à dos* and with silent
lips; for while leaning back, I speedily found that my resting-post
was of a soft nature, and of a moveable character.   But methought
my female neighbour, from whom I was only separated by the linen
of the tent, took no umbrage at my making use of a position so
innocently acquired.

Thus sat I, then, the plain German wanderer, in the midst of
these brown children of the desert, warlike enough in their accoutrements.   Had I thought of Schiller's diver, I should have said,

> There I hung and the awe gather'd icily o'er me,
>   So far from the earth, where man's help there was none;
> The one human thing, with the goblins before me —
>   Alone — in a loneness so ghastly — alone!
>   Sir Bulwer Lytton's Schiller.

Indeed I was wholly exposed to the absolute power of these wild
and energetic hordes, which long vigorously resisted the powerful
arm of Mehemet Ali, and who have now been gained over more by
his sagacity than conquered by his power.   But my feelings were
very different.   The features of these people bespoke so honourable
a character, such honest uprightness, that I sat amongst them with
the sentiment of as much security as if in my own home.

At first, naturally, all eyes were directed to the stranger guest:
those among the Bedouins who are not habitually accustomed to
guide strangers, extremely rarely see an European traveller.   I, for
my part, did not delay complimenting them, as celebrated warriors,
upon so friendly and agreeable a festival.   One cup of coffee, and
then a second, was presented to me, as well as to all the rest who sat
in the circle.   The pipes were smoked in accompaniment.   But
speedily there arose opposite to me an animated and noisy discussion.
My guides, namely, had here fallen in with two members of a tribe
from the neighbourhood of Jerusalem, with whom they were at war.
Slen, my guide, had during the feud displayed considerable valour:
two of the enemy had fallen by his hand.   But here both parties
found themselves under the inviolable protection of the hospitable
roof, and neither had occasion to entertain any fear of the other.

In the course of a brief hour the festal procession around the tomb
of the prophet commenced.   The women were present, most deco-
rously clad, and wholly concealed.   To the sound of that oft-mentioned
music which Oriental women produce by their own mouths, the procession ascended the hill, passed around the tomb, and then entered it,
where the women appeared to pray for a short time.   In the procession, young fellows led the sacrificial lambs, from which, upon the
summit of the hill, a couple of locks were shorn from the brow, and

an incision made upon it. This was followed by the general slaughter
of these fifty or sixty lambs, the real sacrifice of which is effected
indeed by means of the teeth and stomach. They were then hung
up at the tents, skinned, and cut into pieces by means of the large
knives which served also as weapons or short swords.

Whilst the meal was being prepared at the fire, the interval was
occupied by dromedary races. This was an attractive spectacle.
From four to six cavaliers galloped past the tents upon these noble
animals, which were caparisoned with costly carpets and ornaments of
mother of pearl. The women, who were again seated behind the drapery of their tents, upon every fresh race raised their jubilant music.
The dromedary, which in speed surpasses the swiftest horse, can here
scarcely be recognised as the brother of the camel, whose measured
step gravely advances along the sandy desert, as if lost in the profound meditation of the ass. During the last race a storm arose,
which from the neighbouring mountains pealed down into our valley
with its wild music. This indeed interrupted the anticipated pleasure of the dance of the women, which I was told would take place
in the evening, after the meal.

The feast was now discussed. All the meat had been cooked. I
waived accepting a piece to be prepared according to my own wish,
civilly replying that I ate only in company. All lay around in a
circle: from four to six grouped themselves together in a smaller
circle, and a lamb's skin was spread out in the centre. The meat
was served on large wooden trays, and placed upon the lambs' skins.
Of course there were no knives and forks: each took his share with
the instruments supplied by nature. I followed their example as
well as I could. After the meat came a pilau kneaded together of
oatmeal, and certainly improved only with but slight adjuncts. I
declined partaking. A jug of excellent water slaked the thirst during
the meal. This is a complete description of the entire repast of these
little princes of the desert at their great festival of Salech: the gout
can scarcely be a result of such banquets.

After the feast the storm increased in violence, it was with
difficulty that the tent was saved from being upset. The smoke and
ashes of the fire were blown into our faces, and large drops of rain fell
also. Under such circumstances it was impossible to hope that I
should see the Bedouin women dance: it may well be imagined how
much this disappointed me. I discoursed for some moments with
the superior chieftain. His imperturbable good-humour and absolute
faith delighted me. He was far from complaining of the storm:
" God sent it, and therefore it must be good," said he ; and in his
eye was written, " I believe what I say." Together with the conviction of the providence of God, the sphere of his religious senti-

ments embraced the consciousness of the duty of hospitality. Upon speaking of Mehemet Ali with him, he was full of veneration for that ruler. Of our affairs on the other side of the Mediterranean he knew little or nothing. Under the general name of Franks he, like most Orientals, comprised all Europeans collectively : the Russian alone seemed to stand forth in distinct colours from the great combined race.

It was still early when I lay down to rest. My dragoman constructed for me a strange dwelling for the night. Between the cooking apparatus and my travelling chest he spread the tent covering, beneath which I crept. Around me lay the Bedouins, with their wives and children, their dromedaries and camels, their lambs and goats. I shall hardly see such another festal night.

I avail myself of the nocturnal quietude to furnish some further particulars about my hosts.* They belong to the race of Tawarah, as the Bedouins of Sinai or of Dschebel et Tur collectively call themselves, and indeed to the chief race of Sawalihah, whose ancestors, after the conquest of Egypt by the Turks, migrated from the Egyptian frontiers to these districts ; and one of the three branches of the Sawalihah tribe, precisely that also whose relations with the monastery of St. Catherine are more distant, or rather, more inimical, than that of the other two, namely, the Karraschy, numbers amongst its members the present chief sheikh, or the general chief of all the tribes of Tawarah. His name is Salech, the same as that of the venerated sheikh, who subsequently became prophet, and whose festival was this day celebrated. The Tawarah are considered poor among the Bedouins. Doubtlessly, between the bare mountain, of Sinai and Akaba, no great treasures are to be acquired, although they maintain the exclusive privilege of being guides to the pilgrims to Sinai. They comprise, according to Burckhardt's and Rüppel's estimate, about from four to six thousand souls. Their adherence to Mahometanism is but loose and capricious. In addition to the wars they have with other branches of the Bedouins, sanguinary feuds frequently occur amidst themselves. It is only when they seek his mediation that the Pasha of Egypt mixes at all in their dissensions.

A very unusual concert aroused me on the morning of the 24th of May. The camels were singing their morning song, and that chiefly in an incomparably deep bass : a jumping tenor was kept to it by the bleating of a few goats.

After taking a most friendly farewell of the collected sheikhs, I hastened with all despatch to the immediate goal of my journey. The morning was pleasantly cool. The difference of temperature I had

* See Robinson's Palestine, vol. i. p. 219, &c.

felt during the last two days was strikingly conspicuous to-day. To be sure, the Sheikh-valley, wherein we now were, is several thousand feet higher than the Garandel valley, where the heat was insupportable. I did not see the monastery until we were close upon it. It lies in a long narrow valley, situated between the Mountain of St. Epistemius, called also Dschebel ed Deir, and Horeb. But its presence is most agreeably made known by means of its superb garden, which, with its cypresses, pomegranates, and orange trees, peers forth most refreshingly from the grey stone walls. The monastery itself has the appearance of a small fortress, from the elevation of its walls, which are forty feet high; and the want of an especial entrance strengthened this impression. The door is thirty feet high, to reach which it is necessary to be wound up by a rope. Several Bedouins were grouped upon my arrival, beneath the door. They did not omit announcing my appearance by loud cries and firing of arms. Before I was permitted to ascend, I was required to show my letters. The two letters from Suez, which I tendered, were immediately drawn up: but as the prior knew that I came from Cairo,—for I had been already announced to him from thence,—he thought I should necessarily bring a letter of introduction from the parent monastery there. Niebuhr, as is well known, was not admitted, owing to his being without such introduction. I interposed, that I had certainly received a letter from the monastery at Cairo, where I was advantageously known, but that, unfortunately, I had left it behind, enclosed with other papers; and I therefore availed myself of the letters from Suez. To tell the truth, by the way, I had purposely left that letter behind; for, with all its friendliness, it had a trait of a Uriah's letter. (2 Sam. xi. 14.) My explanation may not have been quite satisfactory, yet they hesitated no longer to draw me up by the rope to their cheerful asylum.

SINAI AND ITS MONASTERY.

How striking is it, in the midst of the barren desert, cheerless with its sand and rock, suddenly to abide within these hospitable walls,— in these well-arranged and ornamental pleasure-grounds and chambers, surrounded by men of serious aspect, with long beards and black gowns! The present superior of the monastery, who, notwithstanding the delicacy of his features, bears the strongest expression of duplicity in his glance, instantly accompanied me to a spacious chamber, furnished all round with a divan and gay carpets. This chamber was assigned to me as my drawing-room, another adjoining

it as my bed-room, and a third as my dining-room and study. The
superior also introduced to me, as my ordinary companion during my
stay in the monastery, a young man, who wore nothing but a short
hair garment, striped with brown and grey. I soon perceived that
I had to do with a half-witted fellow: the first question he asked
me was, if I had already travelled in the sun and moon. This
" Signor Pietro" is a native Greek, of a good family : he speaks,
besides Italian and French, a little English, German, and Arabic.
Some few years since his relatives conveyed him to the monastery
to be taken care of, and he daily awaits their return in vain. Notwithstanding his mad *capriccios*, he is doubtlessly one of the most
witty and intellectual individuals in the monastery. His society was
interesting to me, although he was occasionally a bore.

Next to me dwelt a brother of the name of Gregorius, a friendly
venerable man, with a stately white beard : to him the waiting upon
strangers was confided. Forty years previously he had been the
commander of a thousand Mamelukes : like a Rhodian knight of
St. John, he had withdrawn from the din of war to this humble
office in the tranquil monastery. He looked the soldier the instant
he saw arms : almost daily he shot with my double-barrelled gun,
amid the thunder of repeated echoes ; and usually hit a tile which was
placed as a mark against the cloister wall. He also possessed sufficient literary zest to take interest in my enthusiasm for Greek
manuscripts.

My windows, which looked beyond the monastery, commanded a
view of Horeb : there it lay before me in the full nakedness of its grey
granite and in its terrific ruggedness. Yet a few solitary crucifixes
glanced downward from the heights : nothing was too rugged,
nothing too daunting to the pious enthusiasm of the hermits. Upon
stepping forth from the door of my chamber I saw the court
beneath me, with a fountain in its centre, and surrounded by the
luxuriant foliage of a green vine. Between four and five in the
morning, when the little bell had already rung, I invariably saw by
the side of the fountain the worthy brother Cyrillus. This fountain,
with its vine and the good Cyrillus, are still present to my eyes.

With this man, who is between forty and fifty years of age, I became exceedingly intimate. He had first located himself upon Mount
Athos ; but, a short time since, he was brought by force to Sinai for
some unexplained act of insubordination towards the patriarch. He
is here the librarian. I have learned to esteem him as an honest,
well-informed, serious, benevolent man. During the latter days of
my residence in the monastery, whenever I met him he surprised me
with a neat Romaic poem, which he had composed in honour of myself, and transcribed upon embellished paper. He allowed me the

use, in my own chamber, of all the manuscripts I wished from the library. When I apologised for the disarrangement this would occasion in the order of the books, he sought to soothe me by saying, that he should be agreeably reminded of my visit when engaged in replacing the manuscripts in their former order. He was, without doubt, very rarely disturbed in a similar way ; and scarcely will any one but himself in the monastery think of its rich library.

I found there were altogether eighteen brethren in this monastery, each of whom had his especial office. The œkonomus, or steward, visibly did ample justice to his post, for his *enbonpoint* was perfect. I do not know whether the mode of living practised by these monks of the order of St. Basil, may be called strict. Its distinctive features, given by Rudolph von Suchem in the 14th century, might easily mislead. He says, " They do not drink wine on the high festivals ; never eat meat ; but live upon herbs, peas, beans, and millet, which they cook with water, salt, and vinegar : they eat together in a refectory, from a table without a table cloth." In this category is forgotten fish, which, from the proximity of the sea, is never wanting ; rice also, which I never saw finer than here ; and dates and almonds, as well as coffee and many other things. In lieu of wine, they adequately compensate themselves with the excellent date brandy, of which each monk is allowed an ample weekly ration in his cell. The cloister bread is so excellent that it can scarcely be equalled throughout the East. Nor did I trace in any of the brethren the least indication of want.

The number of chapelries exceeds the number of monks by four : formerly the relative proportions were very different. Troilo, in the 17th century, found seventy monks here. Besides the twenty-two chapelries, the monastery possesses a lofty church, rich in splendour. Two rows of granite columns support the arched roof, which is sprinkled with stars upon a blue ground. The floor is tesselated with black and white marble. Many gold and silver lamps and candlesticks glitter around. Innumerable pictures cover the walls : but more tasteful and more beautiful than all these is the mosaic in the arch of the ceiling, where are deposited the choicely guarded reliques of St. Catherine. This mosaic represents on both sides Moses : on the left, before the burning bush ; and, on the right, with the tables of the law : and exhibits in the chief group the transfiguration of Christ, with Moses, Elias, and the three disciples. In the two corners above the group, Justinian and Theodora are represented in two medallions. Both are reputed, and that with justice, to be the founders of the present monastery ; although, even so early as the fourth century, Sinai was built upon and occupied by many anchorets, who, as is related by the Egyptian monk, Ammonios, lived only upon dates, berries, and other similar fruits, and suffered severely under the Saracens.

The mosaic in question, probably co-eval with the period of the foundation, proves that the monastery was originally dedicated to the transfiguration, wherefore even to the present time many travellers adopt that name. But now it is evident that the worship of St. Catherine, who, according to Eusebius, fled to Sinai in the year 307, whence an angel bore her body, after her martyrdom, to the summit of the mountain of St. Catherine, has not only obscured the picture of the transfiguration which stands directly over her relic-shrine with the smoke of her incense and tapers, but has also usurped the name of the monastery; for even the sacramental loaves of the monastery, one of which I possess, are impressed with the "hagia Katherine."

The chief curiosity of the church I have not yet named; viz., the chapel of the fiery bush. It is said to be built on the very spot where the Lord appeared to Moses. The pilgrim is not allowed to visit this chapel with his shoes on. "Draw not nigh hither," it says; "put off thy shoes from off thy feet, for the place whereon thou standest is holy ground." (Exod. iii. 5.) Even though it be only pious faith which has so accurately found the consecrated spot, yet who is there whose heart and lips would not repeat the prayer, "Lord, penetrate me also with fiery zeal for thy holy word, even as thou once didst penetrate thy servant Moses."

The monastery most surprisingly holds within its walls, in conjunction with its churches and chapels, also a mosque. It looked now somewhat desolate. It is said that, by building this mosque, the monastery escaped destruction when Mahomet the prophet visited Sinai. It has served doubtlessly for the Mahometan serfs of the monastery, several of whom fill menial offices here. Besides, it may also be of use upon the visits of such men as Ibrahim Pasha.

I hasten now from the monastery to its garden. The road to it is gloomy; for about the distance of forty steps it passes through a narrow, low, subterranean tunnel, hewn in the rock. But this contrast enhances the effect of the garden, which is laid out in terrace upon terrace. There all is glowing, blooming, and fragrant. The freshest water flows through its canals; the dark and high-towering cypresses stand beneath the silver-coloured olives; by the side of almonds and figs and oranges and citrons, apples and pears are clustering in maturity; but, above all, my eyes were arrested by the bushy pomegranates and their fiery red blossoms. I gathered from them tokens for my dear ones afar off.

WHITSUN MORNING ON MOUNT SINAI.

The 26th of May was Whitsunday. Never in my life possibly did I awake so happy to the Whitsun festival. But once only was I conscious of my heart beating fervently in its anticipation : it was when the birthday of one now deceased, whom I intensely loved, fell upon Whitsunday. When I awoke this morning, my whole soul was absorbed by the memory of the departed one. With what joy would not her maternal eye now sparkle, did she know that I was on this day at this holy spot. I felt as if I knew she were still faithfully performing her domestic duties at the paternal hearth. I imagined to myself our re-union ; and a burning stream flowed down my cheeks. " God cannot make a mortal so happy," said I to my-self. That instant should have been the last of my existence.

It was the monastic bell which had aroused me with its solemn clang. With this exception, not a sound disturbed the sabbath rest. Thus may it be within the heart of a departed wayfarer, around whom, hushed in repose, the noisy turbulence of life is still. How happy must we be, if, when such instants are graciously awarded to us, they find a responding harmony in our hearts !

I purposed ascending to-day to the summit of Mount Sinai. I heartily rejoiced in the anticipation. It had so long appeared to me such an unattainable hope that I had not expected its accomplishment. I now saw it glittering before me, beautiful as the sky itself, but in the same friendly proximity to me as the church is to my paternal home.

My Ali was early prepared for starting. He had put on his scarlet collar, embroidered with gold and silver ; the sunshine of the festival beamed in his cheerful features. Signor Pietro was happy enough in our accoutrements. Mohammed carried the provisions. With these companions I wandered forth, through the garden at the foot of Horeb.

We shortly began to ascend perpendicularly. The road mounts between two precipices forming a ravine, passing over numerous rocky fragments, with remains of hewn steps, originally made possibly in the time of Helena. Shrubs, grass, and flowers were sparingly dispersed. About a thousand feet above the monastery, we rested by the side of the clear fountain of St. Sangarius. Shortly afterwards, having passed two small chapels, I saw with surprise in the heights above me the road crossed by a stone arch, with a crucifix ; and immediately afterwards by a second, to which we ascended through abruptly projecting rocks. My thoughts were wholly lost

in those early times when so many pious hermits, fervently dedi-
cating themselves to the Lord, lived and died upon this mountain.
We now stood upon the oasis of Horeb, which, amidst the grey
granite rocks, spreads forth a cheerful wreath as if in compensation
for its solemn expression.   In the centre, close to a basin of fresh
spring water, stands a solitary cypress.   What more agreeable image
can be conceived than this cypress, with its dark unfading foliage,
its lofty unbowed crown, its foot planted upon Horeb, and its eye
fixed on the summit of Sinai !   It stands there like the most recent
prophetic messenger entrusted with the heavenly promise of a holy
and a happy future.   Close by is the deserted chapel of the prophet
Elijah, who dwelt here when he fled from the wrath of Ahab and
Jezebel.   " Go forth," said the angel of God to him ; " Go forth
and stand upon the mount before the Lord." (1 Kings, xix. 11.)
" And, behold," it is said, " the Lord passed by, and a great and
strong wind rent the mountains, and brake in pieces the rocks before
the Lord."   " Yes, here has the Lord passed by :" thus did my
soul, with Geramb, exclaim upon this consecrated spot ; these rent
rocks, these fractured mountains, bear the marks, even to this day, of
the footsteps of the Lord.

From this point we ascended nine hundred feet higher, over bare,
rugged masses of rock, to the summit of Sinai.

When some few years ago I stood upon the Rhigi, the panorama
of a never to be forgotten scene lay before my eyes and my soul.
In the north reposed the deep broad valley, with all its lakes, over
which the morning had cast its fragrant veil.   In the south stood
the Swiss mountains ; their summits covered with eternal snow.
Day broke : its first rays beamed from behind light blue clouds.
Wonderfully beautiful rosy stripes transpierced the glittering snow:
methought I saw the thoughts of angels ranging to the virgin earth.
A maiden brought me Alpine roses ; a shepherd lad played upon the
horn.   Thou happy Swiss, thy longings I can comprehend, thy tear
is sacred.   My own eye wept with delight in the very eye of the
Swiss.

Two years afterwards I ascended Mount Vesuvius.   The dawn
still prevailed around us as we sat beside the crater.   From its triple
mouth gushed forth the fiery shower ; fearful crashes rolled around ;
the entire mountain smoked.   The hour of sunrise was at hand, but
the eye of day was hidden behind tempestuous clouds.   The neighbouring group of mountains clothed itself in a singular blue robe, as
if a conflagration were raging in their entrails.   My flesh crept with
a mysterious shudder, as if anticipative of a future pregnant with
misfortune.

I was now standing upon Sinai.   The hurricane raged with

fury. Grey and angular masses of granite surrounded me; white clouds rested amongst their jagged points, on which the Whitsun morning sun now shone. Close beneath the deserted rocky summit rose the splendid cypress, with its dark green foliage, from the oasis of Horeb. Here I did not experience the delight of the Rhigi, nor was I thrilled with the mysterious feeling of Vesuvius; but prayer— fervent intense prayer—was necessary here. It seemed as if the Almighty were nearer here than elsewhere on the earth. His sublimity, his reverential majesty, his love, his mercy, all combined in one superb ideal. Such did I feel Sinai to be. As a throne which God has raised for himself upon the earth; unchangeable since the day of the creation; and built by the same hand that formed the heaving ocean, and arched the eternal heavens: this is Sinai. It stands there like a holy fortress removed from the forums of the world, far from the habitations of man, alone amid the desert and the sea, towering upwards to the clouds.

The eye of the Swiss turns mournfully back to the Rhigi, as does the Alsatian dream longingly of his cathedral upon the Rhine; but to Sinai the hearts of all the nations of the earth are collectively attracted. Thither flee, as to an eternal sanctuary, the children of Israel; thither urgently press the Christians of the icy north of Europe and from Africa's glowing heats; and thither do the worshippers of the prophet faithfully make their pilgrimage. Upon its summit the mind unconsciously contemplates in calm serenity the advent of that glorious day when the feuds of the nations shall have ceased, when all the children of the earth shall collect in fraternal union about the impregnable rock of salvation,—when, from temple and mosque, and synagogue and church, one universal hallelujah shall peal in joyful unison.

Had I ever dreamt in childhood of some instant of the future, holy above all other instants, and elevated above the murky present into the pure region of bliss, I must have dreamt of the celebration of this Whitsun festival upon the summits of Mount Sinai. And might I express a wish in behalf of those who accompany me with their love in my wanderings, that wish would be, " May ye all pass an hour of Whitsun morning upon the summits of Sinai ! "

But it was not I alone who solemnised to-day this festival upon this lofty point. The prior of the Monastery of St. Catherine, with two other brothers, was already there before me. They celebrated mass in the small Christian chapel, which stands upon the northern summit. Opposite this chapel, upon the southern summit, there is a little mosque, with a fountain of excellent water beside it. Therein, possibly, religious solemnities would be practised, when upon the following Thursday the Bedouins who reside in the vicinity of Sinai make their pilgrimage, with their wives and children.

A stone, immediately behind the chapel, is pointed out as the seat of Moses after he had received the tables of the law. I sat long upon it. I was thus withdrawn from the eyes of my companions, and wrote here, wholly immersed in my feelings, a couple of sheets of filial endearments to my paternal home. How fervently does one who travels alone, like me, cling in solemn moments to those distant beloved ones whom he cherishes in his heart!

The view from the summit of Sinai which I had, may not compare with the panorama of the desert seen and described by Schubert. I did not see the Red Sea, with its African coast; nor the mountains of Akaba; nor did my view extend as far as Suez. But the immediate circuit around me was grand and powerful enough. In the south, at a short distance from us, was St. Catherine's Mountain, a thousand feet still higher than Mount Sinai. It looked of a blackish red, and was sparingly sprinkled here and there with low green herbage.[*]

Towards the west was the mountain Humr. Between it and the western declivity of Horeb lies the Monastery of the Forty Martyrs (El Erbain), in the valley of Bostan. Towards the north it is that the eye ranges the furthest; and indeed from Horeb, at our feet, away in a north-westerly direction to Aaron's Mountain, behind which lies the Serbal, and north-easterly to the Mountain of St. Epistemius, which is also called the Mountain of the Monastery. Between both wide desert tracts extend, which are again enclosed by mountain chains. In the east, lastly, quite close beneath us, we had the Wadi Sebaye, which reposes like an insulated asylum between rocky mountain walls. North-westerly, whither runs the road to the monastery, the Wadi is fringed by the Mountain of God, upon which Moses is said to have tended the herds of Jethro, his father-in-law. (Exod. iii. 1.)

This Wadi Sebaye is considered, and not without reason, as the

---

[*] Rüppel thus describes St. Catherine's Mountain, to which he applies in preference the name of Horeb. "This mountain mass is totally distinct from that of Sinai. It consists of horizontal layers of reddish feldspar in which small hexagonal double quartz pyramids of a kind of porphyry are interspersed. No mica is seen in it, and only occasionally are there to be found little reddish feldspar crystals. In the fissures a very needy vegetation has developed itself." Compare his Reise in Abyssinia, b. i. p. 121. Immediately before he thus describes Sinai: "The entire mountain consists of vertical strata of a fine-grained grey granite, comprising equal parts of feldspar and quartz, and with very little intermixture of mica; and between all the fissures low shrubs grow in abundance. The summit of the mountain is an insulated cap with a narrow flattened space." See p. 117.

place where the children of Israel encamped, while Moses was receiving the tables of the law.   It is of wide circumference, and
formed, as it were, for such a solemn purpose.   It also affords
an admirable explanation of the words of Moses: " Whosoever
toucheth the mountain."—(Exod. xix. 12.)   In Wadi Sebaye,
namely, the mountain admits of being touched in a peculiar sense,
as it rises so perpendicularly that it may be seen, as it were, from
head to foot as a distinct individuality.   It is the same with the
words, " And they stood at the nether part of the mount."—
(Exod. xix. 17.)   Rarely is it possible to stand so absolutely at the
nether part of a mountain, gazing at the summit rising several thousand feet high, as in the Wadi Sebaye at the foot of Mount Sinai.

The ascent of the mountain direct from the Wadi is almost impossible; which agreed equally with both Moses' wish and design,
and whereby " the bounds about the mount" so much the more
perfectly corresponded with its holy destination.   The road which
Moses took in ascending the mountain is probably the same as that
by which pilgrims ascend in the present day.   Moses then first went
through the narrow pass leading from the south-east to the north-
west, and then from the north to the west.   His whole course,
therefore, was seen by no eye, nor even from the distance.   It must
have been very inconvenient to pass through these rough cleft rocks;
and in the present day we may well congratulate ourselves upon the
remains of the before-mentioned steps.   We must therefore think of
a second road for Moses; a third would not be possible: it is that
which comes from the valley of Bostan, and passes the Monastery
of the Forty; and by this road the side of the mountain opposite
to the Wadi Sebaye is attained.

But shall I state what has led to the adoption of this Wadi as the
great encampment of the Israelites?   It is the narrow dangerous
way which the Israelites would have had to pass through in coming
from the Sheikh-valley.   And the words, " And Moses brought
forth the people out of the camp to meet with God; and they
stood at the nether part of the mount" (Exod. xix. 17), appear
to refer to a considerable space between the camp and the mountain.
For this the Wadi Sebaye, how much soever may be deducted
from the assumed numbers of the host of Israel, will not absolutely afford room.

Upon passing through that imposing portal of perpendicular
granite precipices, several leagues distant from the monastery of
St. Catherine, into the plain beyond, interrupted in its uniformity
by some scattered masses of rock only, the idea struck me that
here possibly Israel encamped during the holy festival.   Yet even
here several difficulties arise.   Whereas the Wadi Rahah presented,

upon visiting the Monastery of the Forty (to my great surprise at the majestic splendour of the rugged precipices of Horeb to the north), every other particular that inclined me to assume it as the place of encampment of the Israelites. For even here the mountain can be " touched:" here also it may be approached below, and it admits of being encompassed by a boundary. Here was ample room for two millions, for it is right to take the number strictly; and here could Moses, in fact, " Bring forth the people out of the camp to meet with God." *

That Sinai might thus be confounded with Horeb offers no real difficulty. The name of the two summits of the mountain group is not definite even at the present day. Thus has Russegger, in the Strangers' Book of St. Catherine's Monastery, called Sinai " Horeb," and Horeb " Sinai." And in the Bible itself both names, Horeb and Sinai, are found as that of the mountain whence the law was promulgated.†

Besides, according to Moses' description, the divine revelation took place amid thunder and lightning, whilst a dense cloud enveloped the mountain. Even an ordinary storm must present a spectacle here, whose sublimity would surpass all description. To compare great things with small, I never heard an echo so rich in its reverberations, or whose impression was so astounding as that which took place upon firing my gun at Sinai. This may be explained by

* See further below.

† I remember that Rüppel, when, in 1843, I enjoyed his instructive intercourse at Milan, considered the present Horeb absolutely as the mountain of Moses, and indeed because at Sinai there was no plain for the encampment. I also observe that Robinson, upon approaching Sinai by the Wadi Rahah, was impressively struck with this being the encamping place of the Israelites. His description runs thus : — "As we advanced, the valley still opened wider and wider with a gentle ascent, and became full of shrubs and tufts of herbs, shut in on each side by lofty granite ridges, with rugged shattered peaks a thousand feet high, while the face of Horeb rose directly before us. Both my companion and myself involuntarily exclaimed, ' Here is room enough for a large encampment !' Reaching the top of the ascent, or water shed, a fine broad plain lay before us, sloping down gently towards the south south-east, enclosed by rugged and venerable mountains of dark granite, stern, naked, splintered peaks and ridges of indescribable grandeur ; and terminated at the distance of more than a mile by the bold and awful front of Horeb, rising perpendicularly in frowning majesty from twelve to fifteen hundred feet in height. It was a scene of solemn grandeur, wholly unexpected, and such as we had never seen ; and the associations which at the moment rushed upon our minds, were almost overwhelming. . . . Still advancing, the front of Horeb rose, like a wall, before us ; and one can approach quite to the foot and touch the mount. . . . As we crossed the plain, our feelings were strongly affected, at finding here so unexpectedly a spot so entirely adapted to the scriptural account of the giving of the law." Vol. i. pp.130—132.

the form and grouping of this whole mountain chain; from the rent
character of its numerous summits; from the wild lofty peaks into
which, as it were, it is split. A very characteristic image of it presents itself to me, possibly a reminiscence of the description of the
Trappist father, Geramb. It is as if the ocean had heaved turret
high its storm-beaten waves. In the midst of its fury a magic word
conjures it, and the surging waves stand petrified. A tempest which
deposited its heavy clouds upon this mount of God, and which besides
was thoroughly impregnated with a miraculous purpose! What a
solemn and striking spectacle! far surpassing any experience must
that not have been for the people of Israel, who had just escaped
from the plains of Egypt, where even rain but rarely falls, and
where a tempest scarcely ever discharges its vehemence.

I am far from wishing to deprive the miracle of its glory; but, by
the natural thread which Moses has himself given us with his own
hand, he draws us up also with his own hand to contemplate the
miracle.

The nearer it approached mid-day, the clearer did the environs of
Sinai stand out before me: the booming storm had dispersed the
light clouds, and the sun cast an enlivening glitter over it. The
scene was surpassingly beautiful: my thoughts were absorbed in its
contemplation. I now felt doubly painful my separation from the
holy spot; and I could thus well comprehend the pious sentiments
of the hermits whose enthusiasm bound them to Sinai for life.

Upon descending the upper granite summit of Sinai, my dragoman
showed me the imprint of the footstep of the dromedary which the
prophet rode upon to the mountain. The genuine outlines of these
traces are plainly discernible in the midst of the rocks: but this is
nothing more than a satire — an ironical sneer at the Christian worship of relics. It struck me that the Koran, by many a trait, had
the same relation to the Bible as the imitator has to an original
genius: this admirably illustrates this much-worshipped footstep of
the dromedary of Mahomet. Besides this footstep at Sinai, there
are three others; namely, at Damascus, Cairo, and Mecca.

In the Strangers' Book at the monastery, this Mohametan relic
has had special notice dedicated to it. An Englishman, in the
first place, wrote down that he never found any thing that surpassed
this chief of relics, amidst the multitude of holy tokens, in countries where religious faith has its peculiar domain. A second
Englishman, vexed with his countryman, thus apostrophised him:
" O thou stupid fellow!" A third, — and he the celebrated missionary, Joseph Wolff, — forgot, in his pious enthusiasm, both himself and the liberal nation to which he belongs; for he decreed to
the writer of the sneer upon the dromedary, " three times forty

bastinadoes." A fourth, lastly, sorrowing over all three, exhorts to
peace and tranquillity by many scriptural passages. And it is now
reserved to a fifth, quietly to put into his pocket all the *pros* and *cons*
of these pious and impious knights, and thus emancipate the pilgrims
of the future from the whole vexation.

We stayed yet some time upon the oasis of Horeb; around the
large, full, fountain basin, named after the prophet Elijah, multitudes
of mountain partridges flocked. I sat a long time beneath the venerable cypress : here I gazed for the last time upon the lofty Sinai.

About a thousand feet below we were surprised by two *feus de
joie* : it was a welcome sent to us from a party of monks assembled
in a cavern to enjoy the happy festival. I found this circle very
jovial ; even the prior exhibited an amiability for which I should not
have given him credit. The special luxury consisted in salt-fish, red
and white eggs, beans, date-brandy, and a delicate wine which is produced upon Sinai itself, and is not unlike the wine of Cyprus. Nor
were pipes wanting. A special mark of amity and good fellowship
consisted in striking the eggs together. The brethren drank with
me from the Sinai grape, to the happiness of all that I loved at my
distant home. I told them these were its sky, its mountains, and its
hearts. I wonder, said I to myself, if my friends at home sympa-
thetically feel that I to-day so festively call them to mind.

At the entrance of the grotto sat an aged but still cheerful singer,
born upon Sinai and a serf of the monastery. Thus was he "an
old man of the mountain." He sang a couple of songs, which
edified our symposium. I much regretted that my friend Cyrillus
was not of the party ; I found him, not indeed among his books, but
within the narrow compass of his cell, which he had inscribed all
over with proverbial sentences.

I had some conversation with Cyrillus about the history of the
monastery ; the study of which, indeed, during his short sojourn at
Sinai, he had not deeply penetrated. An ancient document of the
monastery is said to emanate from the prophet Mahomet; the
original is stated to have been conveyed to the seraglio at Constantinople, in the time of Selim I., at the commencement of the sixteenth
century ; but a copy of it, confirmed by Selim, has remained to the
monastery. Cyrillus had not seen it, nor does he believe a word
more about it than I do. Many years ago, the text of the document was published in Germany ; but, in my estimation, it could
not possibly have proceeded either from the pen or the brain of
Mahomet.

The regulations therein for the care and maintenance of priests,
bishops, and others, as well as privileges of various kinds referring

to the Christian religion, evince the style rather of the Romish chancelry than of a document of the prophet.

I was most anxious to see another remarkable MS. of Sinai : this is a gospel said to have been extant in the palace of the Emperor Theodosius. Cyrillus had not seen it, notwithstanding his function of librarian ; but another brother, as well as Signor Pietro, gave me a precise description of it. Thence, as well as from previous communications made to me about it at Cairo, the MS. I conceive may be of the eleventh century. But all my exertions, both conciliatory and imperative, were in vain. The explanations ran that the MS. was in the archiepiscopal chapel, whose comptroller, who had but recently taken office, was not to be found. Upon my return to Cairo, the bishop there assured me that it had been sent a few years before to Constantinople, to the archbishop, for the purpose of being copied. But even in Constantinople I found no trace of it.

This was a genuine instance upon all sides of the *Græca fides*. Pointedly as I taxed the brotherhood with falsehood, they quietly submitted to the accusation. The prior is a native of Crete ; St.Paul's notorious character of the Cretes (the Cretes are always liars) he seems to verify, even in the present day. I now believe that the manuscript for which Lord Prudhoe offered some years ago two hundred and fifty pounds, and which was not accepted only because they could not agree about the division of the proceeds, has really been sold to the English. As it would be a disgrace to the monastery, they fancy, they dare not admit it. But if it be in England, I wish Christian literature joy of the acquisition of the new treasure ; for, that it may be speedily communicated to the real Christian church, is a wish towards whose fulfilment erudite men are doubtlessly already labouring.

I was told of another very interesting document ; it is said to consist of the original deed of foundation of the monastery by Justinian. Its existence is possible enough. To my astonishment I discovered amongst the Greek manuscripts which I brought home, a document with the superscription " Golden Bull which the celebrated Emperor Justinian gave to theAbbey of the Monastery of the Holy Mount Sinai." This may be the copy of an original deed, although by no means may it be called a title-deed. I shall not defer its publication. But this is not the place for an account of my own labours respecting the MSS. in the monastery, and I shall merely mention that I found in a modern Greek manuscript treatises upon astrology, natural history, medicine, and other similar studies, treated of in a peculiar manner. Under an article headed " Upon the Eagle," it is stated that the heart when dressed and secretly administered to a wife with her food, has the property of concentrating her whole love and friendship upon her

husband. Other secrets I will not betray. When the old Mamaluke
Colonel Gregorius read the note in the manuscript, wherein it is
characterised as a "Satanical book, full of wicked, godless, soul-
corrupting maxims ; a book which is not burnt as it richly merits,
only because it may protect those who read it from the practices of
such magical arts," he made a very considerate grimace at it ; still
he left it in my hands.

The regulation of my *cuisine* in the monastery occasioned me some
embarrassment. There were no chickens, and fish was very scanty.
The Bedouins, therefore, brought me a fat lamb ; but finding their
demands exorbitant, I made them my offer, and explained that at
any other price I should refuse the purchase. After delaying from
morning till past noon, they agreed to my terms. I, for my part,
was aware of the superstition prevalent among them, which prohibits
them from taking home again a lamb that has been offered for sale.

I will say but a word or two of my wanderings in the valley
around the monastery. My constant companion was Signor Pietro
with his dull countenance.

The promenade to the Valley of Gardens, the Bostan Valley, is
very charming. Pietro told me that he had always heard the great
plain Rahah mentioned as the biblical Rephidim. With this must
be conjointly considered the singular Moses' Rock, close to the Monastery of the Forty Martyrs, in the narrow arm of the Wadi, from
south-west to north-east. Remarkable enough is this insulated
enormous block of red granite. A vein runs completely through it
from top to bottom, which gives it the appearance of being rent as
with a crack. These apertures doubtless formed similar fissures
when first precipitated from the neighbouring mountain, owing to
the softer grain of the veins. It is no wonder that monastic credulity should consider this rock as that whence Moses' rod caused the
water to spring forth for the murmuring children of Israel.—
(Exod. xvii. 1. &c.) But Rephidim, although it must be sought for
in close proximity to Sinai, cannot be placed at the very foot of
Horeb. The Israelites, in all probability, approached Sinai by the
same route as myself; namely, by Feiran and the Sheikh-valley.
Rephidim must therefore be looked for in this direction. And in
my opinion no locality is more suitable than the great amphitheatre
of the plain, interrupted only by solitary blocks of rock, which I met
with immediately after passing the sublime granite portals previously
described. This plain may be without hesitation considered as the
spot of the battle with Amalek ; where " the top of the hill," upon
which Moses stood during the battle with uplifted hands, cannot
occasion any difficulty. — (Exod. xvii. 8, 9.) The insulated rocky
hill, beneath which I reposed at mid-day, on the 23rd of May,

completely commands the plain, and may have been the solemn post which Moses occupied.   From thence to Sinai is exactly a short day's journey, well suited to the progress of the Israelitish army.

At the point where the enormous block of granite lies, we can less surmise than anywhere else a deficiency of water.   Even the cheerful gardens in its vicinity testify against it.   The mountain range of Sinai is remarkably copious in excellent springs, otherwise it would have been far less attractive formerly to the numerous hermits who settled there.

The impressions which I felt when visiting the Wadi Mokatteb were renewed upon beholding this rock ; and they here admirably harmonised with the reminiscences of the great events in the history of Israel.   What if indeed the genuine origin of those inscriptions referred back to these distant days, and that the apparently intrusive interpolations were subsequent additions ?   At least, upon their being referred back to the fourth century, their enigmatical character becomes the more surprising, being found here upon this site of hermitages and monasteries, which were deducible from still earlier periods through which it was so easy for an explicit tradition to have been preserved.

Even my Pietro was incredulous as to the grave of the swallowed-up company of Korah (Numbers, xxvi. 10.) ; which also, despite the Bible, is placed here.   But two other remarkable places he pointed out to me, with much earnestness ; viz., the rock whereon Moses upon descending from the holy mountain, broke the tables of the law, and the mould of the golden calf.   Were it even a part of my function, I should scarcely concur with the Bedouins in digging around the rock, with the hope of discovering the rare fragments of the tables.   One point there is, indeed, in favour of the supposition, inasmuch as Moses, upon descending from Horeb, or from Sinai, could have had, just in this place, a good survey of the sinful proceeding.

I held the same opinion of the stone mould of the calf as I had previously entertained of the footstep of the prophet's dromedary. I could not make up my mind to investigate critically these ridiculous traditions: and yet, among European travellers, more than one enthusiast has given himself to the task.   By way of compensation for this loss, I enjoyed myself in the gardens of the valley, beneath the superb green trees — the sycamores, the pomegranates, and the cypresses ; nor was I tired of indulging in the reveries so forcibly suggested by the forms of the rocky mountain, with its melancholy wildness, its sombre sublimity, and its solemn majesty.

The very first garden that we entered, to the left of the monastery, was untenanted, save only by a young Bedouin, a serf of the monastery, and the conservator of the garden, and by his very juvenile wife, who, however, hastily retired from view. I could have indited an idyl upon this Bedouin in his paradise; I even almost envied him his lot. What a happy solitude was his here! with "ample space in simple cot for a happy loving pair." I was told by Linant, when at Cairo, that he possessed one of these gardens in the Bostan valley, and frequently in summer sojourned there for a short time. Even although it sound perilous, that the road thither lies through the desert, one might still indulge the desire for such a recreative trip.

My visit to the Wadi Sebaye involved me wholly in biblical researches. There lies Sinai! like the gigantic structure of infinite power, — like a temple of the far, far distant past! in comparison with which the very pyramids appear but infantile imitations. Its summit looks down like a threatening giant; but, softening its harsh expression, the chapel and the mosque cling round it, like playful children. It is true that the space is, without any doubt, too small for the camp of a host of two millions; but this difficulty may be explained away by transposing the camp itself to the broad plain, where the Wadi Rahah and the Wadi Sheikh meet immediately in front of the entrance to the valley of the monastery; and we may assume that Moses "brought forth the people out of the camp to meet the Lord" in the valley Sebaye.

DEPARTURE FROM SINAI.

Towards the end of Whitsun week I prepared to quit the monastery. Although I had experienced much that was disagreeable amongst the monks, and in their peculiar habits. How abhorrent did it sound to me, that in this consecrated solitude they should have introduced a sort of duel with sticks! a desecration like a blemish upon a picture of a Madonna. Yet, upon reading Schubert's words inscribed, on the 6th of March, 1837, in the Strangers' Book, "As long as I live I shall remember the days spent here with joy and gratitude," I felt them to be the perfect expression of my own sentiments.

I required fresh guides for my return to Cairo. Two sheikhs accosted me for this purpose in the garden of the monastery. The French camel-doctor's assertion was not lost upon me, that he had paid seventy piastres for a camel from Sinai to Cairo; whereas I had agreed to give a hundred and twenty for the same journey. I therefore offered only ninety, upon their demanding one hundred and fifty, with express reference to the camel-doctor. "Oh!" said they, "if you would be our camel-doctor, as the Lyonnais apothecary was, we would also take you for seventy." But as I was unwilling so suddenly to change my calling, I broke up the conference.

Two days afterwards I made an agreement with sheikh Hussein Erhebi. He also demanded a hundred and fifty piastres ; but was satisfied with the offer of a hundred and twenty, upon condition that the English consul could show that the same price had been paid during the current year for the same journey. But as I myself gave the required proof, which I had previously stated, the bargain was struck forthwith. Moreover, upon our arrival at Cairo, the sheikh, the brother of the contracting party, behaved most handsomely. After the English consul had inspected my previous contract, with the assistance of his dragoman, and had found it correct, he gave it as his opinion that my guides should be satisfied with a hundred and twenty piastres. The aggregate had, however, to be divided into eleven portions, for to this number of Bedouins did my convoy gradually increase ; and the subdivision had been calculated by them, throughout the journey, upon the basis of a contract for a hundred and fifty piastres. Notwithstanding this, the sheikh, upon the consul's decision, offered no opposition, but displayed the respectful signs of unconditional concurrence.

The monastery has an indisputable liking for the gratitude of pilgrims entertained therein. Signor Pietro admirably conduces to the gratification of the brethren's taste in this particular. I asked him to advise me as to what I should offer to the monastery. " I would," said he, " give a hundred piastres *per diem.*" Upon this I took counsel with myself. Besides, the monastery is considered to be, and is really, very rich ; for, in addition to the benefices it enjoys at a distance, and the costly presents of pilgrims, especially of the Greek Christians, it has other sources of revenue, in productive gardens, olive plantations, and date groves, in Feiran, in Tor, and elsewhere, which it confides to the charge of its serfs.

These serfs of the monastery, who are called Dschebelijeh, constitute a peculiar class of the inhabitants of the peninsula of Sinai, and comprise possibly more than a thousand souls. They both are, and are not, Bedouins; for they are considered by the genuine Bedouins as not *full-bred.* Their origin is traced back to the two hundred Wallachians and the two hundred Egyptians who were presented by the Emperor Justinian to the monastery, as serfs, upon its endowment. Although they have become Mahometans, through the incursions of the Arabs, yet they have remained the menial attendants on the monastery. A few Christians only, and those indeed newly converted, are to be found amongst them : their presence, in their Bedouin costume, and officiating at the Whitsun service of the church of the monastery, perfectly astonished me. Those who dwell in the vicinity of the monastery receive from it, several times during the week, rations, consisting chiefly of baskets full of bread, of an inferior quality to that consumed within it. On the very first day of my residence at the monastery, I noticed, late in the afternoon, a great clamour. This proceeded from the Dschebelijeh — men, women, and children — assembled in front of the monastery, who announced their arrival, exacting their established claims, with clamorous din. Robinson describes the reverence with which an old mountain guide, of the name of Aid (the Dschebelijeh enjoy the privilege of professed guides to Sinai, Horeb, and Mount St. Catherine), accosted the venerable prior of the monastery upon meeting him one evening at El Erbain. Aid knelt down and kissed the naked toe of the prior, who had taken off his shoes ; and seemed perfectly rejoiced to have met the revered patriarch beyond the cloistral walls.

The relation of the genuine Bedouins to the monastery is, upon the whole, friendly ; although the duration of this feeling can by no means be insured. The monastery, consequently, is prepared for defence ; and it even possesses a small cannon and a well-furnished armoury. The Bedouins, with their camels, are the regular and frequent carriers between Cairo and Sinai, for which the monastery remunerates them. The Bedouins, besides, invariably evince towards the fraternity all the marks of genuine esteem ; and they also put faith in many holy mysteries affirmed to be possessed by the monastery. Thus, for instance, in case of continued drought, they apply to the brotherhood to supplicate Heaven for rain with their unfailing prayers.

I quitted the monastery early on the 1st of June. The requisites for my journey had been attended to in the most friendly manner, and a part of the supply consisted of the peculiar date-bread of Sinai, certainly the most agreeable product of the monastery. It is made of the dates and almonds of the valley of Feiran, kneaded together, and sewed up in leathern bags ; thus closely resembling in appearance our brawn, both internally and externally. Amongst the presents made by me in return, a couple of pairs of spectacles were especially acceptable.

On reaching the base of the monastery, I found some twenty Bedouins, with their camels, who collectively wished to form my convoy. Their swords were drawn in the dispute, which made me feel somewhat uncomfortable ; but they soon agreed together ; and instead of four camels, which I required and had bargained for, I was accompanied by eleven, they having arranged that matter among themselves.

RETURN FROM SINAI TO CAIRO.

After holding our first siesta beneath the shade of the darfa trees, in the western portion of the Sheikh valley, and when prepared to proceed, the sheikh Hussein, upon mounting, injured his saddle. This was no trifle. He came to me and earnestly begged that I would take his brother instead of him, as leader of the caravan; for, in addition to this ominous sign his wives had predicted, by a peculiar game, that this journey would be unlucky to him. This reminded me of the anecdote of the ancient Greek philosopher, who, spraining his foot in falling, obeyed this call to return to his mother earth, and I therefore considered my Hussein a perfect philosopher. I asked him, " But is your brother also brave ?" He replied, " My brother is braver than I am." I consequently yielded to the force of his appeal, and allowed him to return home to his wives.

These Bedouins, like my first guides, practised the utmost simplicity in their mode of living. They broke their fast with coffee; at noon they made new bread of meal, shaping it into little round cakes, which were ready after remaining for some hours in the hot ashes; they then again drank coffee, and towards midnight they repeated this mid-day repast. On the journey they indulged in a pipe, and I also frequently saw them drink camel's milk. It was quite an exception if they accepted a portion of my meal, which was any thing but à la Parisienne. They speedily accustomed themselves to accede unconditionally to my wishes. I know not whether I should admit it, but certainly my intercourse with the Bedouins is among my most agreeable travelling reminiscences. These children of the desert live in many respects so honourably and so nobly, that they put to shame European civilisation. I will cite a few traits of their manners.

Family respect is very strictly enjoined; the father, the head of the house, is always revered, and served by his wives and children; the mothers also are highly honoured by their children; a pleasing feature, which gently modifies the usual disesteem in which the women are held.

The women are also extremely respectful towards strangers. Niebuhr relates of one whom he met in the desert, near Sinai, that she descended from her camel and went aside from the road on foot, until his caravan had passed. Under such circumstances I always encountered faces turned away, certainly an unwelcome mark of deference. But who, in the manners still existing, is not reminded of Moses' narrative of the bride Rebekah ? " And Rebekah lifted up

her eyes, and when she saw Isaac she lighted off the camel." (Gen.
xxiv. 64.)   Naturally out of respect.   I will not here refer to the
differences of customs in our brides.

Maiden chastity is rarely infringed among the Bedouins; the
penalty of the infringement is death : to be sure their early mar-
riages are a great preventive.   On the other hand, the rare exceptions which occur amongst matrons are looked upon less severely,
and, indeed, with some degree of favour.

The Bedouins consider honesty sacred.   In the Nasseb valley I
saw garments hanging on the trees ; and we also elsewhere met with
camels, both singly and in herds, browsing without a guard.   My
dragoman told me that they are frequently left for a long time thus,
for no one robs another.   Disputes amongst them are settled simply
by means of arbitration.

It struck me, as a proof of great affection, that when they meet
they frequently kiss each other.   Nor were they sparing in friendly
shakings of the hand.

The Bedouins live so free, so independently, that they would never
agree to exchange conditions with the constrained life of a German
courtier.   They love their desert and their camels above every thing.
They are unhappy if compelled, even but for a short time, to dwell
within the narrow walls of a city.   Withal they are constantly
prepared for war ; their arms always accompany them.   Like
Orientals in general, as highly as they venerate the duties of hospitality, just as implacably do they pursue their revenge.

What rendered my intercourse with the Bedouins still more interesting was the reminiscence of the ancient patriarchs, traits of
whose habits are still distinctly recognisable amongst them.   The
aversion which the inhabitants of towns, and also the fellahs, who
constitute the agricultural population, bear to the pastoral tribes, still
prevails to the extent mentioned by Moses upon the arrival of the
family of Jacob in the land of Goshen : " For every shepherd is an
abomination unto the Egyptians." (Gen. xlvi. 34.)

The idea repeatedly occupied me whilst wandering in their company through the desert, that these Bedouins might be easily converted to a simple and pure state of Christianity.   I have already
mentioned, that their practice of Mahometanism is of a very lax
character.   Their esteem for European travellers would considerably
facilitate the work of conversion.   I wish, from my heart, that Protestant missionary establishments may speedily share my sentiments;
then would my hopes soon be realised.

Together with the Bedouins the camel occupied much of my observation.   I believe modern physiologists have as yet accorded him no
chapter in their multifarious systems.   He, nevertheless, offers the

richest materials. It is by no means my intention to write an essay upon the subject, and I will merely observe, that there would be no misdirected career in the world, were every one as distinctly in his place as the camel in the desert. His power of enduring thirst for many days is well known ; possibly early habit comes here into play : no other animal is capable of sustaining so long the frequent deficiency of water in the desert. The camel also finds sustenance everywhere, almost, in the sandy unproductive waste, for he contents himself with any kind of herb, leaf, or shrub, which rarely altogether fail during an entire day's journey, and which, like the harsh and prickly thistle, are only adapted to the firm gristly structure of his mouth. Even in case of positive want the camel is supplied in a very peculiar manner ; and is supported, as it were, by the intervention of a reserve store, its own hump catering to sustain it, this hump being, in fat camels, largest and fullest, and in thin ones smallest.

His long neck is admirably suited to glean the food which may lie on either side of the road, without interrupting his progress or disturbing his rider. It also assists the Bedouin by letting him spring lightly over it on to his back.

The step of the camel through the desert is as soft as if on cushions ; at a few paces' distance scarcely any thing is heard, even of a caravan of a hundred camels. His foot is covered beneath with a soft yet rough skin, and he therefore prefers going upon the hard flint sand of the desert, yet he strides along dangerous rocks, if not too smooth, with all the security of a mule.

The burdens he can carry vary ; I saw loads of nearly ten hundred weight. Being too tall to be loaded standing, he is provided with hard knee-joints, upon which he readily kneels, and which gradually become less sensitive from his habit of reposing and feeding in this position.

The milk of the camel has an agreeable flavour, and is also nutritious. The flesh of those that fall on the journey, for it is but rarely that others are slaughtered, is also used by the Bedouins.

The camel is the very image of patience ; it is not easily exasperated to flight ; but, in the desert, a camel that escapes is not readily found again.

Thus the camel would furnish a far better text for a sermon upon divine Providence, than the dog which a Jesuit took into the pulpit to illustrate his sermon on the talent for shrewd discovery possessed by the order of the Jesuits. We may now, therefore, readily conceive why the birth of a camel is welcomed by a family with as joyful a festival as the birth of a child : for with the words, " A young child is born unto us," is it greeted upon its appearance in the world. It may also be understood how the exclamation, " Thou art my camel !" or,

"O thou, my camel!" becomes the expression of endearment with which a wife delights her husband.

Locusts are another interesting novelty that I became acquainted with in the desert. They certainly had not accumulated to a plague of Egypt, which would have been for a critic and commentator on the Bible too flattering an experience; nor did they appear to me, as they had done to other travellers, to advance in the serried array of an army, leaving melancholy desolation and naked brand-marks behind them where they touched. They now only clung in numerous small swarms to the shrubs of the desert, and fluttered away like a light cloud past us as we approached. Those which I saw in the Arabian desert, near the Red Sea, were probably of the same species which Shaw and Morier have described. Their bodies were three inches long, and their thighs bright yellow, and they had brown spotted wings. But, in Palestine and Syria, I met with a species which was a little smaller, and of a grey and light red colour. When they flew, their under wings scattered a reddish glimmer. They were not easily caught, and were strong and active.

Very recently, indeed, Egypt has again suffered from a plague of locusts. Mehemet Ali offered a small reward for every basketful collected of these insects: this admirably helped to remove the evil. But this crafty prince contrived to indemnify himself for his out-lay; for, as I was told, he devised a scheme for being repaid his money.

Nevertheless, the visit of the locusts has also its pleasing features, as many Orientals, for instance, the Arabs and Persians, eat them with considerable zest. The preparation of them is very various. They are eaten fresh or salted, or, as is most usual, roasted. Those which are roasted are sometimes seasoned with salt and spices, and sometimes mixed with rice and dates. Their flavour is differently described, but it appears most closely to resemble that of the lobster.

In spite of this, however, we cannot blame the peasants when they observe a caravan of these warlike guests approaching upon the wings of the east wind — which Moses also mentions in his narrative of the Egyptian plague of locusts (Exod. x. 13) — meeting them with loud tumult and clamour, whereby they sometimes prevent their settling in their gardens, fields, and cultivated grounds. And they also consider it a crime to touch the beautiful golden-yellow bird Sa-marmar, which consumes the locusts with still greater appetite than even the Arabs themselves. But their surest and strongest destroyer is still sent by the Lord, as in the days of Pharaoh, in the winds which drive these oppressive swarms into the sea, especially the south and south-east, which sweep them into the Mediterranean, for locusts are not very noted swimmers. But by far the greatest peril met with in the deserts are indisputably the snakes. These I also repeatedly fell in with. Twice upon my return from Sinai to Cairo my Bedouins raised their cry of terror—" A snake! a snake!" My dragoman instantly sprung from his camel, and poising his double-barrelled gun upon the back of his submissive animal, discharged both charges whilst the guide hastened to drive the camels away from the spot. These snakes were neither of them an ell long; but they are considered the most dangerous and the most poisonous of all. They were of the horned genus, Cerastes, which derive their name from the two small tentaculæ upon their heads. When these tentaculæ only are seen above the sand, they attract birds, which mistake them for worms; but the poisonous seducer speedily coils about them. The tracks of snakes seen in the sand are innumerable: extensive districts are completely scored with them.

One of my camels was suffering from a wound caused by the bite of a snake, which still bled every day. The Bedouins did not seem to care greatly about it; but they told me that the camel usually dies speedily from a thorough bite. As it is so easy for these animals to be bitten, especially during the night in their exposed position in the sand, I had carefully obtained from my physician at Cairo the necessary instruction as to the measures to be adopted under such circumstances. He considered the sucking of the wound as the only certain remedy, and this is only dangerous in the event of the agent having a wound on the lips or within the mouth. Ammonia is considered as the next best application.

A deviation that we made on the return to Suez, on the evening of the third day, from Wadi Taibe to the Wadi Garandel, I think deserves mention. We made a circuit round the high rocky mountain in the west, which lies opposite to the hot Pharaoh's bath, and so close to the sea for a considerable distance, that, notwithstanding the prevalent ebb tide, one of two camels going abreast was obliged to wade in the water. I attached no credit to the danger of the way which my guides, who wished to wait for the moon, alleged to exist; but I now found that foresight was really required. The circumstance of the sea approaching so close to the mountains is important to demonstrate the impossibility that here the Israelites could have skirted the Red Sea.

Upon arriving, on the fourth day shortly after noon, in the Garandel valley to the east of the spring, I experienced the highest temperature that had occurred during the whole course of the journey. Before we stopped, my face felt as if I was holding it to the intense heat of a furnace. It was impossible to endure the naked foot upon the sand. We did not break up again until after sunset; neverthe-

I 3

less, I had scarcely re-dressed myself before my clothes were wet through with perspiration, from the continuance of the sultriness.

On the afternoon of the following day, when about to break up from the Wadi Sadr, I witnessed a terrific spectacle. I am happy at being fortunate enough to have survived to record it. It was the notorious Chamsin ; as dangerous as the roused lion, as fatal as the tooth of the tiger, is it to meet this terror of the wilderness.

I had ordered my tent to be struck about five o'clock, that I might reach Ayin Musa before midnight, to avail myself on the following morning of the ebb-tide to ford the sea, when, suddenly, a gust of wind blew down my tent and me with it. After disentangling myself I looked about me, and found I could distinctly see but a few steps around, and I was speedily enveloped in the bright red sand-dust as in a cloud. The hot oppressive air nearly suffocated me, and a noise raged above and around us wilder and more fearful than when the sea foams in its fury : it reminded me most vividly of the eruption of Vesuvius with its accompanying thunders. This tumult was the more singular, as we were very distant from any buildings or forests ; and it was only from the sea that we were not very far. The Bedouins had hastily collected the camels together that they might not be dispersed by terror ; we ourselves crouched close to a low but bushy sand-hill, which was our salvation, and I also caused myself to be covered up as much as possible.

This condition of things could not last long, or I should have been conveyed in travelling costume, and in such good society, from the Wadi Sadr to the valley of the shadow of death.

I had fallen asleep ; towards eight my dragoman aroused me, telling me that the danger was over, and that the storm had much abated, but that it would be scarcely possible to proceed before the rising of the moon. I again fell asleep, and awoke after midnight ; one quarter of the disc of the moon stood brightly and clearly over me. I started as it were from an oppressive dream. With deep gratitude my eyes surveyed the cheerful sky of night ; but my presiding star, thought I, has not aroused me in vain. I therefore wished immediately to proceed, that I might execute my original purpose. Indeed, to my Bedouins, this was as incredible as it was disagreeable. I myself felt equally uncomfortable, for I now found that my eyes, my ears, my mouth and neck, were completely filled with the sandy dust, and that it had worked its way even into my sleeves and all over my body. But in the course of another half-hour we recommenced our journey towards the Moses' springs, without either rest or repose, and throughout the cool night, which speedily became exceedingly damp.

When talking with the consul-general Costa about my adventure, he also considered the danger which I had escaped to have been very great. He told me that, about four years before, a young Swiss, heedless of his expostulations, started upon his journey for Cairo just as the chamsin commenced; but he paid for his temerity by his death, which took place within a few hours. I was also told of entire and large caravans which had been overtaken by the chamsin in the midst of the unprotective desert, and buried in the sand. I cannot, therefore, by any means recommend travellers to follow my example of selecting, for a journey across the desert, the period during which this wind rages, namely, from the middle of April to the middle of June.

When we had got a day's journey beyond Suez, three of my former convoy returned ; but they came as from battle, laden with a rich booty. The tribe of Tor located on the shores of the Red Sea, to which tribe also those Bedouins belonged who had claimed so energetically upon my journey through Suez the right of convoy, in opposition to my engaged guides, had long entertained hostile sentiments against the settlers from Palestine, along the Mokattam. The latter had now executed their revenge. My three guides, in conjunction with seventeen of their tribe, had fallen upon the camel herds of the Bedouins of Tor, and had conveyed them away as booty. Three hundred pursuers were on their track and, in the village El Bada, some of them had fallen in with my Attayo, and had asked him — naturally without knowing him — which road the freebooters had taken ? They had not, however, overtaken them. It is scarcely to be conceived how twenty Bedouins could carry off so safely a herd of four hundred camels, through these deserts and rocks, and wholly escape the vigilance of three hundred pursuers. They were now quite safe, for their home lay but one day's journey distant.

As this noble troop of four hundred camels, many of which had such beautiful and bushy hair that they appeared as yet totally innocent of a burden, passed by us, and my Bedouins heard the history of its acquisition, they became not a little anxious. They speedily drove their own eleven animals together. But my old guide came to visit me for a few minutes in my tent, and their sheikh ate bread with my convoy, who had baked it with the greatest expedition and solicitude. This cheered their courage. I learnt that it is a strict law among the Bedouins to consider him as a friend with whom they have eaten bread. They nevertheless watched the livelong night by their fires. I supplied them with sufficient coffee for the purpose. I myself slept tranquilly ; for I was sure of a friend in my former guide, and rejoiced that I had had these valiant people in my service.

This predatory expedition was indeed a surprising afterpiece to the great peaceful festival of Salech.

I subsequently heard, in Constantinople, that the Bedouins of Tor had solicited the intervention of Mehemet Ali, who, upon certain conditions, restored to them almost the whole of their lost camels.

JOURNEY TO JERUSALEM.

On the 21st of June, at five in the afternoon, I again bade farewell, and probably for the last time, to Cairo. Jerusalem was my goal. I regret that I did not go thither direct from Sinai, across Akaba, Petra, and Hebron; but, together with other motives, the chief object of my return to Cairo was to visit the Coptic monastery of Damietta, in the prosecution of my MSS. researches. I now gave up this plan, as my expectations had been damped by my preceding exploration; nor did either the visit to Damietta, the very home of the plague, nor the journey thence by water, in a Turkish coasting vessel, present any greatly attractive motive.

An adventure was linked with my departure from Cairo. I had scarcely been an hour's journey from the gates, when suddenly several Arab cavaliers sprung around, with no minor object than to detain me. I rode in advance of my caravan, and received in the most hostile manner the incomprehensible, and yet also right easily comprehensible, demonstrations of these cavaliers. Upon receiving the explanation of this movement, I saw already behind me a troop of many riders upon asses, and a swarm of people on foot, advancing with the greatest precipitation. The secretary of the Austrian consulate rode in advance, and told me that an Italian of rank, of the name of ――, had pocketed, instead of paying into a banker's, a sum of ten thousand florins, and that it had been reported that he had joined my caravan to proceed into Syria. Probably my dragoman, who, notwithstanding his Oriental costume, betrayed the Frank, had been mistaken for the plunderer. I received now an accurate description of him, and was invested with authority to seize in case of falling in with him. The disappointed expedition returned, and I had no opportunity to use my deputed authority.

Upon arriving at the wells of Mataryeh, I saw once more the ancient venerable sycamore, to which is attached the tradition that it miraculously sheltered the holy family during the flight to Egypt; and I caused my water-skins to be filled with the excellent water of the celebrated Fountain of the Sun.

The following afternoon I discovered how unfortunate the selection of my guides was to prove. We stopped opposite Kanka. I wished to proceed some leagues further ; but my convoy constrained me to stay, confessing their invincible fear of the robbers beyond Kanka. They alleged, as their reason, that a few days before a highwayman had been decapitated at that place. But, apart from their real timidity, the main cause was, their wish to join themselves to a caravan that was following us, which consisted of forty camels, and was friendly towards them. This Arab party, to whom women and children made convenience a duty, was very unpleasant to me. I insisted that we should separate on the following morning. But my present convoy were not Bedouins, for they invariably spoke contemptuously of the Bedouins who met us, and whom they called Arabs. Two of them were natives of El Arisch ; the third was a black slave.

But I must also give some account of my dragoman. I had already engaged my brave Ali of Gizeh for my journey into Syria, when several friends recommended to me in his stead a countryman of my own, who was without the means of travelling to Jerusalem, whither he was bent. He was a native of the Baltic provinces of Prussia, and by trade a tailor. He had domiciled himself for a considerable time both in Constantinople and Cairo, and spoke Arabic fluently. I had been told that the many gallant adventures of the handsome young German had made his departure from the ancient city of the caliphs exceedingly desirable. As he—a genuine *homme a tout faire*—was also skilled in cookery, and appeared to have the requisite energy for the caravan, I allowed myself to be persuaded to the exchange, notwithstanding the precaution requisite against such people in such countries, and I took " the handsome Frederick" into my service.

No one could possibly discern that he was a knight of the needle, and not of the pennon, as he rode along beside me upon his camel, clothed from head to foot in the Turkish costume, and decorated with a glittering and trailing sword, and with a brace of pistols in his girdle. I had no occasion to regret my selection, although he was not exactly *au fait* in the command of the convoy. But he had a thousand anecdotes to tell me. I also learnt from him that German wanderers of his condition, and of other similar ones, formed a sort of combination in distant countries, the force of which I should never have surmised. Unfortunately I heard too late from him, that the ass-drivers of Cairo entertain an especial respect for the " rude Germans." As far as I can remember, they did not certainly detect my nationality. An anecdote which may have tended to effect this, I take the liberty to relate :—

A German of the same trade as my dragoman had " too moistly"
celebrated the Sunday — one of the superfluous preliminaries for a
Christian missionary service.   On riding back from Bulak to
Cairo, he cleared his passage through the streets with a naked
sword.   Every thing made way for him — for, in the East, everybody
passes for what *de facto* he is — excepting one seis, who, with the
same steady conscience as his grey quadruped, tranquilly pursued
his road.   But the rampant cavalier reached the ass, and cut off
his nose.   The seis complains, — he demands compensation for his
ass.   The tailor, as well as the ass without a nose, are impounded:
but in consequence of the customary reference of the Franks to their
consuls, the affair became procrastinated ; whilst the impounded ass,
notwithstanding his noseless visage, displayed the heartiest appetite.
The result was, that the seis was informed that his animal would be
sent away, in case he did not remove it ; but the German hero not
only retained — contrary to the ordinary custom of Oriental justice —
his own nose, but received also, on the part of his consulate, another
in addition.

The first four days of our journey our course lay through animated
and fruitful districts, for we were traversing the land of Goshen,
that jewel of Egypt.   We passed by noble forests of date palms —
one in particular astonished me, for it was entirely surrounded with
sand.   This proves how thoroughly, in this fertile land of Egypt,
even apparently desert tracts of sand are capable of cultivation
wherever water is to be procured.   Among the field fruits I observed
large plantations of gourds and water melons.   Upon reaching the
last small branch of the Nile, my guides did not omit apprising me
of it ; and they themselves took hearty draughts of it.

For three days before we reached the Egyptian frontier fortress,
El Arisch, we journeyed constantly through a deep soft sand, which
nowhere yielded a firm hold for our tents.   It had formed here a
multitude of hills and valleys of a peculiar shape, and it was not at
all easy to keep to the proper track.   After nightfall the stars always
served for our guides; occasionally we lost every indication of a track,
and without the lights above it would have been impossible to avoid
being lost.   We also once went astray : we stood upon the edge of
precipices, which, from their unstable sand, looked very fearful ; but the black slave' knew how to extricate us, and in all
doubtful cases I subsequently left the determination of our course to
him.

Our supplies of water we several times drew from the residue
preserved at the post stations which had been constructed by Ibrahim
Pasha, when ruler of Syria, for maintaining the intercourse with
Egypt.   But it was never entirely free from a taste of salt or salt-

petre. Our camels relished it better, for these animals can far less dispense with water than the camels of the Bedouins. A delusive compensation for bright clear water was offered us repeatedly in the spectacle of the Serab, or the celebrated mirage. My dragoman was not unacquainted with it and yet he once surmised that we should now at last reach a lake. We, in fact, saw so distinctly the waves crisped in the wind, and glittering in the sun, that a person unacquainted with the delusion must have been deceived.

We also fell in with an Egyptian guardpost, still distant from the frontiers ; it was garrisoned with Albanian soldiers, who immediately visited me in my tent, and for safety brought their own pipes with them. They were stationed near a wood of tamarisks, where we disturbed several gazelles, which we vainly endeavoured to shoot. On seeing these animals, clothed as it were with such maidenly modesty, and yet exhibiting such graceful forms in their rapid motion over the wide waste, it is easy to conceive the prepossession of Oriental poets for them. I have also studied their mild yet fiery eyes, such as those of a beautiful eastern *inamorata* must surely be. In Cairo tame gazelles are kept, which appear to be happy in their thraldom amongst the peacocks, storks, and fowls of the court-yards. It is known that the name of " gazelle" has been conferred on maidens : its equivalent in Syriac is Tabitha, the name of the pious female at Joppa, whom Peter recalled to life. (Acts, ix. 40.)

A solitary rider upon a dromedary, whom we met, excited my interest. He carried the mail of the French consul at Jerusalem, who usually in from five to six days traverses with his swift bearer the long distance from Cairo to Jerusalem. It is to be feared that this same rider whom we met probably into the hands of the hostile Bedouins beyond Gaza, for neither upon my arrival, nor during my stay in Jerusalem, did he make his appearance. The consul told me that he was not the first whom he had vainly expected, although for some time past he had made terms with a sheikh of the Bedouins of that vicinity to protect the mail.

Before we reached El Arisch, we met several small Arab caravans. My convoy put the same question to each : " How goes it ? What's the news?" And the same reply was made by each : " War ! war !"

On the morning of the 28th of June we arrived at El Arisch, the ancient Rhinocolura. My convoy even put on their sandals to play a respectable part before their friends. I caused my tent to be pitched at some distance from the walls, beneath some palm trees, and went immediately into the town to learn the state of matters. The only European there was a Greek of the name of Riso, an adjutant, and the solitary remnant of the board of health. Of the establishment of the physician, a young Italian, nothing remained but his black wife and a female slave: he himself had become bankrupt and had gone to Alexandria. According to the adjutant, the following was the explanation of the rumour of war. On the 16th of April, the Bedouin tribes of Suerke and Asasme, on the Egyptian side, had taken the field to revenge themselves upon the tribes of Telya and Sarbim, of the Turkish side. On the 25th of May they had renewed their hostilities. Since then, the former, the Egyptian Bedouins, some thousands in number, had moved for greater protection into the immediate vicinity of El Arisch: their tents were pitched upon the eastern side of this strong town, garrisoned at present with a hundred and fifty soldiers. With respect to the security of the road, the intercourse of the Bedouins themselves was in the greatest degree dangerous, and many instances of attacks upon travellers had occurred. But the attack of Franks was limited to the exaction of a tribute, varying in amount. About a fortnight before me an Englishman had arrived at El Arisch, who subsequently wrote to the adjutant of his lucky escape and arrival at Gaza. Three months before a thousand dollars and various effects were stolen during the night from a Russian colonel, just before reaching El Arisch. The Englishman, consequently, who had a considerable sum of money about him, had been induced to stop eight days in El Arisch, that he might receive before starting certain intelligence from Gaza. All this did not convince me of any real danger, and even did it exist there was no apparent probability of its being speedily removed, I was therefore not at all inclined to yield to the wishes of my convoy, who desired that I should await the arrival of the other Arab caravan of forty camels, with the women and children. But I readily comprehended why my delay in El Arisch would be most agreeable to my guides, where Mustapha had two wives, and Mohammed a wife and family. Yet, notwithstanding my incessant and serious threatenings, which the adjutant strongly supported, — while, from the governor, as he was described to me, neither aid nor military escort was to be obtained,— I found myself compelled to submit to the pleasure of my guides. I shall subsequently narrate that I did not remain their debtor for a just retaliation to their refractory conduct.

I endeavoured for four days to amuse myself as much as was possible in this wild and warlike vicinity. The sea, the road to which lay through a noble wood, was scarcely a league distant. On its strand I observed multitudes of those small crabs, of which I had read in Belon's travels, made in 1555. He writes of them, that they are not much larger than a chesnut, and run faster than a man ; and, what is most singular, that by day they lie exposed upon land to the excessive heat of the sun, and go at night into the water. It is the running crab of Aristotle, which, on account of its speed, is called the runner, or dromon. Their appearance might place them between the spider and the crab. The waves flowing over the precipitous shore brought them always with it, but it required a rapid foot and an active hand to seize one of them.

The large well at El Arisch possesses the peculiarity of containing leeches within its excellent water. During my stay here I observed both a camel and an Arab bleeding at the mouth from the nip of a half-swallowed leech. The water, therefore, always requires to be filtered. But I was one evening still more alarmingly surprised whilst lying upon my couch within my tent: a young snake, not more than eight or ten inches long, was creeping close beside me. My dragoman struck at it with his sabre, but every piece of it retained life until hewn into innumerable fragments.

I also became acquainted with the soldiers in El Arisch, who were all excellent horsemen ; but I familiarised myself still more with their beautiful steeds. I was not at all accustomed to the peculiar gallop of these animals, which is an incessant flight ; yet I soon became familiar with it.

The evenings invariably offered me a splendid spectacle. I then seated myself upon the tallest of the white tombstones of the cemetery, which lay upon a high and rocky hill. In the west I had the glittering silver mirror of the Mediterranean ; in the east the large camp of the Bedouins, consisting of about a hundred black and white tents with flaming fires ; in front of me arose out of the sand the little fortress with its walls and palm-trees ; and behind me the pale sandy plain extended to the horizon. Over all shone the most magnificent full moon, and the darkening sky was, as it were, enveloped in a blue veil.

But I must also notify the gallant hospitality of El Arisch. It consisted, in the transmission by a fair hand, on the evening of my arrival, of a festal meal, which comprised an excellent broth of boiled chicken, a couple of roasted pigeons, and a rice pilau. My dragoman apprised me that this was a custom practised towards welcome strangers. And, as an especial condiment to flavour its enjoyment, I was told that these delicacies were prepared by the hands of the matron of one of the first families in El Arisch. I need not asseverate that this lent the meal additional zest. But I have reason to apprehend that I was not favourably remembered by the hospitable inhabitants of Arisch ; for, upon my arrival in Jerusalem, I informed the French consul of the misconduct of my guides, who already thought all forgotten ; he confirmed me in my intention of prosecuting them for their refractory conduct on the road, to which was conjoined a malicious attack upon my dragoman, who, but for my intervention. would have done summary justice with his sabre.   They were, indeed, perfectly astonished at all this; but as their humiliating entreaties were of no avail, they laid a complaint before the Pasha of Jerusalem, who, on their behalf, made application to me at the monastery.   But I had already prepared my appeal to the French consulate at Cairo, in which I enclosed the three still outstanding napoleons, eventually intended for the poor of Cairo ; for, doubtlessly, my guides, upon their return, received the change in a different coin.

I am convinced that this proceeding will be beneficial in its results to European travellers.   Almost all suffer from the conduct of the camel and horse drivers of these parts ; and it is usually only the cheerful moment of arrival that obliterates the remembrance of the vexations of the road.   By these means these selfwilled, lazy, and deceitful men are only confirmed in their capricious obstinacy towards us.   But the beneficial results of repeated proofs of absolute severity to be derived to the improvement of their manners, may be estimated from the effect of Ibrahim Pasha's proceedings on a large scale.

The insecurity to travellers coming out of Egypt, which, in fact, commences at the Syriac-Turkish frontiers, is one of the unfortunate results of surrendering of Syria to the Sultan.   Under Ibrahim Pasha I was assured, at every place in Syria, that a child laden with money might have been sent forth with safety to travel.   I should have thought that it would have been but a just and meritorious act on the part of the great powers, in their friendly and victorious progress in Syria, to have obtained from the Porte the requisite guarantees, or at least a constant military escort for travellers in that country, who are always under their combined protection.

But to return to my travels.   At mid-day of the 2nd of July we at last left El Arisch, and that in company with the great Arab caravan.   On the 3rd we were subjected to one of the already-mentioned hostile exactions.   I certainly had not erred in supposing that I should have travelled far more advantageously had I gone alone, instead of in this company; for at first, (without doubt, upon special prompting,) I was required to pay as much as was demanded from the whole of the second caravan.   I knew the necessary answer to be made, and I paid at last a tolerably moderate sum.   On the 4th the exaction was repeated.   At first it had an ominous appear-ance, when the cavaliers on horseback encircled the caravan, with their long spears, and constrained us to halt.   But the whole affair terminated peaceably.

But I must mention a very agreeable surprise which happened to me on entering Palestine.   The waste and desert sandy tracts had just assumed the indications of a scanty vegetation. We had passed a hilly district with a scrubby wood, resembling the effigy of vegetation, where I had seen at one single glance thousands of active rats and mice, rather more white than grey.   This necessarily reminded me of the plague of the Philistines, when they deprived the Israelites of their ark; but I saw no trace of the "five golden mice." (1 Sam. vi. 4.) But suddenly, near Khan Yunes, like the joyousness of life conjoined to the shadow of death, the fields of Gaza, with their cheerful fertility, were linked to the edge of the desert.   It seemed a magical delusion—like a joyful picture starting suddenly from the colourless canvass.   There a broad plain of pasture-land lay stretched before us, with fields offering their golden harvest, and still sown all over with flowering stems, with tobacco plantations in the splendour of their richly coloured blossoms, with luxuriant melon plantations, with hedges of the productive fig-cactus, with olives and pomegranates, sycamores and fig-trees.   It was the impress of the promised land; it offered indeed a festal greeting.

I then hailed that small and yet so remarkable coast of the Mediterranean lying between the reddish mountains of Edom and the snowy summits of Lebanon.   What country of the world can compare therewith in the great events it has beheld?   Shall I condense into one word how it stands forth in history?   It presents itself as the holy arena for the combats of the intellect, for the conflicts of religion; and thus does it exhibit itself, from Abraham's far distant times on to the very gates of the future.   There did the pure faith sustain its first trials against the Canaanites, against the Philistines, and against the Phœnicians.   There the worship of Jehovah was divided between the Temple and the Garizim.   There salvation flourished upon the cross, moistened by much precious blood; and there the Church endured the hottest hours of its conflict.   There Mahometanism obtained energy; there the Crescent and the Cross were occupied for centuries in enthusiastic conflicts.   We there behold, at the present day, as in no other country, Christian and Jew, Turk and heathen, beneath increasing divisions, on the same hearth fanatically embrace his God.   There also will, even for the time still unborn, the great and saving word resound, and sanctified power arise.

On the 4th of July I entered Gaza, the ancient metropolis of the Philistines.   The reception I met with would have been worthy of that people.   I was quartered in miserable quarantine; I, who had come out of healthy Egypt, and had been exposed for a fortnight to the healthy air and ventilation of the winds of the desert. The French quarantine physician received my letter with the firetongs, and passed it over the brazier.   I begged to be separated as far as possible from the Arab mob, many of whom, to avoid the quarantine, had taken a circuitous route ; so that now one Turk only visited his two imprisoned travelling companions, consisting indeed of his two wives, with the cautious observance of the prescribed distance.

I had, however, chosen an evil lot. The place accorded to me had previously served for various animals, of which at night many reminiscences became evident. Early in the morning I apprised the physician that I was apprehensive that such a quarantine was more likely to produce sickness than to restore health. The physician replied, that he had himself complained in vain to the same effect. I and my tent were consequently, for the next day and night, transplanted to the roof of Ibrahim Pasha's stables, where, for security, I was obliged to maintain two guards.

I thus passed through this ordeal of the caricature of a quarantine, and thereby obtained free liberty to amuse myself in the aboriginal Gaza, whilst my camels still underwent quarantine in their pasture. Aboriginal, I call Gaza, for it is one of the cities whose names have descended to us from the remotest period. Canaan, Noah's grandson and his race, as it is said in the tenth chapter of Genesis, occupied all the land from Sidon, as thou comest to Gerar unto Gaza. Gaza was then not only the chief city of the Philistines, but also their greatest fortress. Joshua's career of conquest was stayed before the walls of Gaza, and subsequently the relation of this city to Israel was more frequently one of command than of servitude : whilst towards Egypt it stood as the true frontier guard of the promised land. Even Alexander the Great, with his troops, accustomed to victory, was obliged to fight for five whole months for the possession of Gaza. After that period it was repeatedly subjected to misfortunes ; it sunk in ruins ; and it once more arose out of its ruins.

Christianity early fixed a firm footing in Gaza. Nevertheless the still remaining temples of the heathen gods were destroyed only at the commencement of the fifth century, when upon their site was built the splendid church of the Empress Eudoxia. Even now the walls and pillars of this structure are standing, though since the commencement of the seventh century it has been turned into a mosque. During the Crusades Gaza endured many severe vicissitudes, and it was here that the Templars especially made their stand against the Saracens.

At the present day Gaza is a busy city with a population of about sixteen thousand souls, somewhat similar to that of Jerusalem. It has no longer any gates, and does not lie so much upon the round height whereon the ancient city stood, as in the broad plain which lies to the north and east of this height. Traces of the earlier structures are found dispersed about the city in the many fragments of marble and granite lying here and there, and even traces of the twelve gates of antiquity may be recognised around the above-mentioned height.

That which made Gaza chiefly celebrated was Samson, the theatre of whose deeds it was. It was there that he took the doors of the gate and carried them up " to the top of an hill that is before Hebron." (Judges, xvi. 3.) It was also by, in the valley of Sorek, that he loved the woman whose name was Delilah, who enticed from him the secret of the cause of his gigantic strength, when the Philistines put out his eyes, and led him down to Gaza; and there, lastly, stood the temple of Dagon, within whose ruins he buried himself with his enemies. Therefore even to the present day, the memory of this beloved hero, who for twenty years was one of the judges of Israel, is a precious jewel in the estimation of the Gazarenes. The mountain up which he carried the doors of the gate, called in the Book of Judges "the hill that is before Hebron," is supposed to be the insulated elevation lying to the south-east of the city. It is there also that a Christian bishop is said to have dwelt, where at present nothing but the tomb of a saint is to be found. The door that was carried away is supposed to have been in a corresponding direction with the hill, where also a grave of Samson has been raised, although another called after him was shown me in a mosque.

Towards noon on the sixth of July I quitted Gaza. My caravan had increased by one companion. It was an Englishman, who deprived Germany of its exclusive reputation of sending poor devils abroad on their travels. Upon quitting quarantine he possessed nothing but five piastres (about $1\frac{1}{2}d.$), and a small bundle of linen and a few books. His clothing consisted of light, white, summer raiment. He was thirty years of age, and recently came from home, and was now proceeding from Egypt to Jerusalem, purposing either there or in Damascus to study Arabic. He showed me a certificate wherein he was described as a sort of teacher of languages. I perched him upon one of my camels, and took him to Jerusalem: he had reached Gaza with the large Arab-caravan by means of the contributions of his patrons at Cairo.

The vicinity of Gaza through which we passed was beautiful and luxuriant. Tobacco plantations especially are numerous, and palms are not wanting among the trees. But which ever way I looked, I observed great hedges of the fig-cactus, which, from the fine spines of the envelope of their fruit, are not to be touched with impunity by any hand that wishes to remain unwounded. Shortly after we had quitted the city our way lay through a long olive wood, where we rested.

Towards night-fall the former anxieties of my guides were aroused.

K

Indeed at Gaza I had myself heard the French quarantine physician confirm some of the El Arisch narratives of predatory and murderous attacks; but my timid guides had lost all credit with me. I was nearly punished for this on this very day; for, as about ten o'clock of an intensely dark night, we were passing close to a large encampment of Bedouins, we came suddenly so near a discharge of fire-arms, that some of the balls whistled about our ears. I was thus within a hair's breadth of entering the heavenly instead of the earthly Jerusalem. Our falling in with this hostile volley was naturally merely an accident. But that the Bedouins, who had us here completely in their power, would exact an adequate tribute, was more than probable. My guides were noiseless; the least sound produced by the camels increased their anxiety. I myself took my girdle, filled with French gold coin, into my hand to cast it on the first alarm into the sand. Watch-fires were burning for a considerable distance, and the dogs barked. Nevertheless it seemed they had not noticed us; but I suddenly saw, after having scarcely lost sight of the lights of the tents behind the hills, at about fifteen paces from our road, two men, lying flat upon the ground, but who now most cautiously rose up, and keeping a close eye upon us, made some steps backwards. I leaped from my camel, as did also my drago-man. We advanced with our swords drawn, and guns and pistols cocked, with our looks directed to the suspected point. Against two highwaymen force would have availed us; but in case of an attack of the Bedouins, whose encampment was doubtlessly several thousand strong, our arms would have been ridiculous, if not dangerous to ourselves. Two persons on foot, who had joined us a few hours before, were suspected as belonging to the fellows upon the road; we therefore acted with the greater caution and deter-mination, and continued on foot until midnight, in constant prepara-tion against an attack. It was certainly less our number than our resolution which scared these footpads away. Although we pitched our tents near a village, still I and my dragoman alternately kept watch until the dawn of the tardy Sunday morning; and then, in the very depths of my heart, I offered up thanks to God.

In Jerusalem I learnt that the Bedouins of Bethlehem were en-gaged in a war of retaliating revenge against those of Gaza, and on that account the road we had just passed was considered as insecure. The recently missing Cairo post had probably fallen into the enemy's hands between Gaza and Ramleh. Two Frankish travellers related to me the causes of this sanguinary revenge, which they themselves had witnessed at Bethlehem. A Gazarene had arrived there leading a dromedary by the bridle, which carried a corpse enveloped in a white cloth. This corpse already emitted an offensive odour.

The population immediately collected together ; speedily the wake-women came howling around, and an aged woman hastened from the midst of the mob to the corpse, raising the winding-sheet so that the horridly mutilated head might be seen to some distance. In the impetuosity of her grief she then tore the veil from her face, plucked the hair from her head, and with yells of woe beat her breasts till they bled. Speedily a fresh incident was added to this melancholy scene. A young and powerful man forced his way through the crowd ; waved his sword over the corpse, and solemnly vowed to revenge the murdered man ; very shortly afterwards, when the funeral ceremonies took place, many others also took the solemn oath of revenge. The death of the man was the result of an amour.

On the seventh of July I took my siesta beneath the walls of Ramleh, in a large olive grove in front of the city, the soil of which consisted of coarse sand overgrown with nothing but thistles. The city lay before us at the distance of only a few minutes' walk. A European flag waved in sight from the summit of a consular dwelling. At a short distance behind our encampment stood a remarkable ruin with a lofty tower. I stayed but a short time in the city, but paid a longer visit to the tower. The city itself appeared to be attractive enough, for Ramleh is considered as the Arimathea of the New Testament, whence Nicodemus and Joseph came ; and also as Rama, the birthplace of Samuel. The Monastery of the Fathers of the Holy Sepulchre is built, as it is said, precisely upon the spot where stood the house " of him who came to Jesus by night." (John, iii. 1. &c.) But there are important doubts as to the correctness of referring Ramleh to the period of Christ, and the time antecedent, although both Arimathea and Rama must be sought in its vicinity, although Ramleh presents itself as one of the earliest positions occupied by the Saracens in the Holy Land. It is only in opposition to one point, which the learned Robinson adduces in proof of the differences between Rama and Ramleh, that I must explain myself : that, viz., which he deduces from the etymological differences of the two names. Ramleh signifies " the sandy ;" Rama, an " elevation." But Ramleh is sandy, and is situated at the same time upon an elevation : it is very possible that the modern Ramleh may have sprung from the ruins of the ancient Rama. The affinity in sound must have conduced the more to the preference of " the sandy ;" as that in fact gives a distinctive character to this elevation, in comparison with the fruitful plain which skirts it : a circumstance which probably did not prevail in the earliest times.

But I hasten to the ruin with the tower. Its historical explanation presents difficulties. Possibly no church ever stood here, (the monument of Helena's piety, as the monks declare,) but that it was a large and

splendid mosque.   The " White Mosque," at Ramleh, is described
by Arabic writers as grand and splendid : its origin they refer back
to the foundation of Ramleh, at the commencement of the eighth
century.   There now exist, only in ruins, outlines of the quadrangular structure in walls and pillars ; yet these are sufficient to indicate its by-gone splendour.   The wide subterranean vault has a
peculiar interest ; for it is here that the Mahometan considers
that the forty companions of his prophet lie buried ; and here also
it is that the Christian monk places the tomb of his forty martyrs ;
viz., those of Sebaste in Armenia.   I do not conceive it probable
that it was, as Robinson supposes, originally a caravansera ; for as
such it would consequently have lasted to the present day, as even
now the course of the large caravans lies by way of Ramleh.   I concur, however, with him in considering the stone square tower, which
is of considerable height*, strongly to indicate its having been a
Turkish minaret, instead of, as has been supposed, the remains of a
Christian belfry.   But what words can describe the view that I
enjoyed from the top of it ?   To the north and to the south lay
before me the plain of Sharon, in all its luxuriance.   Who would
not recognise this celebrated plain, the beauty of which Isaiah lauds
(xxxv. 2.), together with the magnificence of Lebanon ; one of
whose roses the beloved of Solomon states herself to be : " Comely
as the tents of Kedar, as the curtains of Solomon ? " (Song of
Solomon, i. 5.)

The crops now lay piled up in many fields ; other fruits still
stood joyfully upon their stems ; the meadows were green and flowery.
But I sought in vain for a rosebud of Sharon ; these must doubtlessly have faded before the heat of July.   Nevertheless, I saw mentally
a rosebud at this instant : it was as dear to me as was to Solomon his
celebrated rose of Sharon.   It was she on whom I thought as I
gazed far westward towards the silvery flood of the Mediterranean, and
whither I wafted an ardent greeting for my distant home.   Opposite
the sea, to the east of us, the view was limited by the rugged mountains of Judea ; but at their feet, nearer to us, there lay around upon
the hills forming a vast amphitheatre stately villages, which looked
cheerful with their olive-groves and minarets.   Above all the rest, my
eyes were fettered by the Diospolis of the Romans, the Lydda of the
Bible, where St. Peter cured the palsied Eneas.   (Acts, ix. 34.)   It
lay apparently nearer than it really was : it was the ancient city of
the Benjamites, which, during the Christian era, has become most
celebrated through St. George.   St. George is said to have originated
from Lydda ; and therefore, at a very early period, a costly tomb

* Robinson states it to be a hundred and twenty feet.

and a splendid church were erected to him, of which even at the present day many beautiful fragments are to be seen.

Towards evening, as we advanced some distance further towards the wished-for goal, Lydda looked long kindly towards us from its hill. That I dreamt of Jerusalem when I fell asleep this Sunday, need not be stated.

ARRIVAL AT JERUSALEM.

The morning of the eighth of July dawned. I lay encamped with my camels and Arabs beneath a leafy olive grove, in the valley Ajalon. My Arabs delighted in it on account of its fresh spring-water. I transferred myself to the time of Joshua, who has associated with this landscape the memory of his glorious achievements. Who remembers not his words, "Sun, stand thou still upon Gibeon; and thou, moon, in the valley of Ajalon?" (Joshua, x. 12.) Latrun which is indebted for its Arabic name to the old monkish description as *domus boni latronis* — as the home of the malefactor pardoned upon the cross (Luke, xxiii. 43) lies to the south-west of the hill. Still further to the west, the ruins of a castle look down from the round summit of the height upon Latrun. No finer situation could have been selected for a watch-tower. If it belonged to the ancient Emmaus (not that of the New Testament), the subsequent Nikopolis, it may possibly have been very serviceable to the Maccabees.

We now ascended the mountain chain of Judea: for some distance it was picturesque enough. There was no want of forest trees or of tall shrubs. The character of this district greatly resembles that of the Oden forest; broad round hills lay beside and around each other; but it speedily became more barren, more rocky, and more precipitous. After a fatiguing ride of several hours, we stopped at a considerable ruin near a precipice of the mountain; I should think once a church of the Templars. I visited its interior, where stood many thick pillars, and some paintings were also still visible. It lies close to the stately Kuryet el Enab (city of wine), which is built of stone, and which some consider with Robinson to have been the ancient celebrated Kirjath Jearim (city of the forests), which in Samuel's time received the ark from the predatory hands of the Philistines. (1. Sam. vi. 21.) Upon our right we saw Saba, throned upon a beautiful mountain summit, which, according to Robinson, is identical with Samuel's birthplace, Rama; and the Arimathea of the New Testament. For some distance we continued to enjoy this exciting prospect.

We now descended so precipitously from one of the highest summits that we were compelled to dismount. We reached a fruitful narrow valley. Upon our left lay several groups of buildings, and also one of prominent eminence : this was Kulonieh. At a few paces in front of me a roe bounded over a vineyard. Upon our road there lay by the side of a fountain, which flowed out of an ancient ornamented stone enclosure, a Turkish horse at the point of death. The poor animal's mane and tail were cut off, and the blood flowing from its mouth in profusion. Our camels were compelled to pass over it. Thus cruelly could Turks only, certainly not Arabs or Bedouins, leave it to die. Unconsciously the idea occurred to me that this dying steed, convulsively heaving itself up, but always falling languidly back again, was an image of the present condition of the Turkish empire.

After having passed over a stone bridge, which was arched across a rushing stream, with a garden on our right richly glowing with figs, olives, and other trees, another very precipitous and rocky elevation lay before us. Our camels were quite exhausted on reaching the summit : the sun burnt hotly ; it was near noon. How my heart throbbed ! — soon shall I see the city of God with its sacred habitations !

It is true that around us was no land flowing with milk and honey. The land about us much resembled Malta, where the naked rock often peers through the thin soil. I asked myself, did these masses of stone always lie so naked here ? They looked as if washed smooth by torrents of rain ; and certainly they had here and there been formerly clothed with a much richer verdure. We may have proceeded for a couple of hours beyond the bridge in the valley of Kulonieh, when we beheld in the east the bold sandy red mountain chain of Jordan, the Pisgah of Scripture. (Deut. iii. 27.) Upon our right we recognised amidst green foliage, in a verdant landscape, the monastery of the Holy Cross : now the Mount of Olives raised its olive-crowned head, together with its sacred buildings, above us : to the north of it, tolerably high, stood a mosque upon the site of the ancient Siloah. A few paces further, and we beheld walls, towers, and cupolas — there lay Jerusalem ! What more memorable moment have I felt in my existence ! I exclaimed from the depth of my heart, in the words of the inspired David ; " I was glad to go into the house of the Lord, that my feet shall stand within thy gates, oh, Jerusalem !" (Psalm cxxii. 1, 2.) But what is the impression, I shall be asked, made by Jerusalem itself, when viewed merely as any other city ? Who could satisfactorily answer this question ? Should we ask a child, who casts himself into the arms of his mother, whom he has never seen, but yet loved, from his earliest infancy, " How does thy mother please thee ?" Pilgrims from all climates acknowledge now, as for centuries, that a profound and mysterious trace of sorrow hangs over the holy city with inexpressible sadness, and fills both heart and eye. The many cupolas surmounting the flat roofs give Jerusalem a peculiar effect. Its grey stone-colour reminds me of Italian cities, and especially of Avignon. Its lofty walls, which on several sides bound the horizon, made an impression upon me similar to that made by the monastery of St. Catherine at Sinai, just as if the fortress at the foot of the mountain of Moses were a Jerusalem in miniature.

The Pilgrim or Jaffa Gate faced us ; upon its left it has, like a true and faithful guard, the ancient strong castle of the city, from whose background peers forth a group of cheerful green trees from the garden of the Armenian monastery. On the right of it the very first glance surprises us with a view of the high cupolas of the church of the Holy Sepulchre. Both on the right and left are tombs. Thus the Holy City receives us with the true symbol of its character. On the left are the graves of the martyrs of the crescent, and soon afterwards on the right is seen, in the valley Gihon, a Turkish cemetery surrounding a square reservoir.

Close to the Gate of Pilgrims we had to deliver our certificate of health from the quarantine of Gaza, and at the gate itself we dis- mounted. Mid-day was just past. We were urgently invited to become guests in an Italian hotel, quite recently established ; but I preferred making the Casa Nova of the Latin monastery my domicile whither we went through a long, narrow, but clean street, to the left of the gate. I was soon welcomed in the most hospitable manner : a large light chamber on the first floor was appropriated to me, and my dragoman with the baggage was deposited in another on the ground floor.

JERUSALEM.

Where shall I commence, and where terminate, a description of Jerusalem ? What tale do these stones, these mountains, these valleys, tell ? If Rome be called "the eternal city," what shall we call Jeru- salem ? It seems as if man had sprung from Jerusalem. The features of a loving, sacred home speak there to the heart of every one.

Abraham beheld it. Melchisedek, the king of Salem, blessed the patriarch on his return from his heroic deeds. What Joshua's army could not effect, although it entered victoriously, nor Jebus, by the expulsion of the Jebusites, could make it again, Salem, the city of peace, that did David accomplish. "From Zion bursts forth the splendour of God:" thus durst his soul chant; and far away from the holy mountain resounded the hymn. Solomon's splendid temple completed David's song of praise; and henceforward, to all times, Jerusalem became the centre of both the religious and political energy of the people of Israel.

Unhappily, it speedily passed to mourning and to sorrow: the swords and chariots of the enemy overpowered the daughter of Zion, and laid her in ruins. But, like eternally green palms in the midst of the naked desert, thus stood the prophets, with their effective religious zeal, over the ruins: "Awake, awake; put on thy strength, O Zion; put on thy beautiful garments, O Jerusalem, the holy city." (Isaiah, lii. 1.) And after many conflicts, labours, devastations, there arose, under the captives returned from Babylon, a new city, — a new temple. Zerubbabel, Ezra, Nehemiah, these were the names of the noble triumvirate from whose zeal the new creation emanated. True, the ancient splendour never was restored. Foreign domination maintained a firm footing: robbery, plunder, disgrace, and oppression were its result. Alexander the Great, too, trampled with his iron foot over the sacred soil. The short period of freedom obtained by the valiant arm of the Maccabees was but a beautiful garland unfolded in the storm, and in that storm reclosed. Pompey planted the Roman eagle over the conquered city; Crassus seized with avidity the treasure of the sanctuary; and Herod the Great alone clothed once more the favourite daughter of the East in a regal robe. Thus, in due season, was she decorated like a bride; for that was as it were a last great festival for Jerusalem. No, that was not its last; but it was its greatest. The Light came.

Alas! in vain the Temple re-echoed with the eternal words of life; from the Mount of Olives resounded the farewell of the despised Saviour to the lost ones: — "O Jerusalem, Jerusalem, thou that killest the prophets, and stonest them which are sent unto thee, how often would I have gathered thy children together, even as a hen gathereth her chickens under her wings, and ye would not! Behold, your house is left unto you desolate." (Matt. xxiii. 37, 38.) And it was left desolate. Titus's arm stretched itself as it were in judgment over the gates of the city. Out of one single gate the foreign victors bore, during the fatal summer of the year 71, one hundred and fifty thousand eight hundred and eighty dead. As if in bitter sarcasm of the seller of the Son of God for thirty pieces of silver, about a hundred thousand prisoners were offered at the the the rate of thirty for the denarius. Smoking piles remained the sole melancholy memorial of a million corpses.

But the redemption of the nations of the earth issued from Zion. Although the city lay in ruins, still shone the eternal star in unfading beauty over the pile. Ælius Hadrianus in vain built his Ælia over it, and vainly did he fill it with the temples of idols; Jerusalem stood graven within the hearts of the Christian nations of the universe.

Under the pious Helena and the energetic Constantine, Christ celebrated, with the wreath of thorns around his brow and the triumphal crown upon his head, his second entry into Jerusalem.

But, as a type of the Church Militant upon earth, she, the mediator of peace, was not herself destined to find peace beneath the sun. False prophets marched in upon her like sanguinary conquerors; the crescent expelled the cross, although neither Israel nor the Church, despite of all the ferocity of the barbarians, have ever wholly fled from the precincts of Jerusalem.

But what the East, its fatherland, denied to Christianity, that did it obtain ten centuries later from the north, when the whole of Europe prayed in the name of the Sufferer upon the cross. Then suddenly the flame of enthusiasm spread throughout the countries of the North; faith dwelt deeply within the heart; the fire of youth glowed within the veins; chivalry, with its valour and its energy, burst from its native castles, with the cross upon its breast. For the sake only of Jerusalem; Jerusalem, the everlastingly old, the everlastingly new! And Jerusalem once more saw the cross victorious upon its mountains; the great and holy deeds of antiquity sprang forth again vigorously and splendidly as the cedars of Lebanon.

But, alas! the brief dawn was speedily swallowed up by a long night. Saladin's conquest was more durable than that of the noble Godfrey; and since the end of the thirteenth century Islamism has held firm possession of the city of David.

But it still stands holy there, like no other structure of man's hands. For even the Mahometans call her El Kuds, *the holy one;* the Christians of the north and of the south have there their sanctuaries, and monasteries, and chapelries; the bereft children of Israel incessantly convey thither their lamentations, their sorrows, and their tears. Who may compute the tears that have been shed upon the hills of this city in the course of three thousand years? Who can measure the blood that has flowed over the stones of this city? There she stands like a sublime and solemn fate, the prosopopœia of the day of judgment. " Though the earth be removed," as once the inspired minstrel chanted, " though the mountains be carried into the midst of the sea. There is a river, the streams whereof shall make glad the city of God, the holy place of the tabernacles of the Most High! " (Psalm xlvi. 2.) And she has remained, in spite of all that has sunk and fallen, even though the thick cloud of mourning envelope her joy.

If, pursuing my slight indications, we run over the train of events that have happened to Jerusalem, it is difficult to comprehend how we should, in the present day, identify the localities to which these great reminiscences are linked.   The prophecy has here almost found its absolute fulfilment : " There shall not be left here one stone upon another that shall not be thrown down." — (Matthew, xxiv. 2.)   Without being in the least sceptical, we may anticipatively doubt much which the pious happy pilgrim is infatuated to believe he has seen, even in the present day.   Nevertheless the peculiarity of the situation of Jerusalem is of that kind that many characteristics are indelibly preserved ; although even many others of her holy places have received their present names from the most groundless causes.   I expect, therefore, to excite nothing less than suspicion of wantonness if I, without hesitation, declare myself opposed to the admission of the identity of many of the supposed sacred places.

Jerusalem, like Rome, lies upon hills, or as we may most simply state, it is supported by two hilly eminences, one in the east and the other in the west, but both are united by a deep valley, which, with them, takes a course from north to south.   Zion, in the west, extends far towards the south ; that which I call its northern half— it is indeed a separated half—it has been customary to call by the name of Akra.   Opposite Zion, in the east, lies Moriah, the hill of the Temple and which extends to the south by its promontory Ophla, and to the north Bezetha, or, as it doubtlessly is more correctly called, Akra. The position of Jerusalem at present is, without doubt, upon the whole, the same as that which it occupied eighteen hundred years ago, and still earlier, only that Zion's most southern part is now occupied with the castle of David, and a few other buildings outside the walls, whereas in the days of David, as well as in those of Christ, it bore the chief buildings of the city ; and to the north a wide district lies now waste and empty, which was enclosed by a wall that had been built during the first twenty years after Christ.

Jerusalem presents its most unchangeable features towards the east : there Moriah falls almost precipitously into the valley of Jehoshaphat with the brook Kidron, whilst opposite to it the Mount of Olives rises towering above the city and the vicinity.   Equally unchanged must the features to the south and west have also remained.   In the south there rises, as a neighbour to the Mount of Olives, the " Mountain of Corruption," thus called from Solomon having built temples to the heathen deities. (2 Kings, xxiii. 13.)   At its foot lies, exactly opposite Ophla, which, strictly speaking, forms but one whole with Moriah, the very ancient village of Siloam, close beneath which the valley of Jehoshaphat becomes narrowest, where, close to the celebrated well Rogel, the valley Hinnom adjoins the valley Jehoshaphat at a sharp angle. The whole southern portion of Jerusalem, namely, Mount Zion, descends into the valley of Hinnom. This, also, in conjunction with the commencement of the valley of Gihon, forms in the west a necessary limitation to the city, which presents here in the Hippicus, which is now enclosed within the present fortress at the Jaffa Gate, a most important central point for the recognition of the lines which enclosed the city in the time of Christ and antecedently. It is only on the north that the ground has no fixed natural limits. To the north-west lies a precipitous hilly country, whereas the direct north forms a continuous elevated plain.

From all this it follows, that even at the present day we may obtain, without much trouble, a general impression of the position of ancient Jerusalem. It is seen most perfectly from the Mount of Olives. Who could ever have stood there without feeling the most profound emotion? There certainly our Lord often stood, and beheld the holy city at his feet. Just as the eastern wall bounded it to his view, even so is it distinctly bounded at the present day. There, where the Mosque of Omar stands beside El Aksa, upon the broad, bare area, there, doubtlessly, at that period towered the Temple in all its glory. Above all things, I called to mind during my wanderings upon the Mount of Olives, how the Lord as he approached from Jericho to make his entry into Jerusalem, "And when he was come near he beheld the city, and wept over it " (Luke, xix. 31), and how his disciples there questioned him as to the woful hour of the future. Naturally this consecrated spot could not escape tradition : a projecting rock was considered to be the place, and a chapel was built thereon, of which but few traces now remain. But that the identical spot where our Saviour sat during his fearful prophecy (Matt. xxiv. 3) cannot be more precisely defined, leaves the tradition in its naked simplicity.

The Mount of Olives offers another splendid position. It is upon the side where its level summit inclines to the east, and whence the view of the city is intercepted by some buildings.* In front is the sandy-coloured Pisgah, solemn and rugged ; and hence it was — for mount Nebo belongs to the chain of Pisgah — that Moses looked down upon the Promised Land. (Deut. xxxiv. 1.) Beneath that range the Dead Sea spreads its waters like a polished steel plate, and around it the desert glares in its nakedness. To the north-east the course of the Jordan may be traced by the verdure and the trees which line its banks. I also thought I could distinguish some ruins which my guide told me were Jericho. To the south-east lies Bethany ;

---

* I must, however, mention that the summit of the minaret, beside the mosque, commands a view both east and west of Jerusalem as well as the Dead Sea.

nearer to me I observed remains of buildings which I was told was
Bethphage.   How joyfully may not our Lord have lingered with
his disciples in this neighbourhood amid these splendid views !   I
here enjoyed hours never to be forgotten.   The Dead Sea lies like an
immortal forget-me-not, like a dark leaf from the book of fate.   The
pilgrim has beheld it for thousands of years, and to the imagination
of the beholder the tinned roofs of the sunken cities still glitter.
But the dead ascend not from the cold bosom of the sea, and the
doubts of the eternally blind are lost in the cheerless sand of the
desert.   To the north the Dead Sea receives the Jordan ;   close to its
influx St. John baptized;   and here also he hurled his fearful
thunders against the hearts of the hardened Pharisees.   The Saviour
also baptized he here, and yearly troops of pious pilgrims stream
hither to celebrate the remembrance.   But in vain did the voice of
Heaven strike the ears of the unbelievers, and thus the Word of
salvation became the trumpet of judgment.

In returning to the city, the road leads past Gethsemane ; it lies
at the foot of the Mount of Olives, enclosed by low but easily surmounted walls, by the side of which, on the west the brook Kidron
runs.   Eight olives stand within the circuit: great age has hollowed
their stems, and they are propped by stones to support them against
the tempest.   The foreign pilgrim eagerly enriches himself with
a few leaves and a twig from Gethsemane ; but both Catholic and
Greek sedulously protect these venerable trees : although no prominent indication stamps this spot as the authentic Gethsemane, yet
all that we know from the Gospels harmonises completely with the
locality.   Going to the Mount of Olives with his disciples, "Then
cometh Jesus with them unto a place called Gethsemane," says St.
Matthew.   And St. John says, " Jesus went forth with his disciples
over the brook Kidron, where was a garden, into which he entered
with his disciples." (Matthew, xxvi. 36; John, xviii. 1.)   It is remarkable enough that the above-mentioned eight olive trees may be proved
to have stood there at the time of the conquest of Jerusalem by the
Turks ; but still, their existence cannot be traced up to the period of
Christ; for Josephus tells us that Titus upon investing Jerusalem
cut down all the trees encircling the city to a distance of a hundred
stadia.   Yet the certain knowledge of the locality of Gethsemane
admitted the more easily of being preserved in as much as it could
not come readily within the scope of positive destruction.

It is difficult to connect, certainly, the present Gethsemane with the
so-called Cœnaculum, the chamber where the feast of the passover was
held ; but for the genuineness of the identity of the Cœnaculum itself,
there cannot be adduced the least probability, although even before
the period of Constantine according to St. Cyril's testimony, it may have

been held in this veneration. True, indeed, at certain periods it might probably have been found judicious to have placed this apartment exactly over the tomb of David, full of a melancholy desolation, and the scene of an act which it was endeavoured to clothe with the dread ideas of a sacrifice.

The garden of Gethsemane is reached even now, shortly after passing over the bridge of Kidron: upon turning to the right, other similar gardens adjoin the wall enclosing it on the side towards the Mountain of Corruption, whilst to the left of the bridge stands the church of the Virgin Mary, hewn in the solid rock, and mainly subterranean, which encloses Mary's grave, with memorials of her parents, Anna and Joachim, as well as of Joseph. Close by I was introduced by torch-light into the background of a rocky cave, the spot where Christ is said to have endured the bloody agony. (Luke, xxii. 44.) Any other spot of the Mount of Olives appeared to me preferable as the scene of that solemn hour; for, according to the narrative of the Evangelist, how can it have been a cavern?

I returned by the bridge of Kidron to the city along the bald and steep hill: on the left are Turkish graves — there, where Turkish women are so fond of kneeling and sitting, not merely to weep and pray, but also to have a friendly gossip. After having passed through St. Stephen's Gate into the city, immediately on the left lies the so-called Pool of Bethesda; a large, deep, oblong rounded basin (according to Robinson's admeasurement, three hundred and sixty feet long, a hundred and thirty broad, and seventy-five deep): to the north and to the west it is enclosed by houses; to the south it adjoins the walls of the Temple area; and to the east it lies close to the city walls. Within it there is heaped up much rubbish, especially upon its northern half, and upon this grow tall wild pomegranates. Robinson's reasons for denying the identity of this place with the Biblical Bethesda are very weighty, and are rendered the more so, as a few hundred years ago a different pool passed for the Scriptural one. Robinson considers it to be a portion of the deep moat of the fortress of Antonia.

Much probability, however, attaches to the supposition that the Bethesda of the Bible must absolutely have stood somewhere in the vicinity of the St. Stephen's Gate; possibly where Felix Fabri, and still earlier travellers saw it; namely, near the church of St. Anna. What so distinctly marks this vicinity as the locality of the pool Bethesda, is the following consideration. The Sheep Gate, near which the pool lay, must, just as well as St. Stephen's Gate, have stood near the temple; for it was the priests who built it under Nehemiah, and it was close by that the people of Jericho built, who certainly would have built only on the road which led to Jericho. (Nehem. iii. 1, 2.)

But how easily might the unsuspicious investigator be led to put faith in the present Bethesda! for not only near the southern wall which adjoins the Temple area are small round triturated stones found, which necessarily lead to the conclusion that water must have flowed here, but also in the west, or rather the south-west, two open arches are even seen, which seem to indicate the remains of the five porches of the Scriptural Bethesda. (St. John v. 2.) But neither is water an unwonted apparition in the moat of a fortress, nor is it unusual to see vaulted arches supporting the structures raised over them.

With respect to the miraculous peculiarities of the pool of Bethesda, Robinson has recently endeavoured to bring into connection with it the remarkable irregularity of the streaming of the water in the fountain of the Virgin in the valley of Jehoshaphat. The observation is by no means new, although it has often been neglected to be noticed that the water of that fountain, which is also communicated by a subterranean channel to the pool of Siloam, springs forth suddenly sometimes in an unusual manner, and visibly rises. Robinson therefore asks, " May not this fountain of the Virgin be Bethesda, as the Sheep Gate does not appear to have been far from the Temple, and the wall of the ancient city ran probably along this valley?" But may not also this supposition be divested of its significance, in as far as the ancient wall could scarcely have followed the direction indicated by Robinson? Thus a connection appears to me to be discoverable between the scriptural Bethesda and this intermitting spring: and the more so, as from the latter the fountain beneath the great mosque is said to receive its supply, and by this means a communication, sufficiently near, is opened to the most probable locality of Bethesda, a little to the north of the gate of St. Stephen.

But I reserve all further description of Jerusalem, and hasten up the *Via Dolorosa*, that I may spend a few moments within the church of the Holy Sepulchre.

I enter it from the south, where are the two chief portals leading, at the side, into the church. The main façade of the church lies from west to east; so that at the most western extremity, beneath a large cupola, stands the rotunda of the holy sepulchre: thence, towards the east, in the centre of the building, stands the large oblong church of the Greeks, also surmounted by a cupola; and at the most eastern extremity, in a quadrangle, is the chapel of Helena, as well as the spot where the cross was found. On entering, we stand in a long court, immediately to the right of which lies Golgotha. Eighteen steps lead up: in the background, towards the east, is the site of the cross of Christ; beneath which, most remarkably, and with foolish zeal, the grave of Adam, and the place where Abraham meditated the sacrifice of his son, are both shown and revered. To the left of the entrance, stepping towards the west, we enter the rotunda of the holy sepulchre, the ground form of which is that of an ancient Jewish grave; and thence, out of an ante-room, a low door leads into the true sepulchre. Immediately over the entrance to the chapel of the sepulchre hangs a picture of the Resurrection, surmounted by an Austrian two-headed eagle, which stands here, certainly not agreeably to every body's taste. In the interior of the chapel of the sepulchre a split tablet of white marble lies over the cavity intended for the grave. Beside it stands an altar with many lamps continually burning. All is here covered with marble, and otherwise much decorated. Beyond the holy sepulchre two graves are shown as those of Nicodemus and of Joseph of Arimathea, which may, perhaps, be very justly considered as ancient Jewish rocky sepulchres. In the gallery which, to the north, surrounds the splendid church of the Greeks, we meet with places containing relics referring to the facts connected with the sufferings and death of our Saviour; as, for instance, a piece of the pile to which Christ was fixed when scourged, — the place where lots were cast for the sacred vestment. From this gallery we descended twenty-eight steps, to the east, to the chapel of Helena, whence, by thirteen steps more, we still further descended to where the cross was discovered.

There is much that disturbs us in viewing these sacred places. Independent of the Turkish guards, who lie with their pipes and coffee in the ante-court, near the two portals,—independent of the evidently rival tribute-seeking of the Greeks, the Latins, the Armenians, the Copts, which is much to be complained of,—even the harmony is disturbed by the various splendour of the chapels of the churches, and of all the venerated spots, precisely where we should recognise the melancholy Golgotha and the sepulchre in the garden. The identity of these places with those renowned in Scripture is, on many points, subject to doubt, and this I shall below refer to closer investigation. Nevertheless, the heart of the pilgrim beats in these consecrated places with a fervour, an emotion, and a terror, perfectly unutterable. The prayer which here ascends to the lips is like no other prayer. For what, notwithstanding all prevailing doubts, makes the present Church of the Sepulchre an uninfringible and beloved sanctuary, is the veneration it has enjoyed, and still enjoys, from the pilgrims of the Christian nations of the earth since the time of Constantine and Helena, and the all-sacrificing love with which the Christians of Jerusalem have firmly clung to this spot through all the persecutions and oppressions of the Mahometans, as well as the remembrance of the profound sorrow and piety which it has aroused and witnessed in the course of nearly two thousand years.

THE HOLY SEPULCHRE FROM LOCAL INSPECTION AND FROM TRADITION.

Is the Holy Sepulchre genuine, or is it not ? This is certainly an important question. The question may more distinctly run thus — Did Golgotha and the grave of the Redeemer lie where pious faith conceives them to have lain ? that is to say, within the area of the church the description of which I have just attempted ?

This question is not a recent one. It was one which necessarily suggested itself to pilgrims who critically compared the text of the Scriptures on the close of the history of our Lord with what presented itself to them at Jerusalem. The sacred text repeatedly tells us that the Lord was crucified and buried outside the city, but yet closely to it ; whereas, on the contrary, the venerated Church of the Sepulchre is now enclosed by the city walls.

Such doubts as were not strengthened by either an accurate knowledge of the ancient records, or a profound study of the localities themselves, were readily removed by the general adoption of the assertion that the present city has possibly considerably exceeded the limits of the former ; and tradition supported it like an irremovable bulwark.

Jonas Korte, the bookseller of Altona, during the first thirty years of the preceding century was the first who entertained serious doubts as to the propriety of recognising the locality now celebrated as the original site. Since his time this doubt has obtained prevalence among learned inquirers, Catholic as well as Protestant, although recently, among others, Chateaubriand, Prokesch, and Schubert have revived and restored the traditional opinion, prompted, certainly, by no other cause than to favour an opinion which has endured more than a thousand years.

The learned Professor Robinson of New York has recently taken the field in opposition to this opinion, with really a very heavy artillery of reasons and proofs. I myself, indeed, returned home impressed with convictions similar to Robinson's, deduced from my own examination of the tradition as well as of the locality. But the conclusions arrived at within the last few months relative to ancient Jerusalem, by two gentlemen competent beyond all others to the undertaking, have thrown a new light upon my reminiscences, and, so, biassed my judgment. These gentlemen are, Mr. Williams, for fourteen months chaplain under Bishop Alexander, and Dr. Schultz, who has been for more than two years Prussian consul at Jerusalem. The results of their inquiries, as is self-evident, are some of the

fruits, if, indeed, they are not the richest fruits of the establishment of the evangelical bishopric in the Holy City.

I will first treat of the chief proof entertained by the learned
against the admission of the present Sepulchre being the original one.
It is founded upon the supposed impossibility of conceiving the present Church of the Holy Sepulchre to have been outside the ancient
wall in the time of Christ. This ancient wall requires a more definite determination. Jerusalem possessed, according to the precise
information of the Jewish historian, Josephus, in the first century,
at the time of its destruction by Titus, about forty years after Christ's
death, three city walls, the first of which was of the most remote
antiquity, the second could be referred back as standing in the seventh
century before Christ, in the reign of king Hezekiah, and the third
was built ten years after the death of Christ, by Herod Agrippa.

That which concerns us here is the second, the outermost wall, in
the time of Christ, which enclosed the city only to the north and
north-west, just where Golgotha is assumed to have stood. It may
be asked, did the present Golgotha lie beyond this wall?

The answer given by Robinson and others is in the negative.
This wall, according to him, must necessarily have enclosed the rocky
hill of Golgotha. Why? "This wall sprung forth near the Hippicus, the ancient tower in the first wall to the north of Zion, to the
west of the temple and the adjacent Castle of Antonia, and ran in a
circular or curve direction to the north-east of the Castle of Antonia."

The latter, the circular or curve direction in reference to the Castle
of Antonia, is unimpeachable, for Josephus states it expressly. If,
also, the former concur, it would have been absolutely impossible for
Golgotha, from its proximate north-easterly position, with regard
to the Hippicus, to have stood beyond the walls. Besides, which also
considerably strengthens the proof, the position of the pool of
Hezekiah must have been such with respect to the Hippicus and
Golgotha, that both must have been within or both without the
wall. But this pool, which Hezekiah constructed for the purpose
of withdrawing the water from the use of the enemy besieging the
city, into the use of the besieged city, consequently cannot reason-
ably be considered as lying without the walls.

The latter I will first dispose of, namely, the proof supplied by the
pool of Hezekiah. This name has an authority very different from
that of an aboriginal, or even of only an ancient, tradition; for the
Italian monk Quaresmius, in the 17th century, was the first who
maintained that the pool, usually called by the name of the Holy
Sepulchre, was, possibly, the work of Hezekiah. It is still called by
the inhabitants, that is by the Christians, no otherwise than the pool
of the Holy Sepulchre, or as the Mahometan natives call it exclu-

sively the bath pool, because a public bagnio in the vicinity is supplied by it.   Hence, this pool gives no weight to our inquiry; for,
probably, it dates no further back than subsequent to the Christian era.

I must leave uninvestigated here, whether the true pool of Hezekiah be, in fact, as is assumed by Williams, identical with the pool
of Siloam, called also the King's Pool: I will merely mention that
this view is not at all affected by what the prophet Isaiah says
(chap. xxii. 11.) of the position of the pool of Hezekiah as lying
between the two walls, if we admit Williams's plan of the course
of the ancient southern wall.

It may be further asked, is it the case that the second wall commenced near the Hippicus?   Josephus informs us that the first
wall commenced at the Hippicus.   He further tells us that the third
wall commenced at the Hippicus.   With respect to the second he
says, without any mention being made of the Hippicus, that it commenced at the gate Gennath, or garden gate.

This already sounds unfavourably: it would be still more unfavourable could the assumed pool of Hezekiah maintain its authority;
for in that case the wall must, in fact, have commenced in the immediate vicinity of the Hippicus, so closely that it would scarcely be
observed that it did not originate at the Hippicus itself, or, as Josephus has supposed, at least in its immediate vicinity.   But the
error in the assumed commencement of the wall does not require, to
contradict it, an error in the locality of the pool of Hezekiah; for
the most recent investigations have traced, almost incontestably, the
entire course of this wall, both from the traces still remaining of it and
the gates remaining in it.   The garden gate thence appears to have
been situated tolerably distant from the Hippicus, and from the
latter the wall ran in almost a direct line to the Damascus gate, the
situation of which in the wall is distinctly shown without the least
doubt, by the remains still extant.   Golgotha thus remains unen-
closed at the western side of the wall.   No objection can be raised
against the assumed course in a direct line, for the circular bending
mentioned by Josephus is produced by the further extension of the
wall.

This, therefore, is the result emanating from the most recent exploration.   In confirmation of which, we may add what we know
of the two towers adjoining the Hippicus — the towers of Phasaelus and Mariamne, — from the unambiguous testimony of
Josephus.   The two bulwarks, the splendour and strength of which
the Jewish historian describes with exclamations of admiration, were
built by Herod the Great in honour of his brother Phasael and of
his consort Mariamne, in the original ancient wall, and in a line
with the Hippicus.   They stood upon the upper northern peak of

mount Zion, whereby its natural height was rendered still more imposing.

On the one side it is not admissible that Herod should have built these incomparable fortresses in that portion of the ancient wall where they would have been enclosed by the second wall, thereby losing the whole of their military importance at a period when their protection was so much needed. On the other side, it is evident from the description of Josephus, that where the three towers stood, the original northern wall passed over such high ground that its immediate vicinity to Golgotha distinctly could not offer any sufficient elevation which, from military requisitions, should necessarily have been crossed by the second wall.

I might also mention that the spot which Josephus indicates as having been the point whence the second wall started, together with the total omission of any mention of two such posts of strength as Phasaelus and Mariamne corresponding entirely with the Hippicus, seems to prove that this starting-point was beyond them, and consequently to the eastward of both. Just there, where the newly discovered ruins indicate it, may the gate Gennath have stood as the solitary keep.

The name also of the gate Gennath is worthy of note. "Garden Gate" it might have been consistently called, from the royal garden, which was contiguous to it. And the locality also admirably harmonises herewith; for I still saw gardens in the vicinity, for instance, within the former court of the dilapidated hospital of St. John, close to the Church of the Holy Sepulchre.

An objection might be started derived from the signification or purposes of Golgotha. How could the Place of Skulls lie close to the royal gardens? But I am distinctly opposed to the opinion which holds the Place of Skulls as the ordinary place of execution, promulgated even by Cyril, bishop of Jerusalem, in the 4th century. The Greek word used as the equivalent of the Hebrew Golgotha, does not indicate a place where skulls fall or lie; literally translated, it means "place of the skull;" or, as it stands in St. Luke, xxiii. 33., " of skulls." Thence the name appears to be derived from the form of the rocky hill; that is, from its resemblance to a skull. Nor is it very credible that the distinguished Joseph of Arimathea should have had his garden tomb in the vicinity of Golgotha, had that been the ordinary place of execution.* (Matt. xxvii. 60., John xix. 41.)

* In opposition to the explanation of Golgotha as the usual place of execution, I would give weight to the mode of expression used by St. Matthew (xxvii. 33.). He says, " And when they were come unto a place called Golgotha." (Εἰς τόπον, not εἰς τὸν τόπον.)
It should, I think, be called DEFINITELY the place Golgotha, if it might, as

But so much for the autoptical survey of the ground in proof that the present Golgotha in the time of Christ, in connection with the Holy Sepulchre, lay beyond the city walls, and that, therefore, it may consistently be the original locality.

I will only observe, in passing, that it concurs with the erroneous opposite opinion to assume that Akra, or the lower city, lay adjacent, northerly, to Mount Zion. This supposition of Robinson, and of many others, could only be rendered possible by not taking the text of the description of Josephus literally, and by not sufficiently elucidating it to themselves by its comparison with the existing localities. Akra could not lie to the north of Zion, as Robinson asserts; because, in the first place, Josephus says, since the filling up of an intervening valley under the Asmonians, it formed one whole with Moriah, the Mount of the Temple ; but to the present day Robinson's Akra is distinctly separated, and must ever have been so, from the Mount of the Temple, by the Valley of the Cheesemakers; secondly, because Josephus states, that Akra was separated from Zion, or the Upper City, by the Valley of the Cheesemakers ; but the Valley of the Cheesemakers runs, as is distinctly perceptible, from north to south, and has absolutely no arm which from the west, in justification of the expression of Josephus, separated Akra from Zion ; thirdly, because Josephus says, that both the Upper City and Lower City fell externally into deep valleys : now this would be positively incorrect with respect to the Lower City, had that lain where Robinson assumes.*

I dare not here forbear slightly illustrating the tradition linked to the Church of the Holy Sepulchre, and, indeed, its weak as well as its strong points; upon the solitary basis of this tradition have, as is well known, so many past ages firmly clung to the conviction of the identity of the Holy Sepulchre.

One thing is absolutely evident, that, since Constantine the Great, the spots then distinguished by costly monuments, as Golgotha and the Sepulchre, have unchangeably remained identical in the eyes of believers. By command of that emperor a splendid church, with a leaden roof, was raised over Golgotha ; it was decorated with superb

it were, be of itself understood that there, usually or always, criminals were executed, and therefore so was Christ. But the more definite expression with the article which is distinctly found in St. John, xix. 17., as well as in St. Luke, xxiii. 33. (in St. Mark, xv. 22. it is doubtful), is of much less importance than the indefinite in Matthew, xxvii. 33. ; for with the definite article the well-known hill called Golgotha alone is indicated, which by no means must necessarily have been known as the place of execution.

* I hope shortly elsewhere to devote a special essay to this entire subject, and I here take the liberty of apprising scholars of my intention.

marble walls, and greatly enriched with gold and ornaments. To the west of the church there was an open court, paved with flat stones, and surrounded with colonnades.

This probably was intended to indicate the garden which, as St. John relates (xix. 41.), contained the tomb of Joseph of Arimathea and lay close to Golgotha. This court terminated in a chapel upon the site of the Holy Sepulchre, supported by pillars and adorned with a variety of splendour. Whatever disasters might subsequently afflict the Christians of Jerusalem it was impossible, since the favour of the emperor had been extended to the holy places of the city of David, that Golgotha or the Holy Sepulchre could be forgotten, although those costly structures might be destroyed and others built from their ruins. If, then, the correct spot was discovered in the time of Constantine, we may not doubt its present identity supported by its chain of tradition.

But tradition deduces its origin from a still earlier period. In the first place, it is asserted that certainly, even in the first century, those two highly venerated places were especially revered by the apostles and the primitive Christians, and selected as their places of assembly; as also that from James, the first bishop of Jerusalem, unto the time of Hadrian, the builder of the Ælia Capitolina, there was an uninterrupted succession of Judaic Christian bishops, by whose means the tradition was preserved; and the circumstance is cited as a main proof that Hadrian, in derision of the Christians, erected a marble statue of Venus upon the site of the crucifixion, and one of Jupiter upon that of the sepulchre about the year 135. Hence naturally, to the epoch of Constantine, the tradition of the original locality was preserved by a safe, although a desecrating, characteristic.

What may be opposed to this argument?

That the primitive Christians clung with especial veneration to these two spots in Jerusalem, or that they even established places of assembly there, is by no means probable, as Christianity, particularly at its origin, in its very spirit and essence was wholly averse to such modes of publicity. Did it not concern the substitution of a new mode of worship upon the site of the Samaritan mountain and of the Temple of Jerusalem? Nor have we in any of the parts of the New Testament the slightest allusion to any prominent regard for, or veneration of those places, although the preaching of the crucifixion and resurrection of the Saviour presented such opportunities for mentioning them. How closely the primitive Christians adhered to the exhortation of our Saviour upon praying in the spirit, is still very strongly proved by the verbal text of the Evangelists and Epistles of the New Testament having undergone in the course of the three first centuries a large multitude of alterations now lying in many thousands of passages historically developed to us. And if it be wished to make valid the affection with which the apostles clung to the person of their Master, which, being so holy a love, it was impossible should be contradictory to the spirit of the religion, if they sedulously cultivated the remembrances of localities that had become dear to them : yet even this would far more have referred to those localities where the disciples had enjoyed the personal intercourse of our Saviour, as the Mount of Olives and other similar places, than to Golgotha and the grave.

With respect to the uninterrupted succession of bishops from James to the time of Hadrian, in support of it we have but the solitary testimony of Eusebius, who tells us, that, in the total deficiency of certain data, he can only acquaint us with what he had been informed.

Hadrian's idolatrous statues is a still more dangerous matter. It is Eusebius alone, two hundred years after Hadrian, who first relates that desecrating hands had erected a temple to Venus over the sepulchre of our Lord without once hinting at Hadrian. The story of Socrates and Sozomen is the same as that of Eusebius, the latter only adding that as the Christians prayed at the holy places they must have appeared to be pagan worshippers. St. Jerome, however, at the end of the 4th century, cites, instead of one, two heathen statues, that of Venus upon the Rock of the Cross, and that of Jupiter over the Sepulchre. It is difficult to say upon what authority St. Jerome refers this to Hadrian. And what, besides, is the import of what Eusebius and his continuers, as also St. Jerome, say? Nothing more than that the spot where, in the time of Constantine, the Cross was discovered, had the statue of an idol standing upon it, the period being uncertain when it was placed there. But that it was purposely erected over the true Sepulchre of Christ, may only have been stated from the discovery of the Cross indicating this spot as the site of the Sepulchre. To this may be added, that the way in which Eusebius narrates the discovery of the Cross appears to show that before this discovery the holy place was not known, and that divine inspiration, and no external characteristic, led to that discovery.

But, in opposition to these insinuations, it may not be denied that the first Christian community at Jerusalem, so shortly after the transactions upon Golgotha and in the neighbouring garden, must have been perfectly acquainted with these spots. Besides, in the narrative of the death and resurrection of Christ among the Christians of Jerusalem, it was almost impossible to avoid naming the places

themselves, just as neither of the Evangelists records these events
without characterising the localities concerned in them.   That St.
Paul never names them in his epistles may be explained, both from
the nature of his discourse and his own personal relation to the incarnate Christ.   How insipid would it have been for him, in his inspired promulgation of the crucified and raised Saviour, to have referred to the hill Golgotha, or to the Sepulchre in the Garden !   It is
different when St. Peter, in mentioning David, who had been dead
a thousand years, makes use of the expression, "and his sepulchre is
with us unto this day." (Acts, ii. 29.)   The epistles of the apostles
speak as little of Bethlehem and of Nazareth as they do of Golgotha.

But that it was customary at an early period to distinguish with
consideration these consecrated localities is proved by Justin Martyr,
about the middle of the 2nd century, who names in his celebrated dialogue, the cavern or grotto at Bethlehem as the place of
the birth of our Saviour, whilst Origenes, at the commencement of the
3rd century, mentions pilgrimages to the grotto of Bethlehem, and
says that even the heathens considered them as the birth-place of the
founder of our religion.   The conclusion is, however, certain.   If this
occurred to the birth-place at Bethlehem, how much more would
the place of the Crucifixion and the Sepulchre have been faithfully
noticed and often contemplated !

Thus, therefore, it would have been by no means difficult to preserve the precise knowledge of Golgotha.   Even if the first characte-
risation of it as a rocky hill or mountain ascends no earlier than the
year 333, in the Itinerary from Bordeaux to Jerusalem; its very name,
in our opinion, indicates such a peculiarity of situation as does not
admit of being separated from the idea of a hill; concurrent with
which it is a known fact, that the ancients selected prominent spots
as places of execution.   If, now, the knowledge of various localities
in and about Jerusalem have been so certainly preserved that any
doubt of it would be ridiculous, how could a hill, rendered remarkable by its form, and still more so by the crucifixion of Christ, and
which already bore its appropriate name, have been so far forgotten
during the early centuries as to have admitted of its being changed.

Our object heeds not our overlooking the succession of bishops, subject, as we have already shown, to doubt; it is incontrovertible that there
were many Christians in Jerusalem constantly there from the commencement, and that the violent destruction which resulted from the
capture of the city by Titus, could not have lessened the knowledge
of Golgotha among the Christians of Jerusalem.   And that such a
place, a rocky hill with a neighbouring garden, and both, besides,
beyond the first and second walls, should have been so defaced by

the Roman soldiery as to cause positive non-recognition, is contrary to all probability.

I now come to Hadrian's idols. St. Jerome may have erred when he spake of two ; for when he visited Jerusalem, Constantine's buildings were erected, whilst Eusebius saw the heathen monuments with his own eyes : the silence of Eusebius, also, with respect to Hadrian having placed there the statue of Venus, may be left without impeachment ; but it is absolutely decided, that the idol which from probable reasons may be referred back to the period of the construction of the Ælia Capitolina, by Hadrian, stood upon the site of the present Church of the Holy Sepulchre in the time of Constantine. That it really stood upon Golgotha, or, more precisely, over the Sepulchre, and had derision for its object, I believe ; because the Christians, down to the time of Hadrian, were doubtlessly acquainted with the true localities, and thenceforward, when the new community remained unremoved for ever after, from the Ælia Capitolina, would doubtlessly have fixed an eye full of faithful and unchangeable veneration upon it, had it not been thus disturbed. It is also an historical fact, that even towards the commencement of the 3rd century it was customary to assemble upon the graves of martyrs, to practise religious exercises. Besides, the year assumed as that in which the image of the idol was erected, concurs precisely with the time when, in consequence of the fanatical revolt of the Jews, under Barchochba, both Christians and Jews in Jerusalem were exposed to the severity, hatred, and malice, of their Roman lords.

The last assumption that has been considered valid, in opposition to the tradition, is the narrative of the discovery of the Cross. I think that the expressions of Eusebius, and the epistle of Constantine, require strict interpretation, and suffer no derogation from subsequent accounts, evidently capriciously concocted ; such, for instance, as Helena's investigations amongst the inhabitants.

Eusebius says that the emperor, " by divine inspiration, and prompted by the Saviour himself, wished to purify and adorn with monuments the spot where the resurrection of Christ took place, already exposed to entire oblivion and misapprehension." The image of Venus standing over the grave filled up with earth, sufficiently justifies, I think, the assertion of Eusebius that, " the holy spot was already exposed to entire oblivion and mistake." The inspiration and prompting from above is not proposed as the cause of the discovery of the lost treasure, but as stimulating the emperor to consecrate, by monuments of pious reverence, a spot so rudely desecrated.

And if Constantine, in his epistle to Macarius, considers " the discovery of the sign of the holy passion of the Saviour, which had been concealed so long beneath the earth," as a " miracle," " sublime beyond all human conception," he evidently means thereby the discovery of the Cross itself, to which his expression seems to refer, indicating a previous acquaintance with the locality of the original Sepulchre. But the discovery, also, of the so admirably preserved Sepulchre, as Eusebius describes it, notwithstanding the heaping up of rubbish, and the heathen superstructure, may be classed in the category of the wonderful.

Robinson says besides, that Eusebius is entirely silent with regard to the existence of a tradition relative to the Sepulchre. This can not be asserted justly; for when Eusebius informs us that an idol stood upon the sepulchre, has he occasion to define the tradition more distinctly or to pursue it further?

In addition to all that supports the disputed tradition we may advance the peculiarity of the situation of the Sepulchre, which is now venerated. It lies at but a short distance beyond that wall which, in the time of Christ, surrounded the city, but considerably within the present city wall which, at least in the vicinity of the Holy Sepulchre, was the city wall in the age of Constantine. But that Christ's tomb lay beyond the wall was surely known as well in the time of Constantine as now. With a view to deceive, or even in case of a free selection, would care not have been taken for the purpose of safely avoiding all possibility of suspicion on this point, to have fixed upon a sufficient distance from the city? On the other side we may candidly admit, that under Constantine, without doubt, much clearer traces must have existed than at present of the second, once external, wall; so that the position of the Church of the Holy Sepulchre likewise corroborates our previously adduced opinion of the course of this wall, even as it possesses in the latter a proof of its possible origin.

Lastly, it is proved by the tomb of the high priest, John, mentioned repeatedly by Josephus in his account of the siege of Jerusalem in the year 71, (which must absolutely have lain in the vicinity of the Church of the Holy Sepulchre,) that here precisely Joseph of Arimathea's garden tomb may very consistently have been situated.

The result of a serious investigation must be welcome, even should it oppose our prepossessions; for the truth, or what is most proximate to the truth, is the object of all research; but doubly welcome is the result which confirms the sympathies fervently dear to the heart. With such has my inquiry into the authenticity of the Holy Sepulchre furnished me. I think it will be in future difficult to dispute this authenticity upon reasonable grounds. And thus it is confirmed, as an edifying fact, that that grave which resembles no other on the earth—that grave which heralded the victory over all graves, in spite of the curse which prevailed over Israel's Holy City,—

in spite of the war-like scenes which it has witnessed, and of the desolations it has experienced,—has not been able to be removed, even to the present day, from the eye of the faithful.

In conclusion, I will add a couple of words upon the fate of the churches constructed over Golgotha and the Sepulchre.

The splendid structures of Constantine were destroyed by fire three hundred years after their erection, on the capture of Jerusalem by the Persians. It appears they were restored in a more humble style, and, what is remarkable, the rock with the Sepulchre was formed into a hut-like chapel. In the destruction of the year 1010, it is probable that this rocky hut was also destroyed. In imitation of this the Crusaders, when they erected their noble united structure over Golgotha and the Sepulchre, represented the original sepulchre in the chapel, which then received the special name of the Chapel of the Holy Sepulchre. Of this building, of the time of the Crusades, several walls and its predominant form have been preserved, although the fire which broke out in the year 1808, in the Armenian chapel, laid a great portion of the church in ashes.

That which merits in the present day in the Chapel of the Sepulchre an especial notice is the tombs — spaces which are found on the western declivity of the rock that vaults the Sepulchre, and which, in fact, appears to contain ancient Jewish tombs. They have been called the tombs of Joseph of Arimathea and of Nicodemus.

THE INHABITANTS OF JERUSALEM.

Jerusalem is said to lie in the centre of the earth ; a marble wreath in the centre of the pavement of the Church of the Holy Sepulchre indicates its precise position. This calculation is doubtlessly erroneous ; but that Jerusalem is to the nations of the earth's circumference the great maternal heart wherein beat the pulsations of their own hearts, the eye of the pilgrim distinctly feels. Christians of the east and of the west, as various in their confessions as in their languages, Mahometans, Jews, all dwell beneath the roofs of the Holy City. It is not worldly interests that have here drawn them together ; not the promptings of vanity, but the impulse to pray upon a spot sacred and holy above any other spot in the world. Believers in Mahometanism possess here their incomparable mosque elevated over the ruins of the temple of Solomon. All else is open to the inspection of the stranger. Omar's mosque alone is inviolably closed to him.

Christians congregate here beneath the cupolas raised over Golgotha and the Sepulchre of our Lord. What in comparison with this is the magnificence of St. Peter's or the splendour of St. Paul's? The children of Israel come hither from afar. What do they call their property among all the holy things of the city of David? A narrow corner alone remains to them of Jehovah's temple to kneel within and weep. Who could approach this place of lamentation on a Friday when women are never wanting with tears beneath their veils, without sympathising deeply with the fate of this people. It calls the patriarchs, with whom God discoursed, its ancestors ; in David and Solomon it possessed princes whose wisdom the world admires, and the voices of the prophets addressed them in sublime and imperishable language. It stood forth as the chosen people of God, a holy oasis in humanity nurturing in its heart the promise of the Messiah. Madly blinded towards the blessing, it clutched the curse. The Saviour came and bled upon Golgotha. His blood, as they exclaimed, be upon us and upon our children! They forgot that God will not be scoffed at. Since then they carry the curse upon their brow, as did Cain the fratricide. But, notwithstanding all the punishments and terrors which they have endured, they have remained imperishable : they still wander over the earth a living ruin to themselves, an incomprehensible obloquy to the world, a tablet with warnings inscribed by the pen of the Eternal.

Indulging in these reflections, I stood on that remarkable place close behind the Mosque el Aksa. Its general name is no other than that of the Jewish place of lamentation ; it is considered an especial privilege—I may well call it a melancholy privilege, but yet the Jews were not always so fortunate as to possess a similar place in their City of God. For the space of two hundred years after the revolt of Barchochba under Hadrian, until the time of Constantine, even the approach to the city was strictly prohibited. Under Constantine they were permitted to visit the neighbouring hills and thence to behold the city. Later, they were allowed once annually, and indeed upon the anniversary of the destruction by Titus, to visit the ruins of the Temple, and there to weep ; but, as St. Jerome relates, they were obliged to purchase the privilege of weeping from the guard of soldiers. They now occupy the whole north-eastern portion of Zion which is as clean as the Jewish quarters of European cities. The penurious and simple dress which they adopt, has especially for its object to avoid exciting the cupidity of their Turkish lords. Their place of lamentation and the melancholy worship there come down from an ancient period, for even in the middle ages mention is made of it.

I was taken by surprise upon the road from the Jewish quarter to the Jewish place of lamentation, for the perfect ideal of a Madonna stepped forth in front of me from the door of a squalid dwelling, and certainly the most beautiful Madonna I have ever beheld. The Jews of Palestine in general are considered as a race possessing the most agreeable features, but in Jerusalem itself, there are multitudes who come from distant lands, from Poland, Russia, Germany, and who have migrated hither, to die within the Holy City, and to find a grave above the valley of Jehoshaphat.

I must notice a remarkable contrast—whilst there is not a single family of Jews that can be traced to have dwelt for a thousand years, or even for five hundred years in Jerusalem, there are in Egypt Jewish families who have dwelt there in regular succession for a period of four thousand years,—namely, such as did not quit it with Moses. But Jerusalem at present numbers within its walls more Jews than Mahometans; the latter are computed at about five thousand souls, exclusive of the Turkish garrison of about a thousand; whereas there are above seven thousand Jews.

I have still to mention a melancholy adjunct to the Jewish quarter; namely, the dwellings of the lepers which lie contiguous to the Jewish caravansera for pilgrims upon Mount Zion. This sight is not to be forgotten. These poor wretches dwell in huts as squalid as themselves. Pregnant with misery they come into the world, and burthened with misery they quit it. In consequence of their intermarriages, and of their being stringently separated from the rest of the world, and associating exclusively among themselves, they perpetuate the poison of their disease. They now consist of about thirty individuals.

The Christian population of Jerusalem consists of two thousand Greeks, nine hundred Roman Catholics, three hundred and fifty Armenians, a hundred Copts, twenty Syrians, and as many Abyssinians. To these may be added from sixty to seventy Protestants, who, with the exception of the American missionaries, are all Europeans.*

A remarkable custom obtains with regard to real property at Jerusalem. Individual proprietors possess extremely little, and indeed always a very small share of an aggregate whole; every thing else, that is to say, almost every thing, is *wagf* (see above, page 20); viz., the property of mosques, churches, or monasteries, or of other religious institutions; such as, for instance, the Hospital of Helena. Amongst the Christians the greatest proprietors are the Greek

---

* I have followed Dr. Schultz in this census of the inhabitants of Jerusalem. In various respects the most recent calculations differ from it. Whilst Schultz gives a total of 15,510 souls, exclusive of the garrison, the Protestants, and the suite of the consul, Robinson gives 11,500; and Williams 10,920. Earlier accounts varied between 15,000 and 26,000.

6

monasteries. I was told that nearly a hundred houses in the city belong to them. It is this peculiarity in real property which contributes also to make Jerusalem a Holy City.

Unfortunately it would be a mistake to suppose that among the Christian churches at Jerusalem fraternal amity prevails; although the idea is so natural that Christian brethren, though separated by forms of belief, would precisely here, over the sepulchre of the Saviour, if anywhere, offer to each other the hand of conciliating affection. The conflicting strife which prevails amongst all, especially between the Greeks, Latins, and Armenians (for the poor Copts, as well as the few Syrians and Abyssinians, cannot be taken into consideration), presents an exceedingly melancholy spectacle. The scandal is increased by the Church of the Holy Sepulchre being usually made the scene of strife. Since the Crusades, for many centuries the Latins have maintained the upper hand, in as far as they possessed its largest portion as their property; by degrees they have been driven back by the Greeks to a very limited occupancy: other parts are possessed by the Armenians, whilst only one altar belongs to the Copts, and another to the Syrians. Contested claims make the great bodies hostile and embittered against each other: they even do not forbear to disturb and ridicule each other's religious ceremonies — a charge especially made against the Greeks by the Catholics. What in comparison with this desecration of the holy places was the traffic in doves and the money-changing formerly practised in the courts of the Temple (Matt. xxi. 12.), which excited the indignation of our Lord? Still I believe it is but rarely, and then only under the influence of considerable excitement, that these sad exhibitions occur. An instance of the selfishness of the Greeks I was a witness to, in their smearing the beautiful marble pillars and their ornamental capitals, even to rendering these undistinguishable, for the purpose of obliterating Latin inscriptions, and superseding them by Greek ones. In addition to this, the procurator dei Forestieri mentioned an anecdote of contemptible servility on the part of the Greek monks. They had very recently served coffee with their own hands to the pasha of Jerusalem, who had established his divan in the church to the right of the Sepulchre, close to the altar of Calvary.

But I received the most painful shock from what was related to me by eye-witnesses of the so-called holy fire of the Greeks and Armenians during the night of Easter eve; a ceremony which must forcibly destroy all the respect of Mahometans for the Christian religion. The worst of this is not the evident deception practised in the miracle, but the lowness of the debauchery which occupies this nocturnal festival, and approximates it to the orgies of the heathen. It is said that Greek priests forget themselves in sympathy with Turkish dervises, who, it is well known, are uncontrolled by the laws of decency and morality.

At one of these fire-miracles, Ibrahim Pasha, as lord of Syria, played the part which was performed by Napoleon in the blood-miracle of Naples. At Naples the blood of the celebrated relic would not flow; there was in consequence a great disturbance amongst the populace. Napoleon then commanded that it should flow instantly; it did so. Ibrahim did the same with the tardy fire, looking down upon the ceremony from the gallery of the Greeks.

The conduct of the Mahometan inhabitants of Jerusalem would be far more overbearing towards the Christians, were it not for fear of the consuls, amongst whom the French strives to exercise most authority. He considers himself, according to his own expression, as the protector of the pasha himself; yet, shortly before my arrival, a servant of his was assassinated, without even his claiming satisfaction; but it was in a dishonourable amour, wherein the Oriental understands no joking.

The customary expression in Jerusalem—" with respect be it said a Christian"—is characteristic of the sentiments of the Mahometans towards the Christians. The same honourable prefix is applied also to the Jews, and (which will be valued by gallants amongst us) also to the fair sex. " A lady, and with respect be it said," says the Mahometan in Jerusalem.

How very easily travellers get into unpleasant fracas with the Arab population was proved to me by a German painter, who, in sketching an ancient wall, was vexatiously annoyed, and beaten with his own stick, the most convenient instrument at hand.

Albanians, whom I saw striding up and down the streets, are considered as the most dangerous persons to meet. They have a very cavalierlike respect for human life, and this was in fullest force at the time of my residence in Jerusalem, for the pasha was, as it were, then denuded of almost all military strength. It was on that account, possibly, that the closing of the gates took place punctually at sunset; the visits of the restless warlike Bedouins of the vicinity might very easily have placed the Holy City in a state of considerable difficulty.

THE ANGLICAN BISHOPRIC AT JERUSALEM.

The notice I have just taken of the wretched condition of the Oriental churches, as representatives of Christianity, compared with those which are in direct opposition to it, leads me incidentally to the

Anglican bishopric ; for one of the fundamental ideas which suggested its establishment was, to exhibit Christianity worthily to the eyes of Mahometan and Jewish Orientals, as well as to the so deeply sunken Oriental Christians themselves. That the idea was great and noble requires not a word of recognition ; but has the idea been happily carried out since the diocesan's family made their entry into Jerusalem with such peculiar ceremony ? This entry was jocosely described to me by one of the Catholic fraternity, and he related that the " *Ecco il vescovo* " was followed by the spectators exclaiming with astonishment, " *Ecco la vescova,*" and this by " *Ecco i vescovini.*" I might assert that this was absolutely an attack upon Protestantism. It is scarcely questionable that Greeks and Catholics both, as well as the collective Oriental churches, received much annoyance by the appointment of a bishop with such a family retinue, and had thus presented to them an opportunity for scandalising in the very centre of the new territory of conversion. At least, the bishop himself should have been, necessarily, all the more sober and dignified. I hope that my doubts as to the propriety of the selection may be unfulfilled.

It is well known that it has been preferred to select a converted Jew, because the conversion of the Jews in Palestine has been the chief object of the establishment of a bishopric in Jerusalem. If I am correctly informed, both as to the style of preaching of one of the bishop's missionaries and the mode practised in the conversion of Jews in Jerusalem, I do not find that the dignity of Protestantism has been promoted by either. According to that mode of preaching, the Jews are inoculated with a modern Pharisaism ; they seem as those most peculiarly—ay, even exclusively—called to be perfect Christians ; they are invited, by stepping over, to renew their ancient hereditary privileges over us. Naturally, this dogmatical novelty gratifies the Jewish-Christian missionaries themselves far more than all the other Protestants. One of the latter told me that he had openly expressed his disgust to the preacher, and had prohibited his pastoral visits. Here and there similar views may be entertained. An Englishman of distinction had two suitors for the hand of his daughter : one was a baptized Israelite, and he was unconditionally preferred by the father out of respect to his character as Jewish Christian.

With respect to the baptism of converts in Jerusalem it is, as far as I know, framed to an accommodation with the most modern Judaism. Six thousand piastres (about fifty pounds !) are offered to the convert as a premium ; other advantages are said likewise to be considerable. Do they think it to act thus is in the spirit of Christ ? Perhaps rather in the spirit of Christ's temporal viceregent. But what does Protestantism say to this ? Moreover, I consider

Jerusalem as the most unfavourable position for the conversion of
Jews. Here Jewish fanaticism is domiciled; here the Jew feels
happy in being a Jew; here he is surrounded with reminiscences
which from childhood upwards have been dear and sacred to him.
Those Jews who, notwithstanding, have been converted in Jerusalem,
were described to me as persons who had sustained, and that de-
servedly, a degradation by their fellow believers. Thus golden nets
are wrought, and stinking fish are caught. A true caricature of
conversion has been recently given. A Jew was first baptized in
Hungary as a Calvinist, in Vienna he became a Catholic, in
Walachia, a Walachian Christian, and, lastly, an Anglican Protestant
under Bishop Alexander. Who would guarantee that this individual
will not close his career of conversion by a return to Judaism? It is
a fact that recently a baptized Jew became a Jew again very soon
after his baptism. But the most remarkable phenomenon that the
annals of conversion can offer in modern times is that furnished by a
Protestant of Dantzic. This individual was converted to Judaism in
Jerusalem. This is easily understood. If English gold will make
Christians, so can Jewish gold make Jews. The converted Dantzicker
was surrounded by the brethren of his new faith with a halo of
veneration, and sent to Frankfort on the Main at the general cost
to pursue his higher studies.

But I am far from denying that the bishopric, although not
answering to its ideal, still fulfils many hopes and many wishes;
for through the institution, appended to the bishopric, of the two
Christian schools, the one for children, the other specially for new
Jewish-Christian emissaries, it has called into existence what may be
accompanied with manifold blessings.

But the Anglican bishopric in Jerusalem presents other aspects
which require to be viewed. It contains the germ of an attempt towards a union of Protestant ecclesiastical elements, which hitherto
in Europe have remained strictly separated. Episcopal Anglicanism
has hereby connected itself in sisterly union with German Protestantism. Before I proceed to the illustration of this sisterly
connection, I must say a few words in explanation of the distinguishing character of the normal forms of the two Churches; as far, namely,
as it comes within the scope of my plan.

When the Reformation of Luther and Calvin founded the Evangelical Church by the rupture with Rome, it rejected, as a fundamental
principle of the Roman hierarchy, the dogma of the episcopal
succession. According to this dogma, the true church is that
only whose bishops, as bearers of the Holy Ghost, descend in
an uninterrupted line from the apostles and from Christ himself. The bishops, with the primates at their head, represent
conjunctively the true Church, and in matters of faith are infallible.

The bishop, in his peculiar character of bearer and mediator of the Holy Spirit guiding the Church, has the exclusive administration of two sacraments, those of ordination and confirmation, in absolute distinction from the rest of the clergy.

This dogma necessarily was destroyed when the reformers instituted as sole signs of the true Church, the pure promulgation of the Gospel and the just administration of the sacraments, that is to say, of the Lord's Supper and of Baptism, and removed by the idea of the general priesthood of the community the essential distinction between the rank of priests and of ordinary Christians. They could, therefore, far less admit of any distinction among the clergy themselves; thence is it that the ordination which the country pastor receives is valid also for the general superintendent ; that ordination remained no exclusive privilege of the bishop, and that confirmation could be made by all the clergy with equal authority.

On the other hand the episcopal church of England is designated as episcopal ; because, by the admission of the superior authority of the bishops, it possesses a distinguishing difference from all other protestant churches, which indeed have also bishops, but bishops who do not possess any essential superior authority.

The English High Church alone claims for its bishops both the necessity of an especial ordination and the exclusive administration of ordination and confirmation. And she believes, besides, that she stands in holy connection with the primitive apostolic Church by the link of an uninterrupted episcopal succession, and finds in it an excellent wall of defence against the changeableness of human forms and systems ; and also venerates in it the possession of elect mediators and chosen organs of its community ; and finally recognises within it a sure guarantee of presenting the idea of the true Church within her own bosom. All this is an undeniable fact, confirmed both by constant practice and by the language of theology.

Nevertheless the question is asked, Whether the episcopal church considers the peculiarity which approximates it as much to the Catholic church as it removes it from those of Luther and Calvin, merely be a matter of government? or whether it attaches thereto the character and conditions of the true Church?

The course pursued by the Catholic church cannot be, for three reasons, by any means a matter of indifference. In the first place, the confession of the Anglican church contains nothing respecting any difference in the episcopal character between the English and Romish hierarchy. Thus the idea of the identity of the former with the latter lies very proximate, even indeed notwithstanding the rejection of the pope : for, on the one side, the bishops of England have their primate ; and, on the other side, the supreme temporal power

M

authoritatively fills up the bench of bishops. Besides the two solely exclusive offices of the Catholic bishop have also remained those of the Anglican bishop, although throughout all Protestant churches they have been denuded of the character of sacraments. Lastly, the episcopal High Church, which also appropriates to itself the title of the Catholic church, has, during the past centuries of its existence, exhibited towards the Dissenters of its native country a severe tone of exclusiveness similar to that maintained by the Roman Catholic church : a fact which induces us to feel inclined consequently, and not without reason, to apply it also to the relative position of Anglicanism to the Protestant churches out of England. The extent to which the degree of analogy between the Catholic church and the Anglican church in the above mooted question may be carried remains, it is true, controvertible ; but the appearance of Puseyism, the native product of the soil, on the one side, and national works, like that of Mr. Gladstone " Upon Church and State," on the other, give to this analogy a very impressive weight.

After these preliminary observations I may inform my readers how, notwithstanding the peculiar differences between German Protestantism and English Episcopalianism, a bishopric in common, or at least such a one in which the two ecclesiastical elements may unite as allies and friends, has become possible.

The bishopric of Jerusalem is called, and is really, a bishopric of the United Churches of England and Ireland, having a bishop consecrated precisely like all other bishops of the High Church. It has also the function to unite all the German Protestants of the East, whenever they themselves may wish it, in Germanic Protestant communities; and as such to take them under its protection and pastoral care. These communities are specially superintended by German ecclesiastics. These ecclesiastics come to Jerusalem as candidates for the ministry, educated to the extent the Protestant church of Germany requires for ordination. But they are ordained by the bishop of Jerusalem, after a preliminary affirmation upon the three aboriginal œcumenical symbols of faith, the common constituents of the Catholic as well as of the Anglican and Germano-Protestant Confessions. These ecclesiastics thus ordained use in their communities a German liturgy extracted from the formal church-liturgy of Prussia, and carefully examined, with a view to its especial object, by the Archbishop of Canterbury. There is but one exclusive privilege which the bishop enjoys beyond the rest of the clergy in these communities, which is confirmation.

Hence, evidently, German Protestantism has submitted to a certain subordinate position with respect to Anglicanism. This is even expressed in the very name of Anglican bishopric : and the original views of the founders never contemplated any thing else, nor could the tendency of the combined community take a different direction. We may merely ask, In this necessary subordination of German Protestantism to Anglicanism, does the dignity of the former remain undiminished?

The question has been answered in the affirmative on one side, and in the negative on the other. Each speaks according to his apprehension; I speak according to mine. In the "Bisthum zu St. Jacob in Jerusalem" * (Freiburg, 1842), it is decidedly shown that the Anglican church here, as elsewhere, preserves its spirit of exclusiveness. It has distinctly preserved it in the double retention of ordination and confirmation for their bishops. In the "Evangelischen Bisthum in Jerusalem"† (Berlin, 1842), the excluding character of the Anglican church is absolutely denied; and that reservation is only viewed as a component part of external church government.

But how is the view set forth in the latter work, that the episcopal retention of ordination in the Anglican church is merely a question of government, and not of a doctrine, and "that the Church does not certainly declare the necessity of episcopal ordination as a dogma" (see p. 81), consistent with the following observation of the same work (see p. 85)?—"The German church could allow nothing to take place, which should even distantly appear to cast a doubt upon the validity of its own ordination. It was therefore perfectly impossible that she should permit her already ordained clergy to be re-ordained by the bishop of Jerusalem, or by any other bishop. This would have been a confession that she made no claim to a living connection with the entire historical development of the Church; that the consecration of her clergy was but the work of men's hands, to which the seal of a divine calling was wanting; that her servants were but servants of the state, who had no authority beyond that invested by the state. It would be an abnegation of the Church, a contempt of their own spiritual mother, from which the whole church of Germany would turn away with disgust. ... English prelates have never even by the slightest hint made this requisition."

After these observations, will the question of ordination be considered merely as a question of church government, and not doctrinal or dogmatical? In that case, my opinion is, that these observations would have no meaning. Besides experience itself furnishes for our purpose a very useful proof of the view which the Anglican church

* The Bishopric of St. James, at Jerusalem.
† The Evangelical Bishopric, at Jerusalem.

M 2

takes of ordination, wherein indeed the last proposition of the just-cited observations with respect to the " requisition of English prelates," sustains a very important limitation.   The missionary institution of Basle has notwithstanding constant protest, been obliged for many years to send youths already ordained with a view to missionary services to London, there to receive the valid ordination if they wish to serve in English missionary districts.   What does this example of a decided rejection of the ordination of our church on the part of the English church imply, but that the English church thinks very meanly of ours ? but that the English church assumes the admission on the part of the German church " that it makes no claim to a living link with the entire historical development of the Church ?"— " that the consecration of its clergy is but the work of men's hands, and wholly wants the seal of a divine calling ? "   And the one example necessarily shows its general applicability, even should, in other cases, the instance of a second be thwarted or avoided.

The subterfuge adopted for Jerusalem, that German candidates without having received ordination from the maternal church, come to Jerusalem to be there ordained by the Anglican bishop, is yet but a subterfuge wherein English exclusiveness, so universally predominant, distinctly retains its fullest validity.   Should the clergyman ordained in the Anglican church return subsequently to Germany, would he then, to renew his holy functions, receive a renewed ordination? or is the ordination received at Jerusalem valid for Germany ?   In the first case its value is easily appreciated, pursuant to the above observations in defence of the evangelical bishopric (see p. 57).   According to these the case seems wholly impossible.   But, if the second case be assumed, how could ordination be preferred at Jerusalem, to ordination at home, and the former be allowed to supersede the latter, and not much rather the latter the former ?

Thus, in my opinion, even on this point, the subserviency of German Protestantism, relative to an exaction essentially, according to all appearance, linked to the dogma itself of the Anglican church, was sufficiently important to explain the surprise that it caused throughout Germany at the moment of its promulgation.

With respect further to the episcopal privilege of confirmation; this also it will be equally difficult to justify by viewing it as merely an inconsiderable formality; inasmuch as it is too important a procedure in the Catholic church, and has been both dogmatically and absolutely denied on the ground taken up by German Protestantism in opposition to the doctrines of the church of Rome; to this must be added that the combined retention of both individual privileges of the English as well as the Roman bishops for the church of Jerusalem, necessarily increases the consequence of each individually.   But when the

official consecration of the bishop of Jerusalem by the primate of
England, went so far as to commence with the " hope that under
God's blessing it may promote the essential unity of discipline, as well
as of doctrine, between our own (the Anglican) church, and the less
perfectly regulated Protestant churches of Europe," the most natural
consequence was a shout of astonishment from the last-mentioned
" less perfectly regulated" churches.   Did we even modify the expression of the archbishop by attributing it to his position, and apply
the noted deficiency of perfection exclusively to non-essential for-
malities, the majority would still foster the suspicion that they saw
in it the characteristic of an exclusive church, or at least of one
proud of its Roman elements of Catholicism, as exhibited in a way
so derogatory to German Protestantism, in the principles of the
bishopric of Jerusalem, even as it is ostentatiously and superciliously
expressed in the words of the English prelate.

But I renounce the attempt to separate the appearance from the
thing itself, in unmistakeable clearness ; I believe that others see it
with a clearer eye than mine ; and my desire is, if I may be so permitted, that the bishopric at Jerusalem may actually have led the way
to a union of the Protestant churches of the Continent with those of
Great Britain—to a union, in fact, wherein the purity of the protestant principle may be perfectly unstained.

But I still owe a last word to the original thought whence emanated the bishopric in question. This idea originated as is well
known, with an illustrious prince in whom the Protestant church of
the present day beholds its great protector.   It has been fully
detailed in the tract already noticed which has for its title, " Das
evangelische Bisthum in Jerusalem. " (Berlin 1842.)

In 1840, when the East was embroiled in a war which shook to
its centre its political existence, the period was more favourable than
ever to rescue the Christians of the Holy Land, and the Holy Land
itself from its melancholy position. As soon as Frederick William IV.
ascended the throne, he directed his eye towards this object.   By the
course he pursued in conjunction with the other great powers of
Europe, that country to which the entire world is indebted for the
greatest of its boons—salvation, was to obtain salvation itself from its
ancient degrading yoke.   The idea was worthy to be one of the first
entertained by the new-crowned monarch.

But alas ! the bloody decision, effected chiefly by European arms,
merely transferred Syria and Palestine from one barbarian despot to
another ; yet still was reserved what alone appeared possible to gain
by the influential position of the great powers with respect to
Turkey—in the first place, favourable opportunities for developing in
the East, a new future for Christianity ; and secondly, for opening

important alliances in behalf of German commerce and German industry. This second object issued in the mission of a Prussian consul-general for Syria to Beyrout, and of a vice-consul for Palestine to Jerusalem. The first point suggested the establishment of the bishopric at Jerusalem in support of which English influence was obtained, and whose realisation the king's munificence most generously assisted.

The result of all is twofold. The king's original idea stands fixed as the foundation-stone of a new holy alliance which should obtain the triumphs of the crusades, without, like them, costing the blood of millions. Temporary differences in the councils of the great powers, as is shown by original documents, interfered with the carrying out of this idea. What nevertheless remained did not specially refer to the peculiar form of the Anglican bishopric. The idea whence the bishopric emanated remains great and ennobling, although its realisation, owing to multifarious interference, is not what was earnestly desired.

MONASTERIES IN AND ABOUT JERUSALEM.

If Jerusalem had no monasteries, both Catholics and Greeks, as well as all the Christians of the East, would want the most essential link of connection with the soil of the Holy City. The monasteries of the several Churches hold the same place at Jerusalem, as consulates do at Marseilles or Hamburg. They might be called the spiritual representatives of diplomacy. Through their mediation the pilgrim, to whatever faith he may belong (for the Protestant is also welcome), comes into connection with the holy city and its relics. They supply the place of the hotels of the West; for all, who may be attracted to Jerusalem by pious impulses or the spirit of inquiry, resort to the monasteries, with the exception of a few Americans or Englishmen who take up their abode with the missionaries of their countries. There are fewer consulates, properly so called, here than elsewhere, and even those which exist are of a very recent date. On the part of the Catholics there is, besides the French consul, a Sardinian consul possessing a certain degree of importance ; and the Protestants have an English and a Prussian consul to protect their interests.

I took up my residence, as most modern travellers do, at the so called *Casa nuova* which the Latin monastery caused to be built expressly for the reception of its pilgrims. The Latin monastery itself, called San Salvador, and occupied by Franciscan monks, chiefly Spaniards and Italians, is considerable, and is the focus of all the Catholic monasteries of the Terra Santa. Its church possesses many a splendid relic which bears witness to the noble liberality of European princes, chiefly in former times. The good fathers complained to me that Spain, France, and even Austria, rarely now present any thing. Latterly, however, the courts of Naples and Sardinia have exhibited towards it a generous sympathy ; and a fine picture decorates the monastery, representing Louis Philippe, of the size of life, and presented by him as a mark of his devotion.

The course of life pursued in the monastery of San Salvador is very simple ; but Jerusalem is by no means a place for epicures. That which essentially interferes with the pleasures of the table, is the use of oil which is not of the very best quality.

The monastery of St. Constantine takes the lead of the twelve Greek monasteries of Jerusalem. Its spaciousness makes it a palace ; and here at Easter dwell several thousand pilgrims. Its two churches may appear superb to a Greek eye, which is not offended by profuseness of decoration. But to every eye the view from the terrace of the monastery which adjoins the terrace of the church of the Holy Sepulcre is splendid. I thence beheld the city spread before me like a picture. What a past was sleeping beneath the roofs, under my feet ! Variegated minarets rise high above all the surrounding objects, like cheerful thoughts elevating themselves over the Sabbath rest of Israel, and over the sombre aspect of the Christian cathedral. The lower elevations in the north-west recalled to my mind the Roman legions under Titus, for here the day of doom dawned upon the walls of the murderess of ' the prophets. (Luke xiii. 34.) In the east stood forth the Mount of Olives. Its olive trees in the distance looked blandly down upon the melancholy city. How young does it still appear, thought I, although a thousand years of desolation have passed over it !

Besides these two monasteries of the Latins and the Greeks, those of the Copts, the Abyssinians, the Syrians, and the Armenians, lie in the vicinity of the Holy Sepulchre : thus they have clustered all like children around their mother. The youngest of their family is the Anglican evangelical church, whose foundations are planted upon the most northerly summit of Sion close to the citadel.

In the monastery of St. James the Armenians possess a pearl among the monasteries of Jerusalem. It is as wealthy as it is beautiful and large. Its cells for pilgrims of which it possesses several hundreds, are clean and comfortable : its garden abounds in magnificent trees, and surprises by its luxuriance ; its church dazzles with its gorgeousness. This church is said to be built upon the very spot where St. James was beheaded, whence it is that it possesses numerous representations of his decapitation. Its marble floor is

decorated with fine mosaics, and overspread with splendid carpets.
The doors and chancels are inlaid with mother-of-pearl and tortoise-
shell ; and around the numerous pictures upon the walls—not always
in the purest taste — glitters the gold of their frames ; and shining
lamps hang around in profusion. The perforated cupola supported
upon four pillars spreads over the whole a gentle light.

I made a very interesting excursion to the monastery of St. John,
at Ain Karim, two leagues from Jerusalem. Just after break of
day, and as soon as the gates were opened, I rode forth with my dragoman and guide, over the stony heights, sparingly sprinkled with
verdure, lying to the west of the city. At the distance of three-
quarters of a league, lay, in a cheerful valley, the monastery of the
Holy Cross, which enclosed within its firm walls and towers only
four Georgian monks and an aged female. The latter was immediately ordered to procure a pipe and a cup of coffee, for the certainly
very early visiter. Shortly afterwards the complaisant prior conducted us into the ancient church, lighted from its cupola, and
decorated with rich fresco paintings of Scriptural subjects, sufficiently edifying. A narrow lateral apartment, into which we
could only enter by stooping low, constituted the library, which
contained many Georgian, and also some Syriac, Armenian,
and Arabic manuscripts. I discovered no Greek ones ; there only
lay upon the floor several Greek leaves, interspersed with other fragments of ancient manuscripts. What I found amongst it, written
upon parchment, I was allowed to carry away, as a reminiscence of
my visit. According to the description given by Scholtz, more than
twenty years ago, of the library of this monastery, I believe that,
since his visit, much that was valuable has found its way to Europe.*
But I do not doubt that what remains is well worthy the study
of the critic. The monastery itself derives its name of the Holy
Cross, from being built upon the spot where the wood for the Cross
of Christ was felled.

After ascending from the valley to the adjacent heights, we observed in the distance, to the north-west, upon the summit of the
mountain range, the ruins of Zoba, where, probably, the prophet
Samuel was born, and where dwelt the valiant Maccabees. We arrived soon afterwards at Ain Karim, from the centre of which the

---

* Scholtz counted about four hundred Georgian, and these chiefly biblical
manuscripts; fifteen Syriac of the New Testament of the 13th to the 15th
centuries ; fourteen Greek on ecclesiastical subjects, but including also the
work of Johannes Damascenus of the 10th century ; ten unimportant Arabic
as well as twelve Armenian, and four Sclavonic, probably with the text of
the New Testament. See his *Biblisch-Kritische Reise, &c.*   Leipzig and
Sorau, 1823. p. 148.

monastery of St. John stands sumptuously forth. It lies in a rich
and fertile valley, enclosed by lofty cheerful green hills. This monastery, inhabited by Franciscans, and these exclusively Spaniards, has
to thank the beneficence of Louis XIV. for its present condition, and
is considered the finest of all the Latin monasteries of the Holy
Land. Its walls contain a jewel; viz. a church, constructed upon
the supposed spot of the birth of him who was sent to prepare the
way of the Lord (Mark i. 2). This church is supported by four
pillars; the walls and floor are inlaid with marble. Many of the
pictures which decorate it, are excellent; and a St. John, by Murillo,
hangs over one of the altars. The church has also an organ. Marble
stairs lead below to the natal grotto, which is resplendent with
marble, gold, and silk. This is the true sanctuary. An altar is here,
with the image of St. John hanging over it. There is a niche also,
bearing in its centre a marble tablet, with the inscription, " *Hic præ-
cursor Domini natus est.*" (Here was born the forerunner of our
Lord.) Above it, in the roof, which is of black marble, there is a
white lamb, with the words of the Baptist, " Behold the Lamb of
God." (St. John i. 29.) Ornamental bas-reliefs represent upon the
walls around, the history of St. John, from the Annunciation of his
mother to his own decapitation.

Close to the north of the monastery, we visited, under the guidance
of a friendly Franciscan, the Valley of Turpentine, which is considered to be the place where David slew Goliath, the gigantic Philis-
tine. (1 Sam. xvii. 49. and xxi. 9). The valley is enlivened by
the brilliant green foliage of its turpentine trees; it has also a purling brook full of pebbles, which I crossed once before, near Kulonieh, on my road from Ramle to Jerusalem. Hills, clothed with
vines, olives, and fig-trees, command the valley on both sides. But
it is questionable whether it was really here that the celebrated combat took place. In consequence of his determination of the sites
of Socoh (Joshua xv. 48) and Azekah (Joshua x. 11) between
which the Scriptural valley of Elah (1 Sam. xvii. 2) lay, Robinson
considers the latter identical with the present " Valley of Acacias,"
several leagues to the south-west of St. John, in the vicinity of
which he found a remarkable pine tree, probably the oldest in
Palestine.*

A fresh delight awaited us: the desert of St. John attracted us,
although it had become pretty hot. We halted but a short time at
the beautiful ruins of the monastery of the Annunciation, which

* The pine has long enjoyed the celebrity of attaining a thousand years.
Josephus speaks of a gigantic pine near Hebron, reputed to have stood from
the period of the creation.

hang picturesquely upon the declivity.   Herbage and foliage sprout
forth amidst the ruins, and even magnificent trees, especially fig-
trees, jut forth luxuriantly from amongst them.   I visited there the
Chapel of the Grotto, consecrated to the meeting of Elizabeth and
the Virgin, that meeting when the blessed among women (Luke i.
42.) uttered her song of joy.   Still, annually, the festival of the
Annunciation is celebrated here.   " My soul doth magnify the
Lord " (Luke i. 46), sung by the clear voices of the Latins, is
doubtlessly then thoroughly refreshing to the soul.   An hour later
we reached the desert of St. John.   It is indeed solitary, girded by
mountains and rocks ; but it is not destitute of verdure, or springs,
or trees, and in consequence of all this, it is rendered more charming
than many spots of the promised land.   The Cavern of St. John,
where the prophet is said to have dwelt, whilst preparing for his
mission in the wilderness, possesses an attractive charm, and more
especially for me, who had entered it to take my mid-day siesta within
its cool shade.   It lies in the midst of a romantic wilderness of rocks,
which hangs upon a declivity, and terminates in the ruins of ancient monastic walls.   I thence surveyed a wide expanse of table
land, sprinkled with many villages.   Beneath the grotto, the entrance to which is luxuriantly overgrown with a profusion of beautiful foliage, a spring of the clearest water wells, as a rich fountain,
from the face of the unsculptured rock, and precipitates itself down
into a large basin, densely encompassed with reeds and rushes.

The tradition may be erroneous which connects the solitary medi-
tations of the prophetic preacher with this wildly romantic rocky
valley ; but it has made an admirable selection.   Raphael's St.
John in the Wilderness, that incomparable master-piece, has often
found me lost in contemplation before it, when taking a lounging
round in the gallery of the Medici ; but the reminiscence of what I
beheld to-day I would not exchange, even for that sublime picture.

Mid-day was long past when we quitted the charming solitude.
In hastening onward we also saw, close to the juncture of two
Wadis, one of which is called the Valley of Roses, from their exten-
sive culture on the spot, the spring where Philip, on the road from
Gaza is said to have baptized the " eunuch of great authority under
Queen Candace " (Acts viii. 27. 38) ; later we saw upon the left the
revered tomb of Rachel (Gen. xxxv. 19), and at sunset we entered
Bethlehem.

THE SEVENTH SUNDAY AFTER TRINITY.

MORNING EXCURSIONS AROUND JERUSALEM. — EVENING FESTIVAL
AT THE HOLY SEPULCHRE.

This was the first Sunday I spent at Jerusalem. I did not expect to
see any thing new ; but to see once more that which I had already
seen, under the aspect of Sunday, and to enjoy it with my whole
heart.

My guides and I were early at St. Stephen's gate. I had proceeded but a few steps to the right into the narrow street which,
passing the pool of Bethesda, leads directly into the Area of the
Mosque ; but I had scarcely cast a glance through the porch of the
Area when the voice of a guard posted unseen in a corner, squeaked
out a prohibition. We reached consequently all the sooner the foot
of the mountain which had so often heard the prayers of David
before he built a temple to the Lord of the cedars of Lebanon.
(2 Sam. vii. 18.)

Thus I was in the valley of Jehoshaphat wherein flows the brook
Kidron, in that valley which Jewish belief considers will be the
scene of the events prophesied in the parting words of its two seers
Joel and Zechariah. " The Lord shall go forth . . . and his feet shall
stand in that day upon the Mount of Olives . . . and the mount of
Olives shall cleave in the midst thereof." (Zech. xiv. 4.) And the
heathen shall " be wakened, and come up to the valley of Jehoshaphat : for there will I sit to judge all the heathen round about."
(Joel iii. 12.) For these many centuries past, even to the present day,
from all parts of the earth pious Jews hasten hither towards the end
of their lives to be gathered to their fathers within view of this
valley, and to rise again with them upon that great day. The
Mahometans are also tinged with that superstition. They also
expect Jehoshaphat will be the scene of the day of judgment.
And the stone upon which their prophet will stand, upon the
declivity of the Mount of Olives, at the hour of doom, is preserved in the mosque El Aksa. Hence opposite to the great Jewish
burial-ground on the east of Kedron lies also a great Turkish one on
the west.

Thus the mount of Olives is arrayed with imperishable charms ;
it wears around its brow a wreath composed of the reminiscences of
the greatest of all ages, and in its heart it bears the impending hour
of the future.

Yet the aspect of the Mount of Olives is cheerful; even to this day it justifies its name, although doubtlessly formerly its olives stood more thickly crowded than at present.

Before we ascended we got over a low wall and entered the garden Gethsemane, or Dschesmaniyeh, as the Arabs called it. As its locality awakens but little critical suspicion, a fervent remembrance of the hours which our Lord and his twelve disciples used to spend here in the silence of the evening until he was betrayed by the kiss, is readily excited. The very stone upon which Judas stood when he gave his Master this kiss, is mentioned by the pilgrim of Bordeaux as early as the year 333. It is now shown at the south eastern corner of the garden close to a mutilated pillar.

In the midst of the pathway, upon the summit of the Mount of Olives three holy spots are marked out by tradition. The first was formerly indicated by a chapel of which the ruins still remain. It is there that Christ is supposed to have taught his disciples the Lord's Prayer. (Matt. vi. 9.) The second, not very distant from the first, is supposed to be the spot where the Saviour wept over Jerusalem and its blindness. (Luke xxi. 6.) The third is the cavern where the apostles are said to have framed their confession of faith.

We speedily reached the flat surface of the mount where the chapel of the Ascension stands, with the ruins of an ancient church as well as the deserted walls of a mosque. We caused the chapel to be opened ; but I derived from it nothing but an interruption to the fervour of my devotion. It is well known that a stone is exhibited within it, with the impression of the foot of our Lord, made at the moment of his ascent. This impression is certainly as readily recognised and as natural as that of Mahomet's dromedary upon mount Sinai. Independent of the offence caused by this impression, it is questionable whether this locality may be considered justly as the spot whence our Saviour ascended. Precisely upon this point we possess in the Gospels of the Evangelists more definite information than upon many other subjects. At the end of his Gospel St. Luke says (xxiv. 50, 51), "And he led them out as far as to Bethany, and he lifted up his hands, and blessed them. And it came to pass, while he blessed them, he was parted from them, and carried up into heaven." According to this statement, the tradition which caused the chapel of the Ascension to be erected at the summit of the Mount of Olives appears to be an evident error. But St. Luke speaks a second time of the Ascension at the commencement of the Acts of the Apostles (i. 12). He there says, The witnesses of it, "returned unto Jerusalem from the mount called Olive, which is from Jerusalem a Sabbath day's journey" (i. e. six stadia, or 2000

ells.) In my opinion*, these words are to be understood no otherwise than that Christ ascended into heaven at the point whence
the apostles returned into the city. The position of the chapel
admirably harmonises with this view. But can the passage in the
Acts be made to harmonise with that of the Gospel ?   I reply, yes,
within a little certainly.   Even now a path leads over the summit
of the mount of Olives to Bethany.   Hence, our Lord may have led
his disciples across the Mount of Olives towards Bethany ; that is
to say, to the point where Bethany which is situated fifteen stadia
from Jerusalem, lay within view.   Yet may my interpretation be
exposed to many objections ; at all events, it was too rash upon the
faith of the passage in the Gospel to utter so decided a condemnation
of the tradition, especially as the latter had the recommendation of a
very high antiquity. For, shortly after the close of the third century,
Eusebius relates that even then innumerable pilgrims flocked to Jerusalem from all quarters of the world that they might pray on the
Mount of Olives, upon the spot where Christ ascended into heaven.

The ancient minaret, by the side of the mosque, tempted us to the
enjoyment of the incomparable view from its summit. Here the
eye ranges over a complete and distant panorama. In the east we
beheld the Dead Sea, and close to it the verdant shores of the
Jordan ; in front, the pale sandy hills of the desert ; and beyond
the desert, the Moabite mountains, clad in the golden rays of the morning sun. Towards the north we beheld, beyond the Mosque of
Samuel and the neighbouring mountain peaks, and slightly veiled
with vapour, the distant mountain range of Samaria. To the south
we had the mountains of Judah ; the round conical summit of the
Mountain of the Franks, called in Arabic, the Little Paradise,
bordered on the horizon ; and not far distant from it we saw the
heights of Bethlehem ; and lastly towards the west, Jerusalem itself
fixed our attention. Its flat cupola roofs lay indeed closely thronged
together before us ; yet could we readily distinguish, a little to the
right of the Temple Mosque, which presents itself here in an imposing attitude, the Church of the Holy Sepulchre over Golgotha. Immediately in front of it, and in our direction, was the celebrated
Golden gate, by which, it is said our Saviour made his triumphal entry into Jerusalem, and which is now kept carefully walled
up, that no unbeliever should pass through, to the prejudice and detri-
ment of the Crescent, according to Mahometan superstition.

In the small village, immediately behind the chapel and the
mosque, we fell in with some industrious agricultural labourers,
such as I had not seen for many a day. Corn lay in sheaves, to be
beaten out by oxen. After enjoying a cup of milk, offered by

* In opposition to Robinson, see his Palestine, vol. ii. p. 6, note 1.

kindly hands, we descended again by a path bearing to the south-west, into the valley of Jehoshaphat, and arrived at the Jewish cemetery, which extends to the south of Gethsemane, at the foot of the Mount of Olives.   The two ancient monuments, usually now called the tombs of Zecharias and Absalom, necessarily occupied us more than the numerous grave-stones with Hebrew inscriptions. These offspring of a grey antiquity have remained untouched during all the tempests which, for the space of two thousand years, have raged against the Holy City.   They stand there like strange dream-ers: like the hermits of a holy secrecy.   They are the symbol of their nation; a symbol of its tenacious clinging to the soil, and of the faith of their fathers, and of their indestructible hopes and pa-tience.   It is as if their eye was fixed immovably upon the hour which, when it shall rise upon this valley, shall avenge and glorify the House of Israel.

That these tombs are at least as old as the Christian era is incon-testable, although there is but little authority for the names which they bear.   In the 4th century the pilgrim of Bordeaux dis-tinguished these two monoliths as the tombs of Isaiah and Heze-kiah, a proof that even then their origin was referred back to a very high antiquity.   The affinity of their style of structure with that of the monuments of Petra, induces me to connect them with these, and confirms the supposition of their being constructed contempo-raneously.   Yet I do not feel astonished that it should be attempted seriously and learnedly with Williams, to connect the memory of Absalom at least with the one which bears his name.   Besides the passage in the Bible (2 Sam. xviii. 18.), where it says, " Now Absalom, in his lifetime, had taken and reared up for himself a pillar, which is in the king's dale. . . and it is called unto this day, Absalom's place," Josephus also says (Ant. vii. 10. 3.) that the pillar of Absalom, which stands in the king's dale, is two stadia distant from Jerusalem.   The expression " pillar," may, without hesitation, be applied to the monument of Absalom, and the calculation of the distance concurs very well with its position.

But I will compress into a few words a description of these mo-numents themselves.   The two I have named, those called after Zecharias and Absalom, are hewn from the very rock itself, so that to the north-east and south they are enclosed by rocky walls.   The first, that of Zecharias, called also by others that of Jehoshaphat, is a perfect monolith, about thirty feet high.   Upon its four-sided base, whose cornice, decorated with the claws of bears, is supported on all four sides by pillars with Ionic capitals, stands a pyramid twelve feet high.   The whole is about eighty feet in circumference, and presents itself like a small temple, built in the most solid style.   No

entrance is to be detected, although there may be one beneath its present quadrangle, concealed under the ground.

The tomb of Absalom presents a far more striking appearance
than its neighbour. It may be seen even from the Mount of Olives ;
for the rock behind it reaches only about half-way up, to the height
of about twenty feet. Up to this elevation this monument resembles
that of Zecharias ; thus high also it is hewn out of the rock ;
but this is succeeded by two layers of gigantic workmanship, and
above them rises a tower like a cupola, whose apex takes the form of
the calyx of a flower. The upper portion is of the same height as
the base, so that its elevation altogether is about forty feet. At the
height of several feet, one of the four sides has been opened, although
beneath there is also an entrance, now nearly choked up. My dragoman ascended without difficulty, through the upper aperture, into
the interior, which has quite a deserted appearance, and only contains a mass of stones that have been thrown into it. Also outside,
close to the monument, lie heaps of stones, which are referred to a
peculiar custom. Mahometans, even to the present day, curse
any disobedient child who has rebelled against his father, and in
token of their contempt cast a stone at his monument.*

Close behind this monument there opens from the flat surface of the
rock a sepulchre, the door of which is ornamented with some decorations. It passes for the tomb of King Jehoshaphat. But there is
another sepulchre, or rather grotto, far more considerable, to which
the name of St. James is applied, and which is situated between the
two monoliths just described. Two Doric pillars adorn its entrance, which stands tolerably high above the base of the rock. The
cavity itself consists of a fore and back compartment, and contains
several chambers. St. James the apostle does not lie buried here, as
its name might be supposed to imply ; but it was here that he found
a place of refuge at the time Christ lay in the sepulchre.

From tombs we came to tombs. Immediately behind the large
Jewish cemetery we ascended a little upwards, in a south-easterly
direction, and shortly afterwards we stood in front of the so-called

* It may possibly be still remembered that not very long since a very ancient Hebrew Pentateuch is said to have been discovered in this monument.
The particulars were very circumstantial. The distrust I entertained,
and which I immediately unhesitatingly published in the journals, has been
subsequently confirmed, that it was wholly impossible that such a document should be preserved in such a situation, and discovered through
an opening made gradually by the rain. The lucky finder himself has
corrected his first account by stating that it was in one of the sepulchres
of the rock, on the road from Jerusalem to Bethlehem, instead of in the
before-named monument, that he discovered it. I believe he might just as
correctly have named any other hole anywhere else.

sepulchres of the prophets. This very ancient mausoleum is mentioned by Josephus, in his account of the siege of Jerusalem by Titus. He always calls it, from its peculiar construction, the Dovecote, a name still justifiable, for the niches of the tombs are excavated like the apertures of a dovecote: they form a semicircle, placed in two rows, one above the other. Each separate niche is narrow, and runs horizontally into the rock. The whole forms a subterranean structure, excavated in the limestone rock. The larger and smaller chambers, which extend in various directions far into the rock, form it into a real labyrinth.

We descended, exactly opposite the south-eastern wall of Jerusalem, again into the narrow valley, and wandered towards the village of Siloam. Siloam presents a remarkable appearance. It looks as if its origin were deducible from the very commencement of civilisation; as if it stood upon the confines of Troglodyte existence. It consists exclusively of rocky huts and rocky cavities, and abuts upon the foot of the " Mount of corruption." (2 Kings xxiii. 13.) Many sepulchres have here been converted into dwellings for human beings and their flocks; other sepulchres lie in neighbourly contiguity to the dwellings of the living. Upon beholding figures peeping forth from these black rocky grottoes in their picturesque nakedness, amidst flocks of sheep and goats, one fancies himself to be in the midst of the savages of some island in the ocean, to which not the faintest sound of civilisation has hitherto penetrated.

Close to the village is the celebrated stream Shiloah, whose waters " go softly," and from which the prophet Isaiah derived such a beautiful image of the house of David; which, with the semblance of weakness, but possessing the protection of God, made the little brook more powerful than the waves of Euphrates. (Isaiah viii. 6, 7, 8.) It may once have been the confidant of the mysteries and of the prayers of the Temple of Jehovah, as it gently and softly trinkled from the bosom of the rock which bore the Temple. It still flows as gently, as humbly as formerly, now that the proud splendours of Solomon's wondrous work have sunk into ruin.

The pool of Siloam could not well lose the celebrity of possessing especial virtues, since the time that our Lord sent the man born blind thither, that he might wash himself therein and gain his sight. Its virtues were not, however, limited to the eyes: for a French traveller, at the commencement of the 16th century, says, that the Saracens used it in their ablutions, that they might give themselves a more agreeable odour. At all events, even at the present day, Mahometans as well as Christians have a reverential attachment for Shiloah, which their prophet has asserted to be one of the fountains of Paradise.

This spring possesses a remarkable peculiarity in the irregularity and intermittency of its flowing, which was observed at an early period, although what Pliny relates of it is not correct, for he says, that in Judea there is a brook which is dry every sabbath. Nor even is the account given by the pilgrim of Bordeaux exact, that this water flows regularly for six days, and stops on the seventh. This intermitting peculiarity, to which the wonder is restricted, the spring Siloah derives from its parent, the fountain of the Virgin, of which I have before spoken*, and there mentioned that the miraculous pool of Bethesda, in the Gospel of St. John, may have stood in connection with it. (John, v. 2, &c.)

That which is called distinctively the spring of Siloah lies exactly where the hill Ophla terminates in a point between the valley of the Cheesemakers and the valley of Jehoshaphat, and is a small basin hewn in the rock, which is fed by a subterranean canal from the fountain of the Virgin, situated to the north. From it the water flows into the neighbouring pool of Siloah, or King's pool, which is an oblong quadrangle. The numerous fig and olive gardens which lie at the south-eastern foot of Zion, are indebted to the neighbouring waters of Siloah for their luxuriant freshness.

At the distance of only a few paces to the south of the pool stands a magnificent mulberry-tree, and stones placed around its bole furnish a customary resting-place. Tradition says, that it was here that the prophet Isaiah was sawn asunder. We met there to-day a large party of country people, both men and women; but we vainly intreated them for a draught of the water of Siloah from their water pitchers. They absolutely asked for a fee (backshish), which our guide considered in this instance as a positive impertinence. We therefore descended several steps down to the source, and found the water we took up in the hollow of the hand of a very agreeable taste.

The last halting place of to-day's excursion, the Aceldama, that is to say, the field of blood (Acts i. 19), led us through a very ill-famed locality; it is the valley Kessel, into which the Mount of Corruption (2 Kings xxiii. 13), and by the side of it the Mount of Evil Counsel, and opposite, the south-eastern declivity of Zion, all descend. It is here that the idol of the Ammonites, Molech, with the ox head and human arms, stood; to whom Solomon, misguided by strange women (1 Kings xi. 1—8), sacrificed children (Jeremiah vii. 31, 32); and whom even the people of God, together with their king, so far forgot themselves as to worship. The spot is called Tophet, from the beating of the drums intended to drown the

* See page 142.

N

screams of the victims when they were placed in the glowing arms
of the idol. The Mount of Corruption also derives its name from
this profane worship of Israel; whilst its neighbour and ally, the
Mount of Evil Counsel, is named from the villa of Caiaphas having
been situated there, and wherein the evil counsel against Jesus was
held. (Matt. xxvi. 3; John xi. 47, &c.)

But Tophet is likewise the commencement of Gehenna, or of the
valley of Hinnom, which, according to the passage in the discourse
upon the mount, was then a symbol of hell fire. (Matthew xxv. 41.)
For when the Israelites had recognised the error of the worship of
Molech, they were accustomed to exhibit their horror of the infamous
valley by casting the corpses of vile malefactors, as well as of dead
animals, into it; and to purify the mephitic vapours thus caused,
fires were always kept burning, I shall never again read of the fire
of Gehenna, in the sermon on the mount, without having this remarkable valley before my eyes. In fact, to-day an atmosphere
prevailed in the valley, out of the sweep of which we were very glad
to escape. The explanation of its odours was readily found in the
heat of a summer's noon, endured in the centre of the great burial-
place of Jerusalem.

Upon the Mount of Evil Counsel lies Aceldama, or the potter's
field, which the high priest bought with the blood-money of the
betrayer, for the burial-place of strangers. (Matt. xxvii. 7.) I
believe that St. Jerome's corroboration of the identity of this locality
is perfectly well grounded. Quite close to the numerous graves even
now a white clay is dug from the soft limestone rock. Besides, the
Potter's gate of Jeremiah appears to have led hither. (Jer. xix. 2.)
We did not inspect the graves, nor even the remarkable ancient
rocky structure usually called the dead-house, which Dr. Schultz,
through the allusion of Josephus, supposes to be the sepulchre of the
high priest Ananias. The uses to which the potter's field, or rather
the field of blood, was originally appropriated subsequent time has
confirmed; for even during the Crusades it was made use of by the
Western adventurers, as the place of sepulture for pilgrims. How
many a pious heart may not since then, in the midst of its joy at
seeing its most ambitious wish accomplished, have found here upon
this spot rest from all its anxious sorrows and wanderings! I cannot
divest myself of the thought that it must be delightful to die in
Jerusalem: so anticipatory is the indulgence in the idea that our last
moment will be our most delightful one, and yet how rarely is this
hope realised!

The uses of Aceldama have been recently usurped by the south-
western border of Mount Zion. Thence did the supposed sepulchre
of David look down upon us in the valley: close to it the Americans,

and immediately behind it the Greeks, and yet closer to the walls of the city the Armenians and the Latins, have each their cemetery. We contented ourselves to-day with viewing them from a distance, for it wanted but little of high noon. I was therefore rejoiced at reaching the Jaffa gate, through the valley Gihon, and thence in a few minutes we were at the Casa Nuova.

I had promised myself to spend a couple of hours of the evening in the church of the Holy Sepulchre. I was determined to allow nothing to-day to disturb my devotions; neither the observation of an unworthy clergy, nor their sensual forms of religion, nor even learned doubts of local identity. Were this but the place for which the enthusiastic hosts of the Crusaders sacrificed the happiness and love of home,—for which so many of the most valiant swords have glittered,—for which millions of hearts have bled; were this but the place which, since Helena's pilgrimage, has attracted the eyes and hearts of every pilgrim, — received their tears and heard their prayers; where, on the whole surface of the earth, is there such another spot? And, if tradition be correct, upon this very spot the Saviour hung upon the cross; and here, after the brief sabbatic rest of three days, he burst the bonds of the grave for ever : who could approach it without feeling that he here beholds the very countenance of his Redeemer, or without celebrating the entire festival of Easter in the very depths of his soul.

Before entering the church I examined its antique porch. I saw upon one of its pillars the name *Dandolo* inscribed. Six hundred years ago the valiant Doge stood at the same porch of the church of the Holy Sepulchre. We found the doors open, although the Turkish guards were not wanting to the left in the antechamber : the Christian community possess on this day the privilege of a free entrance, we consequently met with a pious congregation already assembled within its area.

When once my departed mother led me by the hand into church, I durst scarcely move my lips; I was affected as children are, with a perception indistinct to themselves, but heartily fervent. When subsequently after many years of study I stood before the expecting community in the same church, I was solemnly affected. I felt conscious of my calling, to speak imperishable words to the hearts of my brethren. Here to day I oscillated in my feelings between man and boy, as I stood at the entrance of the chapel of the Holy Sepulchre, in the midst of a multitude of Orientals prostrated upon their knees, and with their heads uncovered.

We shortly entered the small but brilliantly lighted and richly decorated chamber, containing the rent marble cover of the tomb

A Latin priest performed mass ; standing near him I read with inaudible lips what was deeply graven upon my own heart. A year previously I had written to my distant friends, whilst glowing with the idea of seeing Jerusalem, " When I shall stand praying by the tomb of our Lord, I shall think of you all." To think of those we love, in the highly excited moments of self-dedication, I have always felt to be the most fervent pledge of affection. To-day I did not forget what I had then written.

When Geramb, lost in the contemplation that in the church of the Holy Sepulchre all the Christian sects, by means of their representatives, incessantly elevate their voices in praise of God, he exclaimed, " Strange that one voice still is not heard here—that of the Protestants !" It is true indeed that I myself did not chaunt a hymn of praise, but I rejoiced in the conviction that this instant negatived the assertion of the Trappist.

The whole church was full of devotional emotion. The Greeks assembled in greatest force in their gorgeous church. In the chapel of Helena we beheld Armenian priests magnificently apparelled. Solitary Copts also wandered about, indigent in their raiment, with suffering expressed in their physiognomy, as if performing an incessant act of penitence. The Franciscans, in their dark brown cowls, were parading in procession, which several pilgrims had joined. I was also handed a noble wax taper, that I might participate ; but I preferred to visit, in company with the beloved Padre Lorenzetti alone, the several objects of attraction. The procession went from the altar of the mass, in the small Latin church, to the pillar of scourging ; thence to the prison of Christ, where the soldiers divided the garments ; thence to the spot where the cross was discovered ; then to the chapel of Helena ; to the pillar where Christ was crowned with thorns ; to Mount Calvary ; to the place where the cross stood ; to the stone where the corpse was anointed ; to the Holy Sepulchre ; thence to the place where the Risen One was seen as a gardener ; and to the chapel where Christ, after his resurrection, appeared to his mother. What pleased me in the procession was the edifying chaunting of the Franciscan brotherhood, which reminded me of their musical and song-loving native land. In the sacristy I observed several rituals for all professions of Franciscans at Jerusalem : the prior presented me with a copy as a memento.

From the Sacristy we ascended a staircase higher to a chamber where are preserved, in addition to the festal habiliments of the Latins, two costly relics, namely, the sword and spurs of Godfrey of Bouillon.

Upon returning to the church, which by this time had become tolerably empty, I resolved upon stopping there an hour alone. It

was to me a delicious hour of meditation. I thought for an instant
upon the sceptics of my fatherland, who imagine they have severed
the nerves of positive belief with their sharp knives; and I questioned myself as to the principle which binds me myself to the letter
of the Bible. In spite of my critical calling, which for six years
has entangled me in the complex combinations of the existing spirit
of inquiry, I have not yet attained the vaunted progress; but have
lingered in the convictions I entertained and expressed six years ago.
" The Christian life," as I then said, " and still more the Christian
Church, is thoroughly rooted in the complete historical individuality
of the incarnate divinity; the splendidly iridescent soap-bubble of
poetical belief to which confused philosophical schools have reduced
it, flutters in the air in short-lived joy. Not purposeless is the comparison with the vine. (Matt. xv. 1, &c.) ' Abide in me, and I in
you.' To abide in him is effective. All miserable or sickly attachment to the Prophet of Nazareth, devoid of the Divine nimbus, is
either farce or treachery. Judas also kissed the Redeemer, but close
behind him stood the centurions with swords and staves." (John
xviii. 3, &c.)

Whilst thus wandering solitarily, yet more solitary in my steps
than in my faith, through these localities which were the terrestrial
foundation for the preaching of Him who bore the cross and rose
from the dead, before the eyes of that small troop to whose hearts
nothing was so foreign as a lie, and whose heads without doubt
were incapable of inventing a single star in the firmament of mind:
how bold did the denial of the truth, that Jesus is the Christ, appear
to me upon that spot to be! It is true indeed that Scripture has
many points to which doubt may attach, and which produce even to
innocent faith many vexations. Is it not, it is asked, an internal
contradiction that the revelation of the Son of God, the message of
Redemption, has been conveyed for the instruction and reformation
of the world, in forms which are so uncertain, and which bear more
interpretations than any clause of any statute of a temporal state?
The solution, I reply, lies not far from the contradiction. The
Church of Christ is a living act of God; it was so from the commencement, and is so still. The spirit is its principle, but the spirit
never can be fettered by the letter. As Christ formerly appeared on
earth, combining in his earthly body his divine mission, even so is
he still present. One cried, " He is possessed by a devil." Others,
his wisdom attracted. (John iv. 41—42.) A third confessed, " Thou
art the Son of God." Many saw with open eyes the miracles he performed and the miracle he was, and yet they believed not. Only he
whom the Father chose came to the Son. As was then the case, so is
it now. The Gospel statements, many-sided though their interpreta-

tion may be, have preserved for us the authenticity of Christ's public appearance. The door must be left open to opposition, if faith is to remain perfect faith.   And the various modes of comprehension of St. Matthew, St. John, St. Paul, and St. James, correspond admirably with the variety of human minds.   It is precisely thence, whence so many inconsiderate attacks upon the authority of the Bible have sprung, that we obtain so great a guarantee of its universal destination.   Truly Scripture is not in fault when infidelity despises it, and wisdom treats it superciliously.

But the sorrowful contest in the very bosom of the Church is yet a melancholy fact.   Many a heart throbs sadly that beholds it; even the lamentations of grief are not wanting, and crying aloud that the life of the Church is endangered.   Is there real cause for this ?   It will then commence having a real cause when conscience shall deny, that, above all eyes which are fixed upon its transitory existence, an Eye watches which is eternally open.

Thus have Golgotha and the sepulchre of the Redeemer led me to a confession of the grounds of my faith. When standing upon the dead stones above which the Christian church is built, we are led unconsciously to think of the living pillars whereon the structure rests.

The hour had passed rapidly upon this spot. Although I had not yet commenced my study of the actual sites, yet my repeated visits had familiarised to me the localities of the garden sepulchre and the rocky hill, and in my mind's eye I beheld them as they may have appeared before they were enveloped in the mask of their highly decorated Church.   I did not to-day take a last farewell of the Holy Sepulchre.

DEMANDS ON OUR FAITH AT JERUSALEM.

There is assuredly no city in the world whose surface, with its stones and ruins, offers at this moment to the strictest historical investigation so many characteristics of the past as Jerusalem. Yet this has not sufficed for the desires of leisure minds : for they have recklessly ventured upon discoveries which range far into the domains of the incredible. But credulity has given the heartier welcome to these discoveries, from their appearing to cherish a species of sober piety, which in its day numbered many proselytes. This day has not long been over under every zone ; may there be few amongst my readers who will not too seriously reflect upon what I call *Demands upon our faith !* Indeed those would certainly err, who, on account of the weak side of tradition, should therefore tax it with absolute caducity and penury. To destroy the body because of the deceased limb is unadvisable.

The Via Dolorosa,—who knows it not from its many representations in Catholic countries? That at Jerusalem will naturally be the identical one which led the Saviour to his crucifixion : it runs past the house of the governor, close to the gate of St. Stephen, and terminates in the church of the Holy Sepulchre. I will not adjudicate upon its authenticity : it is at all events probable that the real road, along which Christ walked to death, took this direction and was similarly constructed. For my purpose a few will suffice of the peculiarities which make the Via Dolorosa recognisable, independent of its several chief points. In the house of the governor, the chamber is to be seen wherein Christ sat in bonds before he was led to judgment. Close to it, in a ruinous condition, is seen Pilate's dark judgment hall (John xviii. 28) ; and upon the first story is the balcony whence Pilate uttered the *Ecce homo* to the people. (John xix. 5.) About the middle of the Via dolorosa is the house of the rich man, at whose door Lazarus lay. (Luke xvi. 19.) Probably the representation of this house was suggested, in consequence of such celebrated fathers as Tertullian and Origen giving a positive existence to the parable of our Lord. Near the Temple the spot is identified where Christ absolved the adultress. (John viii. 11.) On Mount Zion a church has been built where Jesus laid the clay upon the eyes of the blind man. (John ix. 6.) A street was formerly named from the archway where Judas is supposed to have hanged himself. (Matt. xxvii. 5.) The house of Zebedee is as well known as that of the pharisee where Mary Magdalene anointed the feet of our Lord. (John xii. 3.) The church of St. Anna contains the grotto of the conception of the Virgin. (Luke i. 31.) Even the very spot where the cock stood when it crowed, and where Peter stood when he heard it, as also the identical one where he wept so bitterly ; all this can be pointed out. Beyond the walls is recognised the spot where Solomon sat when surveying the labourers at work upon the Temple: a stone is also shown which is said to have been the usual seat of Elias ; and the accursed fig-tree (Mark xi. 21.) stood close to the spot where Christ taught the Lord's Prayer. (Matt. vi. 9.)

But the boldest dive into antiquity marks the spot where Abraham and Melchisedeck met (Genesis xiv. 18) ; the scene of the intended sacrifice of Isaac (Gen. xxii. 9) ; and lastly, the tomb of the great parent Adam. This tomb lies exactly under the spot of the cross at Golgotha. It was indeed ingenious to unite the commencement of the human race to the act of its redemption as closely as the root of a tree to its summit. As in former times the very skull of Adam was found, so Golgotha must necessarily possess qualities the very reverse of Aceldama ; for the latter (of the earth of which the Campo Santo in Pisa is formed) is reputed to consume a corpse within twenty-four hours.

But I must not dwell longer upon the idle fondness for such superfluous singularities. We may readily reconcile ourselves to these assertions, by seasoning them with a grain of salt.

OTHER REMINISCENCES OF ANCIENT JERUSALEM.

No reminiscence is more fondly cherished by the children of the Holy City than that of its once glorious Temple of Jehovah; and none so incontestably even yet presents itself to the pilgrim, whether he loiter within the city or survey its cupolas from the adjacent heights. For the large and "noble sanctuary" (El Haram es Scherif), surrounded on the east and south by the city wall, with the two large mosques upon its extensive area, occupies almost one-fourth of the present city. But that the Temple stood here, who of all that dwell within the walls of Jerusalem knows it not, be he Mahometan, be he Christian or Jew. And yet over none of the antiquities of Jerusalem does so thick a veil hang as over this Temple, of which many a fragment and many a trace may still be found, especially under ground. The haram is unapproachable by all who do not hold the faith of the prophet. Only two travellers, and these Englishmen, have succeeded in modern times in visiting the subterranean vaults which once supported the Temple. Any attempts, such as have already been made, to inspect the sanctuary by means of artifice, would in the present state of things scarcely be possible without the danger of absolute destruction.

The best position possible for viewing the haram in its vicinity is the house of the governor, now a barrack, lying at its north-western corner. In one of my first excursions through the city, Padre Lorenzetti led me to the flat roof of this house. As we ascended the steps a halting invalid very conveniently joined us, who, by means of his crutch, subsequently used to our advantage, maintained a certain authority and became our complete Cicerone in the survey of the site of the Temple.

The mosque of Omar, usually called Kubbet es Sachrah (cupola of the rock), occupies the centre of the area, and is considered one of the grandest and most tasteful temples in the world. Between it and the mosque el Aksa, which is contiguous to the southern wall óf the city, there lies at equal distances from each, and enclosed by olives, oranges, and cypresses, a large marble basin with spring water, which invites pious promenaders both to drink and to bathe. The area itself is chiefly paved with marble ; the green turf which here and there sprouts forth, and here and there a few trees, especially cypresses, contrast agreeably with the flat stone surface. Besides these two large mosques there are several small houses for prayer spread over the area.   The one named after Fatima is especially distinguished.   Lastly, there are two peculiarly venerated spots on the eastern wall of the city : that upon the left of the Sachrah mosque is called the throne of Solomon, and that upon the right is held to be the place which Mahomet will occupy on the day of judgment.

The celebrated mosque itself is an octagonal building, sixty-seven feet high, with windows almost equally high in the walls.   It rises above a platform to which eight steps ascend, and the length of which from east to west is 450 feet, and from north to south 550. The octagon is arched over by an elegant cupola covered with lead, at the summit of which a golden crescent glitters.   Upon the external walls of the mosque, mosaics glittering in green, are observed, and around them many sentences from the Koran inscribed in golden letters upon a blue ground.

The three porches of the mosque, situated to the north, the east, and the south, are severally called the gate of Heaven, the gate of David, and the gate of Prayer.   In front of the gate of David stands David's judgment-seat.

In the interior, that which is most remarkable and most sacred stands immediately beneath the great cupola, viz., the rock es Sachrah, from which the mosque derives its name.   Even the pious Crusaders believed that Jacob rested upon this stone when he dreamt of the ladder to heaven. (Gen. xxviii. 12.)   The Caaba at Mecca alone surpasses this rock " of Paradise" in the veneration of the faithful ; for upon it the prophet is said to have stood when he passed hence to heaven.

The mosque el Aksa (that is to say, " the most distant," namely, from Mecca) properly forms in conjunction with the Sachrah mosque but one entire whole. Its style of architecture is that of a church of the early Christian centuries.   It was probably the splendid church which Justinian, about the middle of the sixth century, built and dedicated to the Virgin, and which, a century later, was converted by Omar into a mosque.

The contemplation of the consecrated sanctuaries of the present day leads me necessarily to a retrospect, however brief, of the sanctuaries of the past, which once rose above the same foundations.   It is three thousand years since Solomon built to the God who had given him "wisdom and understanding exceeding much, and largeness of heart, even as the sand that is on the sea-shore" (1 Kings iv. 29), that temple which was " of fame and of glory throughout all countries." (1 Chron. xxii. 5.) David even relates that in " his trouble" he contributed thereto " a hundred thousand talents of gold, and a thousand thousand talents of silver." (1 Chron. xxii. 14.) Lebanon contributed its cedars; Tyre helped with its ships; Sidon sent cunning men and labourers; and thus, in seven years, the holy building was complete and admired at a period rich in wonderful works. But its duration was brief. At the commencement of the 5th century of its date, after the rude hand of plunder had repeatedly ravaged it, Nebuchadnezzar buried it amidst flames. (2 Kings xxv. 9.)

Upon the return of the Jews, fifty years afterwards, from Babylon, they brought with the permission the desire also to build a new temple. It was immediately commenced by Zerubbabel (Haggai i. 14.); but only completed twenty years afterwards, after a variety of interruptions. (Ezra vi. 15.) This second building did not by far attain the splendour and magnitude of the first. Solomon's temple was ardently and longingly remembered, especially since Zerubbabel's temple had been plundered and desecrated to the worship of idols. (1 Maccab. xxiii. 68.)

Herod the Great shared and availed himself of the sympathies of the people. Among the structures with which he renewed the splendour and beauty of the ancient city of David, he determined also upon the plan of a new and splendid temple. For this purpose he caused the greater portion of the remains of the preceding one to be removed, and renovated by his new structure (the description of which Josephus has given us) many of the splendours of that of Solomon.

It was through the halls of this temple that our Saviour wandered, and it was here that many of the discourses out of his divine mouth were delivered to the people. It was its walls and its stones which were regarded by the admiring eyes of his disciples when our Saviour uttered his terrific prophecy. (Matt. xxiv. 2.) Forty years afterwards this prophecy was fulfilled. For the destruction of the city by Titus extended also to the temple. It was the last bulwark of the despairing combatants: it was even still maintained when the strong keep was taken. Every inch of its area cost the Romans fire and blood; and it was only when the flames soared above it that itself became the prey of the storm.

What first occupied its site after this great catastrophe was one of those ironical acts in which Hadrian delighted to indulge. A temple

to Jupiter and an equestrian statue of the emperor were fixed where
the Holy of Holies had stood. Both idol and statue lasted as long
as the temple of Solomon, for it was Justinian who first adorned the
ancient sorrowing mount of the temple with a Christian church.
This church became before the middle of the seventh century, under
Omar, a Turkish mosque ; and by the side of it rose, fifty years
later, the venerated " rocky cupola."

Both survived the centennial episode of the Christian dominion at Jerusalem. But before the cross supplanted the crescent
upon the haughty cupola, Tancred deluged its marble pavement
with so terrific a bath of blood that a contemporary informs us,
" they rode into the temple up to the knees in blood." Justinian's
former church was presented by Baldwin the Second to a new order
of knighthood, which derived from it its title of Knights Templars.

But when Saladin's sword glittered over the holy city, together
with the Christian arms, the cross also speedily disappeared again
from both the houses of God, whose areas desecrated according to
the Moslem by Christian unbelief were purified with rose-water.
Since Saladin, Haram es Scherif has become without dispute what
it still remains at the present day.

Such is the history of the sanctuaries upon the Temple Mount of
Jerusalem, where first the celebrated temple of Solomon stood. Its
duration was indeed short ; the course of twenty centuries has seen
so much restored and re-destroyed upon it. Yet notwithstanding
all this, the walls of the Turkish sanctuary bear witness, even to the
present day, of that wonderful structure : for upon many spots,
especially upon the south-eastern and south-western corners of these
walls, are still observed such colossal and yet artistically sculptured
stones, that we may unhesitatingly consider them to have been
portions of the external walls of the original temple of Solomon.*
Remarkable trophies are they ; trophies of the conquest of human
art over all-powerful time. As they were placed three thousand
years ago, so lie they still as immovable as the rock which supports
them : as if the living God, whose temple they enclosed, had laid
them with his own hand, and had there placed them as a token that
He dwelt upon his mount amidst his people.

I must still once more discourse of tombs, these most faithful and
often such eloquent witnesses of the past. A tomb suggestive of

* Compare Robinson's Palestine, &c. vol. ii. p. 62. where measurements are given of several of these stones. The corner stone of the western
side (to the south-west) measures 30 feet 10 inches in length, by 6 feet 6
inches in width ; several other stones vary between 20½ and 24½ feet of
length and 5 feet of thickness.

much reflection is the tomb of David.   Peter, in his discouse upon
Whitsunday, exclaimed, " David's sepulchre is with us unto this
day," (Acts ii. 29.)   If the sepulchre of the great king had been
preserved for a thousand years, it must have been considerable and
prominent.   Besides, the Books of Kings and Chronicles both speak
frequently and definitely enough of the royal sepulchres, wherein
David and Solomon, as well as eight of their princely successors,
with a high priest, were all placed together.   And, in fact, to the
north of Jerusalem, about a quarter of a league from the Damascus
gate, there is a noble tomb, which bears the name of the Sepulchre of
the Kings.   I, as well as many other travellers, have visited these
dark rocky vaults, which I might call a subterranean palace of tombs.
They are not like other tombs about Jerusalem, excavated in the
rocky wall of a valley ; but they are excavated in the depths of the
rock itself.   To descend into them you first pass through what resembles a large quadrangular cistern, sunk into the rock, in the western side of which a porch is carved, which, although deprived of its
pillars, is still admirable for the splendid carvings that surround it.
The porch leads first into an arched hall, an oblong quadrangle,
and from this you pass through a low door-way, on the southern side,
into a large square chamber, from the three sides of which passages
emerge into the real chambers of the dead, which have spacious sepulchral niches hewn in their sides.   All that I here saw exhibited
unusual pomp and art, attested also by the fragments of marble sarcophagi which lie strewn about.

Our visit to it was accompanied, however, with annoyances
enough ; for instance, the first door-way, after passing the porch, we
found almost wholly choked up with stones.   Besides, my guide,
who was a native of New York naturalised in Jerusalem, had suggested the additional anxiety that we might possibly be fallen upon
by Bedouins or Albanians within this rocky prison ; a fear excited,
doubtlessly, by our having met with a small troop of the latter, to his
infinite alarm, in the olive grove between the gate and the sepulchre.

Does, however, this noble sepulchre bear its right name ? and did
it really receive the remains of the Jewish sovereigns ?   Its splendour, and its peculiarity, speak in favour of this supposition ; but
its position is against it.   For the sepulchre of David, and of the
children of David, lay upon Zion ; of this there can be no doubt,
for it is expressly testified.   With greater justice the sepulchre in
question may suggest other royal funereal monuments ; namely,
those of King Herod.   The Herodian sepulchres, whose costliness
is undoubted, are mentioned by Josephus, in his History of the
Wars of the Jews, in such a manner that they must have lain
near the then northern city wall, traces of which are still found to

run close past the so-called Sepulchre of Kings. I therefore know nothing that may be against the supposition, that the latter are the sepulchres of Herod : it is also further confirmed by Schultz having shown, upon very good foundation, that the sepulchre of Queen Helena, of Adiabene, which Robinson sought to refer to the Sepulchre of Kings, lay upon the north-western rising ground, beyond the city.

Still the question, where did the sepulchres of the Jewish kings lie, remains unanswered. Is possibly the tradition credible, according to which, the sepulchre of David lies upon the southern declivity of Zion, and which is guarded by a sheikh ? There stands, namely, beside a mosque and a former Franciscan monastery, a very ancient church of which it appears mention was made, even as early as the 4th century. Within it, an apartment is venerated as having been the scene of the Lord's Supper, as also of the descent of the Holy Ghost, and other sacred proceedings, and under this apartment it is assumed, the sepulchre of David lies. I did not myself see it, for its Mahometan guard very jealously conceals it from the eye of any Christian.

On this assumption it is easily explained that this monument, the form of which resembles the sepulchre of a Santon, or Turkish saint, is nothing more than a Turkish superstructure, beneath the floor of which the real sepulchre must be concealed within the rock. But whence springs the tradition linked to it ? An historical investigation shows, that the reminiscences of the Last Supper and of Whitsuntide, even as early as the 4th century, were associated with this locality, whereas the assumption of its being the sepulchre of David dates its origin subsequently to the crusades. I am induced, therefore, to suppose; that the Whitsun address of St. Peter (Acts ii. 29), " his sepulchre is with us to this day," occasioned the finding of the sepulchre at the very feet of the orator, especially as the ancient accounts of it raise no contradiction.

But a different supposition is opposed to mine. The Rabbi Benjamin, of Tudela, in the 12th century relates the following singular circumstance, in his travels which certainly does not merit the suspicion of being a forgery :—

" The Patriarch of Jerusalem replaced a fallen wall of the church of Zion by stones from the ancient wall of Zion. Two labourers at mid-day disrupted the stones, without their comrades, and discovered beneath one the aperture of a cavity : they went in, and found a palace standing upon richly decorated marble pillars, and in front of the palace a table, upon which lay a golden sceptre and a diadem. Similar monuments were adjacent to this, and several closed chests also lay there. But as the two men were about to enter

the palace, a violent wind which blew from the aperture of the
cavity, threw them down senseless upon the ground. It was not
until evening that they recovered and quitted the cavity. They
communicated the incident to the Patriarch, and he informed the
Rabbi, Abraham the Pious, of it. The Rabbi asserted the discovered
monuments to be the sepulchres of David and of Solomon. But
when the two labourers were solicited to make further research they
became bedridden, and were not to be persuaded to any further inspection of the remarkable cavity, from their religious fears. Upon
this the place by command of the Patriarch was completely closed
up again." Benjamin of Tudela further adds, that he received the
account of the matter from Abraham the Pious himself.

Dr. Thenius, who has recently devoted a special treatise to the
sepulchres of the kings of Juda*, gives credence in the main to this
narrative, and deduces from it by the conjunction of several reasons
the existing tradition of the sepulchre of David. Many doubts,
indeed, might be easily raised in objection to it. Nevertheless, I also
participate in the opinion that, somewhere in the immediate vicinity
of this traditional sepulchre, the genuine sepulchres of the kings are
concealed in the bosom of the rock. Their discovery would without
doubt amply reward even a laborious investigation, by its weighty
results. According to Josephus treasures have been found in it
twice since its origin; the High Priest Hyrcanus is reputed to have
taken three thousand talents from it; and Herod, a rich raiment of
gold and jewels: statements which at least may not be wholly destitute of fact. For my part, I wish to make it as credible as possible, if thereby the proper hands might be won to undertake
energetically the discovery of the sepulchres of the kings of Juda.
Thenius advises excavations within the walls of the American cemetery, under the pretext of erecting a charnel-house. As long as
Jerusalem lingers in its present condition it would be commendable
to follow this advice.

BETHLEHEM. SAN SABA ON THE DEAD SEA.

I have already announced my arrival at Bethlehem.   I came with
my two companions out of the desert of St. John, the sun was going

---

* See Ilgen's Zeitschrift für die historische Theologie, 1844, Part i. pp.
1—60. Die Gräber der Könige von Juda, vornehmlich durch Berichti-
gung der Topographie des vorexilischen Jerusalem nachgewiesen von
Otto Thenius.

down as I greeted the town, which is seated upon its rocky hills above a carpet of brightly glittering olives, and which the tongue of the prophet had called, "not the least among the Princes of Juda." (Matt. ii. 6.) The view of Bethlehem was indescribably delightful to me, the impression made by its appearance harmonised so thoroughly with the ideas I brought with me. It wore, as it were, the halo of transfiguration; all was as silent around me as if an instant of devotion had wholly absorbed the tumult of the day. Bethlehem seemed a Sunday, at once solemn and lovely.

Sunset necessarily suggested the sunrise for which the world was indebted to this town. Who could approach it without being full of it? What would the world have been had not light arisen out of Bethlehem? As the poor Virgin became the "blessed among women" (Luke i. 28), even so was this modest mountain town of Judea selected to become the most venerated of all the cities of the earth.

Since the birth of our Saviour not only has its name remained impressed in the memory of all; but its hills, its rocks, its walls, have remained irremovably fixed, before the eyes of all who have made the pilgrimage of the Holy Land, for doubt has not endeavoured to touch Bethlehem. But its celebrity extends far beyond the Christian era; a thousand years before it gave the world the King with the crown of thorns, the King of the realm of truth, it bestowed upon the house of Israel its royal Psalmist and divine hero. Both David and Christ sprang from Bethlehem; it was this landscape which their eyes surveyed when they were first opened beneath the canopy of heaven: full of these impressions I rode forward to the monastery which, with its high walls, towers above the deep valley to the north, like the defensive Castle of Bethlehem, opposite to which, upon a neighbouring hill about a hundred paces distant, it stands in an imposing attitude.

In front of the gate of the monastery, upon the broad area paved with flat stones, we met with numerous inhabitants of Bethlehem, all of whom presented a respectable appearance: upon the stone bench, close to the monastery, sat also a Franciscan, who greeted us with a friendly welcome. The monastery in its extensive area is inhabited collectively by Latins, Greeks, and Armenians, although any thing but fraternal unity prevails amongst them. Complaints of the unfriendliness and assumptions of the Greeks were among the first communications made to us by the Latin prior, after our introduction to the monastery.

This same evening I visited the church. Its chief nave has a noble aspect; four rows of marble pillars, the splendour of which, however, no longer dazzles, adorn it; its roof is not arched, and

rests upon a frame-work of beams of cypress-wood : the walls are un-
adorned, but they appear to have been divested of some former decoration.   In the arches of the windows are discerned glittering remains
of the beautiful mosaics of golden glass, which still adorn the mosque
of St. Sophia, at Constantinople, as well as other ancient ecclesiastical
buildings.   The whole nave of this cross-shaped church is deserted
and waste ; the wings only of the cross are in use, and of these the
Latins absolutely possess the smallest portion in their little church of
St. Catherine.

This little church which, to my delight, is furnished with an
organ, is connected by means of a subterranean passage with the
sanctuary, which lies fifteen steps below the high altar of the
Armenian and Greek church.   The sanctuary is a low rocky cavern,
arched at the roof, its floor paved with white marble, and its marble
walls hung with silken draperies.   In the midst, between the two
flights of stairs which lead upwards to the high altar of the church,
lies, in a niche, the spot which is revered as the birth-place of our
Saviour.   The little flames of many silver lamps light it up night
and day ; a little marble table, supported by low pillars, serves for
an altar ; in front of it, a spot upon the floor is distinguished by a
glory of inlaid jasper, and inscribed in Latin with the words—" Here
was Jesus Christ born of the Virgin Mary."   At a few paces from
the niche of the birth-place, stands the marble manger, and opposite
the crib lies, clothed with slabs of marble, the stone upon which the
Virgin sat when she received the worshipping Kings (Matt. ii. 11);
an oil painting hangs over it, representing the scene, and another in
the background of the grotto, depicts the Virgin with the Child in
her lap.

I confess the grotto made a solemn impression upon me.   And I
do not doubt that the text in St. Luke (ii. 7), although it only speaks
of a manger outside of the inn, admits the assumption of a grotto as
the birth-place of Christ ; for nothing is more common, even at
the present day, in Palestine and the adjacent countries of the East,
than the conversion of grottoes into stables, so that St. Luke would
not specially point out this circumstance.   Besides, this grotto so
revered, as I before mentioned *, can be proved to have acquired its
actual celebrity about the middle of the 2nd century ;   and the
church itself, which was raised there for its distinction, is a memorial
of the piety of the Empress Helena.

In the subterranean passage, from which about twenty steps lead
upwards into the church of St. Catherine of the Latins, besides the
altar of Joseph, the altar of the innocent child, the graves of Euse-

* See page 151.

bius of Cremona, as well as of the noble Roman lady Paula and her daughter, still further a chapel especially, and a sepulchre, are regarded as sacred. The latter have both reference to an individual, both monk and presbyter, hermit and learned man, whose memory is also very dear to me. The chapel, which receives its light from above, through an opening in the rock, was originally the monastic cell wherein, in spite of the rancour, contempt, and charge of heresy with which his contemporaries repaid the gratitude due to him, he for many years pursued, with iron industry, his learned labours upon the text of the Bible. The adjacent grave is the bed of repose where he, the venerable patriarch of ninety, laid down his weary head. Who does not perceive that I am speaking of St. Jerome, the translator and critic of the holy original records? I seated myself upon the stone bench in his rocky cell, my heart replete with joy that the same calling which he exercised had procured me the happiness of seeing Bethlehem.

On the following morning I left early for the purpose of visiting the monastery of San Saba. It is true that the tales of the insecurity of the road were deterring enough to check its prosecution; for, as San Saba lies about the middle of the road running to the Dead Sea, the notorious hordes of Bedouins who dwell upon its coasts are reputed to extend their predatory incursions even thus far. But I was too much interested in making myself acquainted with the celebrated library of that monastery to allow myself to be prevented by uncertain dangers from visiting it.

As soon as we had passed the vicinity of Bethlehem, which even at the present day justifies, by its olives, figs, and vineyards, as well as its corn and rice fields, the name of " Ephratah," the fruitful, which was formerly given it (Micah v. 2), we were encompassed by the desert. Yellow sand surrounded us in the valleys, as well as upon the hills. Mountain deposits of limestone with a whitish glitter, and rarely a shrub or a tree : such was the character of this district. A rude morning music speedily assailed our ears ; this was the howling of jackals, which are not unfrequent here. Subsequently an old jackal with three young ones, in the consciousness of perfect security, ran along the heights which closely bordered our road. We also met some Bedouins ; and even came across two small encampments in black tents, with their flocks of goats and sheep. But beyond our own considerable fears nothing molested us.

After a journey of three hours we stood upon a summit of considerable elevation, in view of the neighbouring bold mountain fortress which bears the name of the monastery of San Saba. Beyond it the Dead Sea did not appear to be further off than half a league. That sea makes a sublimely beautiful impression, with its flat black mirror-like surface, lying at the foot of the waste

o

and desert sandy mountain chain as at the feet of a rough and heart-less guard.

When surveying this melancholy land where sand succeeds to sand, one limestone hill to the other, and one rock to another, how difficult is it to believe we stand upon the scene of events which are so dear to history! I hence surveyed the desert in which David, when he fled from Saul, ran through his youthful adventures. The Desert of Engedi, with its rocks and chamois, could not be very dis-tant to the south of the sea. (1 Sam. xxiii. 29.) It was there that the proscribed youth (1 Sam. xxiv. 1, &c.) excited by his noble con-duct his persecutor to tears: so that he exclaimed, " Thou art more righteous than I." (1 Sam. xxiv. 16, 17.) Thither hastened, also, the beautiful Abigail, and became David's wife. (1 Sam. xxv. 18.) But the scene of other reminiscences not less romantic, yet imbued with Christian solemnity, lay close before my eye. For the wild rent mountain chain, whose precipices form the bed of the Kidron, and whose precipitous declivity in the west bears the monastery of San Saba, has been the witness of the enthusiasm and barbarous bloodshed of many martyrs whom even these comfortless and soli-tary rocky ravines did not secure against the murderous steel of the Saracens. Distant from us as, in this age of philosophy and the sobriety of utilitarian selfishness, the melancholy enthusiasm of the Christian hermits may lie, upon beholding with one's own eyes their dens, their recesses, in the midst of the terrific desert where nothing dwells but want and danger, who would not there admire the holy zeal which nerved such heroes !

In a few minutes a voice saluted us from one of the two monastic towers, and directed us to a deeper portal. Upon entering I pre-sented my letter of recommendation from the parent monastery at Jerusalem ; we were received in a friendly manner, and led into a light reception-room.

I called the monastery a mountain fortress: such it is in its fullest sense. On the declivity of the rock, which looks down several hundred feet into the ravine of the Kidron, the stony struc-ture commences, supported upon massive pillars ; it thence ascends the mountain in a succession of terraces, until at the summits its strong walls are surmounted by two towers. Upon one of the towers a vigilant eye watches the approaches of the Bedouins. For, although a basket of small black loaves hangs down constantly for the use of the hungry sons of the desert, yet they from time to time make hostile attacks upon the harmless asylum.

After having refreshed myself with a little wine and bread, I took a saunter through the interior of the monastery. I was surprised by the sight of a palm-tree, and several small garden-parterres in this building of rocks, and upon rocks: to effect this it was requisite to fetch fertile soil from a distance. Close in front of the church, upon the paved area of the court, lies beneath a cupola the tomb of San Saba. This, as well as the church and chapel, is richly decorated in the usual style of the Greeks. From the nave of the church, which is mainly hewn out of the solid rock, I ascended some steps into an upper side-room, where there are arranged, upon trestles, about a hundred Greek and Arabic manuscripts, intermixed with some printed books. I took a hasty glance at each of them. After this I visited the chapel of St. John of Damascus, who wrote many of his learned works in the monastery, and lies buried in the chapel which bears his name. But, as a remarkable object for inspection, I was shown a dark chamber, wherein many hundred skulls lay piled up. They are said to be chiefly the remains of the last sanguinary attack which burst out upon the poor monks, during the Crusades, and which thoroughly extirpated them.

I now had a slight dispute with the monks. Having expressed my astonishment that the contents of their library was so small, the librarian replied that there was another, in the tower above. Upon wishing to see it, I was told the key was not at hand, as the individual, to whose custody it was committed, had gone this very morning to Jerusalem. I was incredulous, and became still more so, upon hearing immediately afterwards a violent dispute amongst the monks themselves, about the matter. It terminated in my being conducted to the tower; an undertaking, indeed, of some trouble and labour, during the noontide heat of a July day in this climate.

But I had not been deceived; this library was, in fact, more considerable than the first. Here, also, I inspected each manuscript, and the two monks who accompanied me speedily found that I was more conversant with the subject than themselves. The contents of this library were very like that which I found upon Mount Sinai. Among the many patristic, ecclesiastical, and Biblical manuscripts, of which not a few were of the tenth and eleventh centuries, and many neatly executed, I found once more the ancient Hippocrates. Besides some Greek manuscripts, I observed several Russian, Wallachian, Arabic, and Syriac, as well as ten beautiful Abyssinian parchment manuscripts. Intermixed with the latter, I discovered a Greek uncial codex, an Evangelistarium of the eighth or ninth century. My companions, however, would not believe that the work was Greek, until I read them several lines of it. Such is the extent of knowledge in a celebrated Greek monastery!

My investigations did not terminate favourably. I found a heap of manuscript fragments swept up into the corner as worthless. I asked if I might select some of them as reminiscences of my visit.

The monks consented. But having made my selection, and with
their consent having removed a fine ancient uncial leaf from a modern manuscript, they cited to me the prohibition against withdrawing any manuscript, but were evidently rejoiced at my skilful selection.
They further told me that, not long since, a Russian Archimandrite
had made a complete list of all the manuscripts.* I, for my part,
contented myself with the notices gleaned from a very superficial
inspection.†

After these warm studies in the library, I found the mid-day
repast prepared. It was neither meagre nor penurious, and I enjoyed it exceedingly.

An hour later I visited the rocky grotto of St. Saba, at a short
distance from the monastery. He continued still to inhabit it, even
after he had founded his monastery containing room for several
hundred brethren. Saba is the Corypheus among the saints of his
age. A contemporary has left us an interesting biography of him.
During the hostilities commenced by the church against the Mono-
physites and Origenists and which resulted from the synod of
Chalcedon, Saba, with his monastery, constituted the focus of orthodoxy. He knew neither limit nor fear in his orthodox zeal. Hence,
one day he did not hesitate to hasten from the quiet concealment
of his cave in the desert to Jerusalem, there to utter his anathema,
within sight of Golgotha, against the heretic patriarchs, in the very
presence of the patriarchal convocation and their imperial guards.
A humane trait of his character is also evinced in an anecdote, still
current, respecting him. The solitary patriarch became familiar
with several foxes of the desert, which returned regularly every
evening to the ravine of Kidron, to receive their daily stipend of a
morsel of bread. The descendants of these clients come even now,
in the 13th century, after Saba's death, for the same purpose daily,
to the foot of the monastery, which the monks readily interpret into a
miracle of their good father.

I would willingly now have visited the dry deep ravine of the
Kidron, as well as some of the many caverns of the eastern declivity,
which had all been inhabited by pious hermits. But I wished to
return again to Bethlehem to-day, consequently time pressed. After
presenting a gratuity to the monastery, we re-mounted our mules
between four and five, and rode up the rocky heights. Thence had
we first beheld it, and thence we took our farewell from the hospitable monastery, from its inhospitable environs, and from the mys-

* Scholz has also given in his " Biblisch Kritischen Reisen," pp. 143—
148. some account of the manuscripts at San Saba.

† Some weeks subsequently I heard of a concealed treasure of manuscripts
at San Saba. I should have much liked to have followed up the matter.

.terious Dead Sea. I now almost regret I did not make an excursion from San Saba to the sea. Several of the so-much-feared Bedouins sat, at our departure, in the hall of the monastery. I think it would have been very easy to have come to an understanding with them for a safe conduct.

For the second time I awoke beneath the sun of Bethlehem, and consequently in the bosom of a Christian city, in the midst of the great anti-Christian empire ; for Bethlehem, since Ibraham Pasha destroyed the Turkish quarter, numbers only Christian inhabitants There may be in all about 3,000 souls, of which there are equal numbers of Greeks * and Catholics, and about 50 Armenians. Who would not rejoice that precisely Bethlehem forms this Christian oasis in the midst of the Turkish wilderness ?

The occupation of the inhabitants of Bethlehem has a marked Christian tendency. For instance, they manufacture the delicate pilgrim-tokens out of mother-o'-pearl, the beautiful black stone found in the Dead Sea, of ivory, compressed camels' hoofs, and the wood of the olive. Upon large oystershells their favourite subject is the Last Supper, or Paul and Peter, the Resurrection, or the Archangel Michael, and other similar representations. The black stone is chiefly carved into drinking vessels, or into the form of a small Psalter, inlaid with Arabic characters. The majority of these objects of *virtù* have not essentially an artistical value ; yet, among other things, I purchased a cross that would have done honour to a Parisian artist.

Besides these occupations, the inhabitants of Bethlehem know how to avail themselves of the fertility of their soil. They cultivate wine and oil, and pursue agriculture and grazing. The Hebrew name " Bethlehem " is therefore as well founded as the more cus- tomary Arabic name of " Beit Lahm." The first means " Bread- house," the last " Meat-house." Meat, as well as bread, has never been wanting to the natives of Bethlehem, although they have thoroughly experienced the weight of the iron rod of the Turkish government.

Travellers have informed us, that the costume of the women of Bethlehem corresponds with Raphael's type adopted in his pictures of the Madonna. I can but confirm this observation. Above a blue vest or frock, supported by a girdle, they wear a red garment, to which they often add a white veil. In the stability incidental to

* Williams (The Holy City, 1845, p. 498.) gives in his extract from the Diocesal census of the Greek Patriarch of Jerusalem only 280 as the number of orthodox Christians in Bethlehem, as at Jerusalem he enumerates only 600. (See in contradiction, vol. ii. p. 42.)

so many customs of Oriental life, it is not impossible that the costume now prevalent is the same as that worn more than two thousand years ago.

In the walk we took to-day through the town, we were frequently
greeted by the inhabitants with a friendly *buon giorno.* They
appeared to delight in being able to address us in the language of
their spiritual fathers.   Their stock of words, however, would not
have reached far*; though I met with a lad of fourteen who accompanied the hawking of his mother-o'-pearl ornaments with an Italian
commentary, and informed me that in Europe we possessed neither
a Holy City nor Holy Places.

I made a rapid ride through the vicinity of Bethlehem.   The
field in which the shepherds were (Luke, ii. 8.) on Christmas eve,
surrounded by the rejoicing hosts of Heaven, is shown near the
village, Beit Sahur, which, like Bethlehem, is inhabited only by
Christians.   The field lies enclosed by a low wall, in a valley rich in
olive gardens, posted upon a cheerful wooded declivity.   A consecrated grotto, also, is not wanting.

Another grotto, celebrated under the name of the Milk Grotto,
and furnished with an altar, lies at a short distance beyond the
monastery.   Turkish as well as Christian superstition derives thence
a beneficial powder, and it is formed into the little cakes called
terra sigillata impressed with the Spanish cross.   It is here that
Mary is said to have lain concealed before the flight into Egypt.
(Matt. ii. 14.)   The grotto is hewn in the soft limestone rock; its
moist chalky walls suggested the singular idea of milk.

More interesting than the grotto and the field were the gigantic reservoirs, at a league from Bethlehem, and called Solomon's
Pools.   These pools, three in number, lie in a high rocky valley,
and the grandeur of their design and the magnificent structure of
their walls, proclaim them to be of the highest antiquity.   They lie
upon terrace-like projections, one above the other, the highest being
the smallest, and the lowest the largest.   The length of the last is
nearly six hundred feet, its breadth about two hundred, and its
depth fifty.   In all of them three steps lead to the bottom, which,
as well as the sides of the pool, is covered with mortar.   The water, I
found, in the lowest pool was very deep; in the middle one it was
deep; and in the upper one it was wholly wanting, as a conduit had
been found from the source itself.   The main object of these reservoirs is to be learned from the aqueduct, chiefly subterranean,
which hence, for a distance of four leagues, runs to Jerusalem.

Not less remarkable than the pools is the well whence they are
supplied.   It lies close to the ancient Saracenic fortress, El Burak;
its orifice is closed with a large stone, and it contains, at a depth of

twelve feet, two beautifully arched cavities, whence a subterranean canal leads to the pools.

The unpoetical fancy of the monks has raised this well into peculiar celebrity. When, namely, the author of the Canticles called his Spouse (iv. 12.) "a fountain sealed," he had, according to the monks, this well in his eye. And as together with the sealed fountain, a "garden enclosed" is used to characterise "his fair love," the monks have also discovered this in the immediate vicinity of the well and the pools, in a spot where, even now, gardens full of oranges and figs glow in luxuriant profusion. These reminiscences of the Song of Solomon will not, it is true, be to the taste of every one ; but, in fact, every probability speaks in favour of the opinion that Solomon possessed here his favourite retreat, the splendid Etham, in the valley of these gardens watered by a babbling brook — a rarity in these lands — and rich in traces of ancient buildings.

From reminiscences of this prince, whose virtues have made him more renowned than his vices, I passed by rapid transition to the last of his successors, who still, with some appearance of independence, wore the regal mantle. Remarkable structures have made his name as glorious as that of his great ancestor, but, unhappily, they only served to house his vices. About a league and a half from the pools of Solomon's tower, with its singular conical summit, is the so called mountain of the Franks, upon which Herod constructed his pleasure seat, which was equally distinguished by its splendour and its strength, and which gradually grew into a considerable city. Its remaining ruins are without form and inconsiderable ; — fit fingerpost to the resting place of the tyrannical ruler. Its present name has been given to the mountain from its appropriation by the Crusaders.

In the afternoon I quitted Bethlehem. But little of all that I have seen has remained so permanently impressed upon my soul as this city and its vicinity.

The road home to Jerusalem conducted us through a richly cultivated landscape, close past the grave of Rachel, for there is no doubt that a monumental tomb was erected to the beautiful mother of Joseph and Benjamin precisely in this locality: and tradition may very well have preserved the identical spot, and have led to the Turkish sepulchre now there. With Rachel I did not forget the devout Moabite Ruth for one of the fields in the neighbourhood of this monument was the scene of her story. But immediately beyond the tomb, an arid stony district begins, where it would be difficult now to glean corn with Ruth. Half an hour afterwards, on our right, was the Greek monastery, Mar Elias, which commands the neighbouring valleys, and springing from the bosom of groves of

olives and fig-trees, looks towards Bethlehem as well as towards
Jerusalem. Whether it is exactly to this locality that the memory of
the prophet is linked as he fled from Jezabel, may be very doubtful
(1 Kings, xix. 4); but it is certain that in the plain Rephaim, or
the valley of Giants, which lay close upon our left at a distance of
about a mile from this monastery, as far as the valley Hinnon, was
to be recognised the field of battle where the newly crowned David
twice defeated the army of the Philistines (2 Sam. v. 20. 25); and here
was "a sound of going in the tops of the mulberry-trees" (1 Chron.
xiv. 15), which even now are not wanting, and which proclaimed the
aid of the Divine arm.

BETHANY. DEPARTURE FROM JERUSALEM.

Bethany I had repeatedly greeted from the Mount of Olives,
before I went over to it. It is exceedingly pleasantly situated as
seen from the summit of the Mount of Olives, on the side which
declines to the east. From this point it made upon me an impression
similar to that felt and described by Schubert,—a feeling that one must
repose there a while before proceeding onward to the Holy City; or
as if it were a tranquil holy Easter eve.

It was only on the day previous to my departure from Jerusalem
that I visited Bethany. It lies to the south east of the city, at a
distance of about two miles. The Mount of Olives declines a little
in this direction, and then extends into a flat and gradually ascending
ridge towards the east. Here lies the small village, which, from its
elevated position, enjoys a beautiful view over the desert valleys in
the east as far as the Dead sea.

I entered into conversation with several country people whom I
met on the road to Bethany; they were wholly ignorant of the
ancient name of the village, which is supplanted by the Arabic El
Azirijeh "Place of Lazarus," which may be explained by the constant pilgrimage to the sepulchre of Lazarus.

That in an excursion to Bethany the most fervent reminiscences
of our Lord irresistibly throng upon the soul, I have myself experienced. The path thither his foot had so often trodden, when the
setting sun called him from the temple; here he found amongst
loving hearts a welcome home; it was here, also, that he gave to the
world the most miraculous testimony that he was the Son of God. It
occurred to me at that instant that a celebrated sceptical philosopher
of the preceding century had repeatedly asserted " Could he believe of
the entire Bible only what St. John relates in the eleventh chapter

of his Gospel, he would at once unconditionally subscribe to the belief
of Christ being the Son of God." Singular testimony of a clear-headed
sceptic ! would that it were acknowledged and taken to heart by a
thousand others !   That eleventh chapter, according to my own conviction, admits but of the choice, that either St. John was the most
adroit and absolute liar, or that He upon whose bosom he rested was
the Son of the living God.

The home of Lazarus is now a poor and quiet village ; even its
walls have retained but few indications of past greatness.   The
supposed house of Martha and her sister gives with its leafy grove of
fig-trees quite a romantic appearance to the small group of houses ;
two slight ruins, resembling the remains of towers, project upwards in
solitude from its walls.

The grave of Lazarus (St. John xi. 18), it is to be regretted, does
not make the impression of the cavern or vault wherein Lazarus lay
for four days in the slumber of death.   We descend by many steps
into the limestone rock as into the confined vault of a cellar. Towards
the end of it the steps terminate in a flat surface several paces wide,
and the cavity of the sepulchre is hereby rendered so dark that in
broad day light we required a torch.*   Against the genuineness of this
grave testifies, besides its form, the fact that it lies within the village;
whereas, according to the account of St. John, it must be considered
as being at a short distance from it.   Nevertheless, the pilgrim of
Bordeaux, even as early as the year 333, speaks of the veneration paid
to this sepulchre, which was further confirmed after this period by
the building of a church and monastery.   Later still, these structures
were enlarged, until at the period of the crusades they attained their
greatest splendour before the middle of the twelfth century, when
Queen Melesinda of Jerusalem bestowed especial favour upon them,
and in addition founded a Benedictine convent for black nuns. These
establishments, however, it appears, were but of short duration. Now
instead of all these monastic edifices and churches, a little mosque,
with a cupola, alone stands near the entrance of the grave. Yet at
certain periods, even now, the grave is surrounded with solemn
devoutness, especially at Easter, when the monks and pilgrims proceed from Jerusalem to Bethany during the obscurity of night lighted
by torches.   This procession would form a touching spectacle.

* Even Peter Belon expressed great surprise at this supposed tomb of
Lazarus.   You descend, he says, as in a chimney eighteen steps perpendicularly down into the earth, and then reach a small chamber ; hence you further go down seven or eight steps into a narrow space which is reputed to
be the grave.   Of all the graves that I have seen round about Jerusalem,
in Galilee, near Sidon, and in Egypt, I have never met with one which it
was so difficult to descend into as this.   See Paulus Sammlung, t. ii. s. 72.

In my road back from Bethany, I passed over the summit of the Mount of Olives; thence I passed by Gethsemane, and renewed my reminiscences of its ancient olives. Thus has this little garden, since it witnessed that moment of most solemn struggle (Matt. xvii. 46), through a long course of ages, bestowed upon the pilgrims the delightful token of peace. I reached the Casa Nuova in safety, with a treasure of green twigs.

How rapidly had the fortnight passed away, which I had spent at Jerusalem! and yet had the result made me rich for all my life. I could now the less conveniently defer my departure, as I should thereby have lost the company of a French traveller, which was desirable from the insecurity of the road to Naplus. This morning we had both of us, by means of the French consul, intreated from the pasha a military escort. The pasha was, however, wholly without troops; he evinced his sympathy merely by counselling us against the journey, as, at this moment, he could not be responsible for any occurrence. We, however, adhered to our resolution, as the timid pasha had become alarmed by his own mishaps; and even had we had the escort, in the event of a positive attack a couple of soldiers would have offered but little help. We were besides told that some Syrian merchants had very recently passed the same road unmolested, and we were also aware of the great respect entertained by the Bedouins of this district for Europeans. An interesting proof of this had just transpired. Two months previously, a couple of Englishmen had gone by land to Nazareth. Between Naplus and Djenin they had left their dragoman alone with their baggage, while they made a short excursion. Meanwhile the Bedouins came to plunder the baggage; but apprised by the dragoman that his masters were Englishmen who were travelling with a firman, they refrained from plundering it, and merely took from the dragoman his own little property. The dragoman himself told us this anecdote, and the Englishmen had likewise notified it in his certificate.

I had to-day again to thank both the French and Sardinian consuls most particularly for their kind attentions. With both I had found, according to my notions, a well furnished table; but both much complained, and doubtlessly with justice, of the difficulty of maintaining a good kitchen at Jerusalem. To my regret I entirely missed the Prussian consul, who was on leave of absence. My regret was the greater, as he was represented to have the best knowledge of Jerusalem.

Of the several missionaries with whom I became acquainted, including Bishop Alexander, I was most pleased with the American Lanneau,—a man of taste, skill, learning, and undoubted tact. The principles adopted by the American missionaries have my fullest

concurrence. Their sermons are less doctrinal than Biblical, and
they unite to illustrate them every variety of faith, Armenians,
Greeks, Syrians, and Catholics ; but they are by no means bent on
making converts. This is truly serving the spirit and the truth.
All the so called conversion among Christian communions has something abhorrent in it ; and yet a proper conversion is everywhere a
sacred duty.

I was under many friendly obligations to the Catholic monastery,
to the president, and especially to its foreign procurator. This very
evening the, latter brought me two Hadji certificates. I had not expressed any wish for one ; but as my German dragoman had begged it,
he brought two for form's sake. The nature of the certificates has been
frequently made public. It is drawn up in the ancient style of Roman
piety, and speaks of the *massa damnata totius humani generis* as well
as of the *miserabilis dæmonum potestas.* Many pilgrims take another
besides the written Hadji certificate, engraved and branded upon
the arm, in the form of a cross. But the third testimonial, that
which is neither engraved nor branded, yet so true and sure, is
certainly the best.

As I was mounting my horse, on the 22nd of July, about three in
the morning, the friendly Padre Lorenzetti came to take a last farewell. Partings differ, and essentially when we can give a hearty shake
of the hand ; I rejoiced that I could do so upon my departure from
the never to be forgotten Jerusalem.

At the Damascus gate we met with the late backshish heroes of
Kuds. The watch had been desired to open the gate for us ; for this
purpose, or rather for the backshish, which was attached to it, they
had congregated in numbers. I had now the opportunity of making up for what I had neglected, with respect to the guards of the
Holy Sepulchre. For it had been impossible for me to give a gratuity to the Turkish guards for the dishonour they do to the Christian
sanctuary.

Leaving the Damascus gate behind us, we rode close past the
remarkable rocky sepulchre, which bears the name of the Grotto of
Jeremiah. Shortly afterwards the sepulchres of the kings lay close
at hand ; I looked in at the open porch. Graves had met me first
as I advanced from Ramleh ; and graves were now the last. From
the grave speaks at once sorrow and hope. And what else should
the pilgrim have in saluting and departing from the Holy City, but
sorrow and hope? Jerusalem goes on sighing beneath the Turkish
yoke. The enthusiasm of the Crusades was a fanaticism, for which
our century has only a contemptuous smile of compassion. In the
cabinets of Europe much is said about the rights states, which are
dear and sacred. The fleets of England and France do not hesitate

if there is a question of defending these rights to proceed to the uttermost ends of the earth. Has Jerusalem no rights, no claims upon the great powers of Christendom ? Or are they become superannuated, because they have been so long neglected ? Christian feeling in the hearts of men may be different ; mine whispered to me that that positive faith which fortunately kings and kingdoms least of all despise, demands a very different sympathy from what has hitherto been shown to Jerusalem, so long as material interests have not absorbed all genuine patriotism. For it is the concern of nothing less than Christian patriotism to wrench that city, whence sprung the Christian faith, out of the hands of those who have trodden this faith under foot for the last thousand years, and most exasperatingly still continue to do so.

But what happens at a time when the ancient enemy of Christianity is so humbled, that he himself comes to solicit the protection of the Christian powers ? The Holy Land is, by means of overwhelming force, taken from the hands of Ibrahim Pasha, to be delivered over to those of the Sultan. And even already barbarism has taken such a stride beneath the sceptre of the latter, that Syria sighs for its restoration to the iron hand of Ibrahim Pasha. An off-shoot of the Apostolic Imperial House, aided with his cannons to effect this melancholy transfer of the Holy Land from one barbaric ruler to the other ; and for this he wears the glittering nischar upon his breast. Would Godfrey of Bouillon believe his eyes ? Will not future generations ask, is this truth or fiction ?

Nevertheless, it is unquestionable that, at this day, it scarcely requires so many pens, as it formerly did swords, to attain the object of the Crusaders. But this is the puzzling question. To whom shall Jerusalem be annexed ? Well, probably the greatest part of the disgrace is, that personal jealousy triumphs over the sacred cause of all. One thing is clear, Jerusalem must be Christian. But, to avoid all family disputes respecting this common patrimony, let Jerusalem be declared to be the city of Christian union ; or a free city, under the protection of the Christian powers. This would be a magnificent act of the century ; it would be an act of Holy Alliance, which would convert into a reality that oft-repeated word of great cordial union. What a future might spring thence for the collective Church ! The melancholy want of Christian confessors which now prevails in the East, would be repelled by the rays of the new Christian life, which enthusiastic troops of European pilgrims would diffuse. A new unity of Christianity would arise in Jerusalem ; like dispersed flocks, the nations would find themselves there collected ; there would then resound the Gospel of a glorious peace of the Church. And what results would thence ensue for the Maho-

metan population of the East! The great Christian city, however
various in its customs, but one in spirit, practising earnest Christianity before the eyes of the stranger — that, indeed, would be the
most effectual missionary sermon.

EPISTLE TO AN ILLUSTRIOUS PATRONESS UPON.
MY BIBLICO-CRITICAL RESEARCHES.

Whilst seated in the rocky cell at Bethlehem, where the pious
Jerome devoted so many years to his Biblical labours, I heartily rejoiced in my own calling.   Well did I think of what Gregory XVI.
sympathizingly said to me in May, 1843 :—" Do you not remember
St. Jerome, and the dangerous opposition which his undertaking
called forth ?" But I reflected upon it only to bless this age, which, instead of the persecutions of the fourth century, has an eye of friendly
recognition for the serious task of Biblico-critical inquiries.   It is
true that the same century has also a very different eye, which, however, as well as the former, insures such inquiries against persecution.
This once occurred to me under the strongest colours in Upper Italy.
A renowned astronomer, who believed in all the stars of the firmament, only not in the star of the wise men which stood over the
manger at Bethlehem, openly confessed to me that he could not
conceive how a man of talent could expend his costly time in the
study of a book like the Bible, which so clearly bore on its forehead
the character of good-natured fables.   It is singular enough, even if
not new, that in the home of unconditional credulity, unbelief should
start forth in such melancholy nakedness.

But I must look wide apart from this point of view, whilst endea-
vouring to show you the sense and signification of my undertaking
relative to the text of the Bible.   The apologetical phasis of my letter
refers to views differing from the fabulous assumption of the Italian
astronomer as widely as heaven is separated from earth;—views, which
may belong to that zeal for God which dwells in ignorant simplicity.

When, more than seven years ago, I began to bestow a critical
study upon the Greek original text of the New Testament, I soon
adopted the twofold conviction that, an historical error, as it were
an hereditary sin, of three hundred years standing, clings to our customary editions of the text, and that a correction of this, at least to a
certain degree, does not lie beyond the bounds of possibility.   The
interest which endeavours having for their object the promotion
of this correction, must have for the entire Church, but especially
for evangelical Christianity, lay distinctly before my eyes.

I now hasten to explain myself more fully respecting this hereditary sin of three hundred years duration. When, in the sixteenth century, the original texts of the New Testament, preserved up to that period in MSS. alone, became much more extensively multiplied, by means of the printing-presses of Guttenburg, the manuscripts at hand were treated in a way that had but little reference to a strict examination of what might be correct and what might be erroneous.

The great Erasmus, who, in strange antithesis, has been called the Voltaire of his age,. presented the world, in March 1516, with the first printed edition of the original text of the New Testament. The few manuscripts which had served him for this purpose had collectively been transcribed a thousand years or more subsequently to the original composition of those Holy Scriptures. Nineteen years later, towards the close of his life, Erasmus published his fifth edition, which he had formed, indeed, by a comparison of the works of the Fathers, and of the Latin version used in the Catholic church, but which, nevertheless, differed very unessentially from his first edition.

Shortly afterwards the form of the text of the New Testament obtained further circulation, by means of the learned Parisian printer, Robert Stephens, who was, nevertheless, singularly enough catalogued in the *Index Expurgatorius* : this text, indeed, after passing almost untouched through the hands of Beza, became signalised at the commencement of the 17th century, by means of the Elzevirs, celebrated printers at Leyden, as the universally adopted text. This honourable distinction, the Erasmo-Elzevir text bore throughout the 17th and 18th centuries, and justified it, in as far as it was that which was in common use.

But even during the same period much was done in England, in Germany, in France, in Holland, and also in Italy, of high importance towards the critical study of the text of the New Testament. Manuscripts, written but a few centuries after Christ, were discovered and examined, very ancient translations of the Greek text into Latin, as also into several of the Oriental languages, were extracted from libraries and compared ; the ancient Fathers, and their citations from the New Testament, were examined and used. The result of all this was, that editions of the Greek text were published, giving the various readings extracted from the original, together with endeavours to glean from such readings corrections for the text in use. Yet the latter maintained not merely the right of usage, but had also gradually obtained with those who were not acquainted with its origin, or were incompetent to form a correct judgment upon it, a sort of sacred authority which made it as inviolable as an article of faith. Of this I proceed to give an instance.

Wetstein, a talented and indefatigable inquirer, was upon the point of publishing, in a new edition, the results of the critical investigations of the text made by him during his travels. He had been previously quite unreserved in communicating some of the results, and it was known that in several passages he purposed introducing new readings upon the authority of ancient testimony. He hereby gave so severe a shock to his colleagues, the theologians of Basle, that he was obliged to deliver up the first sheets of his work to a sort of inquisition, and, in consequence, after a protracted process, he lost his trifling situation of deacon, and was obliged to fly to Holland, whence he in vain solicited permission to return to his native city. This occurred in the year 1730.

About the same time the great critic Richard Bentley of Cambridge, wished to procure paper from France, free of duty, for an entirely new edition of the original text of the New Testament. He exerted himself to obtain this permission, but it was refused him by the English Government. His annoyance at this refusal prevented the appearance of the work.

But towards the end of the preceding century, a German philologer, Griesbach of Jena, laboured with tact and success upon the correction of the text of the New Testament, and was fortunate enough to secure grateful recognition ; and many a learned divine has, since then, chiefly in Germany, laboured with the same views, and still labours at the present day. Griesbach's fame has, however, remained so great, that a celebrated Parisian Hellenist seriously asked me, " Has Griesbach, then, left any thing to be done ? "

I must now, therefore, prepare myself the more resolutely for my reply to the question, What is, then, that historical error, or, as it may be called more characteristically, the supposititious hereditary sin, the cure of which I said was so desirable even at the present day? It consists herein, that the text of the 16th century, published with an evident disregard of all criticism, even although in many single passages it has been expressly purified from errors, has still remained in such esteem, that the majority of the improvements proposed have only dared, like bold adventurers, to look upon its intrenchments from a distance, without breaking in upon them. What, therefore, Erasmus pretermitted has become the patrimony of succeeding centuries.

The matter stands, therefore, thus. Of the Greek text we possess originals from the 4th century downwards ; in the works of the Fathers we find passages of the text, dating from the 2nd, 3rd, 4th, and following centuries. For the text of the ancient translations, made originally in the first Christian centuries, we have documents concurring almost with the period of their being made. We may say generally of these collective testimonies, that the most ancient contain a different colouring of the text from the more modern ones; or that they, both ancient and modern, more or less considered as a whole, present in at least from four to five thousand passages a difference of text. But the received text, in consequence of its being derived originally from modern manuscripts in the sixteenth century, takes consequently that colouring which the most modern texts bear in contradistinction to the most ancient, with merely the exception that recently, as I have already said, it has been here and there corrected from these.

Allow me, that I may make this clearer, to suppose that at the present time we were still without printed copies, and that we only had upon our right hand the ancient documents, and on our left the modern — Would it not be unreasonable to adopt the text from the latter, and extract from the former merely a few corrections here and there? Would it not be more unreasonable, the more clearly the difference between the two was apparent? And if this mode of proceeding has been adopted, may it not be considered as an unworthy submission to custom, and a denial of justice to the sacred cause, to persist in this contumacy.

It is true that an invention has been stumbled upon which has given to the established form the appearance of an admirable justification. The mass of textual testimonies may be classed as it were in families; some appearing to contain that text which was most in use in one portion of the Christian community, and others the text of the other portion. Hence it is that we speak of an Oriental or Alexandrian text, and of an Occidental or Constantinopolitan text; or also of an African and Latin text, both of which, again, equally correspond with the Oriental or Alexandrian text, and of an Asiatic text, which is equivalent to that of Constantinople. To the so called Alexandrian class — for so it may be called concisely and with good reason — belong the whole of the most ancient testimonies; and to the other the whole of the more modern ones. For the origin of both classes we are referred to the systematic remodelling or recension of a learned individual, somewhere about the 3rd century; and yet the more modern are considered more genuine than the elder ones. And accordingly it is assumed that, in the 16th century, a lucky chance led casually to the publication of the purer text.

But what results from a general examination of these assumptions? In the first place that the most learned men of antiquity, as the Biblical critic St. Jerome, in the fourth century, knew nothing of these works which are the foundation of the classes of the text. Further, that the so called Alexandrian text has been followed by the majority and the most ancient of the Fathers in Asia, as well as by the Africans in their citations; and that the copies made by the

Alexandrian transcribers were in ancient times universally the most esteemed. Moreover, in our copies we find a great uniformity in the mass of modern ones, and infinitely less uniformity in the older ones, although their number is comparatively small. Lastly, the more modern manuscripts in many cases bear about them such a peculiarity of character as distinctly to evince an arbitrary deviation from some of the more ancient.

From all this ensues absolutely that the hypothesis of a classification of testimonies may be by no means made a leading principle in our task of a correction of the text. But, on the contrary, the most natural mode of proceeding must necessarily be to prefer the text of the most ancient document, especially when it agrees both with the Greek manuscripts as well as with the Fathers and translations, as long as this preference is not opposed by weighty internal evidence.

Something similar has been already undertaken. A celebrated philologer of Germany has adopted the principle of taking but a very few and only the most ancient manuscripts as the foundation of a new text. Yet with all its excellencies—and the idea itself is indisputably the greatest—so many deficiencies appear to me still to cling to the work (this I endeavoured to show publicly in 1842*), that the main proposition seems to me to be still unsolved.

By these preliminary observations I am in a position to set forth clearly the object of my own biblico-critical undertaking. In the first place, my object is to collect the few manuscripts of the original text of the New Testament, written before the tenth century, and lying dispersed throughout the libraries of Europe, and print them verbatim. This collection of originals, which would comprise from thirty to forty volumes, appears to me on the one side to present a far safer foundation for the learned critics of the text of all ages than the comparison or lists of various readings; and on the other side I consider it in itself as a valuable possession for the Christian Church. Or is it unimportant that the Church should by this means receive into its hands the most ancient originals of its sacred code, which have been so miraculously preserved through the storms of centuries, which is impossible with respect to the solitary originals themselves, which have been exposed not only to the unavoidable dilapidations of time, but also to peculiar and accidental mishaps? I would then proceed in a similar way with the most ancient and most important translations, namely,— and this falls entirely within my province —the Latin; for which we have very ancient manuscripts, some with the text in use prior to St. Jerome, and that of St. Jerome

* Compare Neue Jenaer Literaturzeitung, 1843, Nos. 80—82.

P

himself. The text of St. Jerome is that which, about the middle of the fourth century, by command of Pope Damasus, he compiled from the multitude of those at his disposal. Further, my plan requires such a study of the fathers of the Church as shall lay before us most accurately the text they used. Out of these threefold labours a text will at length be formed upon the strictest scientific principles; a text that will approach as closely as possible to the very letter, as it proceeded from the hands of the Apostles.

But what interest, you will ask, have we—have the unlearned— have the community at large in all these learned labours? The answer is not difficult. The translation for which we are indebted to the masterly hand of Luther, as well as all other printed translations in German and in the languages of the other nations of the present day, had chiefly for their foundation the above described Greek text of Erasmus; only that those which have emanated from Catholic Christianity have adhered more to the Latin text of the vulgate authorised by the court of Rome than to the Greek text. But the text of the vulgate, chiefly derived from modern manuscripts, has the same relation to the most ancient Latin codices that the Erasmian text has to the most ancient Greek. Consequently the translations of the New Testament at present in use among the nations, need a similar correction in accordance with the best and most original authorities.

But I must at the same time explain myself with respect to the kind of varieties of the text which is here under consideration. I have often, especially out of Germany, heard such questions as the following : — " Well, how does Christ present himself in your manuscripts ? " " What is there in them about the Trinity ? " Elsewhere I have heard severe remarks upon the suspiciousness of individual passages. From these I perceived how little the essence and spirit of the thing were understood. The variations of the text refer more particularly to so called trifles than to matters of doctrine. I say " so called " for I can recognise the character of " trifles" only in contradistinction to that of "doctrinal" importance. Most frequently, that is to say many thousand times in many codices, the question relates to the capricious falsification of expression with regard to grammar and style, and also very frequently to determining accurately what each of the writers of the New Testament individually wrote, especially among the four evangelists, and to removing from his text what has been added during the lapse of time from the others, with a view to the completion of his narrative. Occasionally, however, material and historical matters are in question ; lastly, there are cases, but which are sufficiently rare, where the variety of the readings even affects the doctrine.

Hence you will be able to judge how important or unimportant this criticism is. In my opinion, in the text of the book with which no other book in the world can be compared, from the sacredness of its origin, its high significance, and immeasurable consequences, nothing can be held to be so trifling as to be indifferent. What did the Apostle write? what did he not write? even be it but a particle, or even but a grammatical form, I hold to be a question the solution of which is deserving of the most serious study. Have not, not merely books, but even whole libraries been written, and that without meriting censure, upon the correctness of the text of the Greek and Roman classics.

But I must give you further explanations respecting doctrinal readings by means of illustrations.

In the first Epistle of Paul to Timothy, c. iii. v. 16, the ordinary Greek text has " God was manifest in the flesh." In lieu of which, the most ancient authorities among MSS., the Fathers, and translations have " which or who appeared in the flesh." The passage is rendered thereby especially important, inasmuch as the usual reading gives the strongest support to the opinion that Christ was decidedly called " God" by St. Paul. The other reading does not by any means destroy the doctrine of the divinity of Christ in St. Paul, as the ignorant have imagined and the weak have feared; for, whether the Apostle called the Saviour God, or not, the doctrine is as firm with him as the fact of his conversion.

The passage respecting the Trinity, in the first General Epistle of John, v. 7, 8, is also celebrated: " For there are three that bear record in heaven, the Father, the Word, and the Holy Ghost: and these three are one. And there are three that bear witness in earth, the spirit, and the water, and the blood: and these three agree in one." Hence, according to the collective testimony of the ancient Greek manuscripts, and the collective Greek as well as the most ancient Latin Fathers, as well as the collective ancient translations, the words from " in heaven" as far as " that bear witness in earth" must be removed from the text. These words stand, however, as in the authorised vulgate of the Church, so also in our usual German editions, although Luther by no means admitted them into his translation. This passage is naturally important with respect to the Trinity. And yet Luther had the firmest belief in the Trinity, without requiring this interpolated passage.

Among the questionable component portions of the text are the eleven verses in the Gospel of St. John (John viii. 1—11.), containing the story of the woman taken in adultery. The strongest critical testimonies deny their authenticity, or at least their place in the Gospel of St. John. This dispute is very old, for even St.

Augustin treated of it. He indeed asserted that only the weak in faith would reject it. But the doctrinal question, which is capable of very different replies, does not absolutely occupy the highest position in criticism. It is here exactly that the importance of the examination of the original text is exhibited. St. Augustin did not understand Greek; he adhered to the Latin translation. He was hereby prevented from observing that the whole passage differs so positively from St John's style as to appear like the interpolation of a strange body into his Gospel.

But it would be very erroneous to seek the ultimatum of the great critical undertaking of which I speak, in negatives; although the principle of negation has with great injustice already been subjected to the suspicion of an unholy proceeding. For which is more holy, to leave inconsiderately amongst what is divine that which is human, and which in the course of time has acquired the appearance or the assumption of divine, or to esteem the divine so highly as to wish it denuded of all that is deficient in confirmation? Allow me to say thus much in behalf of negation. But when the conscientious investigation of all the originals of long-past centuries, when the strictest use of these triumphant arms of science, sure of victory, shall have transformed the book of books to a work whose originality is more confirmed on all sides than any classical work of antiquity, am I wrong in believing that thereby the true progress of our age will be as much advanced as an essential service rendered to the holy cause of our faith? And this I confess is the point of view from which I set out on my undertaking, and this is the sense in which I ventured to lay this undertaking, shortly before the commencement of my travels, before Prince John of Saxony, an illustrious prince who has both a liberal regard for the earnest labours of a church to which he does not belong, and holds also out to it the hand of a protector. Since then in the countries of catholicism, not less than in those of protestantism, I have acquired the conviction, that this sense, this point of view, is the true one; for thence only can I explain to myself the general sympathy that I have met with. Thus Coquerel in the " Lien," 23rd Oct. 1841, speaks of my labours. " The Lien will keep its readers acquainted with the progress of labours of such high importance to religion, and which promise to inscribe another name upon the list of those men to whom Biblical criticism owes its progress, and who have given to the Christian faith so remarkable a pre-eminence that no Greek author exists whose text is as authentic as that of the New Testament."

I am afraid I should incur the charge of vanity, did I name to you those individuals who have pronounced judgment upon the publication of the Codex Ephrämi in the spirit of my own views. These have accorded me the most heart-felt satisfaction. I will mention but one — my meeting, in the winter of 1843, with an aged Swiss Theologian, who was deeply versed in criticism and exegesis. This worthy man received me with tears of sympathy; his joy at my biblico-critical undertakings was numbered, it seemed, among the most desirable experience of his old age.

But indeed I dare not suppress the fact that, above two years after the appearence of this codex, I was asked by a celebrated theological professor of Germany " Will the codex soon appear ?" This circumstance may be connected with the view that the so called criticism of the text comes into the category of the most super-fluous things in the world, in as far as the 'Bible springing from the hands of Providence is borne under the protection of these hands through all time. But perhaps the wondrous finger of Providence may be more distinctly recognised in this particular, that, amid the mass of Biblical codices, with such a variety of texts, still a few aboriginal ones have been preserved even to the present day, as certain guiding stars for conscientious searchers after truth. Besides, if theories of inspiration be admitted to extend on the one side to Robert Stephens and the Elzevirs, and on the other side to the supporters of the vulgate and of other translations, further competition may certainly appear admissible.

But between the two melancholy extremes of reckless unbelief and careless indiscriminating credulity, my faith is immovable that the Book of Redemption will be of the same validity to the very latest posterity, thousands of years hence, that it is to me at present, and the same as was its value to the Miner's * son, who raised the treasure with enthusiasm and success from the depth of the mine, where it had lain buried for ages.

I have yet a few more words to say as to the relation that the studies of my travels bear to my Biblico-critical tendencies. All else I pass by. In the first place I set about the compilation of those most ancient Greek codices, or more distinctly, their preparation for the press, through which indeed several of the most important of them have already passed. In this particular I have attained, with a few minor exceptions, all that I have striven for. The Parisian Palimpsest, called by way of distinction the Codex Ephrämi, I completed at Christmas, 1842. It is the dearest Christmas gift that the grace of the Lord has accorded me. The discovery and preparation of old documents for the Latin translation was of great consequence also to me. Besides I formed a bond of friendly union with men, from whom in due time my undertaking will receive

* Luther.

p 3

powerful support; and on all hands, even in other than the learned circles, I sought to excite or to augment friendly feelings towards it.

I need not attempt in this place to describe to you how great was the interest, the favour, the countenance, which I found for my journey and its objects; at Paris, where I became the grateful debtor of the celebrated Letronne, Raoul Rochette, Hase, as well as the generous Emmanuel Lascases, and Guizot; at Cambridge, where, at the recommendation of the duke of Sussex, in the most liberal manner the library of Trinity College was thrown open to me; from the learned Dutch, or from De Witte's genuine cordiality, and other pleasing reminiscences in Switzerland. Nor need I repeat to you, that in Italy I found also many patrons and friends, nor dare I begin to speak of my German fatherland.

That I traversed the East for my special object admits, I think, of an easy justification, even if the richest produce I obtained there served for other purposes. For besides what I really found there, it has helped to clear up my doubts as to how far the latest acquisitions, which in Europe form the groundwork of a critical examination of the New Testament text, may thereby undergo further modification.

I need now only add an excuse for the length of my letter. Your interest in the cause must be great to induce you to overlook its dryness. But I know that it is great; the Gospel possesses so large a share of your heart, that I can readily comprehend how much it concerns you to obtain a valid text of the New Testament Scriptures, the bulwark of theology against the attacks of doubting science and the sacred and indestructible foundation of our faith.

FROM JERUSALEM TO NAZARETH.

(BY WAY OF SAMARIA AND SHECHEM.)

When I perceived the walls of Jerusalem recede behind the hills, thoughts full of sadness came over me. I was returning from a festival, but it was a festival of death. The solemn sounds were still reverberating through my soul: I was lost in the dream of a fair by-gone day; but at the same time I felt an oppression like sorrow for a dead one, whom I fondly loved. I asked myself shall "I again see Jerusalem? Should I ever see it again, God grant that I may behold it in the springtide of a new era, which will convert the holy into a happy city!"

The society in which I went to Nazareth was new and entertaining. Our caravan consisted of four horses, three mules, and one ass. The muleteer, or horse-leader, cut a most interesting figure. He sat upon his mule with the perfect air of a lord, a boy ran by his side, as servant, and carried his long pipe. The muleteer of the second rank rode the ass, and busied himself chiefly with the command of the two laden mules. The Frenchman who travelled with me, had long sojourned in the East, as well as in Spain, and he was now conveying the entire Holy Land home with him in Daguerreotype. His dragoman was the same Arab who had been plundered on the road to Nazareth, in the service of the Englishmen. He had consequently become half-Turk and half-Englishman in his costume; for he wore, over his wide trousers, a short close coat, a present from his master, which looked very ridiculous.

Our present road retained no longer exactly the character of the desert districts and naked heights around Jerusalem. Before us and around us, in every direction, hills and valleys lay stretched, whose soil, although frequently rocky, was not unfruitful. We beheld groups of fruit trees, and among them apples and pears; also verdant meadows, pastured by herds and flocks. Here and there we perceived a village nodding upon an eminence; and still more frequently the ruins of a fortress or of a monastery.

In the course of a couple of hours we had close on our left in the west, and surrounded by a few huts, that mosque of Samuel, which I had already greeted from the summit of the minaret of the mount of Olives. The Prophet himself is said to lie buried there. (1 Sam. xxv. 1.) His sepulchre is not contemplated without devotion by Jews, Mahomedans, or Christians. The doubts of the learned strongly contest its right to this celebrity, although so prominent a locality must have been of importance in high antiquity. Robinson supposes the Biblical Mizpeh to have been situated here, where Samuel (1 Sam. vii. 9), by the sacrifice of a sucking lamb, did not in vain solicit divine aid against the Philistines, and where he subsequently annointed Saul (1 Sam. x. 1), who had become filled with the Spirit of the Lord. (1 Sam. x. 6.)

Half a league to the north of Neby Samwil, seated upon "the great high place" (1 Kings iii. 4) is El Gib, the ancient Gibeon, where Joshua's appeal was made, "Sun, stand thou still upon Gibeon." (Joshua x. 12.) It was chiefly celebrated as being the city of the priests of the tabernacle. It was here where Solomon, as youthful monarch, made the sacrifice (1 Kings iii. 4) a thousand burnt offerings did Solomon offer upon that altar, and the following night offered up his child-like prayer (1 Kings iii. 7, 8, 9), which was so pleasing to the Lord. (10.)

We had travelled four leagues, having previously made a short

halt when we reached Bir, to take our mid-day rest. The village
itself we kept at a little distance before us, upon the hill, and remained in the valley near a spring, behind the walls of a deserted
monastery. The subterraneous vaults of this structure, which I
roamed through, may have had their ecclesiastical uses superseded by
temporal ones, and it is probable that the monastery itself had been
subsequently transformed into a khan. In the afternoon we inspected in the village the beautiful ruins of a church, exhibiting the
architectural style of the crusades.

Bir enjoys distinction in Christian tradition. It formed the first
day's journey of Joseph and Mary (St. Luke, ii. 43) upon their return
from the passover : and it was here they sought Jesus, when twelve
years old, among their friends, and missed him. There is nothing
inconsistent in this tradition ; as from ancient custom even at the
present day the Easter pilgrims extend their first day's journey homeward only as far as Bir ; the pilgrims from Galilee may also long
since have practised the same custom. Our road to Nazareth was
certainly the same which our Lord and his disciples repeatedly took
when he went to the festival. These reminiscences were the dearest
company. In our fequent descent from the precipitous mountain
declivities of this district, I clearly comprehended how correctly the
sacred text, speaking of the paschal journey of Jesus, usually says
(John, vii. 10), " went he also up unto the feast."

From Bir all the way to our night quarters the mountain range of
Ephraim extended at our side : it is far richer in trees and shrubs
than the mountain chain of Judah, and yet it also exhibits desert
heights and rocky valleys, with many abysses and ravines. The further we advanced the more cheerful became the landscape ; it is extremely luxuriant in olives and fig-trees. About half an hour before
we reached the termination of this day's journey, we beheld in the
twilight towards the north-east the neighbouring heights, which bear
the ruins of Shiloh, that place of peace which, like Gibeon, long
retained the ark, and then also witnessed the pious juvenile years
of Samuel. There the fiery sons of Benjamin once engaged in an
adventure similar to the rape of the Sabines by the Romans. At
the yearly feast of the Lord, as it is said in the Book of Judges (xxi.
20, 21. 23) : " Go and lie in wait in the vineyards ; and see, and, behold,
if the daughters of Shiloh come out to dance in dances, then come ye
out of the vineyards, and catch you every man his wife of the
daughters of Shiloh, and go to the land of Benjamin." " The children
of Benjamin did go, and took them wives, according to their number,
of them that danced, whom they caught." We now descended so
steep and precipitous a declivity, that it would have been dangerous
to have remained on horseback. At the foot of the precipice we

found in an extensive verdant meadow a large well, enclosed within
an oblong quadrangle of walls, where our cattle refreshed themselves. Three females, but by no means graces, were fetching water
for the village which lay at a distance of a mile. It began to grow
dark as we diverged to Leban on the left of our road, to pass the
night there. This very ancient village lies upon a stony shruboy
height. Close to our encampment we perceived ancient sepulchral
cavities; not far beneath lay fields clothed in splendid luxuriance.
We were speedily saluted by many of the inhabitants of Leban;
they helped to pile up a large fire, and seated themselves at it to
enjoy, with our muleteers, a pipe and a cup of coffee. They kept
up their conversation almost beyond the bounds of what was desirable.
One of the guests offered to sell us a good English telescope, which
without doubt he had stolen from some former traveller. It was
thence evident that their respect for Europeans might not be very
great. As we necessarily feared we might be robbed during the
night by these people, who stood in the very worst repute with our
guides, we hired four guards out of their own number. Our
bivouac I found here less agreeable than in the sand of the desert.
I lay upon a lamb-skin wrapped in my woollen blanket, but the night
dew fell so heavily that I could have bathed myself in it.

———

Early next morning, about eight, we entered the surprisingly luxuriant valley between Mounts Gerizim and Ebal. About half a
league before reaching Naplus, at the entrance of the valley at the
foot of Mount Gerizim, lies the deep well, which may probably be
justly considered as Jacob's well, where Jesus sat during his conversation with the woman of Samaria. (John, iv. 7.) The sepulchre
of the patriarch Joseph, a little beyond the wall which lay close upon
our right, is nothing but a Turkish saint's monument, to which the
Mahometans pay great devotion. Whether tradition is right or wrong
with respect to the locality no one doubtlessly can say.

The view of Naplus, the ancient Shechem is delightful and grand.
It peers forth, with its numerous white minarets and flat cupola roofs
from beneath olive-trees and fig-trees, out of the narrow valley. The
two neighbouring mountains add grandeur to the sweetness of the
picture; they encompass the city and the valley with their bare
rocky precipices, which are on here and there clothed with olives.
What a spectacle must it have been when Joshua, by command of
the Lord, solemnly sealed his entry into the promised land from these
mountains. (Deut. xxvii. 2, 3.) Six tribes stood upon Gerizim and
six upon Ebal. (Joshua viii. 33.) From Gerizim pealed down the
blessing, and from Ebal was denounced the curse. (Deut. xxvii.
12, 13.) To the blessing as well as to the curse uttered by the

mouths of the Levites, the people shouted, Amen, with their thousands of voices. He who has seen these mountains and called to mind that spectacle will ever have them present to his soul like two incontestable witnesses of the solemnity of the law.

Beneath the gate of the city we had a melancholy rencontre; several lepers sat there begging. I know nothing that could have made a more disagreeable impression than this first entrance to the city.

Immediately after passing the gate we rode through the long bazaar which presented the richest variety of all that is beautiful or costly; it was, however, so confined, and so thronged, that we could only labour through it step by step. We took up our quarters, upon the recommendation of the French consul at Jerusalem, in the Samaritan school. Before we could enter our saloon the children were obliged to be dismissed.

We soon received a visit from the chief rabbin of the Samaritans, an estimable man of more than sixty, with a long white beard and delicate features. He wore a crimson silk garment and a white turban. When we told him that we immediately purposed visiting the pasha of Naplus, he obligingly offered to accompany us. The pasha, a very stout middle-aged man, we found in the midst of a circle of friends upon the beautiful terrace of his house. To my surprise he walked barefooted ; yet he remained as he was and immediately sat himself down with us upon the cushions and carpets spread about. We smoked a pipe and drank a cup of coffee. We solicited him to grant us a military escort for our further journey ; he was willing to accede to it, but he assured us that the severity of his police regulations made the roads perfectly safe. We naturally complimented him upon this state of things. When leaving him we were astonished at finding ourselves followed by two of his servants, who begged for their backshish for the coffee. It was impossible to get rid of them with empty hands. I thus became acquainted with another feature of Turkish courtesy. But I was wrong in feeling surprised at it ; for a year previously, when at Rome, and shortly before the moment of my departure at six in the morning, the servant of a cardinal presented himself at my abode to remind me of a similar backshish.

I was now anxious to visit the Samaritan synagogue, being exceedingly curious to inspect the celebrated manuscripts which it contains. There was no difficulty in obtaining access. A rabbin, but not the chief who had remained engaged with the pasha, led us to a small oratory which was covered with straw mats, and not to be trodden except bare footed. Upon a book-shelf I observed about twenty manuscripts, chiefly upon parchment. To several I unhesitatingly accord an age of many hundred years. One exhibited by many peculiarities, for instance, that of being written in three columns, an antiquity of more than a thousand years. But I was chiefly occupied with the alleged exceedingly ancient manuscript which is said to contain a statement to the effect, that it was written thirteen years after the death of Moses, by Abischua, the son of Phineas, who was grandson of Aaron. The rabbin brought us a tin case, within which lay the manuscript like a large synagogue roll of parchment, enveloped in a costly covering of crimson silk with embroidered golden letters. It bears undeniable traces of antiquity. I examined the parchment, the colour of the ink, the system of the lines, the punctuation, the divisions, none of which have initials, and the characters, as well as they could be examined without a knowledge of the Samaritan. All combine to convey the idea of a manuscript of the sixth century. Even under this supposition it necessarily holds a very distinguished rank among all the ancient parchment codices of both the East and the West. With respect to the alleged statement it may not, if in fact it exist, be considered otherwise than as a transcript carelessly copied from former documents, and incorporated in it as a note founded on a remote tradition. Perhaps this Abischua took some share in writing the original Pentateuch. In that case the statement in question would receive some elucidation from the practice in the Greek manuscripts of the Gospel, wherein is frequently noted that it was written by Matthew, by John, &c., as well as the year in which it was first promulgated. These notices have misled uninformed persons. For instance, I found in a celebrated library, inscribed in a manuscript of the Gospel, a remark from the pen of the librarian himself, to the effect that the manuscript was written by the rhetorician Hebraides, in the tenth century after Christ's ascension, and referred to an ancient commentary. But what stood in this commentary? Nothing more than that the Gospel of St. Matthew was published ten years after Christ's ascension, and that in the Hebrew tongue.*

But I return to the Samaritans at Naplus. I do not believe that it would be impossible to obtain their manuscripts, and I feel convinced that thereby a precious treasure would be gained for even the largest library in Europe.

* On this occasion I must mention what will probably be new to my readers ; an exceedingly remarkable original manuscript that has recently been resuscitated from the grave of oblivion. This is nothing less than the Hebrew original manuscript of the inscription of Pilate over the cross of Jesus. It is well known that the holy wooden cross itself has long been preserved at Rome. A learned propagandist of the house of Israel made the remarkable discovery upon it, and immediately communicated it to the world with commentary and fac-simile. He himself showed me his dissertation upon it, but to my regret he gave me no copy of it.

Our rabbin directed the conversation from the manuscripts to his own learned correspondence with Europe. He inquired particularly, as he had done of several former travellers, about certain learned friends of his resident at Geneva, if we rightly understood him. He had expected for I know not how many years, in vain, a reply to his letters. He became quite impatient that we scarcely understood him, and could give him no information about them. But in return we obtained from him a much better account of those of his own faith. In Naplus he enumerated a hundred and fifty Samaritans, and as many out of it. They still venerate Gerizim as their sacred mountain, and turn themselves towards it when they pray. On their four great festivals of the year, the feast of the passover, pentecost, tabernacles, and the expiation, they proceed in procession, reading the law aloud, to the summit of the mountain: they there pitch their tents and sacrifice lambs, especially at the paschal feast. Besides this, they assemble regularly in the synagogue once a week for prayer, read nothing but the Pentateuch, and keep the Sabbath with great strictness. They have not yet reconciled themselves with the Jews, though they have shared like brethren, for two thousand years, in all their oppressions and vexations. They eat and drink with the Turks, but not with the sons of the house of Israel; a remarkable instance of fraternal hatred. It struck me as singular that the features of the Samaritans, at least of all those whom I saw at Naplus and elsewhere, have by no means the Jewish character. And yet one can see, at the first glance, that they are neither Turks nor Arabs. Several wore handsome white beards, and had a delicate, but animated, complexion. Upon taking leave of our rabbin he had, notwithstanding his learned correspondence with Europe, the bonhomie to beg, like the servants of the pasha, for a backshish.

We took a promenade through Naplus, in the company of an Arab physician, who had been previously known as dragoman to many Europeans. The city is tolerably large, but its houses are closely crowded together; it is profusely surrounded by gardens full of orange, citron, and pomegranate trees. The number of the inhabitants was stated to us to be from six to seven thousand* ; amongst whom there is a small number of Jews, and about three hundred Greek Christians, who also possess a monastery in the city.

Upon visiting a large ancient mosque, it was indispensable to cover our shoes with list; a formality which I had been subjected to in Cairo also. Immediately afterwards, my companion was about

---

* Robinson calculates them at 8000, and includes amongst them 500 Greeks.

to sketch a remarkable porch of the middle ages, when we were surrounded by a large mob of people, not most friendly disposed, and had got into a critical position, but we fortunately made a timely retreat. Our guide informed us that the Naplusians are a riotous, overbearing, and fanatical people. The day before our arrival they had slaughtered the sheikh of a neighbouring village, in the heart of the city, out of malicious caprice, and this without even the shadow of punishment having visited them; for when the circumstance was related to the pasha, he exclaimed, Why did he enter the city? and he took charge of the investigation.

We went to inspect a Kufic inscription, in raised characters, carved upon a piece of marble, which is let into a wall. On the road I diverged for a few steps into a narrow street. Some children immediately came running towards me, crying, Harem, harem ; and it was well that I speedily hastened back.

About five in the evening, much to the annoyance of our self-willed muleteers, we departed from Naplus for the purpose of reaching Samaria the same evening. In Naplus (whose ancient name Shechem was changed, in honour of Flavius Vespasian, into Flavia Neapolis, whence the Arabic name Naplus * is formed). I had again trodden soil consecrated from an early period by great reminiscences. Abraham's first dwelling-place, in the land of Canaan, was Shechem. It was before the city of Shechem that the patriarch Jacob pitched his tent, and bought a parcel of a field. (Gen. xxxiii. 18.) And this parcel of a field became a village which, as St. John says (iv. 5), "Jacob gave to his son Joseph." And here it was (Gen. xxxvii. 12) where the brothers of Joseph went to feed their father's flock, and sold the hateful " dreamer " (xxxvii. 19), who had been sent from Hebron to them, to the Ishmaelites, or merchants (xxxvii. 28), who conveyed him into Egypt.

As towards evening we rode a second time through the luxuriant valley which lies in front of the city, my whole soul was filled with reminiscences of the Old and New Testaments. To whom would the reflections have been unfamiliar, which were suggested to me whilst looking down into the depths of the ancient well of Jacob? The well is deep†; I saw with my own eyes, that the Samaritan woman was right. (John iv. 11.) By the side of this well the Saviour sat, and here he uttered those sublime words touching the " water springing up into everlasting life." (John iv. 14.) The words of our Saviour recalled to my mind other imperishable words, which were also uttered

* I prefer writing Naplus, in consequence of its derivation from Neapolis. Whereas Robinson, following Abulfeda's orthography, writes Nabulus.

† The result of repeated measurements gives it 105 feet. When I saw it in the middle of summer it was almost without water.

within view of this well; but were spoken from the summit of
Mount Gerizim, to the assembled men of Shechem. (Judges ix. 7.)
For here it was that Jotham told his beautiful parable, doubtlessly the oldest that we know—of the trees, that went forth to
choose a king. Above all other trees he named the olive and the
fig-tree, both of which, even at the present day, give a striking
character to the valley of the well.

From Naplus to Samaria we rode up hill and down dale through a
verdant landscape, rich in plants, flowers, and trees, which wanted
nothing but the hand of German industry to exhibit the promised
land in its brightest aspect.

Shortly after seven in the evening we had Samaria in view. Its
position is superb. Isaiah called it " the crown of pride of Ephraim"
(xxviii. 1.), and like a crown it still appears, even though its splendour be long since faded. In the midst of a charming valley, surrounded by hills, rises a round mountain ; upon this lies Samaria.
Not far from the foot of the round mountain, we found in the valley
close to the remains of a Roman aqueduct, a rushing brook, on whose
banks ancient splendid olives were standing. Thence we looked
down with rivetted eyes into the ruins of the church of Samaria.
These ruins are certainly the most beautiful in Syria. We saw in
front of us a wall of a circular form, in almost perfect preservation,
with its beautiful buttresses and its high windows beneath decorated
niches, and Byzantine arches. We rode up the mountain full of
expectation ; the road was more difficult than it appeared. Our first
desire was to enter within the walls of the ruined church : but we
met with unexpected difficulties ; for upon drawing up our horses
before the entrance, which leads directly to the small mosque in the
anterior portion of the walls, it was closed before our eyes. My
companion had an imperial firman, which he exhibited. Who
knows not that the signature of the sultan is all potent in the East?
Yet these people did not heed it at all ; the hand of the pasha of
Naplus, they said, should have confirmed it. We had two soldiers
of the pasha as an escort with us ; but even that was of no avail.
They informed us, that if they were to allow us to enter the mosque
the whole village would rise, and possibly endanger our lives.
And thus it remained. But half an hour after we met with a
bold fellow, who facilitated our admission into the ruins, through
a window, without the necessity of touching the mosque itself.
We there beheld with what art and beauty the Crusaders decorated
the church ; we also saw many mutilated crosses of St. John upon
marble tablets.

The origin of this dilapidated building can scarcely extend beyond
the period of the Crusades, although tradition refers it to the great

creatress Helena.   The church was dedicated to St. John the Baptist, and the Order of the Knights of St. John may have had an especial part in it.   The sepulchre of the prophet, built over, in the Turkish manner, is still preserved and revered within the ruins.   Even St. Jerome informs us that Samaria possesses, besides the sepulchres of the prophets Elijah and Obediah, also that of St. John the Baptist. This tradition contains much that is improbable.   According to Josephus and also Eusebius, it appears to be a fact, that St. John was beheaded in the castle Macheras, close to the Dead Sea.   Are his disciples likely to have brought his body from thence to Samaria? And besides the tradition was soon not satisfied with the sepulchre alone, but transferred the scene of his execution also to Samaria. Even at the present day the report runs thus, that the church at Samaria stands exactly upon the spot where St. John sat, and was beheaded.   Hence fancy certainly took the upper hand of history, when the splendid royal city, upon the mountain of Samaria, after being the witness of so many of the atrocities of Herod the Great, was still further made the scene of one bloody deed more under his guilty son Antipas.

No one thinks longer of the Herods, either father or son, but St. John is dear, even to the Turks : his name is known to and spoken of by even the present Mahometan Samaritans.   Did it ever float before the mind of the king, when surrounded by his splendour, or at least was it ever evoked by a dream within his guilty soul, that a period would come when his name would merely oscillate between curses and oblivion, and the name of the man, whose head he sacrificed to the caprice of a woman (Matthew, xiv. 3—12), would be indelibly impressed upon solemn religious edifices, within the books of mankind, and in the hearts of many millions ?

We pitched our tent within view of the ruins of the church, which lie upon the projecting declivity to the south of the mountain ; the present village lies at a slight distance behind and above the ruins.   The population of the village in prohibiting our entrance into the mosque had shown a trait of their true character ; and this we had the opportunity of soon experiencing in those who were staring into our tent.   In spite of our military escort, it appeared necessary during the night to make a watchman of the thief ; and we therefore appointed four persons to this office.

The present evening offered us still further delights.   We wandered to the summit of the mountain and enjoyed the charming prospect.   We there stood in the very centre of a magnificent panorama. To the north-east and south our horizon was bounded by mountains, enriched with cultivation and villages ; towards the west our elevation admitted of the eye ranging even to the Mediterranean.   The valleys which girdled the mountain, as well as the mountain itself, are luxuriantly overgrown with trees, especially olives and fig-trees. Around the mountain run, like a coronet, the traces of a terrace, which was probably formed as a decoration to the royal residence.

Many a reminiscence met us of those departed glories which had distinguished this city under Herod. In an extensive grove of fig-trees, lying tolerably high up the mountain, many pillars of lime-stone still stand, and others lie in fragments around. Our guide led us to his own dwelling in the village, to show us there some ancient marble remains, still retaining traces of exquisite sculpture. But the noblest ruin of all is a splendid avenue of pillars, of which, at the foot of the mountain, especially towards the west, about a hundred still remain, and the majority of these are in perfect order. These pillars are without doubt of the time of Herod. Perhaps they had some connection with the splendid temple of Augustus, which Herod raised to the same imperial protector, in whose honour the name of the city itself was changed to Sebaste.* We wandered long among these pillars, and thought of the distant days they had beheld. Like plaintiffs before the tribunal of posterity, they testify against him who constructed them. It was in Samaria itself that he doomed to death the two sons of his slaughtered consort Mariamne.

But Herod was not the first who had made Samaria a harsh con-trast with the amenities nature had bestowed upon it, — the theatre of bloody deeds and scenes of horror. Since Omri, who founded it fifty years after Solomon (1 Kings, xvi. 24.), and made it the resi-dence of the kings of Israel, it worshipped Baal more than Jehovah. Here Ahab practised his worship of idols (1 Kings, xvi. 31, 32); here Elijah, inspired by the anger of his God, cursed the weak king and the godless Jezebel. (1 Kings, xxi. 19, &c.) Ezekiel called Samaria the elder sister of Sodom. (xvi. 46.) Punishment was denounced against it by all the prophets. But before the pro-phecies were fulfilled by the arm of Salmanassar, they had died away powerlessly.

Thus have these melancholy columns at Samaria much that is me-lancholy to proclaim. And if we turn our eyes from these pillars to their neighbours, the Turkish inhabitants of the village with the imperial name, whose stubbornness and malice form an old com-plaint, to which I myself can testify, we might almost believe that an hereditary sin clings to it with an inextricable sting.

The following morning my companion took several views of Samaria with his Daguerreotype. That this would be a troublesome affair was to be foreseen. The entire population, old and young, encompassed the astonishing and suspicious instrument, as well as its

* Sebaste is the Greek for Augusta.

master. Each wished to see, and also to earn a backshish. In the interim, I lounged through the neighbourhood, and reposed by the side of the purling brook beneath the olives, in front of Samaria, and lost myself in the delightful thoughts which the unclouded sky inspired. The old favourite of my boyhood, the beautiful torchweed, I found here; I carefully gathered some of its golden blossoms, and placed them in my pocket-book; but in my mind's eye I was displaying them already to the skilful examination of my dear brothers in Voigtland.

On my homeward course to the tent I had an opportunity of observing how early rudeness exhibits itself among the Samaritans. A boy, ten years of age, met me on my road; and whilst I was plucking the blossoms of the torchweed, he stood close to me. He now followed me with the cry, "Backshish, backshish;" and, finding that he laboured in vain, he began to pelt me with stones.

We quitted Samaria immediately after mid-day. But our breaking up was accompanied with a tragico-comical incident. The son of the sheikh of the village had been one of the gaping spectators of the Daguerreotype process; he now demanded a considerable backshish, as he had strictly maintained order. The wordy dispute would probably have closed with blows, had not his wish been ultimately acceded to.

Fatiguing though the way was during the hours of the mid-day heat both for us and for our horses, yet it was equally attractive. From precipitous mountains we descended into charming valleys, encompassed by romantic groups of rocks; we passed several villages, and thick olive plantations glittered around the houses. In the midst of our road to Jenin, we halted an instant to ascend a high round rock, which lies solitarily in the plain, covered with ruins. A Saracenic fortress stood here, which, from its position, could defy both friend and foe. Shortly before Ibrahim Pasha's dominion in Syria, the sheikh who held it resisted the notorious Abdallah Pasha of St. Jean d'Acre; he besieged it for several months, and at last, with the aid of the Maronites of Lebanon, took it by storm. Since then the fortress lies in ruins. One or two people, who belong to the village close to the foot of the rock, inhabit the rocky caverns.

We met with a strange rencontre, an hour later, between two neighbouring villages. It was to all appearance a marriage procession. The bride, veiled in white, interested us less than the camel on which she rode, and which wore a female head-dress of the Frankish fashion. The silly expression of this camel beneath the stately head-dress had a most comical effect, which cannot be described. It was a difficult task indeed to suppress our mirth; and yet a laugh would have given umbrage. The bride was escorted by mounted horse-men, with whose long spears I did not feel disposed to jest.

Towards evening we reached Jenin. We should have preferred bivouacking under some palm trees outside the walls, had due care for our safety not prohibited it. We transmitted to the commandant of the town our letters of introduction from the pasha of Naplus, and he appointed us a residence in one of his houses. This dwelling consisted in a neat terrace, and an adjoining chamber: if a small empty space between four walls, and two apertures for windows, may be called a chamber.

Jenin lies agreeably; its gardens, enclosed with the thorny cactus, display the most luxuriant vegetation. In the town we rode past a considerable reservoir, filled with water, and also a rapid brook. We met large herds, which led us to infer good cattle-breeding. But the greatest beauty of Jenin is its view over the fruitful and cele-brated plain of Esdrelon, with a mountain background in the west, north, and east. I enjoyed, in anticipation, our ride through the plain.

I visited with my companion the large khan of the place. We drank a cup of coffee, and smoked a nargileh. The guests whom we met there were doing the same, and only conversing less than ourselves. The silent contemplation of Turks in a coffee-house forms a complete contrast to the noisy talk in ours: of course we find there no trace of a newspaper.

Upon returning home to our terrace we were made acquainted with the domestic circumstances of our host. He had two wives, who lived exactly opposite to us, yet each in her own small harem. That they did not live in very sisterly communion together we speedily discovered by a noisy dispute we overheard between them, and which our host, upon our return, speedily quelled.

In the night we made a variety of unpleasant acquaintances. Our horses were stabled beneath our terrace, and we suffered be-sides from the usual accompaniments of the dog-days in southern latitudes. Our horses did not seem to have spent a more tranquil night than ourselves, for the next morning, the tempestuous sultriness of the past night still continuing, they rolled their heads fearfully, and mine hobbled constantly on one side, frequently stumbling, re-calling to mind, with longing wishes for the possibility of the ex-change, my noble camels and their sure footsteps.

But the effulgency of the light dissipated the shadows; for to-day we rode through the plain of Esdrelon. Its fertility is as wonderful as its beauty. The wheat was chiefly garnered: in the high stubble of the fields a gazelle might have concealed herself. The durrafields still stood, as well as the plantations of cotton shrubs with dark green and yellow blossoms. Blooming banks indicated brooks which flow into the Kishon. On quitting Jenin we had the mountain Gilboa on our right, on our left the foreland of Mount Carmel, and towards the north-west we greeted Mount Carmel itself. The reminiscences which are linked to this plain and its mountains contend for the entire possession of the soul of him who traverses them. Upon the heights of Gilboa, the unfortunate Saul fell upon his own sword (1 Sam. xxxi. 4.); and his son Jonathan, with two of his brothers, died by the swords of the Philistines. (1 Sam. xxxi. 2.) The beautiful elegy of David for the pride of Israel, and for his brother, the beloved one, has raised to both a memorial which towers high above the summits of the mountain. (2 Sam. i. 17—27.) The stream Megiddo speaks of Deborah's and Barak's valour against Sisera (Judges, iv. 14 &c.), and upon which the heroine herself chanted the immortal song of praise (Judges v). The brook Kishon speaks of Gideon; how the Spirit of the Lord excited him to fight the Midianites and Amalekites. (Judges vi. 34). But who could relate all the battles that have been fought upon this plain from Saul to the Maccabees, from the Romans to the Saracens, and from the Crusades to Napoleon. The west as well as the east has profusely moistened with its blood the soil which at the present day offers such joyous fields to our view.

Our road, which lay a little to the east of the direct road of the caravan, conducted us in the course of two hours to the village Zerin, which, since Robinson's investigations, may be identified with the ancient Jezreel. In this small group of ruinous houses lies buried the memory of the haughty queen, Jezabel; for here was Naboth's vineyard, his patrimony upon which she practised her violence (1 Kings, xxi. 1.) : here stood also the palace, from the windows of which she was precipitated, to fulfil most fearfully the denunciation of the prophet. (1 Kings, xxi. 23. 2 Kings, ix. 33, &c.)

Zerin lies high and is beautifully posted ; the view from its ancient tower is magificent, and extends to Carmel in the west, to the lesser Hermon in the north, to the valley of the Jordan in the east and in the south-east to the mountain Gilboa, on whose declivity it lies. I asked our guide in vain for Mount Tabor ; Hermon concealed it. An hour and a half later also, after we had left the village Solam behind us, where Elijah recalled the dead Shunamite boy to life (1 Kings, xvii. 17, &c.), we saw from the foot of Mount Hermon Mount Tabor rise out of the north-eastern plain. At first sight of it, tears started in my eyes ; this stately witness of the past had so suddenly presented itself to me. " The North and the South, thou hast created them : Tabor and Hermon shall rejoice in thy name." (Psalm lxxxix. 12.) These words of the Psalmist I had retained in my heart from childhood. The mountain's high form, its round summit clothed with the foliage of oaks rising freely and boldly out of the plain, transformed into reality the image that I had long worn in my heart.

We had still a league to traverse before we should quit the plain for the narrow valleys lying embosomed amidst the rocks which surround Nazareth. Upon entering the valleys we halted for a short mid-day rest. We here dismissed our military escort from Jenin, who had served us as a symbol of authority. Once I almost thought that we should have required their actual aid. We were going leisurely along our road near Hermon. I had dismounted, and was on foot at about fifty paces in advance of the caravan, when suddenly, to my astonishment, eight or ten Bedouins, upon dromedaries, sprang forth from behind the heights with their long lances. I boldly advanced, but one of the troop took the liberty, for the amusement of his comrades, to point his lance jocosely at me, and brought it quite near enough to my breast. I took the jest in good part, but preferred in future to remain quietly on horseback and in the midst of the company.

Whilst encamped here, a large vulture perched upon a projecting rock opposite to us; to my regret my dragoman's shot missed him. We had this morning in the plain another similar incident, but new to me. A serpent, from two to three ells long and of the thickness of a man's arm, of a dark brown colour, lay in a field in the sun; upon our approach, it undulated in graceful curves away, and escaped in a fissure of the gaping ground.

About four in the afternoon we beheld the cheerful Nazareth lying before us. On three sides it is enclosed by hills richly covered with foliage and leaning against a hill on the west. It has palms and cypresses as well as a high minaret in its centre. Close to the minaret we immediately recognised the large monastic building. There we speedily arrived, and were made the more welcome, as the Latin prior at Jerusalem had kindly given us a letter of introduction to the prior at Nazareth.

NAZARETH. TABOR. THE LAKE GENEZARETH.

Upon entering the monastery at Nazareth, we were congratulated upon having so fortunately accomplished our journey; for even in this monastery a very bad opinion prevails of the road from Jerusalem by way of Naplus. Among other mischances, the prior told us that shortly before Easter the curator of the monastery, although accompanied by a guide and a soldier of the pasha, had been attacked between Naplus and Nazareth, and had incurred the danger of being entirely stripped. The soldier fired after the attack was made, and wounded a Bedouin. For this he could hardly escape death, for the shedding of Bedouin blood can only be atoned for by blood. Eventually, however, the spiritual father succeeded in soothing the robbers, and he was even so successful as to persuade them to give him a safe conduct. Probably there is not much to be had beneath the cowl of of a capuchin.

We took up our residence opposite the monastery, in a building which, like the Casa Nuova at Jerusalem, is appropriated to the reception of pilgrims. We here met with several Frank travellers, who had arrived at Nazareth from Mount Carmel. A Neapolitan amongst them was joked upon the consideration shown him by the monks of the holy land, in gratitude for the favour of his sovereign.

To-day we took a further walk through the town. The houses in Nazareth have a solid aspect; all have flat roofs without cupolas. We saw upon these roofs small parties enjoying the evening breezes, whose refreshing coolness after the sultry day was also very agreeable to us. Nowhere did we observe traces of the earthquake which had visited the town a few years before. But a terrific impression was made upon me on the western side of the town by the overhanging precipices of the declivity of the mountain where the town itself lies. The incident related by St. Luke at the commencement of his Gospel was unconsciously brought to mind. The Nazarenes, he relates, all wondered at the "gracious words" that proceeded out of the mouth of their fellow-citizen (Luke iv. 22); but when they listened to the severity of the prophet, they drove him in rage from the city, " and led him unto the brow of the hill whereon their city was built, that that they might cast him down headlong." (Luke iv. 29.) More than one of these rocks around the modern town, which to all appearance occupies the site of the ancient one, shows how naturally this expression of their violence was suggested to the Nazarenes. The tradition, however, which places the rock whence they purposed casting him, at a distance from the city is certainly incorrect, as it does not agree with the narrative of the Gospel.

The house or workshop of Joseph is naturally enough shown at Nazareth, as well as the synagogue wherein our Saviour referred to the passage in Isaiah (Luke iv. 17.), and usually delivered his discourses. Also a block of stone in the shape of a table is exhibited, at which he is reputed to have eaten with his disciples. There is also the garden in which Jesus, when a boy, took especial delight. This garden, full of fig-trees, oranges, and pomegranates, suggests at least very agreeable thoughts. But what chiefly attracted me to-day was the well of Mary, a few minutes' walk from the city on the road to Tabor. But few of the venerated spots of Palestine are so sure of their identity as this well. It is now the only one of the city, and probably it was so more than two thousand years ago. I found this evening a great many women and maidens collected for the purpose of drawing water from this well: who can doubt that the most blessed amongst women may have once stood here? Among the present water-bearers I saw several graceful figures. Their heavy pitchers they carried upon their heads with remarkable skill.

Not far to the north of the well springs forth the fountain which feeds it. Over this the Greeks have built their church of the Annunciation, for it is on this spot they believe that Mary received the salutation of the angel. (Luke i. 28.) They follow in this the apocryphal Gospel of St. James, wherein it is expressly said, that Mary had gone with her pitcher to fetch water when she received the divine benediction. But the tradition of the Latins also confirms this Gospel; for after Mary, it further says, had returned home with her pitcher, and had resumed her work, the angel repeated his visit and renewed his salutation. And the Latins venerate a cavern of annunciation, and this cavern forms the sanctuary of the church of their monastery.

Upon returning to the monastery in the twilight we were met by two Abyssinian women belonging to a caravan which had pitched its tents for several weeks past near the city. They instantly began speaking to us. Naturally enough we understood almost nothing of what they said ; but they did not allow this to deter them, and continued with pleasing enthusiasm, at the same time pointing to their encampment at hand. As the sweet, yet melancholy expression of their light brown complexions and black eyes, pleased us, we listened attentively to them for a couple of minutes, and then presented these poor pilgrims with a handsome gratuity, one of our companions having already acquainted us with their destitution.

We slept better at Nazareth than at Jenin with our troublesome bedfellows, or at Leban with the cold dew falling upon our faces. But to our bodily comfort was added a higher one ; for the thought of being under the roofs of the city where our Saviour had passed his childhood and youth, illumed this night of my life with a heavenly ray.

The morning of the 26th of July aroused me to fresh delights. At an early hour I wandered over the eastern heights opposite the city, which is more overgrown with fig-trees than with olives. It was difficult to find the most beautiful view of Nazareth. It had from all points a picturesque and beautiful effect. The eye ever found an agreeable resting-place in the white tower of the mosque with the lofty and dark cypresses by its side. But I lingered with most delight on the spot whence I could view, together with the city, the

well also, in the north upon the edge of the mountain. And thus
I let the eye of my body, together with the eye of my soul, dwell
long upon Nazareth and its hills and valleys. Two thousand years
may possibly have changed much; but as much as I saw to-day
must also have been spread out before the divine eye of the son of
Joseph of Nazareth. How often may he not have wandered where
I was now wandering! his sacred heart full of his great futurity—
full of the conception of his doctrine which, from the narrow mountains of his little home, should fill all the mountains and all the seas
of the earth, and every land and every heart.

Opposite to me in the west lay the crown of all the heights about
Nazareth; from the Turkish sepulchre upon it it is called by the
name of the prophet Ismael. I knew beforehand what splendour
there awaited me, especially as to-day the sky was almost cloudless,
and the air perfectly clear.

A few months before I had stood upon the loftiest pyramid, with
the desert, the Nile, and Cairo, at my feet. I had since stood upon
Sinai, the majestic mountain of the Lord, and had petitioned Heaven
itself, like a bosom friend; from the minaret at the summit of the
Mount of Olives, I had viewed at once the Holy City, with Bethlehem's heights and the mountains of Samaria, the wonderful sea of
Sodom, and the mountains of Moab; yet to-day I felt as a child who
had as yet seen nothing but his own home, and knew nothing of the
world. I was thus overwhelmed by the view from Neby Ismael,
which crowns the heights of Nazareth. I looked towards Tabor in
the east, the lesser Hermon and Gilboa peered upwards in its vicinity, and guided me to the mountains of Samaria in the south.
Thence I looked towards the west and beheld the forelands of Carmel, and in the blue distance Carmel itself. Amid all these mountain heights the broad plain of Esdrelon reposed before me, as if
encircled by eternal walls. But beyond Carmel, to its left as well as
to its right, lay like a festal day, in glittering beauty, the mirror of
the Mediterranean. In the north a second extensive plain spread
forth, with Canna, the little town of the marriage and the " Horns
of Hattin," where the army of Saladin trampled under foot all the
conquests of the Crusaders. In the north-east, lastly, shone down,
like a divine eye, behind desert groups of mountains, the summit of
the great Hermon, enveloped in its eternal snows; and withdrawing
my gaze from those distant scenes, I looked down upon Nazareth,
which clung, like a darling child, to the hill above which I stood.

What were the feelings of my soul during this survey? The admiration and devotion then felt have no words to express them; but a
psalm of the inspired David was rushing to the lips, to resound to
the depths of the unfathomable ocean, and to ascend to the snowy

summit of Hermon. What may this watch tower have been to our Saviour ? A symbol of his kingdom upon earth, of the Gospel of redemption, as it embraced heaven, earth, and sea, with the arms of maternal affection ; as it compressed together both the past and the future, into the one great hour upon Golgotha. The snow of Hermon looks like the grey head of Time — like the past : the sea, pregnant with mystery, like the future. Between both reposes the present, this dew-drop, reflecting infinitely rich images from the rays of the morning sun.

Here did the Saviour, when he looked over the ocean to the west certainly often think of thee, thou beloved Germany ! He thought of thee, because he knew that thou wouldst one day be called on as the holy avenger of the truth, to fight and bleed in opposition to falsehood ; that thou wouldst found, in German hearts, a bulwark for the faith comprised within the Epistle to the Romans, when it had vanished from the palaces of the city upon the seven hills. Would that thou thyself stood here, and heard with me, that to thee the words resounded, " hold fast what thou possessest, that no one rob thee of thy crown."

On my return from this mountain, I visited the little church of the Latin monastery. I found it full of Nazarenes, who lay kneeling around the steps of the altar, and according to the custom of the East, repeated their devotions rather loudly. The windows of the church were, as well as its walls, hung with dark drapery, and the organ solemnly resounded to the singing of the monks. The chief object of veneration in this church is the cavern beneath the high altar in which the virgin is said to have stood when she received the salutation of the angel. (St. Luke i. 28.) This subterranean rocky chamber is fitted up as a chapel, like the cavern at Bethlehem and of St. John. Upon a marble tablet, the following words are inscribed in Latin, " Here the Word became flesh." As a wonderful peculiarity of the cavern, a granite column is shown, which was broken in two by the Saracens ; but the upper half of which still hangs firmly from the arched vault. Above this subterranean rocky apartment, immediately behind the high altar, there were two other cavern chapels. One still stands firm ; the other, as the faith in miracles assumes, was conveyed by angels, in the thirteenth century, over Dalmatia to Loretto, near Ancona, to preserve it from the impure hands of the Saracens.

Possibly the greatest solemnity which this church, or rather that upon the ruins of which the present one is built, ever witnessed within its walls, was upon the festival of the Annunciation, when St. Louis of France, in the garb of a repentant pilgrim, was present, and partook of the Holy Sacrament. It was in the year 1250.

Thirteen years afterwards the swords of the Saracens devastated
where the pious monarch had prayed; and the church of the Annunciation became a complete ruin.   In subsequent centuries new
Christian buildings have been erected over it.   But a bishopric, with
all the importance which Nazareth received under the feudal dominion of the noble Tancred, has, at least in name, survived, and is
still retained at the present day.

The present population of Nazareth is chiefly Christian.   Out
of about three thousand inhabitants *, less than one thousand may
be Mahometans.   Among the Christians there are, besides Greeks
and Catholics, some hundreds of Maronites, who have a small church
of their own.

The Bedouins were described to me as dangerous neighbours.
The town was at present apprehensive of a hostile attack from them:
they had made a claim upon it, and in case of refusal by a certain
day, had threatened to use force.   The Nazarenes had consequently
applied to the pasha of St. Jean d'Acre.   As I wished to proceed
the following day, by way of Tabor, to Tiberias, this intelligence
was not agreeable to me, especially as from the present time I travelled alone, my companion going direct to Damascus.

On the 27th of July I rode, half an hour before sunrise, past the
well of the Virgin; one guide only and my dragoman accompanied
me.   The sky was cloudy and the air was sultry; I feared, that for
my hopes an unfavourable star was in the ascendant.   We went
direct to the east, and had only ascended a few heights, and, behold!
there lay Mount Tabor before us, rising majestically from its environs.   It had now an imposing aspect, which was lent it by the
moment.   Its loftiest rounded summit wore the dark colour of its
oaks; but, immediately beneath, it was enveloped in the dark sobriety
of a deeply louring tempest cloud.   By degrees the clouds and the
sultriness dispersed, and the day became cheerful.   When the sun with
its early rays had unveiled its brow, the mountain then shone in resplendent glory, which recalled more vividly to the thoughts of the
wanderer the moment of that heavenly transfiguration, to the memory of which mount Tabor is consecrated.

In two hours we were at the foot of the mountain; the little
village of Daburieh lay not far off on our right.   We ascended without stopping.   The road is precipitous and fatiguing, although I

---

* Robinson received from good authority the following statement:—Of
Greeks, 260 men subject to taxation; Catholic Greeks, 130; Roman
Catholics, 120; Maronites, 100; Mahomedans, 170. See his Palestine, iii. 421.
Williams gives, from his Diocesal Census, 1000 Orthodox Greeks, which
agrees with Robinson's 260 men liable to impost.   Other earlier accounts
estimate the number of the population higher, but probably incorrectly.

observed, in several places, that it had been rendered more easy by art.
In an hour we had reached the summit, the surface of which looks
as if it had been flattened long ago for the construction of a large
building. And, in fact, on several spots of this surface we find
traces of former buildings. A fortress wall seems to have run
round about it; ruins and rubbish lie dispersed about; the pointed
arch of a gateway may still be seen, which the Arabs call " the
Gate of the Wind." I also found a dark vault, with an altar
concealed beneath rubbish, and I was told that yearly a Latin mass
is performed here; and the Greeks have also, on the opposite side of
the mountain, an altar beneath the ruins of a church, for the same
purpose.

It would be difficult to determine from what particular age these
ruins may date; at all events they spring from different periods.
That a city stood here long before the Christian era cannot be
doubted, from the passage in the first Book of Chronicles (vii. 77),
and the Book of Judges (viii. 18); and Polybius proves that it was
still standing in the year 218 before Christ.* And Josephus, too,
the historian and general, may assume the existence of the city when
he says that he intended to raise fortresses upon Tabor.

The Christian celebrity of the mountain is universally known. It
is thought that in Tabor the "high mountain" of the Gospel, and
the "holy mountain" of the Second Epistle of Peter, may be
recognised.   Under the peculiar character of "the mountain of the
transfiguration" it first presents itself in the apochryphal Gospels,
and in the writings of St. Cyril of Jerusalem; whilst Eusebius and
St. Jerome, although they speak of Mount Tabor, do not mention
it in connection with the scene of the transfiguration. But from
the time of St. Cyril, at the end of the fourth century, pilgrims and
churches appear upon the mountain. Even in the sixth century, in
symbolisation of the three tabernacles which St. Peter purposed
building, three churches were erected; and shortly afterwards a
monastery stood near them. The Crusaders greatly venerated the
mountain; it was the scene of many a bloody broil between the
Crescent and the Cross, whence it preserved nothing but the scanty
ruins which are now found there.

From these circumstances, doubts may be suggested whether, in
fact, it was on Mount Tabor that the heavenly voice resounded to
the beloved Son.   Yet is it possible that our historical accounts of
the origin of the tradition are of a much more recent date than the
origin itself?   The mode of expression also used in the Second
Epistle of Peter (i. 18) indicates that even then a particular moun-

* Polybius v. 70. 6.   Refer, for this and the various other buildings
upon Tabor, to Robinson's Palestine, iii. 462, &c.

tain was distinguished as the holy mountain; but it may not be overlooked that from that time the right one may have been changed for a false one. And yet, even were tradition in error, it would be difficult to renounce it. For the mountain to which it clings stands like a moment of inspiration transformed into an earthly form, and deposited as a memorial stone by God in the creation, as the altar of the land which itself is a temple of God. He who sees it at the present day believes, as firmly as if an angel had told him, that the beautiful mountain, whose brothers stand at a distance as if in admiration, bears a sacred mystery within it, and has been sacredly endowed by him who made it so splendid. But it has displayed its mystery—it has fulfilled its object—if it, indeed, was the scene of the transfiguration of the Son of God. Fifteen centuries have celebrated the memory of this transfiguration upon Mount Tabor. How many a sword, since grey antiquity, has glittered upon it and aroused the bloody contest! How many an eye has beamed from it aloft to heaven and supplicated the peace of God!

I sat solitary beneath the ruins to which young ivy was clinging; firs and oaks cast their shades around me; the plain of Esdrelon lay at my feet; the Kishon, " the brook of the former world," glittered in it like a streak of silver. I beheld Endor with its reminiscence of the prophetic spirit which announced to Saul his death (1 Sam. xxviii. 19); I saw Nain, where the Saviour comforted the widow and restored her son to her. (Luke vii. 11—15.) The nine hundred chariots of Sisera stood not in imagination before me; I sat among the disciples, whose eye was unclouded. The past and the present appeared to me as an obscure riddle. Where throughout the world was there a mountain whence the heavenly proclamation of joy and peace resounded as from Tabor? And yet since this was uttered, every stone and every tree of the mountain speaks of war and tribulation : the mountain stands there like a not understood prophet — like a stranger amidst a strange people. But how did I rejoice in the oaks of Tabor! Tabor greeted me with a German tongue. On the German mountains the word has also found an echo which descended upon it from a cloud; in the land of the oak it is more at home than on the banks of the Kishon.

The view from Tabor approaches the splendour of that from Neby Ismael. It commands far and wide the plain of Esdrelon; farther in the south I perceived the little Hermon and Gilboa; in the south east the valley of the Jordan, and beyond it Mount Gilead; in the north east I beheld for the first time the Lake Genezareth, with the mountains beyond and high up in the north beyond the plains and mountains, and towns and villages, the snow-crowned Hermon itself.

Although we had to-day a long way still before us, yet could I not so soon part from Tabor. I gathered from its oaks some leaves and acorns; both differ from ours.* Besides the turpentine or pistacio trees, I saw also laurels. I thought as I plucked its twigs, how delightful it was to carry the laurel home to Germany from Tabor. I did not meet with any wild boars, although many are said to frequent Mount Tabor ; but dense flocks of sparrows chirping the same musical notes as those of Leipzig, surrounded me. These sparrows, which flew upwards even to the very summit of Tabor, interrupted my thoughts of the laurel. But the world is every where alike. The Tabor sparrows peck at the laurel as pertinaciously as those of Leipzig. But every one has his rights and his renown : throughout my travels in Europe, Africa, and Asia, I have convinced myself that there exists a vulgar cosmopolitanism, of which the sparrow is the representative.

Towards eleven we were again at the foot of Mount Tabor; thence we took the nearest way to Tiberias. In an hour we fell in with two large fortresses, like khans, at a short distance apart; there was indeed no indication of inhabitants ; but they are built as the point of union for the inhabitants of the neighbourhood in the east and in the west, where they hold a weekly fair. These buildings were constructed, however, more especially for the convenience of the caravans travelling between Egypt and Damascus. We sought to obtain some water here, and what we found was better suited for our cattle than for ourselves. Half an hour later we approached several tents which belonged to Kefr Sabt. Here instead of water, we were refreshed with some milk. Shortly afterwards a troop of Bedouins met us, clad in stately military costume ; to our delight we did not at all interest them. At a short league before reaching Tiberias we met with a large well, where we were enabled to satisfy our thirst with tolerable water. We met at the well a young woman who was fetching water in the skin of a wild boar ; she was very willing to assist us from her store. Upon ascending, not far from the well, the height in the valley where it descends into the hollows towards the east, we suddenly obtained a view of the splendid lake of Genezareth. This lake has a very different aspect from that of Zurich or of Lucerne, or even that of Albano ; but its peculiar beauty is great. Its eastern shore is destitute of verdure, and consists of a bright red naked precipice, whose picturesquely solemn expression enhances the splendour of the blue mirror. In the north and in the south where the Jordan flows in and out, the narrow banks are deep and cheerfully green. The western side of the lake

---

* Schubert describes this species of oak as the *Quercus Aegilops*.

is formed by a low mountain crest, which is frequently interrupted
by chasms, and more or less recedes. The city Tiberias lies close
to the western shore a little to the south of the centre of the lake.

I need not mention what gives the Lake Genezareth its chief
charm independent of its natural beauty. The acts of our Lord
described by the Gospels, especially the three first, chiefly took place
upon its banks. Here our Saviour had his favourite abode; now
he wandered upon its shores, and now he floated upon its waters:
here it was that he selected from the class of fishermen his favourite
disciples; here he so often addressed his sacred discourse to the
people — now from the mountain, and now from boats: here by the
numerous miracles which he performed did he glorify Him who sent
him. At this moment the sea was perfectly still; not a sail not a
vessel disturbed its waters; repose and silence ruled the entire scene.
I beheld, indeed, the grey walls and the fortress towers of Tiberias,
but I did not see a single individual, although my eye commanded
an extensive view. But one sound floated above the silence of this
landscape: it was a sacred sound. The star of stars shone here, and
it has faded; the master of all masters taught here, and he has closed
his lips; the anointed of God wandered here, and he has departed. While beholding the country of Genezareth, I felt as if
yesterday had been the festival of Whitsuntide or Easter; as if
impelled by a necessity to converse about something delightful that
we had passed through; as if we understood each other without the
intervention of words; like two friends who, after a long separation,
which had only rooted more deeply every delightful reminiscence in
their hearts, gaze silently into each other's eyes.

Upon entering the gate of the city my dragoman asked a Polish
Jew in German the way to the New Hotel. He was not wrong; he
was replied to in German. Several hundred Jews reside at Tiberias,
the majority of whom have migrated from Poland, and some speak
German. Our host also spoke German; he was now busied with
the completion of an hotel, so considerable in size and of such a
character as was scarcely to be expected at a place like Tiberias.

After taking some refreshment upon the balcony of the house, we
made a promenade along the shores of the lake. At the end of the
city we met with a great number of Turkish soldiers, all on horseback: their barrack consisted of several large green tents. I bathed
in the lake, and found its water agreeable, although a little heavy.
Its taste is delicious; the whole city makes use of it as their ordinary drink.

At half a league's distance from the city are the bathing-places
with the medicinal warm springs, which were celebrated even in
antiquity. The new buildings of Ibrahim Pasha there are excellent

and inviting. The warmth of the water varies between 48° and 50° Reaumur; it smells strongly of sulphur and tastes very bitter; its healing virtues are said to be extraordinary, especially upon gouty patients. Schubert expressed the hope that in a few years, by the intervention of steamboats, sick persons would be conveyed from Europe to the baths at Tiberias. It is clear that the climate of the splendid valley of the lake gives the bath a peculiar advantage; but he who comes hither with a mind impregnated with Christian fervour, if not cured for his western home, will be at least rendered more fitted for his eternal home.

Between this bath and the city lie many ruins; among several overthrown grey granite columns one still stands upright. The ancient city, built and named in honour of the Emperor Tiberias, lay nearly a mile further south than the present one. In the city itself we remarked that the traces of the terrific earthquake of the 2nd January, 1837 were almost all effaced; near the recently built houses others were being built. But the entire city, by the narrowness and filthiness of the streets, conveys the impression of a Jewish quarter; we were met also chiefly by Jewish countenances. Tiberias, as is well known, is one of the holiest of the cities of the Jews, and yet along with its from five to eight hundred Jewish inhabitants there may be as many Mahometans, and not many less Greek Catholic Christians. The Latins have also a church here, but it is only visited from Nazareth, and its interior as well as its courts serve for the quarters of Frankish travellers. We had, however, declined accepting the keys of it, which were offered to us in the monastery; for our countrymen who had just returned to Nazareth had confirmed the notoriety of this locality, through their complete acquaintance with it, not through its great thieves, but smaller and more troublesome annoyances. The race of the latter is so numerous at Tiberias, that an Arabic proverb says their prince holds his court there. I was the more easily consoled as our host made so heavy a demand for supper and lodging that I wholly declined them.

The sun was setting as we quitted the city and rode towards the village Medschdel, the ancient Magdala, which lies at the distance of a league. The full moon shortly shone over the lake; its tranquillity, which I had admired a few hours before, gave place to a storm which drove the waves wildly over the rocks upon our road. Above us on the left towered the mountains of Magdala, rent by fissures; the moonlight gave it a terrific but beautiful appearance. It is the mountain upon which our Lord prayed alone when he had dismissed the people, and had sent his disciples forward upon th lake. Reminiscences of our Saviour were all around us. The waves of the sea foamed to-day as they did when the disciples, in terror, awoke their master, whom wind and sea obeyed. But I was suddenly aroused from my contemplations. About thirty paces in front of us, we beheld, behind the bushes of our road, several travellers advancing towards us in the dark. They halted as soon as they saw us, and called out loudly "Who goes there?" They had taken us for robbers; it was not necessary to confide our similar suspicions to them. It was a small caravan which was conveying goods on asses. That the road was not safe we were now thoroughly convinced, and yet we reached the natal village of Mary Magdalene without any further rencontre. We entered a peasant's dwelling, and made our couches upon its flat roof. So tranquilly modest did the little village lie in the moonshine, that it was scarcely conceivable that once one of its daughters was possessed with "seven devils" (St. Luke viii. 2); but the beautiful and pious Magdalene, as so many pictures have displayed her, admitted of the sweetest association with it. We slept perfectly well in our lofty bivouac; but my dragoman in the course of about half an hour was aroused to join the evening meal of our host, which he told me he tasted out of policy.*

A cheerful morning aroused us; the lake again lay before us in tranquil clearness, reflecting the dark blue sky. We rode along its western shore, through the most luxuriant foliage I ever remember to have seen. On our left we had a dense grove of nebek trees, olives, and figs; on our right, a narrow strip only of trees and shrubs separated us from the glittering lake. But the eye revelled upon the delicate rose-coloured blossoms, glittering in the morning dew of the oleanders which grew on both sides of the road, forming a thick garland. Hastening along I plucked a beautiful nosegay, although I was debarred the pleasure of decorating with it the bosom of a beloved one.

One thing only was wanting to complete the enjoyment of this delicious scene; this was an excursion upon the lake. I looked far and wide; not a single boat or vessel of any description was to be seen; even that had disappeared which had been seen some few years before by a party of travelling Franks.

My Biblical inquiries this morning did not extend beyond those previously made by the learned Robinson. Of Chorazin, Bethsaida, Capernaum, not only have the names disappeared; but even the very stones of the ground, which in the East speak with so eloquent a tongue, here yield us no information. I rode beyond a league to the

---

* No payment is received for such accommodation; a present only is left, as in the monasteries.

khan Minyeh, where I could distinctly see the Jordan, which flows
at about a league and a half off into the lake. The dark-coloured
stones, which lie dispersed about the mountain, close to the dilapidated khan, might be considered as the indication of the spot where
Capernaum stood, as the greatest probability speaks in favour of this
locality; but no ruins are to be seen, and the stones themselves are
shapeless and unhewn. Has not the punishing hand of Heaven struck
this spot? The wail of our Lord over Chorazin, over Bethsaida, and
over Capernaum, exalted unto heaven (Matt. xi. 21—24); must it
not present itself forcibly to the soul of him, who in vain now seeks
for the ruins of a wall or of a pillar, in indication of these cities,
where, according to the testimony of Matthew (xi. 20.), the majority
of the miraculous acts of our Lord were performed? Magdala,
the little village where the pious penitent was born (Matt. xv. 39),
lies as it did two thousand years ago; even its very name may be still
recognised; and yet the three cities, the wickedness of which approached to that of Tyre, Sidon, and Sodom, must have lain in the
immediate vicinity of Magdala.

From the khan Minyeh we retraced our steps to Magdala. After
pursuing thence the commencement of the road to Tiberias, we
ascended through a ravine to the heights in the west, whence I took
a parting view of the lake. The road to Nazareth led us over the
celebrated field of Hattin. I know not what battle-field ever so
powerfully affected me. The termination of the Crusades — for the
battle of Hattin, fought on the 10th of July, 1187, gave the true
incurable wound to the Crusaders — could not be more disastrous,
nor more painful. One of the Christian princes (Reynaud de
Chatillon) infringed the sworn armistice by plunder and robbery.
Saladin had a right to despise his prisoner before he cleft his
shoulders in twain; and lastly, the discord between the princes
and knights must necessarily have frustrated all counsel and consideration, and have led the Christian force as a sacrifice to the
enemy. Has history facts to show more melancholy than these?

The so-called " Horns of Hattin," which command the field of
battle, and which was the scene of the last conflict, are called in
Christian tradition, " The Mountain of Blessings," and is considered
as the mount whence Christ preached his sermon. (Matt. v—vii.)
It is not possible to conceive a greater contrast, or a more bitter irony.

In this neighbourhood, as well as that which we traversed yesterday, between Tabor and Tiberias, I was particularly struck by the
extensive districts growing wild oats, as also with others covered with
burdocks and thistles. Where the hand of culture might so easily
raise the golden grain of wheat, Oriental apathy allows inanimate
nature to languish in despondency. Locusts, very like those of the

Arabian desert, we saw flying in dense swarms across the fields; they even fluttered around our heads, but were not easily caught.

I observed a bird hovering above a thorny bush; I stepped towards it; a snake lay there coiled up, of at least two ells in length, and tolerably thick, and sucking the blood of a small bird, which the wailing mother was probably fluttering over. My guide aimed his pistol at it, but it hung fire; and before a gun could be levelled at it, the snake had crept into a fissure, and left the little bird lying dead.

From the village of Lubieh, prettily situated upon a height, the birthplace of Josephus, to whom the science of history is so deeply indebted, we reached Kefr Kenna, where the Cana of the Bible is supposed to have stood. The house where the marriage took place was shown to me (John ii. 1—11), but not one of the six stone waterpots was forthcoming. The village lies agreeably on the southern declivity of a mountain crest, and is only a league from Nazareth. But its Biblical claims are disputed by Kana el Yelil, which with its ruins lies two leagues north west of the plain El Buttauf.

MOUNT CARMEL.

On the 29th I left the little Galilee town after which the Christians were not only called Nazarenes in the earliest times, but whence they are even yet called Nusa (singular, Nusrany) by the Arabs. From visiting the east of Nazareth I passed to-day to the west; the majestic Carmel was now my goal. A holy padre conducted us as far as St. Giacomo or Yafa, located upon one of the heights of Nazareth, about two-thirds of a league from the monastery. We here saw the little church of St. James, whose birthplace is here venerated, occupied in the celebration of a festival; a few days previously the anniversary of the Apostle had been joyfully celebrated by the Christians of Nazareth and its vicinity.

Our road continuously offered us to-day a more cheerful landscape than yesterday's. The heights were clothed with beautiful woods, and the valleys with luxuriantly green meadows; birds sang upon the branches, and birds of prey sailed through the air. In the first half of the way we passed through a village which abounded in hedges of the Cactus Opuntia. I was inadvertently induced to pluck

R

some of them which hung over the road ; and have since learnt that
there is no surer way to destroy all comfort than to gather a handful
of the Opuntia.   Close to one of the declivities of Mount Carmel
we forded the Kishon, which was not attended with any danger.
Between the two existing monuments of a pregnant past, the Kishon
and Mount Carmel, we rode for the space of two leagues towards
the ancient maritime town Haïfa, against the walls of which dash
the waves of the Mediterranean.   A couple of consular flags waving
over handsome new houses, and some vessels moored in the harbour,
gave the ancient town a cheerful aspect.   Yet formerly no doubt
when Tancred conquered it, it had a more chivalric appearance than
now.   That it possibly derives its foundation from the ancient
Japhet, a member of the Ark of Noah, none of the Turkish inhabitants at all imagine.

We proceeded towards the gate without delay, whence it was a
league to the monastery of Elijah, which looked down upon us as
primly as pleasantly from its heights.   A carefully constructed road
facilitated the ascent of the rough and rocky acclivity.   The monastery is seated at a height of 600 feet.   My first step within its
hospitable enclosure made me feel thoroughly at home.

Thus I again stood upon one of those mountains which God has
made to enchant both eye and heart.   Like a glimpse into infinitude
is the view from Mount Carmel over the sea ; like a transition from
the noisy forum of the world to the courts of heaven which here
extends its embracing arms so widely and so powerfully that no
heart can evade it.   Carmel is like a question to the future : far
behind it lies the noisy conflict of the passions of the earth.   The
pilgrim when he has attained it becomes suddenly tranquil, but he is
immersed in those thoughts whose depths are deeper than the unfathomable sea.   The soul here feels face to face with the Almighty;
no images of saints intervene as at St. Peter's.   The pilgrim thinks
he has arrived at the parting-point of the present and the future ;
and he hears a sacred word with a reverberating echo from heaven
which ever afterwards accompanies him in the very tortuous path
of life.

The illimitable surface of the ocean lies, not only in front of
Mount Carmel, but also upon the right and upon the left ; for
Carmel projects itself forward into the sea, confronting its waves like
the bold breast of an opponent.   The only equally sublime view of
the sea I am acquainted with, is that from the heights of Ingouville,
near Havre, a view which Casimir Delavigne has even compared
with the beauty of Constantinople.*   Behind the monastery to the

---

* His words are, " Après Constantinople il n'est rien de plus beau."

south east, the wooded crest of Mount Carmel gradually rises to a
height of more than a thousand feet; below towards the south, the
ruins of Athlit, the celebrated fortress of the Christian pilgrims,
which maintained upon its towers one of the last conflicts of the
Knight of the Cross, standing upon a rocky promontory of the plain
of the coast cast a melancholy look down into the sea.   Towards
the north lies St. Jean d'Acre, whose white walls glittered gaily in
the rays of the setting sun.   Beyond it, in the north east, towers
Lebanon, and crowns its green declivities in the west with its
dazzling snowy summit.

Carmel and its magnificence temporally absorbed all thoughts of
the monastery wherein I had felt so immediately at home.   I
ascended two stories to the refectory, and inspected the adjacent cor-
ridor of visitors' chambers. The cleanliness, the neatness, the comfort
which prevail therein, surpass all expectation.   The eye of the
wandering stranger is chiefly attracted by the white canopies, supported upon iron frames, for in no other monastery of the East has
he beheld a similar arrangement.   I next visited the kitchen and the
mill, the garden and the church; all is excellent.   The latter has a
cupola, through which it receives its light; it is paved with marble
and has a neat organ.   Several feet below the surface lies the cavern
of Elijah, which constitutes the sanctuary of the church.   A little
garden beside the church serves as a cemetery, and is already
ornamented with two funereal monuments.   One is a small pyramid,
dedicated to the memory of the French warriors who, under Napoleon,
died of their wounds upon Mount Carmel; the second is inscribed with the name of a young French count, who very recently
fell a victim to a sudden attack of dysentery.   I was most agreeably surprised by the dispensary of the monastery, whose greatest
riches consist in medicinal extracts from the odoriferous plants of
Carmel.   Their use is not confined to the service of pilgrims to the
Holy Land, but is extended to the sick of the whole country around.

My conducting padre led me at last to the flat roof of the
monastery.   It was difficult to tear oneself away again from it; for
here the grandeur of the view from Carmel exercises its whole
power.

After being introduced to all the treasures of the monastery, I
was invited to a repast, which surpassed all I had enjoyed in the
Holy Land.   In an excellent glass of the wine of Lebanon I drank
to Mount Carmel and its monastery.

But whither does all this tend? whence is this monastery? what is
it? and what does it possess? He who knows that upon Mount Carmel, twenty-five years ago, there stood nothing but a couple of melancholy ruins, which the notorious Abdallah Pasha shattered to pieces,

to prevent their possible appropriation by the Greeks then in a state of rebellion, puts this question with great astonishment. The monk Fra' Giovanni Battista can reply to it; the monastery upon Mount Carmel may justly be said to be his creation. From a far distant home did he come to Carmel; with him he brought nothing but his enthusiasm, but this enthusiasm was mighty and remained faithful to him.

It was in the year 1819 that Giovanni Battista, commissioned by his order, first visited Mount Carmel from Rome. He then found within the ruins of the monastery, instead of monks, a multitude of French soldiers' skeletons. In the disposition of the Turkish *alentours*, in the tyranny of the pasha of St. Jean d'Acre, and in the explosion of the Greek war of emancipation, there was sufficient reason to banish, for the moment, all thoughts of a new structure. But to know the Holy Mount which had given a name to his order to be thus deserted, thus neglected, was a pain which accompanied the pious monk to his western home, and allowed no peace to visit his soul.

Seven years afterwards, in a more propitious season he again visited the East. He came by way of Constantinople; thence he brought, through the aid of French influence, a firman for the erection of a new monastery. Giovanni Battista has skill in architecture; he immediately sketches a plan, the execution of which demanded a fund of a hundred thousand dollars. And whence does he derive these means? His order does not participate in the rich revenue enjoyed by the Franciscans, as guardians of the Holy Sepulchre; the court of Rome too can accord him nothing but its benediction and its protection. He now takes his way along the coasts of Asia and Africa; he traverses Europe: he goes from prince to people; he begs from the Catholic and the Protestant; and with his own hand he conveys the gifts of a liberal sympathy to his mountain, and there he applies them along with a few similarly minded brethren: thus this monastery arose, a refreshing centre of repose to pilgrims from all countries; to the Christian, as also to him of a different creed: to the sick, both of the neighbourhood and from afar, a kindly hospital: and a festal sanctuary to the memory of the great prophet, whose name it bears.

During my visit to Carmel, Giovanni Battista was engaged in a fresh excursion to Europe, for the promotion of his plan; six months afterwards, he visited me at Leipzig. Having seen the completed building, one is absolutely induced to doubt the necessity of the new structure he contemplates. But to a man who can exhibit so praiseworthy a monument of his pious and patient zeal, a favourable eye and an aiding hand are willingly granted when he wishes to give to his work an extension, which he deems to be essential and necessary. Even at the time that I was at Carmel this new building was already commenced, and was proceeding with energy. About two hundred paces from the monastery, to the north-west, towards the sea, there is an ancient ruin, which Ibraham Pasha, who has in other ways promoted Giovanni Battista's undertaking, has presented to the Carmelites. This he purposes reconstructing, to form a second monastic building, or rather a building for charitable purposes, and especially an extensive hospital for the reception of the sick. As it is very probable that but for this second building of the Latins, the ancient walls would have been appropriated by the Greeks,, and re-built for a Greek monastery, I cannot but rejoice on that account at the new undertaking of the worthy Carmelite. For had a Greek monastery arisen close to the present Catholic one, without all doubt the dissensions, every where prevalent in the East between the western and eastern churches, would have been transplanted to Mount Carmel, renovating these vexations.

I met with but few monks in the monastery. The present Prior is a Spaniard; the superintendent of strangers, to whose friendly advances I am much indebted, is an Italian; a third is a German, a native of Bavaria. This countryman of mine appeared to be no very worthy representative of his country, although, according to his own account, he was engaged in the compilation of an Arabic Lexicon. He had been formerly sent to Bagdad by way of punishment, and he now lived in discord with his colleagues.

The evening of the present day I dedicated to the reminiscences of Mount Carmel, both sacred and profane. Even in the earliest period it appears to have been the seat of religious observances; but it was the prophet Elijah who selected it to be the sublimest and holiest scene, the scene of a veritable judgment of the Almighty. (See 1 Kings xviii. 18.) It was hither that Ahab brought his prophets of Baal, eight hundred and fifty individuals; hither came Elijah; the priests built an altar to their Baal; Elijah repaired the altar of his God that was broken down. Sacrifices lay upon both altars. Fire from heaven was to testify to the divine truth before the doubting people of Israel. And it proclaimed aloud and testified miraculously; the people exclaimed " The Lord, he is the God; the Lord, he is the God." (1 Kings xviii. 39.) Elijah led the convicted lying prophets down to the brook Kishon, and slaughtered them; he then returned to Carmel, and implored in his prayer for rain, which, on his denunciation, had been withheld for one year.

Besides Elijah, his disciple Elisha had also his cavern upon Carmel; it is believed to be still recognisable. The number of caves and caverns, however, upon Mount Carmel approximates closely to two thousand; this labyrinth of cavities would seem the passage to the

R 3

spirits of the lower regions. It may thence be easily understood
how this mountain became a favourite place of resort for an-
chorites, and of refuge for the persecuted. Notices in the classics
show that Pythagoras also, upon his return home from the sages
of Egypt, visited a temple upon Mount Carmel dedicated to the
most sacred purposes; that Carmel was the holy mountain of
Zeus; that the gods of the mountain were named identically with
the mountain itself; that an oracle stood here which prophesied
the throne to the general Vespasian. But whatever there may
be of real and positive fact in all this, it was Elijah, the fearless
zealot of Jehovah, who made it a revered mountain of God: and
even now, when the pilgrim, gazing far away over the immeasurable sea, finds emotion moistening his eye, the name of Elijah resounds within his heart, like the sound of the trumpet of the day
of judgment.

The very next morning I quitted the mountain of Elijah and its
beautiful monastery; I quitted it with the wish to return. The
Italian padre who had so kindly joined me yesterday conducted me as
far as Haïfa. On the road he mentioned some anecdotes of the notorious pasha of St. Jean d'Acre, who fortunately has been dead for several years. Amongst them were the two following. His officer was
ordered to cut off the nose of an official person. The officer fulfilled
the command, which, as it affected a kind friend of his own, he
executed as sparingly as possible. When subsequently the pasha saw
the official, it occurred to him that his nose was only half cut off.
The officer very humbly entreated pardon; but the pasha caused the
deficiency to be immediately cut from the officer's own nose. The
other anecdote is of a better character; it has been already related
by travellers. A Greek Christian, who was in favour with the
pasha, had an aged father who dwelt with him in the same house at
St. Jean d'Acre: when the son married, he expelled his aged father
with harshness and craft from the upper story, the most agreeable part of the house. The pasha heard of this, and cited his
favourite before him. Of what religion art thou? asked he him, and
caused the confession of the Holy Trinity with the three signs of the
cross to be repeated to him. Dost thou not know, he exclaimed, in
answer to the reply, that the Father* occupies the highest place: viz.
the forehead? The ungrateful son saved his head by means of this
Turkish-christian sermon. A third anecdote was an occurrence
which took place between my companion himself and a Bedouin of
the vicinity of Carmel. The monk, a handsome man of about forty,

---

* In Catholic countries, three signs of the cross are made; the first (on
the forehead) for the Father, the second (on the breast) for the Son, and the
third (slightly lower down) for the Holy Ghost.

whose beard was not exactly of Oriental growth, had by means of medicaments cured the Bedouin of a malady. The Bedouin wished to pay for it; but the monk would accept of nothing. Then, said the Bedouin, quite seriously, I will pray to the prophet to let your beard grow.

ST. JEAN D'ACRE. BEYROUT. SMYRNA.

Our road from Haïfa to the celebrated fortress of St. Jean d'Acre led us so close to the shores of the sea, that we were often obliged to give way to its advancing foaming waves. I found in the sand a gigantic tortoise, but the shell appeared useless. About ten in the morning we reached the town.

I purposed after a short stay to ride on to Tyre; but my two muleteers were so full of care and anxiety, first for their horses, and then for themselves, that I allowed them to return hence to Nazareth. I sought in vain for fresh horses; the only ones that I could meet with had no saddles. I therefore rejoiced at finding a vessel laden with corn, which was to sail this very evening for Beyrout. I took my place on board; but unfortunately we waited the whole night for a favourable wind; the next morning, I again landed, and returned to the vessel in the evening. Thus, there-fore, I had far more leisure than I desired, to look around me at St. Jean d'Acre, and to recal to mind the remarkable events, which this very ancient city* has seen since the period of the Jewish Judges.

Of its last calamity, its forcible capture by the cannons of the English fleet in 1840, whereby Ibraham Pasha lost possession of Syria, many a trace still remains, although up to the present hour the greatest activity prevails in the restoration of the battered fortresses. At the bazaar many of the weights consisted of pieces of split shells; similar unsavoury relics of the " untoward " act, I my-self found in multitudes strewed about the fields in the environs.

Had Bonaparte been more successful in the spring of the year 1798, who can imagine what might have been the result? Whether possibly the denounced destroyer of freedom might not have pre-

---

* Its original name was Acco (see Judges i. 31) and Ake; it was sub-sequently called Ptolemais, probably from Ptolemy Lathyrus; now the Arabs call it Akkra; the Franks, Akri, and St. Jean d'Acre. The Akkra, of the Arabs, signifies, the broken; whereas, the Greek name, Acri, refers to the cure which Hercules received there from the bite of a snake.

pared a more happy future for the Holy Land than it has acquired up to the present time, from the protection of the great
Christian powers. Bonaparte stormed the Turkish walls eight
times, yet the skill of Sir Sydney Smith remained impregnable behind them.

During the Crusades the city experienced still more violent conflicts. For three years Philip Augustus and Richard Cœur de Lion
besieged it against Saladin ;   nine battles were fought for its
possession. The conquest cost the crusaders much blood, and unfortunately it was stained by a deed against the Turkish prisoners,
that had been intrusted to them, which was avenged a hundred
years afterwards, by the slaughter of many thousand Christians.

Hastily passing from the remembrance of all these dreadful scenes
I recalled to mind the Apostle Paul, who, upon his last eventful
journey to Jerusalem, whither he went bound in the spirit (Acts,
xx. 22), at Ptolemais, " saluted the brethren and abode with
them one day." (Acts, xxi. 7.)   The present number of " the
brethren" there may exceed a thousand, chiefly Greeks, both schis-
matics and Catholics.*   There are but few Latins and Maronites:
about five hundred Jews and eight thousand Mahometans dwell here.
I visited the Latin monastery, which has a magnificent view of the
sea and of Mount Carmel. The Greeks also have a monastery;
their church of St. George is large and stately.   My dragoman met
here two old acquaintances, German mechanics, who were not dis-
contented with their condition.

Early in the evening of the 31st, the long anxiously hoped-for
south wind commenced blowing ; our bark immediately left the
harbour of St. Jean d'Acre, and coasted towards the north. Besides
myself and my dragoman, there were four sailors on board.   I threw
a woollen wrapper upon the heaped up barley, and there I took my
station. Timid persons would not readily thus confide themselves
to the waves of the Mediterranean ; but here upon the coast of
Phœnicia it was perfectly *apropos* to transplant oneself into those
times when the energy of the human mind first ventured to make a
pathway over the unstable waters.

Towards morning my companions aroused me in accordance with
my wish: on my right I beheld glittering in the light of the full
moon, precipices and shattered walls, with the waves of the ocean
foaming around them. They were the melancholy heralds of that
royal daughter of the sea, of that "joyous city, whose antiquity is
of ancient days." (Isaiah, xxiii. 7.) These were the ruins of Tyre,

* Williams, from the census of the diocese, cites the number of orthodox
Greeks at 500.

"Howl, ye ships of Tarshish; for it is laid waste, so that there is no house, no entering in." Thus Isaiah shouted to the proud city (xxiii. 1.), when its merchants were princes and its traffickers the honorable of the earth. (Isaiah, xxiii. 8.) I shuddered as I beheld the ruins blankly rising above the surf of the sea. Behind them there is now but an insignificant village, called Sur. The chief ruins which still testify to the magnificence of the ancient royal city, consist of piles of granite columns, some lying in the sand of the shore, and some immersed in the water close by.

Two hours afterwards we saw, upon an elevation rising from the coast, Surafend, which refers to Sarepta, where Elijah blessed the widow's cruise of oil (2 Kings iv. 1—7), and raised her son from the dead; and before noon we reached the mother city of Tyre, namely Sidon, or, as it is now called, Saïda. This is still a considerable fortified place. Two ancient keeps, probably of the period of the Crusades, towered upwards, one from the midst of handsome houses, the other from a rock in the sea opposite the harbour. Gardens and woods environed the city with agreeable dark green foliage.

My companions shortly afterwards pointed out to me a white painted Turkish tomb with a cupola. It is dedicated to the prophet Jonas, who, according to the belief of the Mahometans, was here released from the belly of the fish. (Jonah, i. 17; ii. 10.) My companions at the same time informed me, that it was not at all unusual to see sharks on the coast of Beyrout, Sidon, and Tyre.

Towards evening we reached our goal. The view of Beyrout is charming. It was formerly considered as the finest city of Phœnicia: it is so now, without the least doubt. It lies with its stately houses and high minarets close upon the coast, and is mirrored in the waters. Behind it, upon the ascending heights, spreads forth a landscape fruitful in blessings; a thick grove of mulberries, olives, and cypresses, interspersed with many cheerful and chiefly Frankish country villas. Above the sea, and the city, and the grove, towers upwards to the very clouds, like a petrified god of antiquity, the majestic Lebanon with its limestone bald and rugged eminences. *

After passing through the custom-house, I hastened to Battista's Hotel, which has quite an Italian air. I there met with a young Frenchman and a Polish count; we immediately became friends. The count had obtained from beyond Lebanon six horses at an extraordinary cost: one of them was perhaps the most superb

* "Lebanon" signifies "the white mountain." I do not at all doubt that it derived this name from the prevalent whitish appearance imparted to it by the limestone of which it consists. Looking now from Beyrout, there was no appearance of snow upon its heights.

creature now in the East. He told me that one of the shiekhs had offered him without hesitation his horses to take home with him upon trial. The shiekh was perhaps as little conversant with Frankish swindlers as with geography.

The following morning, very early, we took a ride in the celebrated grove of pines. This adventure might have been attended with mishap. My horse, of an old Arabic stem, soon discerned that I had only been acquainted with asses and camels. Had it, like that of the Frenchman at my side, rolled itself in the sand — a feat which affords particular pleasure to these horses — I should scarcely have escaped without injury. But the enjoyment of this morning upon the extensive sandy plain beneath the slender pines, with their dense summits, excited within me an enthusiasm resembling that in which Lamartine indulges in his description of his ride through that grove. Lebanon was now surrounded beneath its summit by a wreath of grey clouds, whence it presented a sublime and melancholy appearance.

On our return we rode between hedges of the Opuntia behind which lay gardens of mulberry-trees, within which no doubt many a silkworm was spinning its cocoon.

What a profusion of fruits of all kinds were heaped up at the bazaar! It is immediately seen what blessings are bestowed upon this land. Even the very nakedness of the declivities of Lebanon is but a deceitful appearance from the distance; for they produce corn and wine, and are decorated with a cluster of villages. Corn and wine flourish here, both in quantity and quality.

In the variegated mixture of costumes which I observed at the Bazaar, I was especially struck by the towering hood of the females of the mountains, Upon seeing such hoods we readily conceive how the Apostle Paul in his epistle to the Corinthians, could have said the woman should have " power on her head." (1 Cor. xi. 10.)

Four quarters of the globe are represented at Beyrout. North America possesses here a chief station for its missionaries, and it has also a consul. Many Europeans, especially Italians, dwell here, and there are consuls of all the great European powers. Of Africans, especially negroes, there is no deficiency. But it is the Maronites and Druses, together with the Turks and Arabs, who give to the city its peculiar complexion. I was told of the capricious contempt of life entertained by the Druses; and here people are as guarded against them as at Jerusalem against the Albanians. Since Ibraham Pasha's departure, the general security of intercourse has as much decreased as the malicious disposition of the Mahometan population against the Christian has increased. For the " Nurse of quiet life," as an ancient Christian poet has called Beyrout, it at present by no means may pass, although the oppressive heat disposes more to repose than to exertion.

Notwithstanding its early foundation, Beyrout has but few anti-quities to exhibit. From the quay several ruins of walls are to be seen standing in the water, whence it may be concluded that the former city must have extended into the sea ; and beneath the quay itself many an ancient pillar lies buried. One very remarkable thing is the exceedingly ancient inscription in three languages which was even seen by Herodotus, situated near the mouth of the Lycus about two leagues north of the city. There is likewise shown at Beyrout a cavern wherein St. George is said to have destroyed the dragon.

I had thoroughly enjoyed Beyrout, and on the evening of the 3rd of August I embarked on board the Austrian steam-boat to proceed to Constantinople. I should have liked to make several more excursions in Syria and Asia Minor. Lebanon and its groves of cedars as well as the ruins of Baalbec ought to have been visited. I should have rejoiced still more in visiting Damascus to celebrate there the memory of the conversion of the great Apostle of the Gentiles. But it was requisite to set a limit to enjoyment : for I still had in view Constantinople and the Isles of the Princes and the Bosphorus, as also Greece ; and, after some important labours to be gone through at Vienna and Munich, I purposed reaching my longed-for home at Christmas, to celebrate there such a great festival of thanksgiving as I had never before celebrated in my life. My soul was so full of the Christmas rejoicings, that the proper hour of my return had been already long deeply engraven on my heart.

The deck of the steam-boat presented an interesting party, with the greater part of whom I was already familiar. The two counts Pour-tales, accompanied by their artist, were returning from their delightful and extensive pilgrimage through Egypt and the Holy Land. The Prussian consul at Jerusalem, who had lost his bride at Beyrout under grievous circumstances, was returning home on furlough. A secretary of the English embassy at Constantinople was pacing up and down in contemplative mood, dressed in the Oriental costume. A Polish Jesuit and a *Lazzarist,* a native of Savoy, on their way from distant missionary stations, were now going to their focus in the West. Lastly, the Syrian patriarch, surrounded by respectful attend-ants, was bound for the Turkish capital.

On the 4th, at eight in the morning, our steamer anchored off Cyprus. The Sardinian consul immediately came off to the vessel. In company with the patriarch and the Lazzarist I got into his barge, and in this reverend society I set foot upon the celebrated island of Venus. But before us were none of those pleasure-grounds where formerly the beautiful goddess may have revelled. A light red mountain chain, entirely denuded of its once celebrated groves, limited our view of the island ; but this gave the freer scope for fancy to picture to itself beyond, the temples of Paphos and of Amathus in all their splendour, or at least in splendid ruins. The clerical society in which I had arrived compelled me to be present at mass in the Catholic church. It was Sunday ; the little church was crowded with worshippers. After the service, we partook, in the consul's hospitable residence, of a glass of the best Cyprus wine, which, cooled in ice, afforded great refreshment during the burning noonday heat.

Early on the 6th of August we were off Rhodes. I cannot, alas ! say with Pindar, " I will now sing in praise of Rhodes the sea nymph, the warlike daughter of Aphrodite and the Sun." I had remained upon deck till midnight to avoid the oppressive temperature of the cabin ; but, upon then ascending into my lofty berth, the stormy waves cast a cold bath over me through the open window. I was consequently unwell this morning, and unable to exchange, for a few hours, the rolling vessel for the terra firma of this island paradise. It is true that five hundred camels have long since carried off the ruins of the precipitated Colossus, and it is very doubtful if the two towers over the strait are really the supports of the feet of the gigantic harbour-guard ; but Rhodes has even to the present day faithfully preserved so many reminiscences of its valiant knights of St. John, that it was with much regret that I could not pay them a visit. But, like the well-known eccentric travellers, I read, whilst the vessel was lying off Rhodes, in the library of the steam-boat, that the knights' street, as well as the large hospital and the palace of the grand master, are still preserved by its Turkish lords ; that the armorial bearings of the knights still remain upon the gates and cannon of the fortress ; and that a single glance at the former church of St. John recals to the mind three religions of the world : for the church itself, with disfigured statues of the saints and mutilated tombs of knights, has been transformed into a mosque; whilst in front of its porch still stands, uninjured by every change of fate, an altar of the ancient Greek worship.

Shortly after we had left Rhodes behind us, my bodily indisposition reached an alarming crisis. I thank God from the bottom of my heart that it speedily and fortunately passed over. I possessed a most careful friend at this anxious moment in the Lazzarist Sapeto, who had acquired considerable experience in dealing with such contingencies during his long missionary travels in Abyssinia.

Upon arriving at eight in the morning in the harbour of Smyrna, I the more willingly deferred my further journey to Constantinople,

as from Smyrna I could best make an excursion to Patmos. Sapeto
persuaded me to take up my abode in the foundation of the Lazzarists.
I here found *temporal* comfort, which the *spiritual* brethren seem
very prudently to prize highly; and, in spite of the striking differences
of our faith, I also acquired a taste for the society of these experienced men. It is well known that the order of the Lazzarists stands
in close relation to that of the Jesuits; but the latter, as far as
I have become acquainted with them, have nothing of the innocent
intercourse of the former.

A residence in Smyrna has much that is attractive; its affluence
in the most delicious fruits of the garden, of the field, and of the
grove, it would be difficult to describe; nor does it require a description,
for, with the fig and the grape in the van, it proclaims itself even to
the most distant localities. The position of Smyrna is as beautiful
as it is salubrious. The mountains, which surround it, modify the
excessive heat of the southern sun, as does also the sea, in whose
mirror it is reflected. Its inhabitants are agreeable. The city of the
Franks and the city of the Turks, stand here in more tranquil apposition than elsewhere. If the latter presents the luxuries of the
East, in carpets, in silk, and other splendours; the former invites the
stranger to the palaces of the consuls to enjoy hospitable enter-
tainment.

But, I have still left unnoticed the greatest treasure Smyrna possesses; that which gives the visitor the most agreeable welcome, and
presents him with the most valuable gift upon his departure. These
are its reminiscences. Who knows not that the genius of science, and
of poetry, and of art, once had their dwelling-place here, which thus
became the birth-place of so much that is glorious and great, and
that will endure eternally upon the earth; and when the blossoms
had fallen from the tree of human wisdom, there sprang up here a
plant of still nobler growth, which has produced blossoms and fruits
more beautiful, and more sacred than the works of man's hands.
Homer, the singer of singers, lived here! with his name many
others also shine, all attached to this soil. It was at Smyrna,
likewise, where one of the first Christian communities dwelt, against
which in the number of those seven, no curse was uttered, but
which received the sweet promise of the crown of eternal life. It
besides venerates, as the allied and enthusiastic witness of its faith,
the holy sage Polycarp. Thus, a crown of laurel intertwined with
thorns shines forth, as the truest and most brilliant evidence of
Smyrna's past history.

Twice were these facts recalled most vividly to my remembrance:
once when crossing the water of the bay to the neighbouring Bur-
nabat, whilst wandering beneath its fig-trees and orange groves, and

visiting its rocky caverns. Here Homer is said to have lingered with much delight, and the picturesque beauty of the spot confirms the tradition. The second time was when I ascended the Mustasia mountain, and visited upon its heights the tomb dedicated to the memory of Polycarp. Tradition relates, that here, in the neighbourhood of the then existing city, the patriarch of 100 years died the death of a martyr ; and much probability supports it.

This mountain, at whose feet Smyrna lies, contributes much to the beauty of its appearance. Upon its heights still stand the considerable ruins of a fortress of the middle ages, which had been constructed upon ruins of a far more ancient foundation. Beneath these, and in the direction of the present city, there are still the distinct traces of the stadium, the theatre, and other structures of ancient Smyrna. But what especially adorns the declivity of the mountain is a Turkish cemetery, which, with its dense grove of cypresses, very earnestly and solemnly gazes over the throng of houses in the gay large city.

But one word out of the many edifying facts I might relate of social life at Smyrna. The fair sex here do not maintain the eastern custom of veiling. In a walk through the animated streets, one might almost suppose the city was peopled only with women and maidens ; all sit at their door-ways engaged either in pleasing gossip, or singing some cheerful song ; many a beautiful black eye, of which there is no scarcity here, sends forth its dangerous glances.

EXCURSION TO PATMOS BY WAY OF EPHESUS.

I had fixed my trip to Patmos for the 11th of August, at two o'clock in the morning. The nearest way thither is half by land and half by water. The ruins of Ephesus lie upon this road ; nothing could be more inviting. It was desirable to make the long distance from Smyrna to Scala Nuova in one day, to avoid the dangers incidentally arising from the malaria of the plain of Ephesus and the robbers infesting the vicinity : hence it was requisite to start very early, and continue the journey very late.

Through the influence of the dragoman of the Sardinian consul, my companion in this journey, the governor of Smyrna had sent me an open letter of recommendation. He had also taken care to provide strong horses, whose owners, upon so distinguished a requisition, did not hesitate to make a demand of a hundred and fifty piastres for a single day.

At two in the morning accordingly I was ready, but not before
five did the horses come.   This was that Oriental punctuality which
has so often brought Frankish travellers, whose time is so valuable,
not merely to impatience, but to despair.   It was now impossible to
reach our goal this day.   I commissioned the dragoman to represent
the circumstance in the strongest colours to the governor : he will
scarcely have let his *protégé* pass unpunished.

The following morning exactly at two we were mounted, and rode
with a turbulent noise through the slumbering Turkish city.   In
three quarters of an hour we reached the extreme guard-posts of the
city.   The guard received us with a doubtful look.   Although we
exhibited the pass of the governor, yet they hesitated to allow us to
proceed.   On account of the insecurity of the road, they advised us
to wait till daybreak ; but at last they allowed us to go forward,
" upon our own responsibility."

The insecurity of travelling is here, unfortunately, greater than in
the Arabian desert.   And who are the highwaymen ?   Greeks, but
especially Samiotes.   Sad enough this for Greek as well as for Christian repute.   Every two leagues we met with guard coffee-houses
or guard-houses occupied by some soldiers ; they always made a
point of asking about the rencontres we had had on the road.   How
sad does it make us to traverse this part of the world, whose fertile
plains are covered with nothing but lank grass in the rudest state !
The golden fruits of culture are despised, and in lieu the bloody ones
of highway robbery are resorted to.   One might fancy that this land
must have sadly sinned to have been visited with so heavy a curse.

Our road was sometimes laborious: our guide made no judicious
selection in diverging from the usual route of travellers.   On one portion of the road we were obliged to thread cleft masses of rocks, and
the oaks yielded so little shade that both horse and rider became fatigued.   But the eye roamed cheerfully around to the magnificent
hills above us, whose names re-echoed in such full tones from the
great period of the ancient Greeks.   The pilgrim from the far West
beholds them now with melancholy; they tell him of many an ancient
tale, many an old song they recal to mind; he listens as to a resonance
from his own early youth.   But to the sons of the country themselves they are strange and dumb: the child, the man, the old man,
behold them ; but they have no reminiscences, no heart, in common.

Shortly after mid-day we quitted the mountains and saluted the
extensive plain of the Kaystros.   In the east it is bounded by the Pac-
tolus, in the north by the Gallesus ; the Prion and the Coryssus in
the south extend towards the west, whither the stream also which
has been made celebrated by its swans rolls its reed-engirdled
wavelets to the sea.   At the foot of Prion and Coryssus lie the

ruins of that city whose reminiscences with their rich images oscillate between God and idols.   Midway between the north and the south of the plain rises a lofty hill, the round summit of which formerly bore the Acropolis, and even still commands with its deserted fortress the ruins of Ephesus.

We rode through the broad plain to a ford of the Kaystros.   On our left, an encampment of Turcomans in black tents was spread forth.   This people of nomadic shepherds, who believe but little and know much less, are reputed to be very numerous in this neighbourhood, as well as in northern Syria.   Camels and flocks of sheep and goats pastured close to the tents ; we rode up to the flocks ; and, in consequence of the ignorance of our guide, took a shepherd with us who showed us the ford.   But this ride through the Kaystros was more dangerous than the passage through the Red Sea, for the rapid stream reached to the very stirrups.

Close to the foot of the hill which bears the fortress stands a deserted mosque, whose walls and cupolas, together with their minarets, have an imposing appearance at a distance.   We rode direct to it. Dazzling marble steps on each side ascend to a porch rich in art. The court, formerly encompassed by a colonnade, retains still its marble basin in the centre ; round about ancient trees stand thronged with luxuriant shrubs and grasses.   The interior of the mosque has its floor and walls of marble ; sentences from the koran, inscribed in golden letters, and beautiful mosaics still shine here and there, but above all the eye is attracted by four colossal red granite columns, which make an overpowering impression.   That they might trace their origin to the wondrous structure of the former temple of Diana, I did not for an instant doubt.

This temple, which still bears the crescent upon its cupola, once bore the cross as its highest ornament, and re-echoed with Christian bells and Christian hymns, for it was transformed into a mosque from a church which Justinian dedicated with royal liberality to the memory of St. John, who here found his grave after his protracted labours.   I was now standing upon the ruins of the Church of St. John.   From the ivy which springs from its marble pavement I tore off a leaf : it grew over the grave of St. John ; thus to me it was a relic of the disciple who lay in the bosom of the Lord. (John xiii. 23.)

The hill with its fortress, whose costly marble works, with reminiscences of Hector, of Patroclus, and of Achilles, were very recently transmitted to Europe, I left unvisited.   Timur Tamerlane, when he bore his ensanguined and conquering sword to Ephesus, perhaps dwelt there, and cursed the very same reminiscence which I celebrated to-day.

A stupendous aqueduct extends from the hill of the fortress to the east: many storks build their nests upon its insulated pillars. In its vicinity lies the present small village, Ajasaluck, which derives its name, it appears, from the " Holy Divine," whilst its houses are built of the marble fragments of Ephesus.

But from the modern I passed to the ancient; I hastened across the plain to the declivity of Prion: there I stood in ancient Ephesus. It is indeed the majestic sepulchre of grandeur, pomp, and fame. Whether I stood upon the site of the ancient temple of Diana, I know not; but I believe I did. The rounded elevation of the surface, the remains of enormous walls and rich marbles, the position as regards the former harbour, for a commanding view of the shipping; all speak in favour of it. The altar, from the hands of Praxiteles, the pillars from the chisel of Scopas, the Alexander armed with the thunderbolt, from the pencil of Apelles, have indeed all long disappeared. Perhaps the earth still conceals many a treasure; for the destroying arm of the conqueror had spared the temple; and it was only by an earthquake that it was overwhelmed.

But what a circle of spirits is convened by the imagination of the pilgrim who stands upon these ruins! Crœsus's gold helped to construct " the wonder of the world ;" Xerxes saw it, and spared it. Themistocles paraded its halls, with eternal fame twined around his brow, and the wound of ingratitude in his heart. Alexander came hither, " one god to the other ;" Lucullus celebrated here his victory over Mithridates; Antonius marched into the ivy-crowned city. And speedily all past festivals were surpassed by one that ever endured. To the first Evangelos a second succeeded*; the first brought the glittering stone; the second the bread of Heaven. It is true that the mob then the more loudly lauded the brazen goddess (Acts xix. 23—41); but the Gospel which St. Paul brought founded, in addition to the marble temple of Diana, imperishable holy houses in many a jubilant heart.

Upon quitting the ruins, the thoughts of St. Paul still long clung to me. How could I have bid farewell to Ephesus without thinking of the farewell which St. Paul took of the Ephesians? " Bound in the spirit," he went hence to Jerusalem. (Acts xx. 17—38.) He there again reminded his beloved community of his anxieties and his tears. That wolves would enter the flock he well knew. But his words have been more sadly fulfilled than he himself expected. With what an eye and with what a heart would St. Paul now stand upon the ruins of Ephesus!

The sun set: we were still several leagues distant from the termi-

---

* The shepherd Pyxodorus was called " Evangelos " when he discovered marble on the Prion.

nation of the day's journey. Fortunately I had recovered from the
painful indisposition which the malaria of Ephesus had made me
pay for ten minutes' slumber. The way still lay over a precipitous
mountain path, and the moon denied its light. But at last, about
nine in the evening, we saw the lights of Scala Nuova shining over
the sea. I was heartily glad, but perhaps too fatigued to be able
heartily to rejoice. I had besides a disagreeable surprise ; the French
consul, to whom I had been especially recommended, was absent. I
went thence to the Russo-Anglo-Greek consul Alexachi, to whom I
also bore a letter of introduction ; his amiable and kind reception
has made me much indebted to him.

The following morning at nine, through the agency of the consul,
an excellent kayik was ready to convey me and my dragoman across
the Egean sea to Patmos. As it was provided with only four rowers,
we could not calculate upon a very rapid passage, without a favourable
wind. When we had got half way across between the main and
Samos in the open sea, we were propelled by so fresh a breeze that
there was no occasion for the rowers. We were at present free from
the dangers this passage has in winter, but we were not so safe from
pirates. The Samiotes, the very same who render the land journey
between Smyrna and Scala Nuova insecure, practise also the noble
craft of piracy. These are the modern countrymen of Pythagoras !
In these waters a French corvette, consequently, was cruising, which
only a few days before had been lying at anchor off Patmos. Our
own vessel conveyed more arms than its collective occupants could
have wielded. But we ran into the harbour of Patmos between three
and four of the morning perfectly unmolested.

I could not forbear instantly casting a glance at the island to
which my thoughts had been so long attached. My soul was moved.
The little island lay mute before me, in the light of the morning
dawn. From its foot to its summit it is covered with groups of
houses of light-grey stone ; a few olives here and there interrupt
the desert monotony of the island mountain. The sea was as still
as the grave ; Patmos lay like the dead body of a saint within it.

We lay for two hours in the haven, before the officials of the
board of health received our pass and permitted us to land. We
immediately ascended the precipitous height to the city properly
so-called, without stopping at all in the harbour town. In three
quarters of an hour we stood before the house of Signor Kaligas,
a distinguished Patignote, to whom we had an introduction. A
black-eyed maiden, whose long and splendid tresses the early morning
rendered quite lustrous, received us : it was the sister of the lady
of the house. Shortly came the handsome young couple themselves,
who had only within the last few days again seen each other after a

twelve months' separation. We gossiped now so agreeably that I
willingly suppressed, for a while, my thoughts of the library. We
scarcely understood each other in our very different Greek tongues ;
the ladies especially had their own peculiar dialect, yet all went
happily off through the intervention of the interpreter.

Signor Kaligas accompanied us to the monastery. As he has great
claims upon it, we could not have had a better recommendation.
The prior, who, in spite of his grey hairs, was still energetic and active,
honoured our visit first of all with sweetmeats, together with coffee
and a pipe. He then led us to the flat roof of the monastery, which,
as it lies upon the most elevated point of the island, afforded us a
complete view of Patmos. Almost on all sides around I could
see the confines of the island, as well as its neighbours in the sea.
Round about the strong monastery the whole city has encamped
itself as around its protector. The soil has but little cultivation ; a
few gardens and vineyards, occasional corn-fields, and olive-trees dispersed about, are all that interrupt the wild waste of this island of
volcanic origin. To the north of it lies Samos and Nicaria, on the
south Kalimnos and Kos, on the west Naxos, on the south-east
Leros. Immediately before us lay a couple of bare blackish rocks,
like bold ideas cast into the midst of the dark blue flood, and
animated by the Patignotes with significant fictions. One is said
to be an undutiful daughter, whom a mother's curse had turned into
stone ; the other a false prophet, whom the convicting eye of St.
John not merely rendered dumb, but transformed into rock. Patmos itself was remarkably still ; it was the repose of the Sabbath
visible to the eye. An inexpressible charm lay in the whole picture that surrounded me. I thought of the words of the Revela-
tions (i. 9, 10), " I was in the isle that is called Patmos . . . I was
in the spirit on the Lord's day." Criticism has attacked these
words ; at this instant, methought, Revelation clung inseparably to
Patmos. Were even this not its native home, yet it was delightful
that the enraptured prophet had conceived the idea of celebrating
upon Patmos the Sabbath of his inspiration.

From the roof we descended to the library of the monastery. I
entertained great expectations, for at Cairo and at Smyrna eye-
witnesses who were not unconversant with the subject, had told me
of the great treasures to be found here. It is true the foundation
of the monastery is not of a very early date : it owes its origin to
Christodulos Thaumaturgus, in the 11th century, under Alexius
Comnenus. But in an original document upon the foundation
it expressly says, that the monks whom Christodulos brought to
Patmos, conveyed with them books from their native monastery.
My expectations were at least not wholly disappointed ; this library

is indisputably one of the richest in the East. I long occupied myself with the inspection of each individual manuscript: the number altogether amounts to two hundred. Many are written upon parchment, and date from the 11th to the 14th centuries; they are of great importance with reference to the literature of the Fathers: I saw forty of Johannes Chrysostomus; seventeen of Basilius the Great; and about twenty refer to the New Testament. Lastly, two manuscripts bear the characters of the 9th century, and consequently may be classed with the most ancient extant. The most important portion of their contents refers to the Book of Job, to Gregory the theologian, and to the biography of St. Peter and St. Paul. A manuscript which the good monks take pleasure in deducing from St. John himself, is probably of the 10th century, and consists of extracts from the Gospels, but is destitute of any critical value. To my astonishment there was not a single document referring to the text of the book of The Revelation. Of the classics I saw Aristotle, Porphyry, Diodorus Siculus, Sophocles, Hippocrates, Libanius, Aristides. But I refer to my more particular labours for an account of my studies in the library * ; and will merely mention that, during this inspection, the oldest monk of the monastery was introduced to me, who was on the eve of completing his hundredth year.

Another monastery we saw standing in solitude upon a distant hill. The prior and my companion assured me that no manuscripts were there, and that only a single monk occupied the building. But in the vicinity of the St. John's monastery of Christodulos I visited a convent of nuns, where there are about forty inhabitants. I confess that the manuscripts pleased me better than these sisters. I had hardly entered when the abbess and her friends commenced absolutely begging. That they did not live in a very splendid condition was manifest from the places which they occupied.

We then paid two other visits to ladies in a state of temporary widowhood, and then returned to Signor Kaligas. Among the many peculiarities of habits and customs at Patmos I will mention one of the chief : the reason, namely, why there are so many insulated women. These women are more deeply attached to their native island than the Swiss are to their mountains; they frequently marry without going to their husband's home. This is the more easy, as the daughters regularly inherit the patrimony, instead of the sons. My host himself has his establishment in Syra, and visits Patmos only once or twice yearly, and this is the case with many other families also. In spite of this, the strictest morality prevails,

* See Wiener Jahrbücher, 1845. Anzeigeblatt für Wissenschaft und Kunst xx., " Die Bibliothek zu Patmos."

and with it a very fervent affection. After the death of the husband, to marry a second is an unheard-of circumstance; the widow mourns for her departed spouse to her death. Mourning for parents also extends to three years, and only the intervention of some family festival, as for instance a marriage, can abridge this period. The costume of the females, independent of the short waists which are to be seen in Germany in old pictures, has its greatest peculiarity in the hood. Schubert called it a grenadier's cap, and it is certainly high enough for one; it has almost the shape of a horn, and is partly interwoven with hair. What I have remarked upon the "power" of woman (of which St. Paul speaks, 1 Cor. xi. 10) at the Bazaar at Beyrout (see above, p. 250), I may thoroughly apply to the hoods of the Patignotes. That the number of the fair sex preponderates at Patmos I did not hear, but I think it very probable.

A political advantage possessed by the island over all the neighbouring ones is, that it has no Turkish governor, and its population is exclusively Greek. My first step upon the island announced as much by my meeting with a herd of swine.

But I must relate my farewell from the house of my host. As my visit happened during the Greek fasts, our mid-day repast consisted consequently of appropriate dishes; but, before I again stepped on board ship, a roasted chicken was sent after me by the careful hostess. During the afternoon, I had exchanged many friendly words with both the black-eyed sisters, and had certainly entertained more kind thoughts than I could express in words. Upon taking leave, the lady herself hastened suddenly to a flowering shrub close to the house, broke two blossoms off, and brought them to me. The blossoms were very beautiful, but the eyes of the giver shone still more beautifully. Her sister ran to an odoriferous plant, and brought me a nosegay from it. It was therefore with tender emotion that I parted from the two sweet daughters of the island of St. John. I thought of the favourite exhortation of St. John with which he was accustomed to address the community, "Beloved, let us love one another." (1 John, iv. 7.) Who would not suppose that these ladies of Patmos bore the farewell of their instructor faithfully in their hearts?

On the way back to the kayik, I visited the school, and within its walls the cavern of St. John, which, like Elijah's cavern upon Mount Carmel, is built into a church. It is here that the evangelist is said to have dwelt during his exile at Patmos, and here he indited the book of The Revelation. The upper part of the cavern has been torn asunder from the tower. My companion informed me, and his faith in his narrative was self-evident, that the rock had split the instant St.

s 3

John had received the divine Revelation. The island possesses and venerates, besides, many other localities, all consecrated to reminiscences of St. John. St John is the whole thought of the island. It belongs to him, it is his sanctuary ; its stones discourse of him, and all hearts contain him.

The same evening I returned to Scala Nuova. The following day about two in the afternoon, I arrived at the harbour ; there the kind consul received me with the honours of a hoisted flag. On the afternoon of the 16th, we reached Smyrna, having returned by a different road, without visiting Ephesus a second time.

How agreeably do I still think, and how pleasantly shall I ever think, of Patmos !

VOYAGE TO CONSTANTINOPLE.

I could easily imitate the manners of the Orientals, who readily promise to set out as soon as the wish is expressed, but yet are indefatigable in proving to the patient Franks that they do not regulate their time by the hands of the clock. But, as I have not yet acquired the Oriental practice, I shall give no account of Lazzarism and its importance to the policy of France in the East; nor of the admirable institution of the pious sisters in the convent of Lazzarists; nor of the antiquities which are constantly being excavated at Smyrna ; nor of the large bridge of the caravan, and the endless train of camels : but I hasten at once to the harbour, and steer without delay over the foaming waves, on board the Austrian steamer. The deck presented a singular spectacle ; I know not whether I shall call it warlike, or war's buffoonery. There lay around four hundred Turkish soldiers with their wives and children. I was constrained to force my way through their thronged harems, to the small space allotted to passengers of the first class. This was more interesting than agreeable. The four sisters from North America, whom I met within the cabin, complained aloud of the popular communication from the Turkish party to our quarters. We thus, therefore, conveyed along with us the fullest consciousness of existence in the East.

It was about four in the afternoon of the 17th of August when I left Smyrna. The archbishop of Smyrna travelled with us; he was going to Mitylene, to consecrate a new church. Mitylene is the ancient Lesbos, which the name of Sappho has made so celebrated. Unfortunately it was about midnight when we stood off and landed the archbishop. I cast but a superficial glance at the mountainous island beneath the glimmer of the stars; but the moment was delightful — to think of Arion, and of Alcæus, and of Sappho, who often from the summits of these mountains chanted forth their inspired lays, beneath this splendid sky!

The following morning aroused me to a noble festival. The land I was about to see — how often had I dreamt of it in the happy years of the dawning intellect! I could not recal those delightful hours without cordially thinking of the free-spirited teachers who had introduced me to the propylæum of classical antiquity. To him who has experienced this, does not the name of Homer recal hours never to be forgotten; for they opened a world to him richer and more splendid than all that encompassed him, and yet a world which so speedily attached his heart, possessing as it did a heart to reciprocate his feelings? That spot where the godlike Achilles chafed in wrath and wept like a brother — where the helmed Hector fell while protecting his domestic altars — each instant brought me nearer to it.

The sacred Lemnos rose out of the blue waves in the west; Tenedos, close upon our left, presented strong ramparts upon its sandy dunes. High in the north west lay the rugged brows of Imbros; behind it arose, high in the air and garlanded with clouds, the rocky peaks of Samothrace, as though even now familiar with the mysteries of Orpheus, or as though Poseidon still dwelt there, his eye glaring over the conflict and the decision of the battle. We now approached the Cape of Troy with the tomb of Peneleus, having previously seen the Scamander, that beautifully flowing stream, pouring its waters into the sea. In a few minutes more we had in view the flowery fields on its banks, where the heroes fought so energetically. We next arrived at the Sigeian promontory, where stood the temple of Minerva; immediately afterwards we greeted, close to the shore, two tumuli — we were close to the strand where Achilles selected for Patroclus and himself a prominent tomb. The poet's prophetical word is fulfilled; for it still stands boldly forth to the view of contemporaries as well as of posterity. The tomb of Achilles recalled Alexander to my mind, who here sprang ashore from his ship, and ran three times round it naked, with his friends, and anointed and crowned it. Give me the lyre of Achilles! he exclaimed, when the lyre of Paris was brought him. The tomb of the great-hearted Hector is not visible from here; but the mound of Patroclus is still to be seen, round which Achilles thrice dragged the corpse.

Looking away from these tumuli, we saw to the right and to the left, upon the two projecting points of Europe and of Asia, two modern creations, the two fortresses with their dark terrors. Thus from those celebrated heroic arms the power of the demon has retired to these Cyclopian gorges, with whose gigantic balls of fire it would be vain to contend.

Close to the Asiatic fortress the Simois now flows into the sea; not very distant from it to the north rises the Rhœteian promontory, and there it is where lies the gigantic Ajax, the hero who resembled the God of war. Behind his tomb lies the valley Thymbra, where the proud Mysians, the Phrygian cavalry, and other nations, were encamped. To the east was easily to be distinguished the beautiful hill (Callicolone) where Phœbus sat with Artemis and Aphrodite.

Precisely where the two worlds, Asia and Europe, stretch their iron hands, filled with misfortune towards each other, precisely there have we the entire scene of Homer before our eyes; on the right the promontory of Sigeium; on the left that of Rhœteium; and between both the Greek princes and their people were encamped. To the left upon the hills, sat the protecting deities of Greece; to the right upon the wall of Hercules, those of the Trojans; between them lies, enclosed by the Scamander and the Simois, the battle-field saturated with the blood of so many valiant heroes; and immediately behind it towers the lofty Pergamos itself, whence the Scæan Gate and the Bay of Zeus so often sent Hector's rapid steeds to battle. Above the fortress, bearing a little towards the north, rises Ida with its sacred summit, where Zeus sat full of wrath within his thunder-cloud, and where also he received his lily-armed Hera in the golden cloud, adorned with the girdle of Venus.

The Turkish buildings which here and there rise out of the ever memorable district, for instance the village Bounarbashi, posted upon the very site of Ilium, would be far better away. Here is repeated that irony of fate which is so conspicuous and so active in the East. Near Achilles' mound a Turk has erected his cypress tomb; perhaps one of those contemptible pashas to whom the past is nothing but a vacant shadow: but the soil, more faithful than the men who occupy it, preserves many a memorial, of which no Vandal from the north or from the south has been able to rob it. Even if the tombs have been broken into where the ashes of the heroes repose, the tombs themselves still stand and still speak to later ages; and even if doubt have tainted with its poison classical as well as Christian antiquity, faith clings only the more tenaciously to its treasures.

We slowly steered past this Jerusalem of Greece, dear to the venerators of the Christian muse. The columns of smoke of our vessel receded far to the north-east, a smoking sacrifice to the venerated graves: but with the sorrowful words of the prophetess, with which, according to the patriotic poet, the smoke of her home inspired her, we mingled other words which had a more happy and cheerful resonance.

The numerous consular flags which were waving on the Asiatic coast upon our entering the Dardanelles, told us at once that, in the proud fortress of the barbaric stranger, we were not without the protection of friendly powers.   But we readily forgot the barbaric Turk; for history has planted the channel we now moved along richly with reminiscences, with which the pilgrim from the West is made familiar in his earliest studies.   How often has this tide, since Helle was precipitated within its depths from the golden ram, borne upon its back men, in whose hands was contained the weal or the woe of entire nations, and of whole ages!

We passed Nogara Burnu, where Europe and Asia most closely approximate.   Even there, opposite to Sestos in Thrace, did Abydos stand, that ancient rocky fortress where Xerxes caused the waves to be lashed.   But, in counter-check to the war tones of the overbearing Persian, the hymn of the love of Hero and Leander resounds delightfully.   For, as Schiller sings,

> " Alone, on Sestos' rocky tower,
>   Where, upward sent in stormy shower,
>   The whirling waters foam, —
>   Alone, the maiden sits, and eyes
>   The cliffs of fair Abydos rise
>   Afar, — her lover's home."
>
>   SIR E. L. BULWER.

Whilst the Chersonese, which upon its rough precipitous rocks still bears traces of the fort of Miltiades, admirably harmonises with the reminiscences of the inimical warrior Xerxes; even as admirably do the Asiatic coasts with their laughing vineyards, their gardens of figs, and their groves of laurel, sympathise with the complaining accents of love.

Two new objects are presented in Lampsaki and Gallipoli. Lampsaki seated upon the Asiatic side with its miserable huts, scarcely reminds us of its former splendour, although its wretchedness is veiled in the rare pomp and luxuriance of nature; whereas Gallipoli, posted upon the European side, has risen with renewed youth from the stormy and unhappy days it has witnessed: with variegated charms it now clothes its ancient precipices.

Upon advancing from the Straits of the Dardanelles into the Sea of Marmora, the sun was just setting; but its rays still glittered upon the snow of Olympus in the far east.   Cyzicus, transformed into a peninsula by Alexander, stretched far forward in the southeast.   But passing all thoughts of the Argonauts who had founded upon Cyzicus a temple to Cybele, I recalled to mind Nicæa, beyond Olympus, and the striking fate of this city.   It was there that

Diocletian gave the commands which were to sweep the Christian name from the face of the earth ; and there, only twenty years later, that Church now victoriously extended over the earth, held its first great council.

On the morning of the 19th we were off Constantinople. As I ascended the deck, we were passing the pleasant Greek village of San Stefano. There lay before us, like a dazzling vision, the seven-hilled city; the nearer we approached it, the more richly, the more splendidly, did it stand forth. Constantinople is a wondrous work; heaven, earth, and sea created it, and art lent thereto a happy aiding hand. What first enchains the stranger I can scarcely say : all enchains him. Constantinople is the eye of Europe. It is as if all the splendours of the world had concentrated themselves to discourse to the eye.

The city lies upon seven hills like Rome, once her rival; but these hills at first appear like a single one, which combines the whole picturesque scenery with magical effect. The whole forms an infinitely rich bouquet with an animated play of colours, although red, the colour of the Turks, visibly predominates. Innumerable towers and minarets, slender and elegant, ascend high above the houses and the palaces, increasing the expression of the boldly arched cupolas, from the summits of which the golden crescent glitters far into the distance. Cypresses, plane trees, pines, and other noble trees peep forth here and there ; close to the strand beyond the rampart which divides the city from the sea, the garden of the seraglio glows in its verdure and exhales its odours. The stranger who has but just arrived readily recognises, besides the other noble mosques, that which he has so long desired to see, the Aja Sofia, whose gigantic crescent with its golden reflection may, it is said, be seen even from Olympus. I also recognised a melancholy towering column ; it was the so-called " Burnt Column," which, like the ill-omened messenger of evil days, has remained to perpetuate, in the midst of the golden present, the memory of their sorrow and of their tears.

We are at the end of the imperial Seraglio, where the marble kiosk looks from three sides upon the sea. On the north-east, the Bosphorus extends with the cheerful gaiety of its shores; to the north-west, enclosed by heights, lie Galata, Pera, and the other suburbs, separated from Constantinople only by a narrow arm of the sea, called the " Golden Horn." To the south-east, immediately opposite the end of the seraglio, lies Scutari, with the largest of all cemeteries, from whose lofty cypress groves a solemn memento mori resounds into the midst of the noisy tumult of this earthly paradise. Upon a cliff in front of Scutari stands singularly above the water, like an envoy from Asia to Europe, Kis Kullessi, or the tower of

Leander. The blue waves at our feet were still; they were moved only by sportful dolphins, and silver sea-mews fluttered around them. But the harbour, the "Golden Horn," presented to our eyes thousands of rapid gondolas, manned with gay gondoliers, who are incessantly crossing between Galata and Constantinople. At the sides of the pier, as well as farther out in the harbour, sailing ships and steam-boats under various colours were at anchor; a profusion of objects wherein the gaze was lost. Above all, lastly, was arched a sky of the deepest blue and the most brilliant clearness; a repose for the eye from the infinite beauties of the spectacle.

Italy has much that is splendid and enchanting — who knows not what Göthe has said of Naples? but as grand and splendid a panorama as that presented by Constantinople, even the *bella Italia* no where offers. Schiller says of the poet —

> " Time's yet undevelop'd mysterious hour
> He spreads to the gaze, like a gay and bright flower;
> And catches the instant, which fleets fast away,
> To impress it with all that shall never decay."

According to this view, Constantinople is the greatest poet, or it is rather the greatest poem; for it comprises at one glance the most brilliant and richly coloured picture of the infinite All.

I have not described Constantinople for the purpose of saying, Behold, that is Constantinople! I have only endeavoured to give, as well as I could, the impression I received. To exaggerate a description of Constantinople would be very difficult, at least for the western European. Any picture of it, whether by the pencil or the pen, could only be an approximation to the beauties of the original.

A RIDE THROUGH CONSTANTINOPLE.

The 5th of September I dedicated to an inspection of the splendours of Constantinople, old and new. I had to obtain the Sultan's firman, which was to make the foreign sanctuaries accessible to Christian eyes. I helped to form a stately caravan, which, under the guidance of a Turkish officer fully authorised, traversed on horseback and in carriages all the seven hills, there to behold and to wonder. Of this ride I shall communicate only a few particulars: an adept in the art of book-making would easily fill a volume with the materials.

One main object of our pilgrimage was a visit to the four most remarkable mosques, and above all to the Aya Sofia. It could not greatly surprise us, even with all its riches and all its splendour ; for who would not expect wonders of that temple whose consecration by the third of its imperial creators, Justinian, was justly performed with the words "I have vanquished thee, O Solomon." Even angels forwarded the structure, and saints added the influence of their relics. A few days before I beheld the Aya Sofia, I witnessed how the tongue of a German could overflow in its admiration. St, Peter's at Rome made a deeper impression upon me. Possibly the variegated Turkish decorations in pendent ostrich eggs and lamps, as well as the gaudy colours which here and there force themselves on the view, may be the cause of this. The eye was ever attracted anew to the bold arching of the cupola, which has not its equal. Of the hundred and seven pillars of the mosque, the handsomest are eight of porphyry with capitals and bases of white marble, from the celebrated temple of the sun at Baalbec, as well as eight splendid green pillars of serpentine from the temple of Diana at Ephesus. The ancient mosaic in golden glass upon the arches and walls, can only now be recognised in parts ; but from the four corners of the dome there gazed downwards four winged Seraphim, whose large dark figures do not diminish the ghostly effect. The prophet's faith has inscribed his own spirit in sentences of the Koran upon the walls and the cupola, in golden letters of the most gigantic dimensions.

When I say that the impression made by St. Peter's is superior to that of the Aya Sofia, it must be wholly without reference to the past, which speaks from the depths of the old temple of eternal wisdom. The longer I wandered beneath its pillars, the grander did they rise before me, whether I recalled to mind Constantine or St. Chrysostomus, the solemn synods or the imperial triumphs, the festivals of joy or the scenes of cruelty, it has witnessed. Many a pregnant leaf of history is twined around these columns. And yet to the historical reminiscences many a pious tradition has been linked, in order to make its area more sacred and rich. One of the most remarkable of these, if not one of the happiest, is a hollowed red block of marble, which is venerated as the cradle of our Saviour.

I took my farewell from the Aya Sofia at the ancient belfry which stands at its chief entrance. It looks its wretchedness ! From beneath it purls forth a stream of pure water ; God grant that soon beside it a stream of better water may flow, which shall restore speech to the dumb petitioner !

The Soleymania is the building most nearly allied to the Aya Sofia in its style of architecture; but the former surpasses it in regularity; it is indeed one of the most perfect remains of Saracenic architecture.   Here also I met with four sisters of those colossal pillars of red granite which still glance in the mosque at Ephesus, as reminiscences of the wondrous temple of Diana.   These columns stand in pairs between the pillars of the dome, and support two galleries. Even the Aya Sofia has no columns of such extraordinary circumference.   One of them bore formerly the statue of a Venus, called the test of purity.   In other respects the Soleymania strives to compete with the Aya Sofia also in the splendour of sentences from the Koran, inscribed in the largest and most skilful characters.

In the mosque of Bajazet I admired the many beautiful slender columns, some of granite, some of jasper, and others of verde antico, all equally deducible from the treasury of antiquity.   This mosque possesses the privilege of supplying the faithful with praying compasses, which always indicate the right position for prayer, namely, the direction of Mecca.   A profitable institution!

The Achmedeya has had especially for its object to produce the effect of monstrosity with its dome of nine cupolas, its six minarets, its four columns combined to one of incomparable girth, and its two gigantic chandeliers.   Yet it possesses a rare work of art in its marble pulpit for the Friday preacher, and the gifts consecrated to it by the princes and grandees of the empire dazzle with their costliness.   It is at the Achmedijia where all the state ceremonies are performed; and it is also hence that the great caravan starts annually for Mecca with its pilgrims, and therefore within it the holy Kaaba garment is suspended, which this caravan brings yearly as a gift from Mecca.

All these mosques contain also the tombs of their founders, partly within and partly without the space devoted to worship. Amongst them there are as venerable as there are pompous objects of inspection.   We also visited the sepulchral chapel of Mahomet the Second, whose superb velvet carpets and artistical tablets surpass all the rest.   The pious people whom we met with on all sides, had nothing particularly appropriate to our eyes, and least of all those who lay sleeping around the marble pavement.   The Turks may possibly believe more positively than even we do, that God bestows abundant harvest fields upon his favourites when asleep.

The two seraglios, the old and the new, can scarcely be despatched in a few words; for the new one more resembles a town than a house—it is a league in circumference.   Among the apartments we saw here was one, the walls of which consisted entirely of large mirrors.   Seats also I observed as ornamental and as costly as in any of the palaces of the princes. of the West.   In a glass-case arms glittered, set with the richest diamonds ; opposite it stood a boudoir library of the Sultan's, with books in superb and beautiful bindings. But what chiefly enhances the charms of this imperial dwelling is its view of the sea — that from the marble palace at the point of the seraglio which commands the Bosphorus, the Propontis, and the Golden Horn at once must, at the proper time, be more delightful than all the other spectacles that the Sultan possesses.

But from the gaudy apartments and odoriferous gardens of the seraglio I hasten once more back to ancient Byzantium, whither our excursion to the mosques, beyond the circuit of 'the temple of St. Sophia, repeatedly brought us.   Indeed nothing remains to the present city of Constantine but a few fragments of pillars of all the artistical riches which both the East and the West, now with willing and now with reluctant hand, presented to the former city, in such profusion as if the muses should have no other dwelling-place than on the Bosphorus.

We now stand upon the celebrated Hippodrome, or At Meidan, within view of the mosque of Achmet, the foundation and site of which once formed part of the Hippodrome itself.   Its foundation dates from a period anterior to Constantine ; but it was under him, on the day of the foundation of the city, that the first of the great races took place, whence it has its name.   It has since remained the scene of these admirable and, as regards their consequences to the entire state, most important national recreations.   It was also the spot where the most distinguished statues of Athens and of Rome were collected together, as to a triumphal festival of art, from all the islands of the Archipelago and the cities of Asia Minor.

That which far transcended all that has been destroyed was the Hercules Trihesperus, which has even been transferred to heaven as a constellation.   That this fell a sacrifice to barbarism under Baldwin and Dandolo, being melted down to make copper money, corresponds indifferently with the reproaches we are accustomed to make against the barbarians of the East.   What still remains of all is threefold. First, namely, an Egyptian obelisk of granite, which came hither by way of Athens, and which, besides its hieroglyphics, contains upon its base upon all four sides a eulogy of the Emperor Theodosius. Secondly, a quadrangular colossal column, once covered over with gilt bronze plates, and, at least according to the words of the inscription, comparable with the colossus of Rhodes.   It now stands but as a naked skeleton complaining of fire and plunder, and threatens to be speedily in ruins.   The third is a short bronze column in the form of a threefold entwinement of snakes, which once had three heads, and is said to have originally supported the Delphic tripod of Apollo.   Of the three heads, Mahomet the Second struck one off at a single blow; the two others were subsequently abstracted during the night.

Besides all this the Hippodrome has two neighbours which deserve to be seen. One is the ancient cistern of the senator Philoxenos, hyperbolically called " *the thousand and one pillars.*" It consists of three subterranean stories, with nearly seven hundred pillars. All are preserved, although the greater portion of them lie buried in mud. The upper story now serves as a silk-spinning manufactory. The other neighbour of the Hippodrome I formerly mentioned upon my arrival at Constantinople; it is the so-called Burnt Column. It was formerly the superb porphyry column of Constantine, entwined with golden wreaths, upon whose summit that emperor had placed a statue, by Phidias, of Apollo with a glory around his head, transforming Apollo into himself, and adding the inscription, " To Constantine, who shines like the sun." When the statue and the three upper pieces, of the eight of which the shaft of the lofty column was formed, were precipitated to the ground by lightning, their place was supplied by a large golden cross. But of all this there now only stands a melancholy column, held together by iron rings, which, from the numerous conflagrations whereby it has suffered, bears the name of the " Burnt Column." It yet conceals within its foundation the rarest treasure, perhaps still uninjured, namely, the palladium formed of the ashes of Pelops, which Constantine transplanted from ancient Rome to the new imperial residence.

To crown our present ride through Constantinople we ascended the tower of the Seraskier, or the tower of the fire guard, in the old seraglio which in fact hovers like an eagle over the city, sea, and environs; and justifies the poet's comparison of it to the nest of a bird of paradise, by spreading at its feet a veritable paradise. But I will not curb the free play of the fancy by describing what I here saw; I will merely mention its extreme point of repose in the south-east, which consists of the snowy summits of the Bithynian Olympus.

THE LIBRARIES. THE PATRIARCHS. THE ISLANDS OF THE PRINCES.

It is an ancient and widely-spread opinion that, both in and about Constantinople, even to the present day, costly Greek manuscripts are concealed. The seraglio of the Sultan, especially, is surmised to contain treasures of the kind. In fact, some curious circumstances are connected with this imperial library. When the learned mission of Pope Nicholas, about the time of the capture of Constantinople, had vainly sought the Hebrew original of the Gospel of St. Matthew, and consequently missed the prize of five thousand scudi, it returned to Rome with the intelligence that it was deposited among the treasures of the seraglio. Almost contemporaneous was the assertion of the celebrated Lascaris, that he had seen in the imperial library at Constantinople the historical work of Diodorus Siculus, in a perfect state. Repeatedly have new inquiries and researches, or rather the preliminary steps to researches, been made. In the 17th century, upon the assurance of an Italian traveller that the lost books of Titus Livius were still extant in the seraglio, an attempt was made to recover them, and thus obtain the large sums that had been offered for them at Florence and at Venice. At the commencement of the last century an Italian ecclesiastic sojourned long at Constantinople, on account of the manuscripts of the seraglio. At last he succeeded, as he says, through the medium of a young assistant, in obtaining the opportunity of inspecting them, and he made a catalogue of them. This catalogue was shown me at Milan as a rarity; but according to it not a single Greek manuscript was to be found amidst a multitude of Oriental ones : thus the secret of the concealed chest of Greek records remained as much a mystery as before. Other accounts, which even determine the number of certain manuscripts, especially of Biblical ones, include that of a French abbé who, about the year 1728, was sent to the East by his government for the purpose of discovering Greek manuscripts, and who asserts that the manuscripts of the seraglio were one and all burnt under Amurath the Second. If I am rightly informed, not long since a German painter, who was in the good graces of the Sultan, spoke to him with regard to the supposed concealment of literary records in the seraglio. The Sultan is said to have replied that he did not think that any such existed, but that he himself would inquire into it. Of course nothing further took place.

At the present day in Germany, together with the belief in concealed treasures in general, the belief also in the existence of the treasures in question has declined; but the incredible is often true in the East.   Who would not discredit the possibility of walled-up libraries? yet the walled-up library at Cairo, of which I have before given an account (p. 30), is a fact.   The Greek Biblical fragment also, which I was so lucky as to discover and bring home, and which in my opinion is not surpassed in antiquity by any of the Greek vellum codices *, has surprised very many who considered the hopes I entertained of such discoveries, as merely silly enthusiasm. All things considered, there is still, methinks, a probability that the seraglio of the Sultan conceals ancient and valuable Greek manuscripts, although complete obscurity prevails as to their contents.   I had some conversation upon this subject (as I shall subsequently relate) with the Greek patriarch Constantius; he strengthened me in my opinion, and thereby confirmed also what he himself had said upon the subject, twenty years ago, in his Greek work upon ancient and modern Constantinople.   In proof that unknown Christian treasures lie still concealed in Constantinople, since the period of its conquest, he alleges that, in the year 1680, a golden case was unexpectedly discovered containing the hand of John the Baptist, and inscribed with " The hand which baptised Christ," and was presented by Solyman the Second, to the knights of St. John at Malta, from whom, in the year 1799, it came into the possession of the Russian Emperor Paul the First.   But with respect to the manuscripts in question, no diplomatic step will certainly be able, in the first instance, to drag them into light; but that instrument which is more dazzling than sharp, would more readily obtain access to them.   The chief enemy which guards the entrance (nor have I any fear of being wrong) is Turkish fanaticism, which might easily surmise that these ancient manuscripts, especially the theological ones, conceal Christian talismans that would precipitate Islamism into some imminent danger; and in matters of faith, as well as in all things that relate to it, the Porte is as inflexible as the Vatican.

I was desirous to pay my respects to the present Greek patriarch of Constantinople.   A twofold cause of a delicate character, and of the highest importance to my investigations, caused me to wish to be introduced to him by that envoy whose influence upon him from alliance of creed is not doubtful.   The intervention kindly offered to me had something about it that disturbed me in my calculations,

* I have given a more particular account of this in the Wiener Jahrb. 1845, b. ii. and b. iv.   Anzeigeblatt für Wissenschaft und Kunst.   Of this manuscript, which I call after his Majesty the King of Saxony, Codex Frederico-Augusteus, and which has become the property of the University Library of Leipzig, a splendid and faithfully correct impression is published.

whilst the mediation of other envoys to whom I had been most strongly recommended, was in itself, in consequence of the circumscribed relations of politics to the church at Constantinople, not favourable to my especial objects. I therefore went without any introduction, and accompanied only by my dragoman, to the residence of the patriarch to see what I myself could do. The patriarch received me in a friendly manner, I found him to be a man of agreeable good-natured features, and at the same time, as it seemed to me, of more candour than I had found in the majority of Greek ecclesiastics in the East. I told him of my visit to Mount Sinai, and showed him the three Romaic poems which the librarian there had addressed to me. He read them with evident interest. I subsequently learnt that it was he who had banished the learned and intellectual author from Athos to Mount Sinai. Upon my asking him if he had any commission for Athens, he replied that there was scarcely any intercourse between him and Greece. I perceived that the question was almost painful to him; indeed the wound is still green, which the regulations of the Greek government, relative to the holy synod and divorce, have inflicted on the patriarchate of the Greek church. The patriarch might be justified in finding the advancement of the Greek kingdom at the cost of the Greek church more important than any less interested person. I then apprised him of my manuscript researches; and as far as I explained them, he received the communication with urbanity. He has no library of his own; but he offered me an immediate introduction to that of the patriarch of Jerusalem. He knew nothing whatever of the puzzling codex of the Gospels belonging to Sinai written in golden characters, which had so much perplexed me, and, which according to the account of the bishop of Cairo, had been conveyed to Constantinople for the purpose of being transcribed; he, however, referred me to his deposed predecessor, Constantius, who, as archbishop of Sinai, must necessarily be acquainted with the matter. I now went direct with the proffered introduction to the patriarch of Jerusalem. The bishop only was at home, a man of considerable intellectual activity, and not deficient in literary attainments. We went through the catalogue of the library together; but precisely of the manuscripts there was no account. After this he allowed me to inspect the library myself, and permitted me to make any use of the manuscripts I found. They were thirty in number, but they were altogether without any especial interest, with the exception of a palimpsest upon mathematics.

A few days later, I made an excursion to the Isles of Princes; this from antiquity downward so celebrated place of refuge for the exiled, who here exchanged purple and gold for the garments of misery. The two deposed patriarchs Gregorius and Constantius are now here. My visit had more to do with the libraries of the monasteries, than with the ancient history of these islands, or the charming landscapes which constitute two of them, Chalki and Prinkipos — very fortunate islands.

About four in the afternoon of Saturday, a steam-boat landed me at Chalki. I had a friendly companion who hospitably received me in his Armenian dwelling, which, indeed, presented a remarkable beginning to my monastic studies. Six Armenian females, a mother and five daughters, dwelt there, of whom it was difficult to say which bore the most dangerous fire in her dark eyes ; but it was not the first time that I had passed unharmed through the battery of such artillery.

The patriarch Gregorius resided near us; I immediately announced myself to him, thinking him to be Constantius, the archbishop of Sinai. It was only when I reached his gay domicile that I discovered my mistake ; but Gregorius is a man of the most cultivated manners ; although aware of my mistake, his reception was very cordial. Certainly, the luxury with which he was surrounded displayed any thing but the household of an exile, and he was also now building a stately church upon his island.

The next morning we embarked for Antigone. It was a pleasant Sunday morning, and the excursion through the tranquil sea, in the midst of the group of islands, was rendered still more enchanting by the innumerable dolphins which gamboled around us, and displayed their sportive antics by the side of our vessel. Antigone was formerly called Panormos, from a castle which was celebrated for a two-headed female statue over its northern gateway. This statue had been preserved uninjured during a conflagration, which raged all around it, and had repulsed the flames from it, whence it was subsequently conveyed to Persia as a miraculous statue. St. Methodius has given to this island its most melancholy reminiscence. After enduring the torture, he was imprisoned here in a cavern with two robbers; and the corpse of one of them was allowed to decay at his side till, seven years afterwards, he was removed from his dungeon and ascended the throne of the patriarchs. Constantius, who is now exiled to Antigone, and whom I visited early in the morning, feels great ennui in his solitude ; but yet he suffers none of the hardships of his predecessor. He is, moreover, a man of erudition, and as such obtained celebrity twenty years ago, by his work upon ancient and modern Constantinople, of which he is now preparing a new edition. He presented me with a copy of his book. Only in his capacity of archbishop of Sinai he does not display a learned figure ; for it was he who several years ago, represented to a German traveller, that the manuscripts there were exclusively Oriental, and that there were no Greek ones among them. It is true, he was never there in person; for the visit of the archbishop to the monastery would not only involve extraordinary expense, but would occasion the unpleasant necessity of opening the walled-up porch. Of the Thedosian manuscript of the Gospels he likewise had not the slightest knowledge *; but he is perfectly conversant with the politics of the day; with Athens he has a closer connection than the dominant patriarch, and he spoke of both Mavrocordato and Coletti as his friends.

Upon his divan lay scattered a variety of French feuillettes, one of which caught my eye, printed in French and Greek. He scarcely permitted me to take it up, notwithstanding his agreeable deportment. It was the pastoral letter which Monseigneur Hillereau, archbishop of Petra, had recently published for the conversion of the Oriental churches of the Greeks and Armenians. When acquainted with the relations which the Greek and Catholic monasteries of the Holy Land at present bear to each other, as well as the hostile disposition of the Oriental Greeks towards the Roman church in general, one can scarcely imagine how it was possible at this moment to conceive the unhappy idea of such a crusade. Constantius found it vexatious that even common sense, or as the words ran, *le propre bon sens*, should be denied them one and all.

The apostolical vicar is certainly right in considering the disputed points, which produced the separation of the two churches in the 11th century, as very trifling, but certainly only as regards progress, and not viewing them with respect to actual practice. He enumerates the fifteen points which the Greeks object to the Latins, commencing with their eating unleavened bread, and that their clergy are shaved, and he closes with the objection, that during fasts they do not sing the Halleluyah. But will he likewise convince the Greeks that the superior ecclesiastical tribunal which, as such, he calls *la garde du corps des pasteurs*, possesses the divine infallibility which enunciates its oracles by the organ of the human mind (*a pour autorité l'infallibilité divine donnant ses oracles par l'organe de l'esprit humain*). It is striking that no mention is here made of the person of the pope, nor even subsequently, where it is said that the divine power over souls

---

* I have recently obtained a satisfactory explanation of it. A German traveller, not unacquainted with these matters, obtained a sight of it in the summer of last year, in the monastery of St. Catherine. From the description I have received, biblical science has lost nothing by my not having had the opportunity of subjecting it to a critical inspection. For instead of the four Gospels, it contains only extracts from the Gospels, made for church service, and with all the splendour of the golden characters throughout, it exhibits distinct traces of having been made in the 9th or 10th century.

which Christ accorded to his Church, is in Catholicism, executed throughout its entire compass by the bishops in council, and in due dependence on the chair of St. Peter, the bulwark of its freedom and centre of its unity (*par les Evêques en l'union et la juste dépendance du siège de Pierre, boulevard de son indépendance et centre de son unité*). Were it even not otherwise clear, this mode of expression would prove that the whole cry for conversion more nearly concerns the French than the Roman church. That the Greek church has given up the indissolubility of the marriage tie is characterised as the undermining of one of the main holds of Christian morality. This indissolubility, it is there said, has, until now, been held firmly by all Christians as a point of faith ; but now among the Greeks marriage may be dissolved at caprice, according to the passions of individuals and the caprice of the higher clergy. And, lastly, it is emphatically dwelt upon, that the patriarchal throne has been subjugated to the slavish yoke of temporal power ; that a certain number of families share the patriarchate among them, and raise in rotation one of their "creatures" for a couple of years to the throne. Thence we have a melancholy glance, first at Russia, where the imperial power has wholly swallowed up the ecclesiastical ; and secondly, at Greece, where the constitutional government has painfully wrenched the church from its patriarchs.

Yet, notwithstanding the truth that may be contained in all this, who can possibly believe that the Oriental Greeks, and especially those ecclesiastics who are cooped up within the wealth of their monasteries, would be hereby rendered susceptible of a transition to Rome ? Is it not much rather to be feared that this lightning, which comes so singularly from an unclouded sky, should exasperate into greater activity and bitterness that "disinclination," that "hatred," which Hillereau already charges the Greeks with entertaining towards the Latins ?

I now return to the Isles of Princes. From Antigone I proceeded to Prinkipos, the largest and the most fertile of all the nine. Pomegranates and cypresses, olives and vines, clothe its heights ; a cheerful village lies at the harbour, and insulated villas environ it. Oriental and Frankish Christians resort hither to enjoy themselves. We visited two of the three monasteries ; both are beautifully situated, but deserted by all but a single monk. None of the few manuscripts that I saw there yielded any critical harvest. Prinkipos possessed

* I have felt the less inclined to withhold, at the present moment, my account of the remarkable incident of the Franco-Greek pastoral letter, or the remarks I wrote down upon it whilst at Constantinople, as they essentially tend to explain the most recent conduct of the Greek and Armenian patriarchs at Constantinople, with their anathemisation of the Catholic conversions.

T 3

its most remarkable cloister-inmate in the Empress Irene. Just as she was about to unite the East and the West in a conjugal alliance by her acceptance of the hand of Charlemagne, she was deprived of her crown by the chancellor of the empire, and exiled to the very monastery at Prinkipos, which she herself had built. A year afterwards she there found her lasting rest.

From Prinkipos we returned to Chalki. Two monasteries there have libraries, whose manuscripts reward research. In that of the Holy Virgin, which has been transformed into a Greek school, I met with a highly educated monk of the name of Bartholemew. He formerly dwelt upon Athos ; thence the Greek revolution drove him to Italy, where he remained seven years ; he is now superior of his monastery, and superintends the excellent school. His manuscripts, which exceed a hundred in number, he has even catalogued. I here found, as in the monastery of the Holy Trinity, some classical, for instance Demosthenes, intermixed with ecclesiastical and Biblical MSS.

This present Sunday evening was full of life in Chalki. This delightful island is inhabited by Greeks, Persians, and Armenians, who here enjoy a cheerful hour far from the oppressive burden of the metropolis. The Armenian ladies rejoice here in being able, without a thought, to lay aside their veils. To-day, however, the Persians of the city gave, upon this island, a festival of fireworks close to the strand where it furnished a doubly beautiful spectacle. A concert of Bohemian musicians played, and attracted many of the charming daughters of the island together. There we wandered in balsamic odours, under pines and firs, beneath the starbright canopy of night, revelling in an hour of terrestrial bliss. The cool sea invited to a bath ; the phosphorescent waves lapped the nocturnal swimmer in a brilliant flood. Here would Jean Paul's Emmanuel have imagined himself to have been transported to another orb with better reason than during his own blissful midsummer day.

FAREWELL TO CONSTANTINOPLE.

I spent three weeks in the Turkish capital. Some of the consequences of venturing to travel in the East during the spring and summer months I had here to bear ; this induced me, although with much regret, to give up a visit to Mount Athos. The friendly house of Madame Balbiani, at Pera, was a real asylum to me during my

indisposition.*   In spite of my illness I had enjoyed myself greatly
at Constantinople, and was much occupied with its many peculiar
characteristics. — A few words only will I still allow myself.

In churches, both Greek and Armenian, Constantinople is still rich,
although the number of those which have been transformed into
mosques is still greater.   Some of the latter have had the singular
destiny of having been originally heathen temples, and then changed
into Christian churches, and in the third period of their existence have apostatised.   Of the many traditions which are linked
to the still extant churches, the most remarkable is that of the baked
fishes, which, in the church of the Virgin of the Fountain, are still
said to be constantly swimming in the water, and are exhibited when
a wish is expressed to see them, though, it must be admitted, by
a very imperfect light.

The two suburbs, Galata and Pera, have their peculiar character.
Galata, which in extent may be compared to the large capitals of
Germany, reminds us at present far less of its worship of " the gentle
goddess of love," previous to the Christian era, than of that of Mer-
cury, or rather of the flourishing commerce which it formerly enjoyed
under the Genoese ; for its narrow streets are as thronged with merchants, as those of Leipzig during the fair.   These merchants are
chiefly Christians, and still enjoy the privileges granted them by the
conqueror of Constantinople.   Saint Andrew is said to have come to
Galata as the first herald of the Cross; from him the bishopric of
Byzantium derives is origin.   In Galata, I became best acquainted
with the ancient high tower which corresponds to that of the Seraskier at Constantinople ; and it but too frequently fulfils its office, for
the alarm cry " Fire" constitutes almost its daily song. I ascended it
repeatedly to fix permanently in my mind the impression of the
splendours which lie around this ancient suburb of the Venetians
and Genoese.

Pera combines singular contrasts, — the most ridiculous beings in
manners and costume, and the representatives of the European
powers.   The high clattering stilted shoes of the women, and the
obliquely-cocked towering hats of the men of Pera, are celebrated ;
and both of these are in proper harmony with the silly fancies,
loquacity, and oddity of the Perotese. Yet these Perotese, from their
dragoman functions, are in incessant intercourse with the rest of
the frankish population of Pera.   But lucky the stranger whose propitious fate keeps him ignorant of them.   The dæmonic interpreter

* Four weeks after I quitted it, this house was burnt down during an extensive conflagration, with such rapidity that scarcely any thing was saved
from it.   But I have recently learnt that this excellent woman has almost
already succeeded in rebuilding it.

of Plato could not, methinks, have undergone a more melancholy metamorphosis in the style of Ovid than in being transformed into a dragoman of Pera. Divine service is performed at Pera in very different forms and languages. I visited there even a German protestant chapel.

The most entertaining resting-places of my stray promenades through Constantinople were the fountains with their rich ornaments of Arabesque art; it is there that Arabic taste may be best studied in miniature.

It requires indeed much self-denial to visit the Turkish coffee-houses; but they gave me a thorough insight into the character of the Turks. The opium booths and their guests affected me almost painfully; on seeing them, I thought how melancholy do their pale faces, in which, as in shrouds, intoxication wraps its departure, contrast with the close of a beautiful day, or with celestial joy!

In noticing the bazaar, I will not refer to its seductive luxuries, but to Turkish honesty. Just as the Bedouin hangs his tent to a tamarisk, in the midst of the desert, where for months he knows it to be as safe as under lock and key, even so the Turkish merchant of the bazaar will leave all the riches of his stall unguarded during an absence of hours.

The slave-market may be visited by the Christian stranger without difficulty. The sight of these black women, both young and old, in their red striped garments, with, perhaps, a ring around the instep or a coral necklace, with here and there one with an infant at the breast, sitting together by scores, in the middle of the market, and playing, laughing, and weeping together, is not easily forgotten.

Impressions of a different character I received from the dancing and howling dervises — singular aberrations of religious sentiment, although by no means recent; for the dance of the Turkish monks is an off-shoot from the ancient Indian mysteries. In its mystical sense it is symbolical of the harmony of the spheres; at least these dancers as rarely come in contact as the stars themselves, notwithstanding the wide sweep of their fluttering garments, as they encircle their sheikh in a narrow compass. Apart from the symbolical meaning of their dance, I confess that it had, beyond all expectation, a very serious effect upon me. The sheikh utters his prayer with the greatest devotion and dignity, and the music possesses a peculiar blending of the lyrical and elegiacal; the dancing monks did not enliven their pale features, and their fixed eyes, with the least symptom of a smile.

Much more might I relate of the Bosphorus, both because there is not in the world a more beautiful sea voyage than that through the strait, and because I retain the most grateful remembrance of joyful hours spent at Bujukdere and Therapia, where European diplomacy suns and cools itself, as also at Bibek. But the shores of the Bosphorus, with their magic charms, demand a picture, for which, at this moment, I have no pencil; and the thanks which I would wish to offer to my patrons are far dearer to him who bestows them than to them who are to receive them.

But that to which I must last bid farewell at Constantinople are the sanctuaries of the dead. How willingly, even now, do I frequently abstract my thoughts to the cypress groves of Scutari, and Ejub, and Pera!

To the carnival tumult of the great city, there cannot be a more impressive contrast. How admirably does the Mahometan know to honour and love the dead! In what neighbourly communion does he continue with the departed! I fear, however, at least partially, that I mistake a fair semblance for a reality; for the visits of the living to the cemeteries, especially at Pera, often present very unedifying spectacles.

The East possesses a treasure in its cypresses: that this tree was formed to stand by the grave, is proclaimed by its entire aspect. It stands there like pious reflection upon Good Friday, enveloped by a cloud of sorrow, in a sombre robe, but with its eye fixed upon the dawning of the Easter morning.

VOYAGE TO GREECE.

From the 8th to the 12th of September I was on board the "Kolowrat," bound for Syra from Constantinople: the sky was cheerful; the passage good. I possessed a real treasure during these days in Count Albert de Pourtales, one of those rare men whom we have only to become acquainted with, in order cordially to enjoy and to esteem them. How delighted I was to gaze a second time on the field of Troy, in his society! Even more interesting than the oil sketches in his rich portfolio were his communications relative to Sardes, Colossæ, and Laodicea. Of the last, amidst unshapely ruins, only three monuments of empty pleasure—three theatres—are still extant. So far, therefore, is that city reduced, to which the words of the Revelation (iii. 15. 17) were directed! "Thou art neither cold nor hot...Thou sayest, I am rich...and knowest not that thou art wretched, and miserable, and poor." Pourtales had likewise visited the Dead Sea. When bathing in it, it bore him steadily and lifted him sensibly upwards. The vegetation on its shores he found by no means so scanty as has been often represented. Neither did he see dead fishes nor dead birds.

On the afternoon of the 12th we lay off Syra.   It was here
that six months before I had first saluted Greece.   What a blessed
and pregnant interval lay between !   I had to be detained here for a
fortnight's quarantine.   Although the idea of quarantine is in itself
disagreeable, yet did this period — may I call it a truce ? — appear to
form an essential link in the chain of the incidents of my journey.
The last year had passed like an uninterrupted debauch, which
indeed during my whole life I shall not be able to sleep off ; but this
spiritual collecting of the mind, this repose of quarantine, was very
desirable.   An abode in the sanatory guard-house of Syra has even
its pleasant side.   Directly opposite my windows lay the beautiful
maritime town, and in the harbour there were many ships.   If a
steam-boat or sailing vessel chanced to pass in or out, the eye and
the heart were both instantly busied.   This going and coming is
full of significance.   At the entrance of the harbour the lighthouse
stands solitary upon its rock.   In the east, behind it, lies Delos ; to
the north, Tenos.   Not a day did I miss looking towards Delos,
when sunset enveloped this holy abode of Apollo in an odoriferous
saffron-coloured veil.   At the foot of the rock on which we were
perched, the sea dashed its surf ; it was repeatedly so rough as to rouse
me from sleep.   But I awoke with pleasure, and ran to the window
to admire by moonlight the turbulent rolling of the waves.   It is as
if the sea had in its breast an unutterable pain which breaks forth
with all its anguish by night ; or as if it were a criminal, whose
wicked conscience allows him no repose.

By day, when the sea was perfectly clear and still, I became here
acquainted with a new source of livelihood, that of the diver or
sponge hunter.   Three men sit in a boat, covered only with a shirt :
they look fixedly into the sea, which is here about fifteen feet deep.
As soon as one of them observes a sponge, he instantly throws off
his shirt, and dives to the bottom, head foremost.   He often remained
so long below that I looked on with considerable anxiety.   But at
last he came up, clung with his hand to the vessel, threw his prize
into the boat with the other, and then swung himself back to his
post.   It is a barbarous occupation, and so injurious that even the
strongest islanders do not live long.

Early on the 28th we arrived at the Piræus, and about ten in
the morning at Athens.   The Acropolis, with its marble ruins,
I had already beheld from the ship.   It now stood close before the
windows of my apartment.   With it arose within my soul a host of
reminiscences ; reminiscences which to mankind, as long as they
shall endure, will be dear and holy.   For have not wisdom and art
both created so much that is great within the city of Athens, that the
entire world still sits listening at her feet ?   Does legislation possess

a wiser guide than Solon? — state policy a more worthy representative than Pericles? Where is the orator like Demosthenes? Is not Thucydides still a model for historians? Were not also Eschylus and Sophocles Athenians? Has any sculptor surpassed Phidias? And who amongst the deepest thinkers of the earth has not enjoyed the divine Plato? But Socrates too was a son of Athens, although it was his mother herself that handed him the poisoned goblet.

I must at once hasten upwards to the ruins of the Acropolis. We pass through the market-gate, upon whose four ancient pillars the market prices of the days of Hadrian still stand inscribed. The guards open the gate of the Acropolis: there stand we upon the ancient marble floor, and stray through the halls of the propylæum. From the tower constructed at a later period, we speedily turn away and enter the area of the Parthenon, or the temple of the virgin Athene. Several pillars, as superb as they are colossal, are still standing: others by the side of them are arising from out the ruins by the aid of helping hands. Every individual spot the cicerone can point out; even to the very spot where stood the masterpiece of the master, the statue of Athene, in gold and ivory, sculptured by Phidias. With most regret, however, may the present Athenians contemplate the empty house behind the Parthenon, where was kept the public treasure, once rich to overflowing. In the immediate vicinity of the Parthenon stands the small temple of the wingless Goddess of Victory, of surprising delicacy and almost perfect, as well as two stately ruins of the temple of Erechtheus. The Acropolis has been transformed also into a modern museum; for statues, and busts, and inscriptions, and friezes, with sculptures of all kinds, have within the last few years been numerously collected and judiciously arranged there.

Had Athens, with all it was and possessed, totally disappeared, with the exception of its Acropolis even as it now remains with all its mutilations and desecrations, it would alone constitute a magnificent testimonial to past greatness; it alone would attract the archæological inquirer and the energetic artist to Athens, and hold them entranced. But around the Acropolis there look upwards to it other monuments which equally speak of past splendour; above all, in the south-east, the pillars of the temple of the Olympian Jupiter, and near it Hadrian's triumphal arch; in the south-west, the almost perfect monument of Philopappus; in the west, the Pnyx, with the place where Demosthenes stood, as well as the sacred judgment-hall, the Areopagus; finally, in the north-west, the temple of Theseus or rather of Mars, which with almost undiminished pillars and walls has wondrously survived all its neighbours, and is now consecrated to be the asylum of all recovered works of art.

I will add to these reminiscences of art, before we descend from the Acropolis, one word upon the works of nature which here surround us.   Athens itself lies close to the foot of the rocky mountain upon which we stand ; in the north beyond it, and behind the valley of the Cephissus, lies Parnes ; and in the east, the marble mountain Pentelikon ; Hymettus, celebrated for its honey, extends from the east to the south as far as the sea ; and in the west, stand exposed to view the Saronic Gulf, with Salamis and Ægina.

The present view of the city is highly refreshing for all who know the state of desolation in which it languished twenty years ago. Its desert suburbs are now delightfully adorned with a young olive grove in the north-west; thus the tree consecrated to Athene still remains faithfully true to the city.   But that which first and last attracts the eye in the view of Athens is a large dazzling white marble house, which shines like a new star in the ancient heaven ; it is the house to which cling the most ardent hopes, not merely of Athens, but of entire Greece ; for therein a heart throbs earnestly and watches faithfully over these hopes.

My sojourn in Athens extended to nearly a month ; it harmonised with the joy and happiness of my Oriental travels ; to the enjoyment of the ancient was added that of the modern.   Although it is only recently that the ungrateful dismissal of the Germans from the new state had taken place, I soon felt as much at home at Athens as in my fatherland.   What contributed mainly to this was the kindly reception I met with during my whole stay, in the house of the Bavarian minister Von Gasse.   This distinguished statesman is attached with his whole heart to Greece ; paternal solicitude, one soon perceives, has attached him officially to the youthful monarch, who would seek in vain throughout his country for a more faithful friend.   Through his means I was so thoroughly instructed in the great questions which concern the kingdom, as well as familiarised with the persons in whose hands the moulding of its immediate futurity rests, that I might almost have imagined that I had come to Athens for political purposes, and not in pursuit of knowledge.   But who would not take a hearty interest in the country with which all of us by the probationary years of education are so fervently and inseparably connected throughout after-life ?   It is true that, at this moment, I can calculate in Germany but upon little sympathy with my words.   Nowhere, it is said, could our sympathy have met with a worse return than in Greece.   And in the development of the state many a friend of Greece has not been in doubt, but in despair, as the anarchical character of the people and their concomitants appear to trample down every seed which the careful hand of its protector has planted.

Neither the reproach on the one hand, nor the doubt on the other, is without foundation; and yet I conceive that in both injustice has been done. Ingratitude in the expulsion of the Germans is certainly evident. It is true that I met with individuals here and there, who unreservedly expressed themselves on the unamiable character of those dismissed; and yet I had the satisfaction of hearing from others this violent act censured, and the merits of the Bavarians held in grateful remembrance. But what must be said in excuse of the conduct of the Greeks is, that much that was arbitrary and improper had got into the government of Greek affairs, and could not remain concealed, namely, the offensive setting aside of natives in situations where no prominent individual skill was evident, together with the mass of the most ill-adapted colonists who had been incorporated with persons of ability. The curing of the evil bore the stamp of southern blood; the wound burst open, and a knife was seized to cut it out.

With respect to the second of the above circumstances, namely, the doubt or despair as to the Greek people, I am far from participating in them. The Greek kingdom, it must be admitted, is a plant nurtured in tempests, whose forced development is seen from all sides; but it must not be forgotten in what soil it has grown. When we have visited countries whose present situation resembles that of Greece previous to its emancipation, and when we also observe how much the same Greece has advanced towards a fresh blossom since the battle of Navarino, we can well value and esteem it. The talent of the Greek people to form themselves into a consistent state, is doubtlessly rooted in the sound understanding, and the correct view which it has repeatedly shown itself to possess. Did it not, in the midst of those days of September when it rioted in its revolutionary consequences, listen to Piscatori's representation that the mere mention of the 3rd of September in the address to the king would be painful to the latter? Did it not after protracted debates determine upon the constitution of two chambers? Did it not on the 4th of August 1844, when armed for bloody battle against absolute injustice, immediately raise a joyful shout for its king when it beheld him, as the avenger of their injured rights, confidingly step forth into their midst? * Did it not relative to the question of the holy synod, which was of the greatest importance in its opposition to the northern propaganda, notwithstanding all foreign influence, decidedly support the ministry of Coletti?

The Greek nation has latterly shown its happy tact in nothing

* I take the liberty here to refer to the detailed article which I wrote at Athens, for the Allgemeine Zeitung, "Zur Geschichte der Ministerien Maurokordatos und Kolettis." See 5th Nov. 1844. I here repeat much that I there said.

better than in its faithful attachment to Coletti. I have been acquainted with no Greek whom I could esteem higher than him. I dare venture no opinion, but I believe Coletti is the man who was still wanting to the resuscitation of Greece. His individuality—any thing greater can scarcely be said of a minister — reminds one much of Guizot. Coletti is more serious and reserved than is customary with men beneath the Greek sky ; he is iron in his business habits ; he is decided in his views ; and what greatly distinguishes him from his countrymen is, that with the possession of all their craft he is without their falsity. Besides he has all the characteristics which insure popularity. He is a great friend of the Palikars ; he would have given, shortly after his acceptance of the ministry, a great banquet to the Palikars, had he not been dissuaded by the good counsel of his friends. And if it be even propagated that Coletti is not without sympathies with France, it must be remembered that he was educated in Paris, and it must be equally well known that, above all and with all, he is a patriot and a thorough Greek.

But perhaps no other foreign influence is so beneficial to Greek interests as the French. For it must be admitted that Greece will not so soon be exempt from foreign influence : this has been sufficiently provided for by the protection of the great powers through those cramping swaddling-clothes which were cast into the cradle of the young kingdom : if, however, it has been observed how the most incongruous foreign influence has uninterruptedly exercised its power, which has chiefly exhibited itself in numberless factions, we must necessarily feel surprised that, in spite of this, the affairs of the country have been able to attain their present position.

My pen has been as much engrossed by Athens as I myself was. Science possesses certainly there its buds and blossoms. I did not omit investigating this, but every pebble at Athens is saturated with politics — one cannot take a step without stumbling upon them.

I must say a word or two about my excursions in the vicinity of Athens. These excursions were rendered doubly agreeable by the friendly society of the court chaplain, Luth, and his amiable lady. Delightful was the enjoyment of Pentelikon, from whose heights we commanded not only the whole of Attica, but could also see in the north-east Euboea, and in the west Acrocorinth. The air was of that wondrous clearness which is reflected in the works of the Attic poets. Close beneath us we most distinctly saw the battle-field of Marathon, where Miltiades obtained the unfading laurel in his fight against a tenfold force. A trip to Daphne and its salt lake permitted us to celebrate the memory of the great Themistocles, for there we stood upon the shore of the sea in view of the site of the battle of Salamis; opposite to us, beyond the semicircle which the sea here makes, we beheld Eleusis ; even upon our road we still distinctly saw the traces on the ground of the chariots which formerly went from Athens to the Eleusinian festivals.

It is difficult to describe the beauty of the view from Acrocorinth ; it is an ample reward for the labours of the precipitous path which leads to this rocky watchhouse with its commanding view of two seas.   In the east, we looked over the sea away to Athens; in the north, the mountains were clothed in superb blue beneath the evening sky. I was especially delighted at beholding Parnassus among them.

One morning we spent at the delightful Ampelokipi, at the foot of Hymettus ; on the road the blooming oleanders which decorated the dry bed of the river Ilissus recalled to memory the Lake Genezareth.

The enormously large stadium of Herodes Atticus to the east of the city, is still recognisable; not far from it we visited the protestant burial ground, which already is inscribed with many German names.

About half a league to the northward of the city lies that " brightly clear " rocky hill Colonos which once possessed the sanctuary of Prometheus ; and beside it lies what is of paramount interest, the venerable hill of the Academy, where Plato taught.   I there passed a joyful hour.   I there also thought of poor Ottfried Müller, so early torn from the hopes of science ; for high minded gratitude has raised his marble monument precisely upon the consecrated hill of Plato.

One word more upon bidding farewell to Athens, and it shall be the concluding word of my travels.   Athens has a hill more holy than all those which once bore its sacred edifices, even more holy than that of the Academy.   How happy was I when I stood upon it !   Once that man stood there, like whom no other held, in the spirit of the Holy Ghost, the sword which conquers the world.   This was the Areopagus whence St. Paul addressed the assembled Athenians. (Acts xvii. 19.) His discourse, which is one of the living stones that bear the structure of the Church, testified TO THE UNKNOWN GOD (xvii. 23.), to whom also the ignorant wisdom of the Athenians paid worship.   The position of St. Paul was grand ; before him the city lay stretched out, nearer to him stood the Theseion, and at his side rose the Acropolis with all its temples.   There did he utter the words (Acts xvii. 24) — " God that made the world and all things therein, seeing that he is Lord of heaven and earth, dwelleth not in temples made with hands;" the words could nowhere have had fuller significance.

I quitted the Areopagus ; from him whose memory I there celebrated I shall never part.

THE END.

For EU product safety concerns, contact us at Calle de José Abascal, 56–1°, 28003 Madrid, Spain or eugpsr@cambridge.org.

www.ingramcontent.com/pod-product-compliance
Ingram Content Group UK Ltd.
Pitfield, Milton Keynes, MK11 3LW, UK
UKHW010348140625
459647UK00010B/923